The Constitution of the Roman Republic (287–133 BC)

To Professor of Law Owen McIntyre,
a great academic colleague and an inspiration.

The Constitution of the Roman Republic (287–133 BC)

A Mixed Polity

Antonios Emmanuel Platsas

EDINBURGH
University Press

Edinburgh University Press is one of the leading university presses in the UK. Publishing new research in the arts and humanities, EUP connects people and ideas to inspire creative thinking, open new perspectives and shape the world we live in. For more information, visit www.edinburghuniversitypress.com.

Edinburgh University Press Ltd
13 Infirmary Street, Edinburgh EH1 1LT

Typeset in 10/12 Goudy Old Style
by Cheshire Typesetting Ltd, Cuddington, Cheshire
Printed and bound in the UK using 100% renewable electricity by
CPI Group (UK) Ltd

A CIP record for this book is available from the British Library

ISBN 978 1 3995 4582 2 (hardback)
ISBN 978 1 3995 4584 6 (webready PDF)
ISBN 978 1 3995 4583 9 (epub)

EU Authorised Representative:
Easy Access System Europe
Mustamäe tee 50, 10621 Tallinn, Estonia
gpsr.requests@easproject.com

MIX
Paper | Supporting responsible forestry
FSC www.fsc.org FSC® C013604

This book is printed using paper from well-managed forests, recycling and other controlled sources

Contents

Part IV Concluding Thoughts

Figures and Tables

FIGURES

TABLES

Preface

Why Rome? What is the point of examining the constitution of the Roman Republic? First, one is free to examine in one's academic endeavours what one sees fit and beneficial to their discipline, society and humanity. Academia, a bit like Athens in the times of Pericles, is like a city thrown open to the world and our city is certainly one that obeys one master alone: the master of academic freedom. Second, Rome, her constitution, is a sort of a constant and eternal reminder of what can go right and what can go wrong in human nature, affairs and endeavours. Rome, never divine, always human, occasionally all too human, still represents human existence in its most fundamental but powerful essence: Rome and all that she symbolises has traditionally represented obscure and mysterious beginnings, greed, power, pragmatism, degeneration, decadence, lust, rise and fall. To study Rome is to study human existence, human character and human nature. To examine the Republic is to examine not only the constitutional psyche of the Romans but also the constitutional psyche of much of our modern world. To evaluate the constitution of the Roman Republic is to effectively understand the phobias, the anxieties, the dreams and the aspirations of the Romans. Even the utilitarian Romans dared to dream. Their dreams went close to the more basic essence of human existence and, yet somehow, the Romans created something great and beautiful despite their humble and rustic beginnings. Their culture, a hybrid culture by all means, stands for one of the three classic pillars of the Western world (the other two being Athens and Jerusalem). Third, perhaps the greatest benefit to one's examination of Rome's constitution is the fact that, through such examination, one can be offered practical shortcuts about political and legal issues in modern times. Rome offers us the magnificent shortcut as to how we can make our world's republics better and stronger. Every true democrat, every true aristocrat, every person in the disciplines of law and political science, every research scholar in the classical disciplines, every politician but also every citizen of the world can learn a great deal as to how the republican ideal and democracy flourished and died in Rome's mixed constitution, a constitution that seems to have been generated out of fear of great individual power for long.

In their efforts to democratise their Republic, the Romans, at least their elites, did all they could to maintain the status quo, a status quo that would tend to be of oligarchic and monarchic nature. For the most part of the Republic, its constitution was controlled by powerful oligarchic elites, mainly comprising Patricians and plutocrats with the democratic elements of Rome being kept under significant control by the same elites. Rome's people would be powerful but it would be

Rome's Senate that would rule city, Italy and empire. From reforming the House of Lords in such countries as the UK to the way political institutions degenerate and fall, but also should operate, there is magnificent benefit in examining the role of Rome's Senate, its people as well as the other institutions in the constitution of the Republic. Fourth, a correction is long overdue: Polybius and Cicero can be partially excused to have idealised the constitution of the Republic but the republic, which they so admired, hid in its heart an adamantine, centralised oligarchy of free Roman male individuals, effectively appointed in their roles on hereditary right and wealth, the Senate, the same senate that was responsible for the rise and the apex of the Republic's constitution but also for its fall. Fifth, Roman law, indeed Roman constitutional law, is *par excellence* an area that matches comparative legal studies.[1]

This is a book about the constitution of the Roman Republic at its best, the period between 287 and 133 BC, when the republic became slightly more democratised and when Rome generated its empire, which continued to rise for many centuries even after the fall of the Republic in 27 BC. The book operates in the realm of law and at the crossroads of constitutional law, history and political science. Inroads to ethnography, laography, sociology, philology and economics are also made, for to master the Roman Republic's constitution, one must take an interdisciplinary approach where appropriate. Nothing less than a composite research methodology would practically suffice for breaking the code of the Roman Republic's magnificent composite constitution. And yet in agreement with modern bibliography when it comes to the constitution of the Roman Republic our focus should be on law.[2] As always, the use of historical matter would be a natural matter in exploring the essence of Rome's magnificent constitution. Also, it would be appropriate for both modern and ancient sources to be considered; so too, we would have to critically analyse what the Romans had to say about themselves[3] but also what others thought of them and their constitution.

The book comes with a number of propositions. These can be reduced to the following: first, the constitution of Rome was a wholly mixed one in the years of the Republic. Rome was effectively a mixed polity or an Aristotelian polity+, the Roman 'twist', in the face of Aristotelian theory, being that Rome's mixed constitution also comprised monarchic/dyarchic elements, when Aristotle would include in mixed constitutions oligarchic, aristocratic and democratic elements only. Second, the Republic's constitutional machinery thus comprised four elements (the monarchic, the aristocratic, the oligarchic and the democratic element); not three as Polybius and Cicero maintained. Indeed, against the Polybian/Ciceronian thesis, the Senate, the Roman Republic's constitutional heart, was

1 Cf. J Harries, 'Law' in A Barchiesi and W Scheidel (eds), *The Oxford Handbook of Roman Studies* (Oxford University Press 2010) 648.

2 C Ando, 'Public Law and Republican Empire in Rome, 200–27 BCE' in E Cavanagh (ed), *Empire and Legal Thought: Ideas and Institutions from Antiquity to Modernity* (Brill Nijhoff 2020) 108.

3 Cf. C Ando, *Roman Social Imaginaries: Language and Thought in the Context of Empire* (University of Toronto Press 2015) 3–4.

not quite exactly an 'aristocracy' but a full-blown oligarchy of plutocrats in perfect agreement with Aristotelian doctrine. Third, in the years of the Republic, there was no such thing as a golden age of Rome Athenian style, but the period between 287 and 133 BC can be identified as the Roman Republic's period of flourishing, its constitutional and political apogee, when the Republic otherwise historically spanned between 509 and 27 BC. It is in this period, the period between 287 and 133 BC, that one observes the apex of the Roman Republic in constitutional and political terms despite failures and mistakes. Fourth, most interestingly, the fuzzy constitution of the Roman Republic is responsible for the rise of the Republic from what was an insignificant and small republic of rustics and peasants, somewhere in the Italian peninsula, into a world empire, only for the same constitution to burn out in the process, as it could not sustain the empire that it generated. The same constitution that offered relative internal stability to Rome could not actually withhold any more, in the twilight of the 2nd century BC, Rome's internal conflicting forces and the external growth that it cultivated. The Roman Republic retreated; Rome did not and actually transformed itself into the Roman Principate.

It is a magnificent privilege to write about the Roman Republic. To write about the Roman Republic is about writing about our modern world's republics, all at once. Rome and all that she represents is to this day the world's constitutional fountain. From the Americans who had to examine the Roman Republic's constitution to the British whose fuzzy constitution somewhat reminds us of the fuzzy constitution of the Republic, Rome and her constitution are very much alive and strong. Nothing lasts forever in nature and human affairs. The Roman Republic too fell, as its constitution could not sustain the weight of the empire which it generated. The constitution of the Republic was good for a city; quite good for Latium, acceptable for keeping the Italian peninsula and Sicily under certain control, but not adequate to sustain the political and administrative pressures of an empire spanning from Gaul and Iberia to Asia Minor and Egypt.

A bloodstained star was once born. A star was once born out of the villages and the rustic populations scattered on seven hills near a river called Tiber: the bloodstained star of Rome. The Roman rustics, the mock of the lay Greeks of the Italian peninsula; Rome, the old protectorate of the Etruscans, the once plaything of the ferocious Celtic tribes frequently raiding much of the Italian peninsula, the initially inferior competitor of majestic and flamboyant Carthage, learnt her lessons well only for her to teach a few lessons to old enemies and the world: those who would be humiliated by the Celts in 390 BC, those who were embarrassingly entrapped by the Samnites in 321 BC, those whose existence would still tremble like fire about to die, when the Epirote King Pyrrhus would challenge them in 275 BC, those who in 216–214 BC lost many of their Italian allies to Hannibal, when magnificent panic ensued in the streets of Rome and in the minds of the Romans,[4] and when he was *ante portas*, persevered, fought back and rose. In one of history's most surprising turnarounds, the fallen became the risen. The bloodstained star of

[4] E.g. PA Zoch, *Ancient Rome: An Introductory History* (University of Oklahoma Press 1998) 107.

the Roman Republic, if there is one thing it ever taught the world, is to never ever underestimate anyone, for History is not forgiving to the arrogant, the complacent or the naïve. Close to Rome's perseverance,[5] Rome's elites and people created in the years of the Republic a magnificent engine: Rome's constitutional engine. It was this engine that was responsible for stabilising Rome internally in order for it to expand externally. Rome's overall internal constitutional stability allowed it to project itself with magnificent force and boldness to the world. And yet, this engine wholly failed by 27 BC. This is a book about Rome and her confident republic, her arising to unimaginable heights of glory, power and constitutional excellence. It is the Roman Republic that established the Roman empire, later giving rise to the Principate and the Dominate. Rome once lost in the Caudine Forks but through the relentless Caudine Forks of History, Rome danced confidently, wild and free. And she won.

Rome is, by far, the best example in human history of an initially relatively backward and humble people that came almost out of nowhere, finding itself interlocked between the leading cultures of Greece and Etruria, it rising, standing confident and proud to the world, falling and destroying itself only for it to rise ever stronger. It was once the Roman Republic against the world, the Romans having seriously upset not just other Mediterranean cultures and peoples but also almost all[6] of their Italic brothers and cousins and, of course, the Gauls, the Britons and the Germans. Humble, proud, arrogant, decadent, world-leading are only a few of the adjectives that best describe the Roman Republic.

The Roman Republic, indeed Rome itself, has been the subject matter of almost complete deification by scholars of major European colonial powers between 1800 and 1945 and almost complete demonisation by scholars from former European colonial and neo-colonial imperial powers beyond Europe from 1945 to date.[7] The book treads carefully between these two worlds, in that it distinguishes Rome's greatest achievement, its stealthy and powerful constitution, from Rome's imperial conquests and expansions that followed after hundreds of years since the original conception of the Roman Republic. Even more provokingly, it posits that, had it not been for republican Rome's constitution, the Roman empire would not have existed or grown but the fact that the Republic's constitution enabled Rome's stabilisation and expansion should not demonise or condemn her constitution as a legal creation. It should also be recalled that the Roman culture was, traditionally, not particularly original; yet the constitution of the Republic seems to have been, at least in its amalgamation, an original product, the product of Roman genius and local unnamed elites, the Romans taking particular pride from the fact that no single person could be identified as the father of the Roman

[5] Cf. A Momigliano, *Alien Wisdom: The Limits of Hellenization* (Cambridge University Press 1975) 43, putting Rome's superiority to her capacity to replenish.

[6] E.g. D Hoyos, *Rome Victorious: The Irresistible Rise of the Roman Empire* (Bloomsbury Academic 2019, reprinted 2023) 8.

[7] Cf. M Beard, *SPQR: A History of Ancient Rome* (Liveright Publishing 2015) 16.

Republic's constitutional design. Thus, the constitutional law scholar must distinguish between the benefit that the Roman Republic's constitution brought to the city of Rome, which it was originally designed to serve, and the wider implications behind the same constitution. The assessment of the former would be in the positive, as the constitution of the Republic stabilised Rome to a great degree for centuries. The assessment of the latter, of course, would be in the negative, in that the constitution enabled *inter alia* Rome's expansion at the cost of human lives and magnificent pain.

Moreover, the book breaks new ground in that it taxonomises Rome's institutions, bodies and magistrates into democratic, aristocratic, oligarchic and monarchic offices, when the overwhelming majority of authors in the area would actually limit their analyses to the description and critical evaluation of such offices.[8] The monograph, thus, balances between strictly analytical elements and taxonomical elements, the latter being maintained with the reader in mind. In this respect, it must be told that the bibliography lacks a coherent, systematised and precise ordering of the Roman Republic's institutions and magistrates, authors traditionally describing Rome's institutions and magistrates in turn without taxonomising and/or categorising them. To the defence of such authors comes the fact that there has been overall lack of interest in categorising Rome's offices, bodies and magistrates from the times of the Republic to date. The fact that Roman public law has always been more abstract than Rome's private laws must have been another reason behind the lack of systematisation and taxonomisation of Rome's institutions, magistrates and bodies. The monograph comes to fill this long-standing gap in the bibliography. Equally, the monograph does so in a non-dogmatic fashion and offers its analytical models on an indicative and illustrative basis. One could also argue that the Romans would not be interested to categorise and taxonomise their polity's structures and offices, so why would we? The Romans were renowned for centuries for their lack of interest in systematic scientific research, that is from writing their own history to exploring their own constitution. From the scientific point of view, however, the traditional apathy of the Romans to explore their constitution would not hold water in the interests of academic enquiry. On the contrary, the fact that the Romans did not examine the academic essence of their constitution would mean that we ought to cover the apparent academic void in the area.

Our monograph additionally departs from Mommsen's optimistic thesis that the Republic came with the characteristics of an objective constitution, the more plausible thesis about Rome's republican constitution being that Rome came with objective characteristics in its institutions, bodies and magistrates that would

[8] EA Posner, 'The Constitution of the Roman Republic' in G Dari-Mattiacci and DP Kehoe (eds), *Roman Law and Economics: Institutions and Organizations Volume I* (Oxford University Press 2020) 35. But cf. C Ando, 'Self, Society, Individual, and Person in Roman Law' in MR Niehoff and J Levinson (eds), *Self, Self-Fashioning and Individuality in Late Antiquity: New Perspectives* (Mohr Siebeck 2019) 378, speaking of taxonomisation in certain modern presentations of Roman law in the context of legal persons, when Roman texts would relate to persons in motion.

come very close to Aristotelian and Platonic concepts and systems of government. Rome's overall constitutional ordering was one that would not qualify as an objective constitution in the strict sense, for example, as a modern constitution would. Why would it? The Roman elites were close to perfectly content with a constitution that was objective in its overall institutional layout but quite subjective in the interpretation of constitutional norms, especially in the absence of concrete legislation (*mos maiorum*, the traditions and the customs of the ancestors and the fathers of Rome, would be Rome's classic device in interpreting its constitutional law). Thus, the constitution of Rome per se was not an 'objective' one in the sense the modern formal constitution of France or the Basic Law of Germany would be, but many of Rome's institutions were objective constitutional realities, in the sense that they would subscribe to forms of political government, all mixed into one, creating the polity of Rome. Polybius was, thus, right about Rome's mixed character in constitutional terms, even though he was rather finite, limited and selective[9] in the way he described Rome's constitutional features, as was Cicero. He got the mixed character of Rome's constitution right but not the components and the number of components thereof right. Nor did Cicero. It would seem that Polybius and Cicero have done so as part and parcel of their job description in presenting Rome as a rounded and idealised constitutional reality. The historical exercise was muddled with the constitutional law exercise in the case of Polybius. The constitutional law exercise was muddled with the political rhetoric exercise in the case of Cicero.

The old Greek dream for an ideal republic[10] flourished more than anywhere else in a city that looked both familiar and foreign to the Greeks: Rome. Yet, the Roman constitution of the Republic made sense to the Greeks,[11] as it would make sense to us in modernity. If ambition is like a dream with a V8 engine, Plato and Aristotle's constitutional ambition must have come closest to the V8 constitutional engine created by the Romans, an engine that went into full overdrive for centuries. The Republic's constitution was as if certain of Plato's and Aristotle's ideas were fully flourished.[12] At other times, the constitution of the Roman Republic would remind us of a more sophisticated and complex version of Sparta's constitution[13] or even the constitution of Crete,[14] as explored by Aristotle. The Spartan ambition, of course, extended to the Peloponnese and central Greece; the Roman ambition, enabled by the Republic's constitution, went to the world. Yet, any engineer would tell us that an engine operating in full overdrive for long will be practically operating at higher temperatures; it will degrade its engine oil at a

[9] TC Brennan, 'Power and Process under the Republican "Constitution"' in HI Flower (ed), *The Cambridge Companion to the Roman Republic* (2nd edn, Cambridge University Press 2014) 20.

[10] Beard (n 7) 188. Cf. MB Wilson, *Dictator: The Evolution of the Roman Dictatorship* (University of Michigan Press 2021) 17.

[11] Momigliano (n 5) 25.

[12] Cf. Momigliano (n 5) 14.

[13] Momigliano (n 5) 14, 39 citing Athenaeus 6 (273a-275b).

[14] T Mommsen, *The History of Rome*, vol. 1 (W Purdie Dickson tr, Macmillan & Co. 1901) 32.

higher rate; its fuel consumption will increase; it will strain the engine's cooling system and eventually it will push the engine to its limits only for it to burn out. The constitution of the Republic was that engine: operating in full overdrive for centuries, it created an empire but the same empire it created caused Rome's constitutional engine to collapse under the weight of the empire it created.

The Roman Republic was born in 509 BC and it faded away to the Roman Principate in 27 BC. Our journey per se commences in 287 BC when the Roman Republic became somewhat more democratic through *Lex Hortensia* (the Hortensian Law), such a process coming to an abrupt end in 133 BC with the assassination of a promising young man, Tiberius Gracchus. This is republican Rome's finest period, Rome at its best, even though, as stated, Rome never had a golden age the way Athens did. It is in this period, however, that Rome almost fully stabilised its Republic in Latium, Italy and the Mediterranean world with its legions becoming virtually unstoppable and its empire rising. It is the Roman Republic that is responsible for the Roman empire. Of course, we know Rome from its imperial times mostly but the dream (or the nightmare, depending on one's perspective) of Rome's empire certainly started and materialised to a significant extent in the times of the Republic. In the classic Republic, the Middle Republic, which this book explores in great detail, Rome rose in almost every aspect of human development, albeit somewhat less in the field of the Arts and the Letters, especially as compared to its great accomplishments in military, civil law and public law terms.

In the vastness of the Hellenistic world, spreading from the shores of east Iberia, southern Gaul, Sicily, Magna Grecia to Cyrenaica, Egypt, Macedonia, Thrace, Illyria, Phoenicia well into Persia, Gedrosia, Bactria, Arachosia and Sogdiana, a once insignificant republic, somewhere in central Italy, thus blossomed in the 3rd and 2nd century BC. Rome's constitutional and military flower blossomed more than any other constitutional and military flower did in the face of human history in relative terms. It is in this period that Rome established its republican empire or imperial republic. And she actually superimposed herself on the Hellenistic world in administrative, political and military terms, albeit never culturally.[15] Of course, Latin was not that spoken beyond the Italian peninsula during the Republic[16] but it was the Romans that now governed the fortunes of the Mediterranean peoples as well as many of the fortunes of certain European peoples in this period of time already.

Having created an Aristotelian polity+ is the Republic's greatest achievement in constitutional law terms. Concurrently, her elites Hellenised by some of the finest Greek educators, Rome the proud, Rome the arrogant, is to this day the constitutional mother of our world's modern republics and it is the case that it is only the mix of comparable republics of modernity that changes based on many

[15] E.g. ES Gruen, *The Hellenistic World and the Coming of Rome* (University of California Press 1984, reprinted 1986) 2.

[16] Cic. Arch. 23.

of the constitutional components and solutions that made Rome's constitution. To paraphrase Victor Hugo, the world of modern constitutions is the expanding constitution of the Roman Republic and the constitution of the Roman Republic is the shrinking world of our modern world's constitutions.

For so many reasons, which we will explore in this monograph, the Republic's constitution and its relative stability between 287 and 133 BC was, by all means, a greater historic achievement than all of Rome's previous and future victories. It was a greater historic achievement even than the great growth of the Roman empire in the years of the Principate and the Dominate that followed after 27 BC and after AD 284 respectively. The constitution was the very historical nucleus from which Rome grew, rose and expanded. Had it not been for Rome's imperial Republic, the republican empire, for which the constitution of the Republic was responsible and which it established in the first place, Rome would not grow further during the Principate and the Dominate; it would have been more of an impossibility then for Rome to build the greater empire which it built on the constitutional foundations of the imperial Republic. In other words, the Republic and its constitution were the conditions precedent for Rome's empire and future empire. Had it not been for the collective genius of Rome's ruling elites found in the Republic's purposefully fuzzy but powerful constitution, Rome would not have been internally stable as a city to confidently project herself to the world.

Rome most of us know from her imperial years during the Principate, the Dominate and thereafter. We also know Rome from the 1100+ years of the Eastern Roman Empire's continuous reign, the Roman offshoot in the Greek speaking medieval world that lasted more than any other empire the test of time. Nonetheless, it was the Republic that offered the Romans the initial constitutional engine for Rome to be registered as a force to be reckoned with in military and constitutional terms. Before the Republic, Rome did not matter much; it was a small, insignificant, rustic kingdom in Latium. So too, during the Principate, Rome already had an empire from the years of the Republic, the finest achievement of the Republic being its constitution.

By the middle of the 2nd century BC, it was absolutely clear to Polybius that the inexorable, imperial-constitutional dragon of Rome was wholly unleashed and could not be stopped any more, him warning, between the lines, his fellow Greeks that Rome was the future. So were other Hellenistic historiographers, who promoted a pragmatic agenda for the Greeks, asking them not to resist the Roman conqueror in the hope that the occupied Greeks would acquire benefit.[17] However, Polybius was not always wholly honest with his audiences, to which one must state that Polybius is dear to us, but dearer still is truth of course. He, for instance, did not always fully and accurately present the Republic's constitutional picture, rounding Rome's oligarchic elements by calling them aristocratic (those same

17 C Steel, *The End of the Roman Republic, 146 to 44 BC: Conquest and Crisis* (Edinburgh University Press 2013) 224, citing LM Yarrow, *Historiography at the End of the Republic* (Oxford University Press 2006).

elements were his paymasters by the way). Cicero, part of the dying soul of the Late Republic (the other part of that soul being Pompey), more than a generation later than the generation of Polybius, went further: not only would he maintain that the Senate was an aristocracy but he also idealised the Republic calling it the best constitution in the world, when rather peculiarly, if not suspiciously, it was not a genuine republic any more, that is during his lifetime and according to his very own deliberations, but in a name only. The Roman Republic was practically dead and it was the same republic that he so idealised that ordered his execution in 43 BC on the instructions of the Second Triumvirate, in all probability on the initiative and the advice of Mark Antony.

A final thing to be mentioned for the reader's benefit is the ideology of the Republic's constitution. Essentially, Rome's constitution was about the fears and the hopes of the Romans. Fear and hope governed the Roman constitutional genius. A constitution of fear but also a constitution of hope is what the Romans created during the Republic. Fear governing the minds and the souls of the Romans resulted in them crafting a sophisticated constitution of checks and balances. There was nothing more repugnant to the republican Roman mind than the rule of a single person, a tyrant (hence the split of Rome's old *Rex* (King's) office into two Consuls with the fall of the Monarchy). Hope in their minds and souls resulted in a constitution that would stabilise Rome and would create the conditions precedent for an empire. That fear of the Romans for a tyrant running their city and their empire sprang again and again in their minds and it haunted them until the final days of the Republic in 27 BC: ultimately, it was the phobia of the Romans for the rule of a single man such as Tiberius Gracchus or Julius Caesar that must have armed the hand of their assassins, even though one could certainly additionally argue that the very reforms advocated by Tiberius and Julius Caesar were not a particularly appealing prospect to the conservative elites of Rome.

Leeds, April 2025

Acknowledgements

This monograph is the product of pure research conducted in the Law School of Leeds Beckett University. I would like to express my gratitude to the School of Law and, in particular, to Dean and former Director of Research, Professor Deveral Capps, as well as incumbent Director of Research, Professor Rachel Armitage, for their continuous support in this project from beginning to end. By extension, I am indebted to institution, Leeds Beckett University, because it has offered me the academic space to conduct research of the highest calibre in the critical area of Roman constitutional law, an area of law that is of central importance to the ways we build our societies and the societies of the future. I am also grateful to Commissioning Editor, Laura Quinn, and Assistant Commissioning Editor, Sam Johnson, for their support throughout all stages of the project, and Desk Editor, Eddie Clark, is hereby acknowledged his support for his excellent work both in front and behind the scenes in order for this project to come to life in its final but most critical stages during production. I wish also to thank my brother, Nikolaos, for his support with figures, graphics and related aspects. Special thanks to Edinburgh University Press for making the whole production a smooth and rewarding process. Finally, I am particularly indebted to the anonymous reviewer of the Press, not least because their fine remarks, their constructive spirit and their encouragement have been crucial in the direction and the character of this monograph. This colleague has my best wishes.

AE Platsas

PART I

THE REPUBLIC'S RISE

Chapter 1

An Introduction to Rome in the Years of the Republic and Analytical Parameters

1.1 INTRODUCTION AND MONOGRAPH'S REMIT

This chapter introduces the reader to Rome in the years of the Republic. It also presents the monograph's subject matter and sets out its analytical goals and parameters. The monograph is about the apex of the Roman Republic and its constitution in the same period of time. The analysis is divided into four parts: Part I (the Republic's Rise), in which the reader will be offered background information and an analysis relating to the rise of the Republic in the first place; Part II (the Republic's Apogee), in which section the reader will be offered a full analysis in relation to the constitutional apogee of Rome in the years of the Republic and other related matter such as the character of the Romans as crystallised into Rome's constitution; Part III (a Mixed Polity of Monarchic, Oligarchic, Aristocratic and Democratic Elements), forming the analytical core of the monograph, the particular section exploring the constitution of the Roman Republic per se as well as the constituent elements behind it; finally, Part IV (Concluding Thoughts) is about solidifying the points previously made in the book, this final part concentrating on the key tenets of this monograph's thesis. For the benefit of the reader and their contextualisation in republican Rome's constitutional analysis, historical addenda are offered closer to the end of this book.

The Romans, in the years of the Republic, have created a magnificent constitution of mixed characteristics combining monarchic, oligarchic, aristocratic and democratic elements to it. In addition to exploring the apex of the Republic and the reasons behind it, this book taxonomises and explores the very constituent elements of the Republic. It does so by offering a detailed analysis as to the precise constitutional nature of the Roman Republic and its institutions in the same period of time. The work's original character can be found in the fact that it reevaluates ancient and modern sources as to the precise nature of the Republic by challenging certain established modalities. For instance, the Roman Republic, even after 287 BC, was more oligarchic and less aristocratic and democratic than ancient sources but, also, certain modern sources would suggest.

Our exposition offers new unique analytical insights into the golden constitutional era of the Roman Republic by exploring the essence, the fundamentals, the historical roots and the structures of its institutions. One can learn a great deal in our times from the way the Romans, over the centuries, designed their Republic, of which many of them must have been so very proud, and mostly with good reason. Far from flawless, however, the Roman Republic's constitution did not, for instance, come very close to the Athenian democratic constitution of the 5th century BC, which was, on the one hand, highly communitarian but, on the other hand, a constitution that would place its emphasis solely on free male individuals assuming personal responsibility for the running of the state. Finally, the text offers novel comparative perspectives and insights, as it compares the constitution of the Roman Republic with elements and aspects of certain other contemporary constitutions, for example, those of Athens, Sparta and Carthage, as well as with elements and aspects of modern constitutions.

1.2 KEY FEATURES

The book's key analytical features are as follows:

- It advocates the mixed character of the constitution of the Roman Republic by putting forward a mixed polity model combining monarchic, oligarchic, aristocratic and democratic characteristics.
- It discards the Ciceronian and Polybian view that the Roman Republic consisted of monarchic, aristocratic and democratic elements only, thereby coming closer to a more Aristotelian perception of things vis-à-vis the oligarchic nature of the Roman Senate.
- It proposes that the Senate was more of an oligarchic body of a closed number of wealthy Roman individuals in view of Aristotelian doctrine and against Ciceronian and Polybian perceptions.
- It further proposes that the apogee of the constitution of the Republic of Rome was the period between 287 and 133 BC and supports such a claim by way of legal, historical and political data, analysis and argumentation and in an interdisciplinary fashion.
- It defends the idea that the constitution of the Roman Republic offered not only considerable initial stability to Rome itself, but it also laid the foundations of its empire.

1.3 ANALYTICAL PARAMETERS AND HISTORICAL BACKGROUND

For the reader to fully acquire the monograph's essence, its analytical fundamentals require a brief explanation. This is a legal analysis, with interdisciplinary elements, on what the author perceives to be the apogee of the Roman Republic's constitutional development: the period between 287 and 133 BC, the Roman republican era otherwise extending between 509 and 27 BC. The year 287 BC was, of course, the year of the full re-enactment of an old democratic law, taking the form of *Lex Hortensia*. About two centuries on, Roman full citizenship expanded all over the Italian peninsula with the end of the Social War in 89 BC, when 'Rome's allies successfully claimed the rights of full citizenship'[1]. However, the Roman Republic's

[1] N Davies, *Europe: A History* (Pimlico 1996, reprinted with corrections 1997) 165.

path towards democratisation was interrupted in 88 BC, when Sulla transferred all the powers of Rome's Plebeian Council to the city's Centuriate Assembly, thereby putting an end to the continuous path of the more democratic Roman Republic between 287 and 88 BC. Concurrently, the Roman Republic's constitution was being reduced, whilst the Roman Empire was expanding, with the Republic eventually wholly subsiding to the Principate in 27 BC.

It was otherwise in the period between 287 and 133 BC that Rome became what it was to be. In the period between 280 and 200 BC Rome had already been taken 'from the fringe of the Mediterranean world to one from which she can be seen, with the benefit of hindsight, to dominate it'.[2] Rome's only major challenger in the East and the Italian peninsula per se, Greece, had now met a formidable enemy, the Romans themselves, albeit still in Italian soil, with the defeat of Pyrrhus in 275 BC. This effectively amounted to the beginning of the rise of Rome over the Greek world.[3] Roman control over the Greek world was established in the 2nd century BC and was completed with the conquest of the last Hellenistic Kingdom in the Mediterranean, the Ptolemaic Kingdom of Egypt, in late 1st century BC. In 146 BC, Rome was also in control of what was once the powerful Carthaginian Empire, Rome's most formidable competitor in central and west Mediterranean.

On the institutional side of things, Rome's Plebeian Council would otherwise survive the fall of the Republic but its powers would be so diminished that it would become a mere shadow of its old self.[4] The final years of the Republic, between 88 and 27 BC, were merely the twilight of the Roman Republic with personalities such as Pompey and Cicero not being able to save it from its final and full demise. The Roman Republic has been, of course, responsible for establishing a spirit of imperial characteristics in Rome and against the rest of the then known world.[5] Thus, '[t]he Roman Republic presided over the city's growth from provincial obscurity to mastery of the whole Mediterranean'.[6]

The Republic's constitution has been a magnificently sophisticated system of governance worthy of our attention. Furthermore, as a comparative example to the constitution of the Roman Republic, the constitution of democratic Athens, was about periodical meetings (on statutory assembly days); not about public gatherings that authorised Roman officials would call at their discretion.[7] In Athens,

[2] M Crawford, *The Roman Republic* (2nd edn, Fontana Press 1992) 46.

[3] Cf. Crawford (n 2) 48.

[4] FF Abbott, A *History and Description of Roman Political Institutions* (Ginn & Company Publishers 1901) 397.

[5] By the end of the Third Macedonian War in 168 BC, the Roman Republic was not just a full-blown imperial power but also a major intimidator in the Mediterranean. Cf. RW Mathisen, *Ancient Roman Civilization: History and* Sources (Oxford University Press 2019) 118. In 146 BC, two of the most renowned cities of the Mediterranean world, Carthage and Corinth, would have been destroyed by Rome. Cf. also F Millar, *The Roman Republic in Political Thought* (University Press of New England 2002) 1: '[o]ne need not feel the least admiration for the ingrained militarism of Roman tradition'.

[6] Davies (n 1) 153.

[7] H Mouritzen, *Politics in the Roman Republic* (Cambridge University Press 2017) 16.

the *demos*' initiatives could be the result of popular gatherings, where citizens could both debate and decide.[8] In Rome, on the other hand, there was a clear-cut distinction between meetings where people could decide (*comitia*) and meetings of relegated status (*contiones*),[9] where people could debate under a strict regulatory framework and under the direct authority of a presiding official, such meetings being more about 'an address to the people than a consultation of it'.[10]

Athens was, thus, about a generally pro-active and sovereign *demos*. Rome, on the other hand, was more about a non-sovereign *populus* of passive characteristics,[11] it being dependent on its leaders.[12] However, at least in the case of the *contiones*, even if one did not have voting rights in Rome, one could attend them: women, non-Romans, slaves, Latins, citizens of Roman Allies and foreigners could in principle attend them and participate in them.[13]

Rome, during the years of the Republic, could not always hide its mostly secret but at other times almost overt[14] admiration[15] for Sparta's severe, strict, military character and mixed-oligarchic system of governance. Indeed, the Sabines, once enemies of Rome to the north-east of Rome, would be compared 'to the Spartans for their bravery and simple morality'.[16] At other times, it would seem that certain characteristics of Sparta's classic system of governance would effectively be followed in the Roman Republic, even though there does not currently seem to be direct evidence that Sparta and Rome were actively interacting or were in political and legal contact with one another except perhaps in legendary terms. For example, for the creation of the Twelve Tables, a Roman commission would have been instituted in the 5th century BC to conduct comparative legal research in Athens,[17] and, in all probability, in Sparta[18] and Gortyna.[19] Moreover, considering the geographical proximity of Rome with Greater Greece in south Italy and the continuous trade exchanges between Rome and the Greek *poleis*, one cannot exclude the possibility of at least passive interaction between the pre-republican

[8] Ibid.
[9] Ibid.
[10] Mouritzen (n 7) 17.
[11] Mouritzen (n 7) 18 (citing E Badian, 'Kommentar: Magistratur und Gesellschaft' in *Staat und Staatlichkeit in der frühen römischen Republik*, ed. W. Eder. Stuttgart: 458–75 at 471); 31.
[12] Mouritzen (n 7) 17.
[13] IE Τζαμτζής, *Ο Μεσογειακός Κόσμος* (Εκδόσεις Σάκκουλα 2014, ανατύπωση 2018) 104.
[14] E Dench, *From Barbarians to New Men: Greek, Roman, and Modern Perceptions of Peoples of the Central Apennines* (Oxford University Press 1995) 86–7 citing Servius Auct. *Ad Verg. Aen.* 8.638.
[15] Dench (n 14) 53.
[16] PA Zoch, *Ancient Rome: An Introductory History* (University of Oklahoma Press 1998) 12.
[17] D.H. 10.51.5; Liv. 3 31. On a modern overview of the influences of Greek legal systems on the drafting of the Twelve Tables of Rome, see e.g. R Scarciglia, *Methods and Legal Comparison: Challenges for Methodological Pluralism* (Edward Elgar 2023) 7.
[18] See n 26 in this chapter for the very similar approach that the Romans shared with the Spartans when it came to the treatment of disabled newborns.
[19] Cf. K Moore, 'Rome's Decemviral Commission to Greece: Fact, Fiction or Otherwise?' (2019) 5 *Athens Journal of History* 123, 132.

and republican Roman world with the Greek world in the sphere of certain legal matters.[20]

In any case, irrespective of the alleged contact of Rome with the Greek world, another common feature of Sparta and Rome was their strong emphasis on the military power of their societies to the point that it would be an omission to not consider such as a separate constitutional law power for Rome. Indeed, '[f]or most of its history the Roman Republic was constantly at war … Its institutions were military in character and function, and its culture was pervaded by a warlike ethos'.[21]

Whilst the Spartan society would traditionally be more militocratic[22] than that of Rome, Rome's nobles, even by mid-2nd century BC, would be required to offer ten years of military service to their country prior to entering politics.[23] Yet another common characteristic that both Spartans and Romans shared would become apparent from the way they would treat certain of their newborns,[24] thereby revealing the harsh and severe character of these two peoples: if we are to believe Plutarch's words on certain practices of Sparta,[25] one observes that both the Spartans as well as the Romans (the latter under the Twelve Tables)[26] considered it an accepted socio-legal norm, to be able to kill or even have the right to kill[27] one's own child, if born disabled or deformed. Beyond this, Sparta's philosophy of life would be both about military training and a dual Kingship, half of it being dedicated to military duties. So too, Rome's philosophy of life, especially about law, discipline[28] and order, would come relatively close to the Spartan one but Rome's overall educational model would clearly be less militaristic than that of Sparta, even though both Spartans and Romans could be readily described

[20] For instance, Cornell argues that, whilst the Roman embassy to Athens in 454 BC may have not been true in a literal sense, the Romans may have been influenced by the laws of the Greek cities of the [Italian] South. He also maintains that Rome's heavy Hellenisation would make it impossible for its Twelve Tables not to have any traces of Greek influence: TJ Cornell, *The Beginnings of Rome: Italy and Rome from the Bronze Age to the Punic Wars (c. 1000–264 BC)* (Routledge London, 1995) 275.

[21] Cornell (n 20) 365. Cf. T Whitmarsh, 'Hellenism' in A Barchiesi and W Scheidel (eds), *The Oxford Handbook of Roman Studies* (Oxford University Press 2010) 736.

[22] But cf. Crawford (n 2) 46, claiming that Rome was more militaristic even than Sparta. Perhaps his point might be that, in absolute terms (e.g in numbers), Rome was indeed a more militaristic society than Sparta was.

[23] RE Mitchell, 'The Aristocracy of the Roman Republic' in R Howarth (ed), *Hearsay, History, and Heresy: Collected Essays on the Roman Republic by Richard E. Mitchell* (Gorgias Press 2010) 125.

[24] Mathisen (n 5) 95. See also n 26 herein.

[25] But cf. D Trikkaliotis, AA Mouratidou and A Anastasiou, 'The Fate of Sickly and Disabled Newborn Babies in Ancient Greece (Sparta and Athens)' [2018] *The Journal of Physical Activity, Nutrition & Rehabilitation* 519, 520–3.

[26] Table IV of the Twelve Tables, Law III: 'A father shall immediately put to death a son recently born a monster or has a form different from that of members of the human race'.

[27] Table IV of the Twelve Tables, Law I: 'A father shall have the right of life and death over his son born in lawful marriage …'.

[28] On the Roman military discipline, see e.g. D Hoyos, *Rome Victorious: The Irresistible Rise of the Roman Empire* (Bloomsbury Academic 2019, reprinted 2023) 8.

as warlike[29] peoples. As stated, Rome would also have incorporated the military power in its constitution; as Sparta would. Moreover, Rome's conservative values of obedience, prudence, temperance, devotion to family and country, fortitude, dignity and honour were very similar to the values of Sparta and vice versa. Also, Rome like Sparta was a society of traditionalist ideology, adding here the fact that the Romans 'were experts at retaining the form of institutions while changing their substance'[30]. Beyond this, Rome's value system was conservative and patriarchal. For instance, '[t]he power of *paterfamilias* remained comprehensive and unbroken'.[31]

Rome was, however, unlike Sparta, one great cultural melting pot in the heart of the Italian peninsula, acquiring a great deal of cultural characteristics from its Italian neighbours, who would pose as friends at certain times and as enemies at other times. Principally, '[o]nly by understanding the neighbours of the Romans can we even begin to understand the true significance of the evolution of Roman culture [and, by extension, their polity]'.[32] Perhaps the very genius of Rome was found in the fact that, even though Rome was traditionally not particularly intellectual or stylish, it was confident and intelligent enough to 'readily borrow … from the cultures of [its] Italian neighbors [and not only]'.[33]

So, too, the Rome of imperial ambitions in the years of the Republic but also in the years of the Principate was intelligent enough to respect the customs, the traditions, the religions and the local city-state forms of government[34] of the conquered. Rome otherwise started rather primitive.[35] Indeed, whilst the first Romans were not, of course, nurtured by a she-wolf, this well-known Roman myth may

[29] A Herman, *The Cave and the Light: Plato Versus Aristotle and the Struggle for the Soul of Western Civilization* (Random House New York 2014) 110.

[30] Cornell (n 20) 25. Also, Crawford (n 2) 13. But cf. HI Flower, *Roman Republics* (Princeton University Press 2010) 22, who argued, in a slightly different context, that '[f]ar from being conservative, Romans tended to be bold in adopting new solutions and policies to meet the changing world that they were shaping by their aggressive foreign policy'. The synthesis of these two apparently opposing theses could occur by reasoning of the fact that Cornell was referring to institutions, whereas Flower was referring to policies. The two terms are interrelated but would not be synonymous. Flower makes a slightly different point later on in her analysis: HI Flower, *Roman Republics* (Princeton University Press 2010) 45, stating that in the context of Patricians retaining exclusive magisterial powers in republican Rome at least up until 367/6 BC, 'Roman society appear[s] highly traditional and slow to change, even under intense pressure from external enemies and from internal social tensions'.

[31] KA Raaflaub, 'Born to Be Wolves? Origins of Roman Imperialism' in RW Wallace and EM Harris (eds), *Transitions to Empire: Essays in Greco-Roman History, 360–146 B.C., in Honor of E. Badian* (University of Oklahoma Press 1996) 291.

[32] Mathisen (n 5) 32.

[33] Mathisen (n 5) 55.

[34] Mathisen (n 5) 133. A similar point was also made by Millar with regard to the respect which the Romans seem to have shown towards the identity and culture of the conquered Greeks: Millar (n 5) 37.

[35] Mouritzen (n 7) 31.

actually pinpoint the very humble and primitive beginnings of the village[36] that Rome once was. The same legend carries a powerful ideological connotation: the Roman identity has been 'a mixture of different ethnic groups, and ... Roman culture [has been] the product of various foreign influences'.[37] At the same time, Rome's interaction and wars with Carthaginians, Greeks, Celts, Italics and Etruscans, its legendary roots to Troy, its claims to the Peloponnesian origins of its first settlers, the profound influence of the Etruscans on Rome's population and culture,[38] all point to the very mixed character that Rome acquired.

For instance, theory suggests that it was the Etruscans that transformed Rome into a city from a village of scattered straw huts on the hills of Rome.[39] Moreover, the Abduction and Rape of Sabine Women by the Romans in the mid-8th century BC was just Rome's mythological packaging to explain that its population comprised Sabine elements too. Chariot races in circuses (racecourses) were borrowed from the Greeks and the Etruscans as late as 211 BC, when they were introduced in Rome to honour Apollo.[40] Additionally, to this day, one would not be perfectly certain of whether the word 'Roma' is of Italic,[41] Etruscan[42] or Greek[43] etymology. That mixed character of Rome, we shall see, was not only found in its culture but also in its polity, the mixed polity, which Rome was in the years of the Republic.

However, the Roman polity's high degree of constitutional sophistication in the years of the Republic became readily apparent in at least one way: for fear of returning to the rather primitive and authoritarian one-man states, especially the last one-man state in the last two to three[44] decades of the Roman Monarchy, a well-established system of multiple checks and balances would be part and parcel of the Roman Republic, from the 3rd century BC already and especially in the 2nd century BC, when the Roman Republic was mature and confident. 'No man to hold too many powers in his hands for long' must have been the secret wish and the motto of all true Roman republicans,[45] except, of course, if the office of the Roman dictator would be necessary, ideally, for a certain limited period of time only. Thus, with the exception of the Roman Republic's extraordinary but

36 Mathisen (n 5) 55.
37 Cornell (n 20) 60.
38 E.g. Cornell (n 20) 159, 169–72.
39 Mathisen (n 5) 61.
40 Mathisen (n 5) 133.
41 Serv. A. 8.63–5.
42 Mathisen (n 5) 62.
43 Mathisen (n 5) 60.
44 Zoch (n 16) 28.
45 Cf. Aristot. Pol. 2.1273b where it is stated that 'it might also be thought a bad thing for the same person to hold several offices, which is considered a distinction at Carthage. One man one job is the best rule for efficiency, and the lawgiver ought to see that this may be secured, and not appoint the same man to play the flute and make shoes'. See also Mathisen (n 5) 79. He claims the Roman Republic's administration was based on the principle of collegiality, i.e. no office in the Republic would be overseen by a single person.

normal and time-limited office of the Dictator, '[i]n the republican period the very idea of a king was viewed with an almost pathological dislike'.[46] Indeed, the more developed and slightly more democratised constitution of the Middle Republic (264–133 BC), especially through *Lex Hortensia* in 287 BC, strived to maintain and mostly maintained considerable order in Rome and the empire through a system of checks and balances, even though the times of political and constitutional strife in the era of the Republic, especially later in Rome's history, in the years of the Late Republic (133–27 BC), were not uncommon to the point that the Republic would eventually give way to the Principate.

The Romans of the Middle Republic were a confident people, full of energy and perseverance. At the beginning of the Middle Republic, however, they would not necessarily wish to become imperial; nor would there be a plan for an imperial Roman republic. Conventionally, Rome became clearly imperial after 201 BC with its victory over the Carthaginians in the Second Punic War and fully imperial with the Treaty of Apamea in 188 BC. The challenges that Rome of the Republic found in its path created the classical Roman character: a character severe and rigorous, somewhat similar to the Spartan character, albeit greedier to that of the average Spartan and, certainly, a character considerably different to the more liberal, more entrepreneurial and more open-minded character of the Athenians and the Etruscans: these challenges made Rome what it came to be, the Romans forging for themselves a 'shared ethic of sacrifice for the community [but] a sense of imperial destiny emerged as the city overcame what surely seemed at some moments to be insurmountable challenges'.[47]

1.4 DEFINITIONS

The monograph proceeds *inter alia* on taxonomising and categorising the institutions, the magistrates and the bodies of the Roman Republic into four types: monarchic ones, oligarchic ones, aristocratic ones and democratic ones. The analysis, thus, follows the Aristotelian division of constitutions, a theory which is largely unitary.[48] As such, the proposed division of Roman magistrates and institutions operates and proceeds in agreement with key tenets, aspects and definitions of Aristotelian theory but also in agreement with the Republic's overall mixed character and mixed constitution (polity), a constitution that certainly comprised monarchic, oligarchic, aristocratic and democratic elements into one.

A democratic institution or office is herein defined as one whose exercise of power comes with a democratic essence to it, one that shows correspondence and respect to the will of the people,[49] the *demos*, the *populus* in the case of Roman

[46] Cornell (n 20) 148.

[47] Flower (n 30) 99–100.

[48] DJ Riesbeck, 'The Unity of Aristotle's Theory of Constitutions' (2016) 49 *Apeiron* 93.

[49] Cf. Thuc. 2.37: '[Our constitution's] administration favors the many instead of the few; this is why it is called a democracy'.

Republic. It would effectively be about the promotion of the interests of Roman Plebeians (even though Patricians were also included[50] in the definition of the *populus* – the reason for this is that the Plebeians would form the overwhelming majority of free Roman citizens).

An aristocratic institution is fundamentally one which comes with the rule of the best in the exercise of its powers. The monograph, thus, remains faithful to the original Greek definition of aristocracy (rule of the best)[51] and decisively departs from the currently prevalent term of 'aristocracy' in the modern English, Greek and many other European languages, which is effectively synonymous to nobility, the ruling classes, wealthy elites and so on.

An oligarchic institution is taken to be one which normally promotes the interests of a few, the few wealthy that are in power and/or the few wealthy behind such an institution. An oligarchy would, thus, be about a closed number of persons in power, normally ones that are not only few but also wealthy, in full and perfect agreement with Aristotelian doctrine.[52]

Finally, a monarchic office would be a body whose exercise of power would point to the sole discretion[53] of an appointed or elected[54] Roman magistrate in the exercise of power.[55] In Rome there were unwritten customary rules in this respect, especially if powers were to be exercised within the same college of magistrates.[56] Moreover, in the case of monarchic offices, because of Rome's great affection to dyarchy in the years of the Republic, we shall take dyarchic offices to be falling under the wider category of monarchic offices but a special note will be made as to the dyarchic nature of any such offices in the Monarchic Elements chapter.

And yet, it would be fair to suggest that our classification of Roman offices would be offered on an illustrative and indicative basis only. The Romans did not have to have read Plato and Aristotle to build their mixed polity; nor would they have to have corresponded to the Greek definitions of constitutional government in any possible way. However, the constituent elements of their sophisticated republic would come very close to the ones explored, analysed and posited by Plato, Aristotle and Thucydides.

50 TC Brennan, 'Power and Process under the Republican "Constitution"' in HI Flower (ed), *The Cambridge Companion to the Roman Republic* (2nd edn, Cambridge University Press 2014) 20.

51 Aristot. Pol. 3.1279a; 4.1293b. Cf. Aristot. Pol. 3.1286b; Plat. Rep. 5.473c–d.

52 Aristot. Pol. 3.1279b–80a.

53 It is to be noted that magistrates that would operate in Rome itself should not exercise the fullest of their powers: Brennan (n 50) 24.

54 Cf. the elective tyranny in the form of the office of the Dictator in Rome; Aristot. Pol. 3.1285b (see third sub-category of kingship under Aristotle).

55 Aristot. Pol. 3.1285b, especially the fifth sub-category of monarchic offices: 'a fifth kind of kingship is when a single ruler is sovereign over all matters in the way in which each race and each city is sovereign over its common affairs; this monarchy ranges with the rule of a master over a household, for just as the master's rule is a sort of monarchy in the home'.

56 Brennan (n 50) 44–5.

Chapter 2

From the Monarchy to the Republic: From Legend to History

2.1 INTRODUCTION

This chapter proceeds on the basis that Rome's beginnings have traditionally been seen as rather obscure and that historical data from the years of the Roman Monarchy (753–509 BC) and from the 5th and 4th centuries BC (the first two centuries of the Roman Republic) is scarce. For instance, it seems that the year of Rome's foundation was more of a conventional point in time, Rome's beginnings being older than that. To the extent that historical data from these centuries exists, such will be used in this chapter, taking socio-political, legal and other contextual matter into account.

2.2 *AETERNA ROMA*

Rome existed long before[1] 753 BC, the traditional year of her foundation. What may have been established in the eighth century BC was the united and designated city of Rome[2] under a common framework of customs and laws, in the form of a *synoecism*[3]. At least that is what the founding of Rome through the ploughing of the city's boundaries by Romulus[4] seems to suggest, for Rome prior to this must have resembled more like the Sparta of Thucydides: a city without a centre, that is a *polis kata kōmas oikoumenē*.[5] As such, the villages and the settlements of Rome pre-existed the conventional date of Rome's founding[6] per se and there have been reports that the area of Rome was settled before that. Of course, the Romans

1 E.g. M Beard, *SPQR: A History of Ancient Rome* (Liveright Publishing 2015) 83–4.

2 Cf. L Capogrossi Colognesi, *Law and Power in the Making of the Roman Commonwealth* (Cambridge University Press 2014) 8.

3 T Mommsen, *The History of Rome*, vol. 1 (W Purdie Dickson tr, Macmillan & Co. 1901) 53–4, 108–9; Capogrossi Colognesi (n 2) 7, 20.

4 D.H. 1.88.1–2; Liv. 1 7.

5 Thuc. 1.5.1, 1.10.2.; M Herman Hansen, 'Was Sparta a Normal or Exceptional Polis?' in S Hodkinson (ed), *Sparta: Comparative Approaches* (The Classical Press of Wales 2009) 389–90; Capogrossi Colognesi (n 2) 7.

6 The original city of Rome was created on the Palatine Hill. Subsequently, Rome expanded to other hills too, even to the West of Tiber. The final three hills of Rome, the Esquiline, the Quirinal and the Viminal Hill, were added to it under Servius Tullius in the 6th century BC: PA Zoch, *Ancient Rome* (Oklahoma University Press 1998) 25.

would occasionally intermingle history with legend and what they considered Rome's ancient history is to our eyes myth.[7]

However, because myths were about Rome's codified messages to the world, one must pay certain considerable attention to Roman myth to appreciate the later development of Roman history. Also, the Romans were not always particularly interested in recording their history, which, of course, started to be recorded hundreds of years after Rome was established.[8] What is important from the constitutional law point of view is that Romulus, the legendary founder of Rome, organised Rome's monarchic 'constitution' in the first place.[9]

Another legend, a pure fabrication of Rome's propaganda machinery,[10] had it that the Romans drew their origins from Troy, as have maintained other peoples in Europe after the Romans.[11] The choice of the 'Trojan descent' of the Romans through Aeneas, was one that also somewhat matched the old stories of Herodotus as to the roots of another Italic people, the Etruscans, from the East, and, in particular, from Lydia in Asia Minor. It was also about the Romans telling the Greeks and the East Mediterraneans that they, as 'Trojans', were both similar and different to them; that Rome could impose her dominion in the Eastern Mediterranean and Greece because that is where the Romans would claim to originate. Also, conveniently, the fabricated Trojan descent of the Romans would therefore fit them well[12] and would allow them to avenge the allegedly Grecoitalian-descented-from-Odysseus[13]-and-Circe Etruscans in the 4th century BC;[14] the Greeks of Pyrrhus in the 3rd century BC;[15] and Greece itself in the 2nd century BC for the destruction of Troy by the Greeks c. 1000 years ago. Finally, whereas Odysseus would wish to return to Ithaca because he would miss family and fatherland, Virgil informs us that the fugitive Aeneas from Troy, the 'Odysseus of the Romans', was destined to wander in the Mediterranean to eventually build a city that would give birth to a great empire.[16]

Rome's fabrications reached new heights, however, by putting Aeneas on a pedestal, while condemning Odysseus: Aeneas was a man of honour, even

[7] Zoch (n 6) 6.

[8] Ibid.

[9] Capogrossi Colognesi (n 2) 9.

[10] Cf. EJ Bickerman, 'Origines Gentium' (1952) 47 *Classical Philology* 65, 68.

[11] Bickerman (n 10) 65, 66.

[12] E.g. ES Gruen, *Culture and National Identity in Republican Rome* (Cornell University Press 1992) 50–1; however, he argues in the same work (30, 48 citing Plut. *Flam.* 12.6–7.), by using the example of Flamininus, that the Romans did not contradict themselves as descendants of Troy and protectors of the Greek freedom.

[13] Gruen (n 12) 10.

[14] E Dench, *From Barbarians to New Men: Greek, Roman, and Modern Perceptions of Peoples of the Central Apennines* (Oxford University Press 1995) 41 citing TJ Cornell, 'Aeneas and the Twins' (1975) 21 (201) PCPS 2 with n. 7.

[15] Cf. Dench (n 14) 41, 72. The Greeks too used the alleged Trojan descent of the Romans to attack them: Gruen (n 12) 44; G Bradley, *Early Rome to 290 BC* (Edinburgh University Press 2020) 87 citing Pausanias 1.12.1 and A Momigliano, 'How to Reconcile Greeks and Trojans' 240–1.

[16] E.g. Zoch (n 6) 7.

though he wanted to give birth to the rise of imperial Rome, to an empire; while Odysseus was relegated to a man of deviousness because he wished to reach his family and Ithaca. Greater still was the fabrication behind Rome's myths when the Roman elites through Virgil decided in the *Aeneid* a major stopover for Aeneas in Carthage where he met princess Dido and fell in love with her. Aeneas, reminded by Mercury of his destiny to create Rome and empire, abandons a heartbroken Dido, who curses him and his descendants, the Romans, asking the Carthaginians to turn against the Trojan settlers of Aeneas in Italy for all posterity.[17] Virgil's choice of the city of Carthage was, of course, no accident, as Carthage was a traditional enemy of Rome, which Rome destroyed in 146 BC. Aside from Rome's fables as to her origins and her raison d'être, the reader would be informed that Rome was almost always a composite reality in her history; four circles would have defined her and her constitution traditionally: the Latin circle, the Greek circle, the Etruscan circle and the Samnito-Sabine circle. These we will explore in another chapter.[18]

2.3 AB *URBE CONDITA* SIGNIFICANCE FOR ROMAN CONSTITUTIONAL LAW

Historians and, by extension, the Romans would count years from the conventional year of the foundation of Rome, that is *ab urbe condita*, 753 BC. *Condita* in the Latin language is the feminine form of perfect passive participle of the verb *condō*. *Condō* is etymologically derived from the Latin prefix con- (together) and dō (to put). Literally, the verb *condō* means 'to put together'. Thus, the more appropriate meaning, the more appropriate translation of the term in the English language, would be 'from the putting together of the city [of Rome]'.

As stated, Rome was not founded in 753 BC; nonetheless, it must have been put together as a city in the eighth century BC. So would its public law, as the putting together of the Roman settlements must have required a co-ordinating authority under a common framework of rules, customs and principles. In other words, the literal interpretation of the participle 'condita' in conjunction with the legendary 'founding' of Rome by Romulus, logically allows us to propose that sometime in the 8th century BC Rome was united into one, under one authority, one set of customs and one religion. All land falling within the *pomoerium* (Rome's religious boundary) was Rome *stricto sensu*. Roman fields (*agri*) beyond the *pomoerium* would be Roman dominion but would not fall, strictly speaking, in Roman religious territory.

The designation of the *pomoerium* must have had wide-ranging constitutional implications for Rome: not only would Rome be given an urban designation, a definition and religious borders but this would in turn have caused the very creation of Roman public law under a single authority, presumably the

[17] Verg. A. 4.621–9.
[18] Chapter 7.

Rex (King). Indeed, the literal translation of *condita* in conjunction with the parallel interpretation of the Roman legend would give us reason to believe that the 'foundation' of Rome (see the putting together of Rome, in most precise terms) was actually the beginning of Rome's constitution. In short, the unification of the villages and the settlements on the Seven Hills of Rome would almost certainly signify their constitutional unification into one. Thus was born the constitution of Rome.

2.4 ROMULUS ESTABLISHING THE CONSTITUTION OF ROME AS A MONARCHY

A constitution now existed but its finer details were still in the making. Eventually, the legendary founder of Rome, Romulus, after he killed his brother, Remus, became first king of Rome and created a Senate of 100 members who were the *patres* of Rome's 100 major Houses, each House representing a clan. The members of the *Rex*'s Senate were called the *patres*, that is the Fathers of Rome, as they would be the fathers of leading Roman families.[19] The ancestors of the *patres* would be called the Patricians, the nobles of Rome, while all the rest of the Romans would be Plebeians, that is the common people of Rome.[20] Practically, while Rome's constitution was still in the making, a choice for their form of government was offered to the Romans and the Romans chose a monarchic model for their city based on the monarchic model of Alba Longa, entrusting the then new kingdom in the hands of Romulus.[21] The Monarchy was thus formally established, it being supported[22] by 100 Senators who would help the ascent of a person to the throne but would not practically have the power to overturn his decisions as *Rex*. The Senate would be the *Rex*'s advisory body.[23] However, the *Rex* was the only person in Rome having *imperium*, being practically unchecked in the exercise of his absolute executive powers. Constitutionally, the *Rex* would hold executive, legislative, judicial and religious powers, his will being the supreme will of Rome. In the absence of the *Rex* from Rome, his regal duties would be performed by the *Rex*'s appointed leading senator, the *Praefectus urbi*.[24] A final point to be noted with regard to the position of the *Rex* in Rome was that he was *mutatis mutandis* the 'proprietor of the state'[25] and managed the finances of the state, even

19 E.g. Zoch (n 6) 11.
20 Ibid.
21 A Fraschetti, *The Foundation of Rome* (Marian Hill and Kevin Windle (trs), Edinburgh University Press 2005) 66.
22 Capogrossi Colognesi (n 2) 19.
23 K Von Fritz, *The Theory of the Mixed Constitution in Antiquity: A Critical Analysis of Polybius' Political Ideas* (Columbia University Press 1954) 196; I Shatzman, 'The Roman Republic: From Monarchy to Julius Caesar' in JA Olsen and CS Gray (eds), *The Practice of Strategy: From Alexander the Great to the Present* (Oxford University Press 2011) 38.
24 Fraschetti (n 21) 66–7.
25 Mommsen (n 3) 84.

though his private property seemed to have been technically separate from that of the state.[26]

There are three versions[27] according to Dionysius of Halicarnassus as to what happened to Romulus as first King of Rome;[28] the first version speaks of him being taken to the heavens and becoming a god (*apotheosis*), supposedly because he served Rome well. The second version speaks of him being dismembered and torn apart into pieces (*aphanismos*) by the senators as he became a tyrant and did not serve Rome well. This duality and ambiguity of the Roman myth here is almost certainly an invention of the Rome of the Republic: a king can be good but his rule may deteriorate into a tyranny; furthermore, one ought to respect the founder and the first king of Rome, Romulus, but the rule of one man, even if that is the rule of Romulus, can be constitutionally perilous. The Roman myth here thus sows the seed for the well-being of the Republic based on a system of checks and balances or, more probably, it was created as a myth because the Republic was based on the idea that kingships can become tyrannies, as even Romulus may have become a tyrant eventually during his reign. Practically, the Republic used myth to explain its main constitutional raison d'être: the fact that the Republic will not accept the rule of a single man, let alone the rule of a single man for long, and that power will be shared predominantly amongst its ruling classes and the people of Rome. As for the third version, this one speaks of the new citizens of Rome being maltreated by Romulus as *Rex*, them finding the opportunity to assassinate him after nightfall when he would not have the protection of his bodyguards.

The years of the Monarchy (753–509 BC) were by all means interesting from the constitutional point of view but the Kingdom of Rome was otherwise an insignificant political and military entity in this era. Rome as a monarchy did not register on the historical radar of major Mediterranean powers, unless one were an Etruscan noble and wished to expand one's territories from Etruria to the South, all the way to Rome and beyond. However, from the constitutional point of view, one can divide the years of the monarchy into two further periods of time: a first period, let us call this the period of the traditional Roman monarchy, which would span from 753 to 578 BC, in which the *Rex*, with the exception of Romulus, would be normally elected by Rome's Curiate Assembly; and a second period, let us call this the period of tyrannical Roman monarchy, which spanned from 578 to 509 BC. This second monarchic period was the monarchic period of the last two of the seven kings of Rome. The last two kings of Rome, Servius Tullius and Lucius Tarquinius Superbus, would not have been properly elected onto the throne. Moreover, not only would Lucius Tarquinius Superbus not have been elected but his kingship would be wholly tyrannical. He and the Tarquins had to be persecuted and removed from the throne and from Rome in 509 BC. Thus was born the Roman Republic.

[26] Mommsen (n 3) 92.

[27] Zoch (n 6) 14; Fraschetti (n 21) xiii, 85–6.

[28] D.H. 2.56.1–5.

2.5 THE FIFTH AND FOURTH CENTURIES BC AS AGES OF OBSCURITY FOR THE ROMAN REPUBLIC

The fact that the Republic was born in 509 BC did not make it any stronger than the Monarchy. In fact, the Roman Republic was not anywhere near a confident and strong republic in the fifth and the fourth century BC. It was merely fighting for its survival. Moreover, the overthrow of the Roman Monarchy in 509 BC did not make the Etruscan influence on Rome immediately disappear and Rome would still be under the influence of the Etruscans for some time.[29] The well-known stories behind such legendary figures as Publius Horatius Cocles, Gaius Mucius Scaevola, Cloelia, Lucius Quinctius Cincinnatus and Camilus, while they were inspirational for future Roman generations, speak of a republic that was merely fighting for survival. Culturally, Rome was still very introvert too at the time and would now be threatened by her next door brothers, the Latins.[30] In these centuries, one otherwise observes relatively underdeveloped forms of republican institutions in Rome and, occasionally, the historical sources are not clear to the point that certain legendary and historical fact may have been used interchangeably. Livy attests to the fact that Roman history before 390 BC was more of a moral lesson than historically narrative *stricto sensu*.[31]

It is also the case that in these centuries there was considerable unrest between the Plebeians and the Patricians. It would also seem that the Order of the Patricians had a much greater say[32] in the running of the Republic, in these early stages of its history, to the point that the Roman *populus* would be more of an ornament to the Republic than a component of it. The Consulate, a central constitutional characteristic of the Republic, did not fully operate between 449 and 367 BC with Military Tribunes with equivalent-powers-to-Consuls running the Republic instead.[33] What was also certain was the fact that in these centuries Rome was more of a historical sideshow than a significant player in the Italian peninsula (let alone in the Mediterranean world). Rome started as an amalgamation, a synoecism of villages, conventionally in the 8th century BC, or even before that, and it would seem that in the fifth and fourth centuries it was more of a well-developed town with city state characteristics in the orbit of the Etruscan and the Greek worlds, superior civilisations to Rome,[34] Rome having previously succumbed to the influence and control of the Etruscans for certain periods of time.

For instance, in 750 BC the Etruscans allegedly came to help (or may have actually been part of the Roman forces from within Rome that helped) against the

[29] Capogrossi Colognesi (n 2) 51.

[30] Capogrossi Colognesi (n 2) 51.

[31] KA Raaflaub, 'The Conflict of the Orders in Archaic Rome: A Comprehensive and Comparative Approach' in KA Raaflaub (ed), *Social Struggles in Archaic Rome: New Perspectives on the Conflict of the Orders* (2nd edn, Blackwell Publishing 2005) 10.

[32] E.g. Raaflaub (n 31) 4.

[33] Capogrossi Colognesi (n 2) 53.

[34] M Crawford, *The Roman Republic* (2nd edn, Fontana Press 1992) 16; Raaflaub (n 31) 16.

Sabines, after Rome provoked a war with the latter. As a matter of fact, it has been argued that Rome may well have been founded by Etruscans in the first place, whilst the Romans themselves have argued that the first settler of Rome's Palatine Hill and, by extension, the first settler of Rome was Evander (his name meaning 'the good man'), a Greek from the Peloponnese. Nonetheless, when Romulus and Remus founded Rome on the Palatine Hill, they seem to have done so following Etruscan traditions.

In any case, these two centuries, the fifth and the fourth century, were quite dark for the Roman Republic.[35] Rome was frequently engaged in wars with its Latin neighbours and with the Etruscans.[36] Its military efforts were occasionally rather appalling and it did not inspire any great fear, let alone respect, to its enemies. For instance, Rome was a historical absentee from Mediterranean conquests of the surrounding-to-the-Italian-peninsula-islands. In the Battle of Alalia in c. 540 BC, a turning point for the conquest of Corsica by the Etruscans, the belligerents were Greeks (Phocaeans) on the one side and allied Etruscans and Carthaginians on the other side. The Greeks won the battle but, with two thirds of their fleet destroyed, their losses could not sustain their settlement and safe presence in Corsica. Thus, they created the colony of Hyele, later known as Elea, in south Italy instead.

The Romans, on the other hand, were absent from the battle of Alalia, as was Rome continuously absent from its humble beginnings until the conquest of the Mediterranean powers to control such islands as Sicily, Sardinia and Corsica in the 6th, 5th and 4th centuries BC. Nor did Rome play any role when, relatively close to its kingdom's territory, the Cumean Greeks engaged in conflict and repelled the allied forces of Capuan Etruscans, Aurunci and Dauni in 524 BC. Also, Rome was again absent in the battle of Imera when the Sicelian Greeks crushed a powerful Carthaginian invading army in Sicily in 480 BC. Furthermore, rather suspicious was Rome's absence in mainland Italy's developments in 474 BC, when the Cumeans repelled with the help of the Syracusans the Etruscans, the rationale of Rome probably being that the Cumeans would sustain all the pain of repelling the Etruscans without Rome having to sustain any losses whatsoever. Rome had clearly not risen yet and its military efforts were concerned with mainly defending its rather limited territory in central Italy.

So too, Rome was not always very successful against its land enemies in the 4th century BC either. Aside from its victory over the Etruscan city of Veii in 396 BC, it actually fell at the mercy of the Gauls a few years after, when it was invaded by them in 390 BC (the Gallic leader Brennus famously exclaiming '*Vae victis!*' ('Woe to the defeated!') at the humiliated and invaded Romans paying extraordinary ransom to the invaders, when Brennus threw his sword on the balance that was weighing the ransom gold for the Romans to pay even more ransom to the Gauls). This event, a major *dies frigoris* to the Roman mind, defined the Roman psyche for

[35] Raaflaub (n 31) 4.
[36] Ibid.

whole centuries, as did the ever-growing Roman hatred in the 3rd and 2nd centuries BC against Carthage and the traditional fear of the Roman political elites for the rule of one man, the *Rex* (king), in the 6th century BC. In the 4th century BC again, in 321 BC, at the hands of the Samnites, the humiliation that the Romans sustained, indeed the humiliation that the two Roman Consuls leading Rome's armies against the Samnites sustained upon defeat, was not negligible either: post the battle of the Caudine Forks, the Samnites sent these two Consuls, all of the caught Roman military officers and all of the caught legionaries under the yoke as a symbolic act of humiliation of the victorious Samnites against the defeated Romans. So too, Roman society was not anywhere settled; nor was what was otherwise its republican constitution: whereas there was a settled distinction between Plebeians and Patricians, this period of time has been characterised by the so-called Conflict of the Orders.[37] Conventionally, this period is marked between 494 BC, when the Plebeians seceded to Mons Sacer (Rome's sacred mountain) and 287 BC, when the Hortensian Law was passed.[38] The Plebeians seceded for the second time in 449 BC, for the third time in 445 BC, for the fourth time in 342 BC and for the fifth time in 287 BC. Most importantly, this era of political and geopolitical turmoil for Rome has also been an era of historical darkness for Rome, '[t]he modern historian of the early Republic [being] faced with a seemingly impossible task'.[39] These dark ages for Rome were also reflected in the Republic: the overall constitutional framework of the republic must have been a mixed one in Greek terms, a republican one in Roman terms, but clearly not as developed as the constitution of the Republic between 287 and 133 BC, which this monograph explores in detail.

[37] Ibid.

[38] Ibid.

[39] Raaflaub (n 31) 5.

Chapter 3

Periodisation of the Republic: Between Classic Periodisation and Flower's Periodisation

3.1 INTRODUCTION

The book adheres both to the classic periodisation of the Roman Republic and to Flower's more precise division of the Roman Republic era into a number of republics. It proceeds and focuses on the more established periodisation of the Roman republican era in the interests of practicality for the reader and as a matter of convention.

3.2 FLOWER'S THESIS

Flower's thesis is about the division of the era of the Roman Republic into a number of republics.[1] Her thesis is certainly more meticulous, more refined and more precise[2] than the classical periodisation of the Roman Republic into three: the Early Republic (509–264 BC), the Middle Republic (264–133 BC) and the Late Republic (133–27 BC). It is, therefore, more scientific. However, this work balances, for reasons of practicality, between her thesis and the more traditional division of the Republic for the convenience of the reader. Thus, every time the term Middle Republic will be used herein, one practically refers to Flower's 'republics of the *nobiles*', especially her Republic of the *Nobiles* 1 and the Republic of the *Nobiles* 2, and vice versa.

3.3 MONOGRAPH'S POSITIONING IN TRADITIONAL PERIODISATION AND FLOWER'S PERIODISATION OF THE ROMAN REPUBLIC

The monograph proceeds mostly on the traditional periodisation of the Roman Republic with the obvious note that our analysis, especially when it comes to the constitution of the Roman Republic, will concentrate on the period 287–133 BC (as opposed to 264–133 BC which stands for the Middle Republic's traditional timeframe per se). This would stand for the book's remit, even though the reader would also be offered information about Rome and her constitution before and

1 HI Flower, *Roman Republics* (Princeton University Press 2010) 33.

2 Cf. C Smith, 'Becoming Political: Middle Republican Quandaries' in S Bernard, LM Mignone and D Padilla Peralta (eds), *Making the Middle Republic: New Approaches to Rome and Italy, c. 400–200* BCE (Cambridge University Press 2023) 256.

after the book's timeframe. This book, thus, concentrates fundamentally on the very late stage of the Early Republic (287–264 BC) and the Middle Republic (264–133 BC). As stated, the remit of the book largely coincides with Flower's Republic of the *Nobiles* 1 (300–180 BC) and Republic of the *Nobiles* 2 (180–139 BC) but obviously it also merely touches for six years upon Flower's Republic of the *Nobiles* 3 (139–88 BC),[3] the period up until 133 BC which came to a close with the assassination of Tiberius Gracchus (see Figure 3.1). The reader would also be reminded that beyond the book's overall compatibility with Rome's classical periodisation (see the Middle Republic's era) and Flower's Republics of the *Nobiles* 1 and 2, it further posits that, while Rome never had a golden age Athenian style in constitutional government terms, the period between 287 and 133 BC would effectively stand for the Republic's finest period in constitutional law terms, despite certain grave mistakes, errors and omissions of the Romans of the same period, in geopolitical, constitutional and socio-economic terms. Finally, the monograph's remit is also offered herein for the benefit of the reader against the periodisation of both first Rome and second Rome, Constantinople and Eastern Roman Empire (see Figure 3.2).

3.4 ADDITIONAL FEATURES OF FLOWER'S THESIS FOR THE UNDERSTANDING OF THE ROMAN REPUBLIC

A key idea in Flower's thesis is the idea of periodisation, which is a central feature of the discipline of history.[4] She concedes, however, that the Romans did not think of their existence in Rome in terms of historical eras and periods in the same way we do.[5] Of course, a further argument here would be that, at least in the minds of the Romans of the Republic, the division of Rome's history under the Monarchic era and under the Republican era must have been a relatively clear-cut one, despite the Romans' traditional reluctance to engage with historical matter in a strict scientific way. Moreover, Flower's thesis is also very precise where she calls the republican systems of Rome during 287–133 BC as the 'Republics of the *Nobiles*'. Indeed, these were not the republics of 'aristocrats', as many authors would wrongly posit or imply, but the republics of nobles at best, effectively wealthy Romans who would mostly come from Patrician clans and so on. These were republics of nobles; not aristocrats in the Platonic sense, unless a wealthy Roman farmer with little formal education, if any, would qualify as an aristocrat as per original Greek meaning. Whether these nobles would be the best persons to run Rome is thus doubtful, in that their degree of education (or lack thereof to be more precise) would hardly qualify them as 'aristocrats'. At most, one could argue that the wealthy rustics of Rome represented the wealthiest parts of Roman society, its *sui generis* high society, so to speak, but considering that

[3] Flower (n 1) 33.
[4] Flower (n 1) 3.
[5] Flower (n 1) 6.

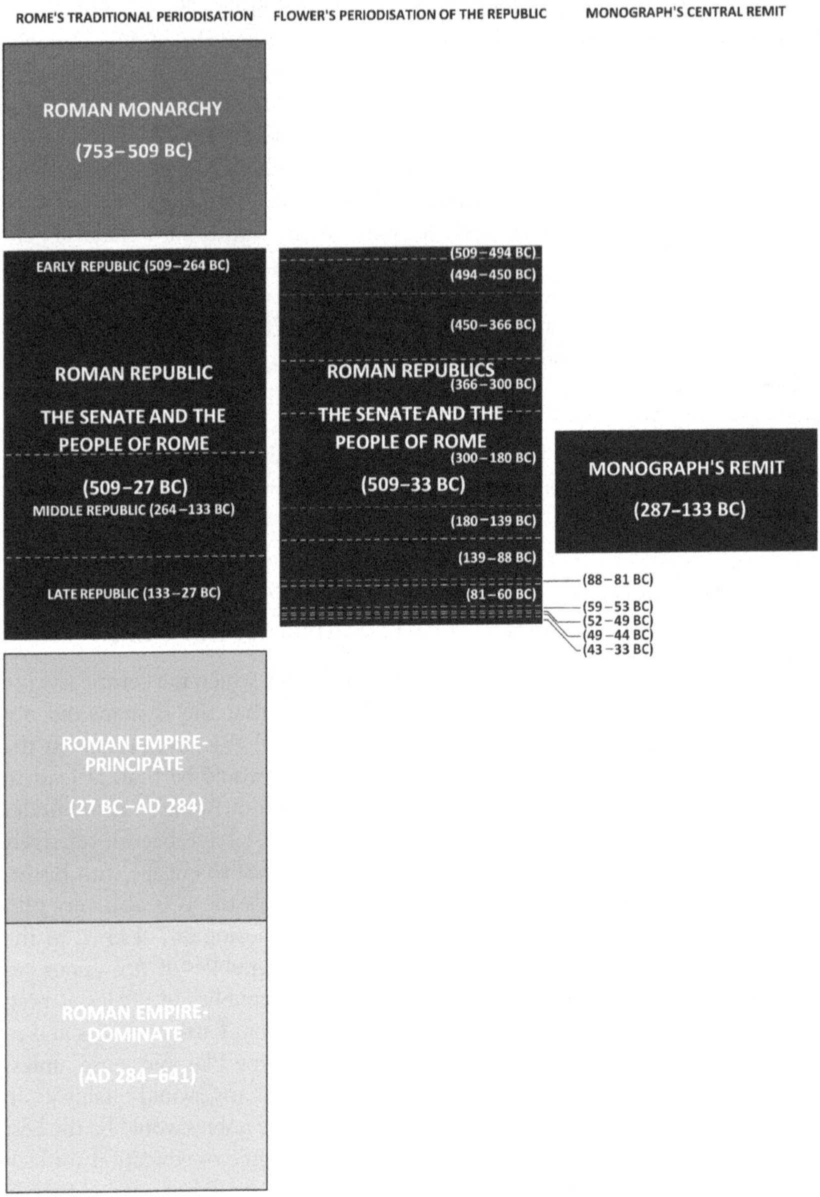

Figure 3.1 Rome's classic periodisation, Flower's periodisation of the Roman Republic and monograph's remit

Figure 3.2 First and second Rome's classic periodisation, Flower's periodisation of the Roman Republic and monograph's remit

Rome's engagement with formal education and the arts *stricto sensu* was a much later advent, even the wealthiest parts of such society would not necessarily qualify as 'aristocrats' in the Platonic and Aristotelian sense.

3.5 THE ROMAN REPUBLIC AS A LARGELY UNITARY HISTORICAL PHENOMENON IN CONSTITUTIONAL LAW TERMS

The constitutional lawyer would have to note that, whereas the Republic could historically be fragmented into a number of republics as per Flower's thesis, the phenomenon of the Republic was a largely unitary one, that is to say the conservative nature of Rome's Republic would allow us to maintain that, as a whole, the Republic presented largely similar constitutional characteristics from c. 500 BC to 133 BC, even though these would be somewhat modified over the centuries.[6] Of course, the Roman Republic of the 5th and the 4th centuries BC would be less developed than the Middle Republic, while the same republic after 133 BC would be manipulated by charismatic figures and personalities[7] and it would be more dictatorial in crucial times of the Late Republic's development. However, all these points do not change the overall conservative character of the Republic, at least prior to the Late Republic (133–27 BC). The Romans, indeed the ruling elites of Rome, were renowned in repackaging old institutions into new realities, the old status quo into a 'new' status quo, only for the old nature of things to ultimately prevail. An exception to this was the *mutatis mutandis* Roman Republic from 509 up until c. 450 BC, which ended with the enactment of the Twelve Tables in 449 BC. In this respect, it is to be noted that aside from the fact that the first fifteen years after the demise of the Monarchy would be ones under a transitional regime for the Romans,[8] the Roman Republic at least up until mid-fifth century BC would be a largely divided one, even from the constitutional point of view.[9] But it would seem that the concessions that the Patricians made to the Plebeians in 449 BC did not alter the republican core of Rome's constitution.

One of the most intriguing characteristics of the constitutional and institutional phenomenon of the Republic was the fact that it would change but it would not necessarily alter Rome's status quo significantly. The Roman Republic was a conservative republic. Momigliano is illuminating on this and reminds us of the fact that even as early as c. 500 BC the Republic had many of the constituent

6 But cf. EA Posner, 'The Constitution of the Roman Republic' in G Dari-Mattiacci and DP Kehoe (eds), *Roman Law and Economics: Institutions and Organizations Volume I* (Oxford University Press 2020) 36.

7 E.g. M Kahlos, 'Charismatic Leadership in Ancient Rome' in JP Zúquete (ed), *Routledge International Handbook of Charisma* (Routledge 2021) 65–76.

8 E.g. Flower (n 1) 33.

9 Liv. 2 44. Also, TC Brennan, *The Fasces: A History of Ancient Rome's Most Dangerous Political Symbol* (Oxford University Press 2023) 22. Cf. Flower's proto-republic between 494 and 450 BC: Flower (n 1) 33.

elements one would find in it in the 3rd and the 2nd centuries BC.[10] A classic example here would be the constitutional revision of the Republic through *Lex Hortensia* in 287 BC, even though the oligarchic elites of Rome would mostly continue to control the Republic even after 287 BC until 27 BC and beyond. Equally, as one would expect, it was also rightly noted in Momigliano's thesis that the 'political, institutional and social realities' behind the same offices of the Republic must have been different to those a few centuries later.[11] However, whereas such realities would change, the Roman constitution would not always follow suit. In fact, despite piecemeal changes to it, the core of the constitution would remain republican and oligarchic. Every rule comes with exceptions and here the dictatorial republics of Sulla and Julius Caesar in the Late Republic are to be noted as major exceptions to the 'normal' Republic which one would observe for most of the Middle Republic or the Republics of the *Nobiles* 1 and 2 under Flower's thesis.

In short, while Flower has a point in maintaining that the perception of the Roman Republic should be one that comes with a number of separate republics over the centuries, especially in the interests of historical precision, it should also be noted that the Roman mind traditionally perceived the phenomenon of the Republic, indeed the *res publica* itself, as a unitary and monolithic phenomenon.[12] One's constitutional analysis also attests to the fact that the Republic changed over the centuries but not dramatically. Of course, we are aware that, over the centuries, the Republic developed but the central constitutional characteristics thereof (except the size of established offices and the fact that Plebeians would eventually be permitted to become magistrates) remained largely similar from the beginning to the end of the Republic: classic examples here would be the Consuls or offices that would look very much like the office of Consuls or come with consular powers (between 449 and 367 BC), the continuous powerful position of the Roman Senate throughout the Republic's era and so on and so forth.

From modern times, one ought to consider the phenomenon of the French Republics. Even though French republican history has not been continuous, the phenomenon of French republicanism, albeit somewhat choppy, could be largely perceived as a unitary one as a whole: the constitutional aspiration for a proper Republic in France in 1792 was as relevant then as it is in modern France. The centrality of the citizen in the French Republic in 1792 was as relevant then as it is in modern France, even though the French citizen's rights have expanded and strengthened for more than two centuries now. Of course, it would be a mistake to expect the offices of the First French Republic to be the same as in the Fifth French Republic: for example, the First Republic in France came with a Consulate which the subsequent French Republics did not proceed with as an institution. It would also be neglectful to overlook the climate of violence and fear in the first

[10] A Momigliano, 'The Rise of the Plebs in the Archaic Age of Rome' in KA Raaflaub (ed), *Social Struggles in Archaic Rome* (Blackwell 2005) 170.

[11] Ibid.

[12] See Chapter 9 for more on the monolithic perception of the Republic's constitution by the Romans.

years of the First French Republic and the fact that there have been a number of republics in France from the historical point of view. But this does not change the overall unitary republican era of France from the more constitutional law perspective, with the obvious exceptions of the French constitutions that were not republican or largely republican in between the five French Republics, especially the regimes between 1800 and 1830 and between 1852 and 1870. As a constitutional phenomenon, however, the Roman Republic was even more unitary in that respect than modern France's republican era, in that at least between 509 and 133 BC, the Roman Republic's constitutional colours were largely similar, even if the period between 509 and 449 BC was transitional. The overall phenomenon of the Roman Republic was thus a largely unitary one. Equally, this does not change the fact that the historian and the political scientist could perceive it as a more fragmented reality in the interests of a more refined and precise analysis in their subjects.

Ultimately, it is how one poses the question here: for instance, would a historical and political[13] fragmentation of the Republic into separate republics justify the Republic's fragmentation into separate republics in constitutional terms? One could do so but that would somewhat oppose the established position of the Republic as a largely unitary constitutional phenomenon, even though the historical, the social and the political circumstances between 509 and 133 BC (let alone between 509 and 27 BC) would range from different to very different.[14]

3.6 MONOGRAPH'S POSITIONING IN TRADITIONAL PERIODISATION AND FLOWER'S PERIODISATION OF THE ROMAN REPUBLIC

To conclude, for the convenience of the reader, the monograph proceeds mostly on the traditional periodisation of the Roman Republic, with the obvious note that our analysis, especially when it comes to the constitution of the Roman Republic, will concentrate on the period 287–133 BC (as opposed to 264–133 BC, which stands for the Middle Republic's traditional timeframe per se). This monograph, thus, concentrates on the very late stage of the Early Republic (287–264 BC) and on the Middle Republic (264–133 BC). As stated, the remit of the book largely coincides with Flower's Republic of the *Nobiles* 1 (300–180 BC) and the Republic of the *Nobiles* 2 (180–139 BC) but obviously it also merely touches upon Flower's Republic of the *Nobiles* 3 (139–88 BC) for six years,[15] the period up until 133 BC, which came to a close with the assassination of Tiberius Gracchus. The reader would also be reminded that despite the book's overall compatibility with the periodisation behind the Middle Republic era and Flower's Republics of the

[13] Flower (n 1) 33.
[14] Cf. Posner (n 6) 36.
[15] Flower (n 1) 33.

Nobiles 1 and 2, it posits that, while Rome never had a golden age Athenian style in constitutional government terms, the precise period between 287 and 133 BC would stand for the Republic's finest period, despite certain grave mistakes, errors and omissions of the Romans of the same period, in geopolitical, constitutional and socio-economic terms.

PART II
THE REPUBLIC'S APOGEE

Chapter 4

The Roman Character and the Republic's Character at its Best (287–133 BC)

4.1 INTRODUCTION

The psyche of the Roman people has crystallised into their Republic's constitution. The constitution of the Roman Republic is about the psyche of the Romans. Any detailed exposition of the Roman Republic's constitution ought to also be about a meticulous and thorough psychography of the people behind it: the Romans. In this chapter, the reader will, therefore, be familiarised with the character of the Romans, especially in the best years of the Republic, but also with the character of the Republic itself at its apex. To understand the Roman Republic, its constitution and the political system that made Rome what it came to be, one must thus be first familiarised with the Roman character. A psychography of the Romans would thus be essential for us to appreciate, assess and comprehend the constitution of the Roman Republic. The constitution of the Republic would be one of the finest reflections of the Roman character.

4.2 EXAMINING THE ROMAN CHARACTER FOR GRASPING THE ROMAN REPUBLIC'S CONSTITUTION

The character of the Romans is revealing of the constitution of the Roman Republic. To examine the Roman character, however, one ought to examine the ethos, the customs and the fears of the Romans, especially as manifested in their history, their laography and their myths. It would also be about examining the ethnicity of the Romans.[1] For instance, Polybius, to justify the divergence in approach, when it comes to conduct, between Greeks and Romans, would put the Roman traits, or what seemed like barbaric acts of the Romans, down to custom,[2] even though he would, at least impliedly, oppose the distinction between Greeks and barbarians (the Romans included) and between ethnicity and ethics.[3] Beyond this, the collective composite of Rome comprised Latins, Sabines and Etruscans in the main. However, in the case of Rome's population (like every city), one could not exclude persons of different descent: for example,

[1] Cf. E Dench, 'Roman Identity' in A Barchiesi and W Scheidel (eds), *The Oxford Handbook of Roman Studies* (Oxford University Press 2010) 267.

[2] A Erskine, 'Polybios and Barbarian Rome' (2000) 3 *Mediterraneo Antico* 165, 175–6.

[3] Erskine (n 2) 165, 172.

Greeks, Italics beyond Sabines and Etruscans, and so on. Furthermore, whereas the significant influence of the Greeks on Rome cannot be disregarded, it would seem that for the greater part the Romans were of Italic stock and a people that, whilst related to the Greeks in one way or another, would be relatively distinct from the Greeks.

The best example as to how the character of the Romans affected the constitution of Rome was, of course, the well-known phobia of the Romans over the rule of a single person for long over the city of Rome. The rule of a tyrant was not a welcome idea in the Republic. The whole of the Republic was based on the idea that it should never deteriorate into a tyranny. This relates, of course, to the deep contempt of the republican Romans for kings and tyrants.[4] Whereas the Romans would accept kingship for centuries prior to the Republic, the deterioration of Roman kingships into tyrannies must have been the crucial factor for the eventual Roman contempt for tyrannical monarchies.

4.3 BACKGROUND HISTORICAL INFORMATION: ROME 287–133 BC

Rome of the Republic never had a golden age the way the Athenians had in the years of their democracy under Pericles' Golden Age. Nevertheless, the period of time between 287 and 133 BC is, by all means, the best period of time for the Republic in constitutional law terms and, of course, in developmental terms for the city of Rome and its empire. Rome had not flourished in the letters and the arts as of yet, but it was in the process of doing so, a relative peak in the area having been reached in the 1st century BC. The names of the Greek[5] poet and writer Livius Andronicus, the Campanian[6] poet Naevius, in the 3rd century BC,[7] and the Greco-Italic[8] poet and writer Ennius, in the 3rd and 2nd century BC, should otherwise suffice as to identifying the first major personalities of intellect of Rome and Italy in the world of the arts and the letters. Also, in the 3rd century BC, one observes the first Roman historian, Quintus Fabius Pictor, while another important Roman figure in the field in the turn from 3rd to 2nd century BC was Lucius Cincius Alimentus. By all means, it is in this period, 287–133 BC, that one observes the best traits of the Roman character, and yet one could not escape the fact that, even at its best, the Roman character was darker

[4] E.g. B Forsén and A Lampinen, 'Barbarians and Empire: Greek and Roman Conceptions of the East' in B Forsén and A Lampinen (eds), *Oriental Images: Stereotypes and Identity Creation in the Ancient World* (Franz Steiner 2024) 21.

[5] E.g. E Fantham, 'Literature in the Roman Republic' in HI Flower (ed), *The Cambridge Companion to the Roman Republic* (2nd edn, Cambridge University Press 2014) 325.

[6] Fantham (n 5) 326.

[7] PA Zoch, *Ancient Rome* (University of Oklahoma Press 1998) 136.

[8] But cf. A Momigliano, *Alien Wisdom: The Limits of Hellenization* (Cambridge University Press 1975) 17, who considered him Oscan.

than the noble and proud one the Romans wished to project to themselves and to the world.

4.4 THE PSYCHOGRAPHY OF THE ROMANS OF THE REPUBLIC

The reader should note that the Roman character at its best, even at its best during the best years of the Republic, came with considerable mistakes, pain and errors for the Romans themselves and, of course, for humanity. As such, the fact that one speaks of the Romans' character at its best would not make the character of this people ideal, at least not from the Aristotelian perspective. Moreover, the Romans clearly lacked the thorough cultivation of spirit, which other peoples in the Mediterranean would display, the educated Romans being aware of Rome's lack of cultivation of spirit and intellect.[9] Indeed, the Roman character came with both the energy and the heated, raw[10] and austere[11] characteristics of a young adolescent who is still in the process of forming the more refined elements of their character and identity as they enter adulthood. The Greeks would be eternal children and young in soul according to the famous Egyptian priest's response to Solon about them,[12] but the Roman character before the 3rd century BC resembled more that of an introvert deserted teenager fighting for survival[13], whilst during and after the particular century that of a wild and rebellious[14] teenager who is driven by ambition in pursuit of success, wealth and power. Historically, the partial degeneration of the Roman character in the second half of the 2nd century and in the 1st century BC affected Rome's constitution but not her empire, which continued to grow. This could be explained from the fact that certain traits of the Roman character (e.g. the traditional Roman affection for a mixed polity of checks and balances) were attacked by powerful personalities and were on the retreat, while others such as greed were on the rise.

[9] E.g. *Verg.* A. 6.847–53.

[10] E.g. Erskine (n 2) 165, 172.

[11] E Dench, *From Barbarians to New Men: Greek, Roman, and Modern Perceptions of Peoples of the Central Apennines* (Oxford University Press 1995) 82.

[12] Plat. Tim. 22b.

[13] Cf. BW Frier, Book Review (1977) *The Classical Journal* 379, 379.

[14] Cf. D Hoyos, *Rome Victorious: The Irresistible Rise of the Roman Empire* (Bloomsbury Academic 2019, reprinted 2023) 1; Hoyos speaks of Roman aggressiveness.

A layer of rusticity[15] and a lack of interest for the letters and the arts[16] would also be key features of the Roman character's original configuration[17] and for much of the Republic; the character of the Romans of the Republic was historically far from flawless and one which did not actually fully flourish in intellectual terms but, equally, one that clearly did not degenerate either, except in the Late[18] Republic; nor was the character of the Romans one that became decadent for most of the Republic. The great degeneration of the Roman masses into a life of 'bread and circuses'[19] symbolically[20] commences in the 1st century AD with the erection of the Colosseum, in the years of the Principate, but reaches new heights of decadence, fall and decline with the rise of the Dominate from AD 284 onwards until the Western Roman Empire's final collapse to barbaric tribes in AD 476/480.

Polybius, despite his overall pro-Roman stance[21] and admiration[22] for Rome, speaks of Romans, contrary to the way Greeks would be, as highly superstitious creatures,[23] yet they seem to be rational barbarians to him,[24] unlike most of the barbarians, who would just be deemed irrational.[25] A similar point to the rational barbarians comment made by Polybius was made by King Pyrrhus more than a

15 Cato the Elder, *De Agri Cultura* Preface; Hor. Ep. 2.1, line 157; Verg. A. 6.847–53; M Rostovtzeff, *The Social and Economic History of the Roman Empire* (Oxford University Press 1926) 13, 13–14; W Kunkel, *An Introduction to Roman Legal and Constitutional History* (2nd edn, The Clarendon Press 1973) 4, 8, 44; J Harries, 'Law' in Barchiesi and Scheidel (n 1) 640; L Capogrossi Colognesi, *Law and Power in the Making of the Roman Commonwealth* (Cambridge University Press 2014) 10, 62; A Herman, *The Cave and the Light: Plato Versus Aristotle and the Struggle for the Soul of Western Civilization* (Random House 2014) 110; M Beard, *SPQR: A History of Ancient Rome* (Liveright Publishing 2015) 145: the particular layer was attested from the Twelve Tables already, which would have been devised with an agricultural community in mind, *inter alia*. Also, N Petrochilos, *Roman Attitudes to the Greeks* (National and Capodistrian University of Athens 1974) 55, 62; IE Τζαμτζής, *Ο Μεσογειακός Κόσμος* (Εκδόσεις Σάκκουλα 2014, 2018 reprint) 85–6 on the calls of certain parts of Roman society to a mentality of austere agricultural simplicity; F Fulminante, *The Rise of Early Rome: Transportation Networks and Domination in Central Italy, 1050–500 BC* (Cambridge University Press 2023) 9, 24–5, 119. But cf. Hoyos (n 14) 10 claiming that Rome by 264 BC was one of the largest cities in the Mediterranean and a major economic centre.

16 E.g. Hor. Ars 323–32. Also, T Mommsen, *The History of Rome*, vol. 1 (W Purdie Dickson tr, Macmillan & Co. 1901) 36.

17 E.g. Juv. 2.6.2–10 (Juvenal, *Satire* 6.2–10).

18 E Dench (n 11) 67.

19 Juv. 4.10.77–81 (Juvenal, *Satire* 10.77–81).

20 But cf. Zoch (n 7) 147, Zoch suggesting that the spirit of 'bread and circuses' was existent at the times of the Gracchi already.

21 E.g. Plb. 3.16.2; Hoyos (n 14) 25, 27. Hoyos calls him a hard-nosed person and a critical admirer of Rome. Cf. ES Gruen, *The Hellenistic World and the Coming of Rome* (University of California Press 1984, reprinted 1986) 2, 57.

22 E.g. Gruen (n 21) 344, 346.

23 Erskine (n 2) 165, 178–9. Cf. Mommsen (n 16) 35 noting that the Latin term 'religio' is 'that which binds'.

24 Erskine (n 2) 165, 182. Cf. T Whitmarsh, 'Hellenism' in Barchiesi and Scheidel (n 1) 735, arguing that the idea that Rome of the 3rd century BC was seen as coarse by its Hellenisers or worthy of 'civilizing' is deceptive.

25 Erskine (n 2) 165, 165.

hundred years before Polybius wrote his work. Impressed with the discipline of the Romans on sight of their military campus, King Pyrrhus stated to his officer Megacles that the Romans were 'barbarians but their order is not barbarous'.[26] The Romans were also highly religious creatures. Their high religiosity would be explained from their traditional tendency to maintain a balanced life between human and spiritual affairs.[27] The Romans could also be described in their interactions with other Romans as creatures of high morality as a whole, but what started as a high moral perception of life, especially in Rome's ruling classes,[28] seems to have eventually transformed into perverse and pretentious moralism, especially in the final two centuries of the Republic. Even more alarmingly, the strict moralism, or more precisely, the abuse of a moral perception of life by the Romans, could be used and was used as an excuse for action against political enemies within Rome and against geopolitical enemies outside Rome.

Ideas and theories did not matter much to most of the Romans during the greatest part of the Republic.[29] '[I]deas exercised relatively little power in the Roman world'.[30] The Roman in the years of the Republic would be a utilitarian creature in the main. The utilitarian inclination of the Romans could most certainly be seen in the fact that the arts and the letters were not particularly cultivated at an early stage of the Roman Republic's history. The flow of ideas, Stoicism, which was embraced in Rome so much more than in the Hellenistic world, from where it originated, the systematic cultivation of the letters and the arts, were rather late trends in the Roman Republic. The peculiar phenomenon of Greek slaves in Rome being frequently more educated than their Roman masters was observed.[31] Stoicism, however, affected Rome's juridical science[32] and, by extension, Rome itself to the point that even slaves would eventually be treated somewhat more favourably than previously through new legislation.[33]

At other times, Rome could not escape openly barbaric traits: for instance, while the Republic formally banned human sacrifices in 97 BC[34] and once again in 81 BC,[35] there were reports of human sacrifices conducted by Romans in 228 BC,[36] in 216 BC after the defeat at Cannae,[37] Livy attempting to save face for the Romans

26 Plut. Pyrrh. 16.4–5.

27 Cf. K Bradley, 'Freedom and Slavery' in Barchiesi and Scheidel (n 1) 629.

28 Harries (n 15) 638.

29 Cf. Zoch (n 7) 137.

30 WV Harris, 'Power' in Barchiesi and Scheidel (n 1) 565.

31 Zoch (n 7) 136.

32 Capogrossi Colognesi (n 15) 139.

33 Harris (n 30) 576.

34 Plin. Nat. 30 3.

35 Julius Paulus, '*The Opinions of Paulus*' 5.23.16 as found in SP Scott, *The Civil Law* (The Central Trust Company 1932) 326.

36 Z Várhelyi, 'The Specters of Roman Imperialism: The Live Burials of Gauls and Greeks at Rome' (2007) 26 *Classical Antiquity* 277, 278 at note 2 citing Plut. Marc. 3.3–4 and Orosius 4.13.1–3; Beard (n 15) 180.

37 Liv. 22 57.6. Also, Beard (n 15) 180.

by maintaining that these were not related to the Roman spirit,[38] and in 113 BC[39] in preparation for attacking Gaul, Plutarch attempting to justify the Romans because of their religious adherence to the Sibylline Books.

Nonetheless, despite the Roman character's often raw, severe and unrefined features, the Roman was mostly a man of honour, *libertas* and courage. The love for honour (*φιλοτιμία*) of the Romans would put considerable pressure on the Roman youth, in that they would be expected to surpass the achievements[40] of their ancestors, as the famous quote of the young Scipio Aemilianus to his friend, Polybius, reveals.[41]

A life of simplicity, frugality,[42] moderation and honour would be the ideal for the Roman. For instance, Plutarch reports that, when Fabricius disclosed Pyrrhus' own doctor's planned betrayal to kill him, Pyrrhus released Roman soldiers without asking for ransom to return the favour. Given the proud ways of the Romans, the Roman response was to release the same number of hostages to the Greeks.[43] Also, before Rome became an imperial power, the Aetolian Greeks would have miscalculated the susceptibility of the Romans to receiving bribes: the Romans in these romantic and honourable times of their history would not prioritise pecuniary benefit over principle.[44] Also, euergetism (to do good acts in a charitable fashion by pecuniary means or otherwise) was strong amongst the Romans.[45] The Roman was also mostly characterised by *pietas*, which would be a composite characteristic that would expect and combine faith in gods, homeland and family.[46] The Roman would also aspire to virtue (*virtus*, the rough equivalent of Greek *αρετή*), clemency, mercifulness (*clementia*) and justice (*iustitia*).[47] To these characteristics one ought to add the ideals of *gravitas*, *constantia* (persistence) and *continentia* (self-restraint).[48] Additionally, *pudicitia* (modesty)[49] and *castitas* (chastity) would be expected of women.[50]

Of course, the Roman elites would occasionally purposefully exaggerate these traits of the Roman character: for example, when they would artificially promote 'their own' Aeneas as a man of honour over Odysseus, who would be presented as a man of deviousness and resourcefulness. Also, *libertas* in Rome, especially in its full-blown application, would be a privilege for the few rather than a right

38 Liv. 22 57.6.
39 Plut. Quaes. Rom. 83; Beard (n 15) 180.
40 N Rosenstein, *Rome and the Mediterranean 290 to 146 BC: The Imperial Republic* (Edinburgh University Press 2012) 30.
41 Plb. 31.23.9–12.
42 Petrochilos (n 15) 56.
43 Zoch (n 7) 88 citing Plutarch, *Pyrrh.* 21.2; also Plut. Pyrrh. 21.3.
44 Gruen (n 21) 348.
45 B Rawson, 'Family and Society' in Barchiesi and Scheidel (n 1) 614.
46 Rawson (n 45) 615.
47 Rawson (n 45) 621.
48 Zoch (n 7) 134.
49 Ibid.
50 P Culham, 'Women in the Roman Republic' in Flower (n 5) 127.

stricto sensu for the many,[51] but the Roman always aspired to liberty.[52] *Libertas* would be tantamount to *civitas*: liberty would essentially stand for a key feature of Roman citizenship.[53] It would also be fair to maintain that the Roman character would practically come with more positive than negative traits. Equally, the negative aspects of the Romans, which one could most clearly observe in the Late Republic, would be significant and would eventually lead to the demise of their Empire in the West a number of centuries after the Republic. At other times, the partial relaxation of the Roman discipline and severity of character, as reported in the years of the Middle Republic by Polybius, post Third Macedonian War in 168 BC,[54] resulted in an overall soothing of the Roman character, even though its strictness peaked yet again in 146 BC. Polybius, it should be recalled, although a great historian, was a former Greek military officer and a Roman strategist, to whom the partial relaxation of the Roman character was a vice not a blessing. Yet for the power-hungry and greedy imperial republican Romans that partial relaxation must have been a bit of a blessing, albeit a temporary one.

Also, Rome's sexuality and, for that matter, the sexuality of the male Roman has had major impact on the Roman constitution. The Republic would have only males in its constitutional machinery, a minor exception being the relatively powerful role of the Vestal Virgins, priestesses of Goddess Vesta, in state religious matters. Beyond this, the peculiar situation where women would be citizens of Rome having private rights but no public rights[55] would be observed but would have never been questioned in the years of the Republic. It was otherwise inexplicable and was never really reasoned.[56] By all means, it would seem that the unfortunate overall exclusion of women from the Republic's constitutional machinery was nothing else but a pure reflection of sexism and the spirit of conservatism that would be prevalent amongst Roman males and society. Women in Rome had a very specific role to play in society and the moral code to which they had to abide was stricter than the moral code to which males had to abide, to the exclusion of women's participation in the core operations of the Republic; so too, women

[51] Cf. Bradley (n 27) 627.

[52] Cf. C Nicolet, *The World of the Citizen in Republican Rome* (PS Falla tr, University of California 1980) 320–1.

[53] M Humbert, 'Libertas id est Civitas: Autour d'un Conflit Négatif de Citoyennetés au IIe s. avant J.-C.' in M Humbert (ed), *Antiquitatis Effigies: Recherches sur le Droit Public et Privé de Rome* (IUSS Press 2013) 83–101, in particular 94–101.

[54] ES Gruen, *Culture and National Identity in Republican Rome* (Cornell University Press 1992) 261 citing Polybius, 31.25.4–6.

[55] R van den Bergh, 'Roman Women: Sometimes Equal and Sometimes Not' (2006) 12 *Fundamina* 113, 127 citing OF Robinson 'The Historical Background' in McLean and Burrows (eds), *The Legal Relevance of Gender. Some Aspects of Sex-Based Discrimination* (Palgrave Macmillan 1988) 43–4. Practically, women, foreigners and slaves were all excluded from the Republic's constitutional machinery: W Kunkel and R Wittmann, *Staasordnung und Staatspraxis der römischen Republik: Die Magistratur* (C.H. Beck 1995) 53–4.

[56] Van den Bergh (n 55) 128.

could be sexistically accused by males for *levitas animi*[57] and would have to live a life under the guardianship of a male and so on. Homosexuality in Rome was not forbidden but males engaging in acts of homosexuality assuming a passive role in such acts would be considered effeminate. The prevailing spirit of sexism and machismo in Rome would mean that the Republic was one that was male driven and constitutional posts and positions would be reserved for free Roman males.

At other times, the Roman would have developed a complex of inferiority:[58] for example, when the lay Greeks of south Italy would playfully tease the Romans by calling them *Οπικοί* (Oscans)[59] or when they would just call them barbarians,[60] when, as a matter of fact, the Romans would be related to Oscans but would not be Oscans; when they would have a city which was very similar to Greek cities[61] and a Pantheon which was very similar to the Greek Pantheon; when the Roman General Marcellus would shed tears over the magnificent beauty[62] of the finally-conquered-by-him Syracuse as compared to the rather pale colours and beauty of the city of Rome of his time.

The mostly rational, pragmatic and utilitarian Romans would occasionally give way to their emotions: the Romans would be dazzled by the statues and the artistic creations of the Greek world, which they would otherwise plunder as a matter of course,[63] or by the riches of confident and flamboyant Carthage when a Roman embassy visited it in 152 BC.[64] A Roman visiting Carthage at the time must have resembled to some extent a Spartan visiting Athens. The cultural outpacing of Athens over Sparta in the classical times was beyond doubt; so was the economic outpacing of Carthage over Rome for most of the 2nd century BC and, certainly, up until 152 BC when the envious Romans[65] were impressed by the rigour, the strength and the energy of Carthage, only six years before Rome destroyed it.

At other times the Roman character would come close to the Greek character. The dramatic display of Greek education over the defeated and the fallen would have, of course, reached a new pinnacle with the tears of Scipio Aemilianus over destroyed Carthage in 146 BC, him bringing to mind the common destiny of all human beings and the potential future fall of his own city, Rome, to barbarians

57 E.g. Gaius, 1.144.

58 E.g. Gruen (n 54) 2, 64.

59 Cf. Mommsen (n 16) 15, 168 opining that the Greeks would use the term for both Latins and Samnites and, collectively, for all the Italians.

60 Plin. Nat. 29.7. Also, see the way the Tarantine Greeks treated Lucius Postumius Megellus when he attempted to address them in less than perfect Greek: D.H. 19.5.1–5; App. Sam. 1.pos=37. From modern sources, see e.g. Petrochilos (n 15) 108; Beard (n 15) 198.

61 E.g. N Purcell, 'Urbanism' in Barchiesi and Scheidel (n 1) 579.

62 Cf. A Rossi, 'The Tears of Marcellus: History of a Literary Motif in Livy' (2000) 47(1) *Greece & Rome* 56, 57.

63 Plb. 9.10; Gruen (n 21) 252, 259.

64 E.g. B Kiernan, 'The First Genocide: Carthage, 146 BC' (2004) 51 *Diogenes* 27.

65 Plut. Cat. Ma. 26.2; App. Pun. 10.69.

after a number of centuries.[66] The Roman constitutional-imperial dragon was fully unleashed in 146 BC but Rome quite clearly started to lose her soul.[67]

That same character that would hide a complex of inferiority even as late as mid-2nd century BC would eventually give way to a character that would hide a complex of superiority and degeneration that would characterise the Roman of the very late Late Republic and the Romans of the Principate up until the full decline of the Western Roman Empire in AD 476. So much so that the wealthier the Romans became, the more they would resemble the ways of the *nouveaux riches* of modernity. For instance, the display of ownership of human property (slaves) by the wealthier Romans would be to advertise their 'power and … prestige'.[68] Envy and extravagance eventually became a Roman trait, in that the Romans, according to Polybius,[69] from a life of great simplicity would eventually wish to conquer the men who always had luxury and extravagance in their life, the Romans becoming like the conquered. At this point, it should be noted that Polybius seems to otherwise echo some of Rome's most conservative voices and circles by making use of the common Roman theme[70] of moral decline.

The Roman character was also fundamentally interested in the art of war[71] and the imposition of a fine system of law, administration and checks and balances, not in the arts or the letters.[72] This had major impact on the constitution of the Republic. The Roman would not even cynically enquire what the point of ideas is. The Roman, for most of the Republic, would just largely ignore these as either thin air or as matter that would not serve any tangible purpose. The Roman was, thus, a man of deeds mostly; words were almost never his forte.

The Roman was also a creature of phobias,[73] emanating from his lust for power and wealth; from the fact that he lived in a particularly vitriolic and antagonistic geographic neighbourhood in Italy; and, of course, from his fear of the rise of a tyrant to power. At other times, the Roman would exaggerate traits of the ideal character he would supposedly have, especially as compared[74] to the supposedly decadent character of the Greeks; thus, the Greeks were fluent in speech and big in words, when the Roman was a practical creature and great in acts;[75] the

66 R Xu, 'Roman Conception of Self and Others' (2018) (10) *Review of European Studies* 139, 142.

67 Cf. Gruen (n 21) 353 citing Latin authors with regard to the decline of the Roman character post 146 BC.

68 Bradley (n 27) 628.

69 Plb. 9.10.

70 Whitmarsh (n 24) 737.

71 E.g. Bradley (n 27) 631; Harries (n 15) 640.

72 '*[T]u regere imperio populos, Romane, memento; hae tibi erunt artes; pacisque imponere morem*': Verg. A. 6.851–2.

73 Cicero referring to Ennius (Cic. de Orat. 3.168): '*At Romanus homo, tamen et si res bene gesta est, corde suo trepidat*' (yet, the man of Rome, even though he has done well in his life's matters, hides fear in his heart). Translation by the author.

74 E.g. Petrochilos (n 15) 36, 55.

75 Petrochilos (n 15) 35–6, 58–9; Xu (n 66) 139, 142.

Greeks would be of immoderate character,[76] when the Romans would be about moderation; the Greeks would be proud and arrogant,[77] when the Romans would be prudent; the Greeks would be fickle, of rash behaviour and about lack of honour,[78] when the Romans would be about *gravitas*;[79] the Greeks would be deceitful, insidious and cunning[80] (rather like the Roman version of Odysseus), when the Romans would be honourable and noble (rather like their 'own' Aeneas); the Greeks would be interested in a life of luxury and dissipation,[81] when the Romans would be about a life of frugality;[82] the Greeks would be about lack of manliness while their sophistication would be really about softness (*mollitia*)[83], when the Romans would be about endurance and manly spirit.[84] Of course, the only thing that was missing from the description of the Romans about themselves was a pinch of salt, while the idealisation of the Roman character would be discarded as mostly a fabrication of the Roman elites, even though there were elements of truth[85] in the rawer aspects of the Roman character in certain of the above. Aside from the exaggeration of the Romans about their character, these exaggerated traits of what makes a good Roman were fundamentally ideals about Roman society and constitution as a whole.

Moreover, when it comes to the character of the Romans during the Republic, one could maintain that it stood for a type of character of composite nature, comprising rigour, vulgarity and ambition. Rome would also perceive the Orient as decadent and degenerate as a whole by reason of the fact that in the Roman mind wealth and luxury would amount to decadence.[86] The Republic too, co-extensively, in the years between 287 and 133 BC was certainly one which could be described as confident, rigorous and ambitious but, also, occasionally arrogant and hybristic,[87] to the point that the Roman elites would order, for instance, the utter destruction of their enemies and the cities that stood in Rome's way (e.g. Corinth and Carthage, which were both razed in 146 BC); to the point that later in the Republic's history massive proscriptions would be ordered and implemented in the streets of Rome, and so on. Hybris was not an unknown characteristic to the Roman character. It could be observed in the plundering of Syracuse in 212 BC. Greater still was the hybris of the Roman character in the destruction of

76 Petrochilos (n 15) 37–8.
77 Petrochilos (n 15) 39–40.
78 Petrochilos (n 15) 40–3.
79 Petrochilos (n 15) 42.
80 Petrochilos (n 15) 43–5.
81 J-L Ferrary, 'La Géographie de l' Hellénisme sous la Domination Romaine' in J-L Ferrary (ed), *Rome et Le Monde Grec* (Les Belles Lettres 2017) 508.
82 Petrochilos (n 15) 45–6.
83 Beard (n 15) 205; cf. J-L Ferrary (n 81) 508.
84 Petrochilos (n 15) 46–7.
85 Cf. Petrochilos (n 15) 35.
86 A Lampinen, 'Explaining the East: Forming and Applying Eastern Stereotypes in the Graeco-Roman Tradition' in Forsén and Lampinen (n 4) 308.
87 Cf. Dench (n 11) 81.

Carthage, if one considered the fact that, if Carthage had not been destroyed, the Carthaginian intellectuals would eventually have condoned Rome, as the Greek intellectuals did previously.[88]

Thus, the Rome of the Republic was not always magnanimous and could frequently be vengeful and power-hungry. However, the Romans could occasionally be magnanimous: for example, when an embassy of three Greek philosophers pleaded the reduction of a fine imposed on Athens by Rome, the Roman Senate responded by reducing it down to a mere 20 per cent of what was owed. Rome, of course, committed historical mistakes despite the magnificent vigour of her constitution. Furthermore, in a similar manner to the way the Roman magistrates supervised one another in their city's sophisticated constitution, especially in the higher echelons of Roman society and constitution, so did the Republic create a complex system of checks and balances which would not allow the presence of the same individual in a given position of power for long. One could, of course, move from one magistratorial position to another, through the *Cursus Honorum*,[89] but the idea of a single man holding the same political office for long was a characteristically repugnant one to the Romans of the Republic. It was politically and constitutionally abhorrent. Nothing would cause greater anxiety to the Roman elites than the rule of the same man in the same position for long – the Senators, appointees for life, being practically exempted from such a 'constitutional' rule as they were a collectivity – let alone one which 'represented' Rome's leading families.

The Romans would also display Janus-faced traits: they would transform their 'disadvantages' into advantages and their supposedly past roots into excuses for action in the present. For instance, the Greeks would call Romans 'barbarians' but the Romans would actually use this to their advantage. The Roman conqueror was quite aware of the utilitarian and raw ways of Latium, when occupying 'civil' Greece, Latium being 'agresti'[90], that is barbaric according to the Romans themselves. Indeed, from Cato the Elder to Cicero and Livy, the Romans were aware of the drawing line between Hellenes and barbarians and that they too would be 'barbarians', at least to Greek eyes, even though educated Greeks would not call them as such;[91] even if Fabius Pictor would claim Greek ancestry for the Romans;[92] even if the Romans too would draw their own line between the world of civilised nations such as those of the Greeks and the Romans and the world of the rest of nations. Yet, the often-difficult-to-justify-connection of the Romans with other nations, especially the ones from which they would wish to draw ancestry, would be best displayed in the story of Rome's Trojan descent. The myth of the Trojan descent of the Romans was quite clearly a pure fabrication[93] of the

88 Momigliano (n 8) 5.
89 See Chapters 9 and 10 for more on the *Cursus Honorum*.
90 Hor. *Ep*. 2.1.156–7.
91 Erskine (n 2) 165, 171.
92 E.g. Dench (n 1) 271.
93 Cf. EJ Bickerman, 'Origines Gentium' (1952) *Classical Philology* 65, 66.

Roman propaganda machinery, to signify Rome's relation but also distance from the Greeks and the East as a whole.

What better propaganda recipe for the Romans to fully impose and legitimise their imperium in Magna Grecia, Greece, Asia Minor and the Eastern Mediterranean than to claim Trojan descent, a descent that would bring the Romans both close and far from the Greeks and the peoples of the Eastern Mediterranean?[94] The fable of Rome's Trojan descent could have been Rome's preparatory act for her imperial maiden flight into Greek lands, initially those in the South of Italy, in the 3rd century BC, a sort of late but precise revenge[95] of the 'Trojan' Romans against the Greeks that once destroyed mother Troy of the Romans on the excuse of Helen's abduction by the Trojans in the 12th century BC. It is also noted that the myth of Rome's Trojan descent may have been connected or simply echoed such narratives as those of Herodotus as to the supposed oriental roots of other Italian peoples as the Etruscans[96] who, according to him, would originate from the East, that is, from Lydia,[97] before they settled in Italy.

Thus, the Roman myth does not tell us about the descent of the Romans; rather it tells us about their character's ambition; about the way the Romans wished to connect to the world of the Greeks and the Eastern Mediterranean peoples by conquering them, through the Romans 'returning' to these lands or avenging for their Trojan ancestors there; it was about Rome attempting to create a narrative that would move away but also come close to these peoples. The Roman narratives, in the form of myth-making, reached new heights of rhetoricism in the Late Republic when Cicero would famously proclaim that *Itaque oportet et eum qui paret sperare se aliquo tempore imperaturum*, that is 'he who obeys may hope that someday he will rule',[98] ruling other citizens being for most Roman citizens a matter of pure imagination.[99] All this found its way to Rome's imperial constitution *lato sensu* eventually.

Even the language of the Romans, Latin, must have affected them, especially as to how they perceived themselves and, by extension, their character against others. For instance, Latin looked both similar and different to Greek. Ancient Greek would differ, of course, from Latin much more than modern Norwegian, Danish and Swedish would differ from one another. Yet, Greek and Latin are not wholly different either. They are sister languages.[100] Aside from close or direct equivalents of Greek in Latin, for example, *πατήρ-patḗr* (*pater* in Latin (father in English)), *μήτηρ-mḗtēr* (*māter* in Latin (mother in English)) and *egṓ* (*egō* in Latin

[94] Cf. Dench (n 1) 272.

[95] Verg. A. 6.840.

[96] Gruen makes the point that Aeneas was a favourite theme in many Etruscan vase paintings but concludes there is no substantive evidence that suggests Rome took the idea of her supposed Trojan descent from Etruria: Gruen (n 54) 22.

[97] Hdt. 1.94.2–7.

[98] Cic. Leg. 3.5.

[99] Harris (n 30) 566.

[100] Mommsen (n 16) 15.

(I in English)), in old Latin one could identify certain very similar words to classical Greek such as *dacrima* ('tear'), when the Greek equivalent would be *dákry*, which later became, in classical Latin, *lacrima* and so on.[101] At other times, Latin preserved with Ionian Greek the sound 'q' instead of 'p' (thus, *quis* and *κοῖος*, in Latin and Ionian Greek respectively, and not *pis*), when most Greek dialects but also, interestingly, the Samnito-Umbrians would use p instead of q (thus, the widely used *ποῖος* in Greek and *pis* in Samnito-Umbrian).[102] The point is that the Romans were both close and distant to the Greeks, the Romans being well aware of this. Their constitution also resembled Greek constitutions to some extent but it was also far apart from them, in that monarchic and oligarchic elements would not be generally recognised in Greek *poleis* in the same way they would be recognised in Sparta and Rome, while Rome would be different to the Aristotelian republics,[103] which would not accept monarchic elements per se either. And yet, despite its differences, as we shall see in another chapter, the Roman Republic looked more like an Aristotelian polity+.

4.5 THE ROMAN FATHER AS A SIGNIFIER OF THE ROMAN CHARACTER

The father figure was of paramount importance in the building of Roman character as a whole. While the woman in Roman society belonged to the household, the man belonged both to household and community.[104] In patriarchal Rome[105] and, of course, in the overwhelming majority of societies and peoples of the ancient Mediterranean world, the father figure was paramount for family, society and ethnos. This seems to be related to the fact that the Roman society was traditionally patrilineal.[106]

It is otherwise no accident that the idea of supremacy of the father figure has found expression in the originally-created-Senate-of-100-members by Romulus, the original senators, and all the senators ever since were called the *patres*, the (fore)fathers of Rome. By extension, *patria potestas* passed down to every single Senate in Rome, whereas the authority of the Senate's authority was practically assisted by [the very existence of] this notion.[107] The future offspring of the original 100 *patres* would be called Patricians, which, of course, relates etymologically as a term to *patres*. The Roman notion in this respect was called *pater familias*, that is, the father of the family or the oldest male of the family, if the father was

[101] JT Katz, 'Linguistics' in Barchiesi and Scheidel (n 1) 79.

[102] Cf. Mommsen (n 16) 16.

[103] P Pasquino, 'Machiavelli and Aristotle: The Anatomies of the City' (2009) 35 *History of European Ideas* 397, 399–400 citing Aristotle, *Politics* III.

[104] Mommsen (n 16) 73.

[105] E.g. Beard (n 15) 35.

[106] Capogrossi Colognesi (n 15) 10.

[107] WV Harris, 'The Roman Father's Power of Life and Death' in RS Bagnall and WV Harris (eds), *Studies in Roman Law in Memory of AA Schiller* (EJ Brill 1986) 89.

deceased. In theory, the powers of the *pater familias* were absolute.[108] His powers were by definition patriarchal, authoritative and extensive, even though the father figure in Rome equally had an obligation not to corrupt or neglect his offspring.[109] Reminding us of C(h)ronos (named Saturn in the Roman Pantheon) who would devour his own children (even though the Latins would consider Saturn as one 'devouring' years and the turning seasons per se as opposed to C(h)ronos who would have devoured his own children, Hades, Poseidon, Hestia, Hera and Demeter),[110] the Greek father Agamemnon's sacrifice of his own daughter to Goddess Artemis to bring favourable winds to the Greeks, the Roman father too could, through *patria potestas*,[111] sacrifice his very children for the sake of Rome.[112] Certain parallels can be drawn here with the Phoenicians who seemed to sacrifice children[113] to deities such as Moloch or Baal.

The Roman father would have rights of life and death over his offspring, adult or not[114] (*vitae necisque potestas*).[115] The classic example of an exercise of such rights would be the ordering by Lucius Junius Brutus to execute his two sons for conspiring with his wife's two brothers to overthrow the Republic.[116] These rights could still be exercised in most of the Republic, that is by the Late Republic, by which point the final remnant of the *pater familias*' rights behind the traditional *vitae necisque potestas* could only be exercised in the master–slave relationship.[117] In any case, the particular notion has had certain dramatic connotations for Rome: the flip-side of the Platonic doctrine according to which 'your homeland is more precious, to be respected more and is more sacrosanct and at a higher level among gods and men … than your mother and your father'[118], the Roman *pater familias* could insist and proceed with the sacrifice of his offspring if that would be critical for Rome, whereas he would do so with impunity. In classical Greece, Plato would report that the sacrifice of children would be a barbaric trait, even though the Greeks of the epic years would sacrifice children and would throw the babies of the Trojans from the walls of Troy. Crucially, the killing of the son by the father would be permitted under the traditions of Rome, if the son committed an unacceptable offence.[119] The killing of a daughter could be justified if a father

[108] Harries (n 15) 640.
[109] Mommsen (n 16) 74.
[110] Cic. N.D. 2.64.
[111] Harris (n 107) 81.
[112] Harris (n 30) 571.
[113] E.g. P Xella, J Quinn, V Melchiorri and P van Dommelen, 'Cemetery or Sacrifice? Infant Burials at the Carthage Tophet: Phoenician Bones of Contention' (2013) 87 (338) *Antiquities* 1, 3–4, 4–5.
[114] Harris (n 107) 81.
[115] Harris (n 107) 81; also, R Westbrook, 'Vitae Necisque Potestas' (1999) 48 *Historia: Zeitschrift für Alte Geschichte* 203.
[116] Zoch (n 7) 41; TC Brennan, *The Fasces: A History of Ancient Rome's Most Dangerous Political Symbol* (Oxford University Press 2023) 15–16.
[117] Westbrook (n 115) 203, 223.
[118] Plat. Crito 51a–b.
[119] Westbrook (n 115) 203, 206.

wished to preserve her virtue or if she engaged in inappropriate relationships.[120] From the way a father in Rome could sacrifice his own offspring for Rome and the centrality of the male leader in the Roman household, one understands that the Roman character was one that would normally prioritise fatherland over the Romans, fatherhood over motherhood and offspring and so on. In short, the male Roman character was patriarchal, authoritative and traditional.

4.6 THE GRADUAL HELLENISATION OF ROME AND THE ROMAN CHARACTER

As constitution and Republic were maturing and as Rome was expanding, a powerful new trend would define the Roman character: its gradual Hellenisation. Aside from Rome's traditional indirect Hellenisation through the Villanovans of Etruria, Rome's initial subtle but decisive process of Hellenisation seems to have started with the Twelve Tables, Rome dramatically re-orientating itself, through them, from Etruria to Greece.[121] The process of Rome's Hellenisation gathered pace in the 4th century BC, if not previously,[122] especially through Rome's contact and trade with the Greeks of Magna Grecia, and much more directly and at an ever-increasing pace from the 3rd[123] and the 2nd[124] century BC onwards[125] and throughout the particular centuries; in the late 4th century BC the Romans would add Greek *cognomina* next to their Latin names;[126] by the 3rd century BC Rome's Sibylline Books would be wholly found in Greek hexameter verses in Rome and the so-called Greek rite would be followed in religious matters relating to them;[127] additionally, from the 3rd century BC, the Greeks would increasingly appear in Rome, whether as slaves or economic migrants.[128] In 155 BC an embassy of three Greek philosophers delivered the first public philosophical speech to ever be allowed in Rome, on the occasion of their visit to Rome in order for them to formally request from the Senate the significant reduction of an Athenian fine payable to Rome, which they achieved.[129]

In the 1st century BC, Rome, in tune with the rest of the Mediterranean world and beyond, was a heavily Hellenised Latin-speaking city: from original pieces

[120] Westbrook (n 115) 203, 208 citing Valerius Maximus 6,1,3 and 6,1,6 and Livy 3,48,4–7 and 3,50,5–7.

[121] A Momigliano, 'The Rise of the Plebs in the Archaic Age of Rome' in KA Raaflaub (ed), *Social Struggles in Archaic Rome* (Blackwell 2005) 180. Cf. J-J Aubert, 'The Republican Economy and Roman Law: Regulation, Promotion, or Reflection?' in Flower (n 5) 171.

[122] Gruen (n 54) 228 citing Liv. 4 25 3 and 4 29 7; TJ Cornell, *The Beginnings of Rome: Italy and Rome from the Bronze Age to the Punic Wars (c. 1000–264 BC)* (Routledge 1995) 124.

[123] Petrochilos (n 15) 15; Momigliano (n 8) 16–7.

[124] Gruen (n 54) 224, 251–2.

[125] Gruen (n 54) 269–70.

[126] Gruen (n 54) 227; Whitmarsh (n 24) 732.

[127] Gruen (n 54) 228; Whitmarsh (n 24) 732.

[128] Whitmarsh (n 24) 729.

[129] D Sedley, 'Philosophy' in Barchiesi and Scheidel (n 1) 701.

of art looted by Roman soldiers,[130] which they would bring to Rome from conquered Greek cities, to copies of Greek art, and from the Roman composite order (based on an adaptation of the Corinthian and the Ionic order) to the modelling[131] of Roman letters and arts on Greek poetry,[132] music,[133] theatre,[134] architecture[135] and urban theory,[136] to the fact that Roman religion was overtly and deliberately affected by Greek religion[137] and the fact that the education of the Roman upper class youth[138] would be entrusted to Greek scholars and philosophers,[139] Rome resembled ever more any other Hellenistic city. At the turn between 2nd and 1st century BC, the Romans were habitually bilingual speaking Latin and Greek.[140] All Roman Senators seemed able to understand Greek by 80s BC.[141] Momigliano offered us a most significant aspect of Rome's massive Hellenisation: the Greek way of thinking and the Greek language skills of the Roman leaders offered them significant comparative advantage over their Greek counterparts who would need interpreters to understand Latin and, by extension, the Roman way of thinking.[142]

Eventually, after the demise of the Republic, it was not just the affection of many Romans to Greek culture but also the fact that one's Greek education and engagement with Greek culture would come with prestige and status amongst the Romans.[143] In this respect, Augustus, the first Roman Emperor, would practically instruct on a daily basis the mixture of Greek and Roman cultures.[144] In any case, Rome's heart was dancing to the tune of Greek culture, arts and sciences, this having had impact not just on the character of the Romans of the Republic but also on the character of the Romans of the Principate and beyond.[145] The Roman character looked increasingly Greek.[146]

130 E.g. Whitmarsh (n 24) 732.
131 Mommsen (n 16) 307.
132 Whitmarsh (n 24) 734–5.
133 Mommsen (n 16) 296.
134 E.g. Gruen (n 54) 232.
135 A Wallace-Hadrill, 'To be Roman, Go Greek: Thoughts on Hellenization at Rome' in M Austin, J Harries and C Smith (eds), *Modus Operandi: Essays in Honour of Geoffrey Rickman* (Institute of Classical Studies – School of Advanced Study, University of London 1998) 90; Whitmarsh (n 24) 732.
136 Purcell (n 61) 590.
137 Gruen (n 54) 229.
138 Gruen (n 21) 257.
139 E.g. Whitmarsh (n 24) 732–3.
140 Gruen (n 21) 259.
141 Wallace-Hadrill (n 135) 82.
142 A Momigliano (n 8) 38.
143 Whitmarsh (n 24) 743 (citing Lucian, *On Salaried Posts* 25), 745.
144 Suet. Aug. 98.
145 The trend continued in the 1st and 2nd century AD; see e.g. Juv. 1.3.60–1 (Juvenal, *Satire* 3.60–1): '*non possum ferre, Quirites, Graecam urbem*'.
146 Cf. Wallace-Hadrill (n 135) 82.

4.7 REPUBLICAN ROME'S PHILOSOPHICAL UPBRINGING THROUGH ECONOMIC AND CULTURAL CONTACTS WITH GREECE

Rome's character was also eventually affected by its encounters with Greek philosophy. Rome, on the other hand, has never acquired the status of an autonomous philosophical powerhouse of the ancient world.[147] For most of the years of the Republic, Rome's contribution to philosophy could be described as rather minimal and it practically never broke free from original Greek thought.[148] Even Cicero, an eclectic philosopher in the main, was, as Sedley put it, 'a non-partisan type of Platonist',[149] whereas we are aware of the fact that his *De Officiis* was heavily influenced by Panaetius,[150] his *Republic* and the *Laws* were conceived as adaptations of the works of Aristotle and Plato,[151] and so on.

In this respect, an important element that is often neglected in analysing the legal and political character of the Republic's constitution is Roman society's philosophical basis, especially in the 2nd and the 1st century BC, when philosophy was more actively taught and welcome in Rome; when Rome's republican constitution would be much more developed than in the earlier stages of the Republic. Historically, when it comes to republican Rome's interaction with the ancient Western world's philosophical systems, Rome must have always had the chance to encounter Greek philosophy through the philosophers and the philosophical schools of Magna Grecia and through its overall interaction with the Greek colonies in the Italian peninsula at the very least. Economic contact between the Greek world and Rome seems to have otherwise commenced as early as 14th century BC, as Mycenaean coins were found from that period of time at Rome.[152] Considerable economic contact between Rome, conventionally founded in 753 BC,[153] and the first Greek colonies of the Italian South founded at least as early as c. 750 BC,[154] must have also taken place relatively early and, most certainly, already by the final century of the Roman Monarchy.[155] Multiple waves of Greek

[147] But cf. Sedley (n 129) 702.

[148] Cf. N Davies, *Europe: A History* (Pimlico 1996, reprinted 1997) 150: 'In speculative philosophy and the sciences, the Romans made virtually no advance on earlier achievements.'

[149] Sedley (n 129) 703.

[150] E.g. CN Smiley, 'Stoicism and Its Influence on Roman Life and Thought' (1934) 29(9) *The Classical Journal* 645, 650. Cf. Fantham (n 5) 342.

[151] J Connolly, 'Political Theory' in Barchiesi and Scheidel (n 1) 715.

[152] MT Boatwright, *Peoples of the Roman World* (Cambridge University Press 2012) 73.

[153] Cf. ES Gruen (n 54) 9 mentioning the encountering of the Greeks with Italics from 8th century BC.

[154] E.g. RW Mathisen, *Ancient Roman Civilization: History and Sources* (Oxford University Press 2019) 59. Cf. Cornell (n 122) 37–8 and 86, who, referring to Dionysius, mentions that the first Greek immigrants in southern Italy were Arcadians and arrived there from about 1750 BC. Cornell otherwise refers to the first historical settlement of the Greeks in the area of Pithecusae or Aenaria in c. 770 BC. Crawford gives a c. 775 BC date for the founding of Pithecusae: M Crawford, *The Roman Republic* (2nd edn, Fontana Press 1992) 18.

[155] Cornell (n 122) 124 stating – by citing Cicero (Rep. 2.34) – that the Greek culture was brought to

settlers reached much of southern Italy and Sicily in the coming few centuries up until the 5th and the 4th century BC. On the other hand, Rome's position towards Greece can be safely described as rather duplicitous in the years of the Republic. Synagonistic initially (5th and 4th centuries BC); antagonistic thereafter (for the most part of the 3rd century BC); hostile thereon (for the most part of the 2nd century BC up until 30 BC and the fall of Hellenistic Egypt) and, ultimately, almost wholly embracing (remainder of the 1st century BC to the first three-four centuries AD) of Greek culture, which the Romans, to their historical honour, left almost completely intact, even when all of mainland Greece was under Rome's full control from 146 BC onwards. So too, in the East, the Greeks were mostly allowed to run the internal affairs of their city states in the same way they would run them prior to Roman annexation.[156]

Greece was always on the Roman mind.[157] It has been said that the Greeks paid relatively little attention to the Romans, when the Romans would often turn their eyes to the Greek world for examples of good governance[158] but also for examples in the arts and sciences. And it is also the case that philhellenism was strong amongst certain Romans in the 3rd and the 2nd century BC.[159] Beyond this, however, the position of the Romans towards Greece seemed to have been of vacillating character, to state the least, especially in the 2nd and the 1st century BC.[160] This rather ambivalent[161] and paradoxical,[162] if not schizophrenic,[163] position of the Romans towards the Greeks, Greek culture and the Hellenistic world was best illustrated in the case of Cato the Elder, who would openly detest Greek culture only for him to 'turn … to Greek models for his oratory and writing'.[164] It initially seemed as if the Romans wanted to be accepted

Rome by Tarquin, the son of Demaratus. Tarquin the Elder's reign was between 616 and 578 BC. Cornell also informs us that archaeological findings confirm that Corinthian craftsmen lived and worked in the centres of southern Etruria at the time.

156 Whitmarsh (n 24) 730.

157 Whitmarsh (n 24) 728; J-L Ferrary, 'Cicéron et les Institutions Rhodiennes (De re publica 3, 35, 48)' 15–20 and J-L Ferrary, 'Les Romains de la République et les Démocraties Grecques' 24 in Ferrary (n 81).

158 E.g. P Matyszak, *Greece Against Rome: The Fall of the Hellenistic Kingdoms 250–31 BC* (Pen & Sword 2001) 20.

159 Gruen (n 21) 250, 270. On the cultural and political philhellenism of the Romans in the 2nd century BC, see J-L Ferrary, *Philhellénisme et Impérialisme* (BEFAR 1988) 495–615. The philhellenism of the Romans continued well into the years of the Principate: J-L Ferrary, 'Rome, Athènes et le Philhellénisme dans l'Empire Romain, d' Auguste aux Antonins' in Ferrary (n 81) 451–75.

160 Boatwright (n 152) 77.

161 Petrochilos (n 15) 15–16, 26, 33; Gruen (n 21) 270; Gruen (n 54) 2, 214. Cicero too posited that Greek philosophy should be considered and used by the Roman political elites on the basis that it is domesticated and Romanised: Whitmarsh (n 24) 741–2 citing *Tusculan Disputations*.

162 Gruen (n 21) 260.

163 Cf. Gruen (n 54) 4, 61.

164 Boatwright (n 152) 78. Cf. Momigliano (n 8) 20; Whitmarsh (n 24) 737–8, 741; see also, Gruen (n 21) 258; Gruen (n 54) 52, 56–7; Beard (n 15) 205.

by the Aegean Greeks, championing their freedom,[165] even though the same people would crush a number of decades later one of the leading Greek cities, Corinth. Like Cato the Elder, however, most of the Romans, as a people, never openly aspired to the Greeks,[166] except in propaganda terms and in the circles of leading Roman intellectuals, especially at the later stages of the Republic, even though almost every single aspect of Roman life was partially Greek or wholly Greek in one way or another[167] from the years of the Roman Monarchy onwards. Apparently, 'there was never a time in the history of Rome, ... when the population who lived there was not influenced by Greek culture, importing Greek pottery, later imitating Greek art, and establishing the cults of Greek gods and goddesses'.[168] The peculiar Roman position towards everything Greek seems to have been the result of *φιλοτιμία*:[169] for love of honour, the Romans would, on the surface, occasionally show contempt for the Greeks, from whom they took the most, because they wanted to excel them; not because they wanted to degrade them. However, imitation is a form a flattery and in the act of flattery by imitation the not-always-very-original Roman culture has achieved certain of its highest academic marks. Also, another plausible explanation is the fact that the Romans wished to draw a line between their affection for things Greek and their foreign policy, which, of course, could oppose Greek interests.[170] The Romans, thus, showed clear preference for Hellenism over the Hellenes.[171]

The wholesale acquisition and embracement of Greek culture by the Romans,[172] however, a move that was led by Rome's ruling classes,[173] did not always produce excellent results: for instance, the Romans never reached the pinnacles of Greek arts, philosophy and the sciences, their cultural production often taking the form of a *kakektypon*, their works of art and scientific writings[174] frequently having been mere imitations or assimilations of the Greek originals. Perhaps Rome and its elites were never interested in competing with Greek culture, for they must have

[165] Gruen (n 21) 5 citing T Frank, *Roman Imperialism* (Macmillan 1914) 138–89.

[166] Cf. Herman (n 15) 110: 'Although they professed to despise the Greeks as a people, the Romans developed a strange dependence on Greek culture and on its two greatest thinkers [Plato and Aristotle]'.

[167] E.g. Herman (n 15) 111–12.

[168] F Millar, *The Roman Republic in Political Thought* (University Press of New England 2002) 12 citing T.J. Cornell, *The Beginnings of Rome: Italy and Rome from the Bronze Age to the Punic Wars (c. 1000–264* B.C. (Routledge London, 1995). Cf. Cornell (n 122) 397.

[169] Gruen (n 54) 80 citing Plut. *Cato* 23.1.

[170] Gruen (n 21) 267.

[171] Gruen (n 21) 270.

[172] Consider here the view of Boardman also, referring to Pliny the Elder and citing Sorcha Carey, 'The problem of totality: Collecting Greek art, wonders and luxury in Pliny the Elder's Natural History' (2000) 12(1) *Journal of the History of Collections* 1–13; he speaks of 'the Roman addiction to collecting, such things [as *mirabilia* rather than relics], especially from the Greek world, as a means of demonstrating Rome's greatness': J Boardman, *The Archaeology of Nostalgia: How the Greeks Re-created their Mythical Past* (Thames & Hudson 2002) 30; also, Whitmarsh (n 24) 728.

[173] Cf. Crawford (n 154) 31.

[174] E.g. PT Keyser, 'Science' in Barchiesi and Scheidel (n 1) 870.

seen it as a ready-made type of culture, which would fit many of the more intellectual aspects of their otherwise mostly utilitarian existence and way of life. And yet, it would also seem that the Romans, for the most part, seemed to have continuously, albeit covertly mostly, admired Greek culture. When it came to Rome's rather weak opposition to Greek culture, the nationalist circles of Rome and Cato the Elder were thus 'waging a losing battle against the Greeks'.[175] In fact, the arrival of the Greeks in Italy 'prompted far-reaching changes in the social habits of Tyrrhenian Italy at the end of the eighth century BC … From now Hellenism was to be a pervasive influence, the single most important factor of change and development in Roman (and Italian) history'.[176]

Concurrently, despite the Roman Kingdom's relative isolation and limited progress in cultural and economic terms, certain economic interaction between Romans, Celts, Etruscans, Carthaginians and Greeks in the Italian peninsula and in the islands surrounding the peninsula must have occurred at different points of time and in variable degrees already during these monarchic times and, of course, in the coming centuries during the Republic. For instance, religious contact of Rome with Greece is said to have occurred already in the years of the Roman Monarchy, when certain Romans visited the Oracle of Delphi to consult it.[177] Moreover, interaction between the Greek settlers in the Italian South and Italic peoples intensified in the 5th century BC, creating an amalgamated Greek and Italian culture.[178] Greek stonemasons from Campania were hired by the Romans to build the Servian Wall sometime after the Gallic sack of Rome in 390 BC.[179] Economic contact further intensified in late 4th century BC.[180] Coins produced in the Greek colonies, settlements and trade entrepôts[181] of the Italian South (Magna Grecia) were otherwise already circulating in Rome's territories since at least 300 BC,[182] Rome producing its 'own' didrachms under the Campanian and the Neapolitan standard since c. 281 BC.[183] In this respect, by common assent, both numismatists and historians 'agree that Roman contacts with important

175 Boatwright (n 152) 78. Also, Zoch (n 7) 140.

176 Cornell (n 122) 92.

177 Boatwright (n 152) 69.

178 Mathisen (n 154) 59. Cf. CP Cavafy, 'The Poseidonians' citing Athenaios, *Deipnosophistai,* Book 14, 31A (632) and Crawford (n 154) 17.

179 Mathisen (n 154) 90.

180 Boatwright (n 152) 73.

181 Crawford (n 154) 18, Crawford making the valid point that the term 'colonies' for the Greek settlements and cities in Sicily and along the coasts of southern Italy might be inappropriate. Pithecusae to him 'was almost certainly intended to act as an entrepôt for trade with Etruria'.

182 RE Mitchell, 'The Fourth Century Origin Roman Didrachms' in R Howarth (ed), *Hearsay, History, and Heresy: Collected Essays on the Roman Republic by Richard E. Mitchell* (Gorgias Press 2010) 13: Mitchell refers to the view that the earliest Roman didrachms 'are variously attributed to the period between 326 and 269 BC'. Also, Whitmarsh (n 24) 732. Cf. WE Metcalf, 'Numismatics' in Barchiesi and Scheidel (n 1) 135.

183 Cf. Mathisen (n 154) 131. See also with regard to Roman coins 'in patterns similar to those found in Greek cities, especially in Southern Italy' HI Flower, *Roman Republics* (Princeton University Press 2010) 75.

coin-using and coin-producing states in the South, especially with Greek states, fostered Rome's own coins and greatly influenced them in matters of type, style, and weight. Neapolis, Metapontum, Thurii, Syracuse and Carthage are but a few of the states frequently cited'.[184]

By now, economic contacts between the Greeks and the Romans must have also led to certain minimum but considerable philosophical and cultural contacts. Naturally, in this relationship Rome was mostly the cultural borrower,[185] Greece being mostly the cultural lender. Interestingly, cultural contact per se seems to have formally started through poetry. Rome's first writer was an educated Greek slave, brought to the city from fallen Tarantum in 272 BC, who then became a freedman,[186], Livius Andronicus; he would translate Homer into Latin verse.[187] The first Roman historian, Quintus Fabius Pictor, was also influenced by the Greek Sicilian historian Timaeus and recognised[188] the effect of Greek historiography in his works; he wrote his historical work in Greek in c. 215 to 200 BC,[189] albeit the particular choice may have been down to both literary and political reasons.[190] Romans and Latins would be quick to adopt and imitate Greek artistic and cultural prototypes, albeit not always with perfect grace. Initially, Rome resembled a young hopeful artist who would not be particularly talented or trained otherwise. Furthermore, Roman playwright Plautus would release his comedies from c. 205 BC and would model such on Greek originals.[191]

To the Romans who developed culture and the arts, Rome being *par excellence* a place full of utilitarian dwellers, one ought to give particular praise: not only certain of them, such as Virgil, Horace and Ovid, were quite exceptional in the process of Hellenising and civilising the rather rustic Rome and Latium, but they actually did so amidst a society that was never great traditionally in the arts and the letters. In this respect, these great minds of Rome were greater than their Greek counterparts, for they were fighting an intellectual war against all odds and, in the face of traditional cultural apathy from the mobs of Rome, they actually won this war.

The Roman character was steadily becoming more Hellenised in the Middle Republic already. In the 2nd century BC, for instance, the famous Scipionic Circle would include a number of philhellenic personalities who would exert

184 Mitchell (n 182) 14–15. Despite Rome's coin system being similar to that of Magna Grecia initially, Rome moved towards a unified coin system with the introduction of its 'own' denarius 'sometime in the last two decades of the century B.C.': WT Loomis, 'The Introduction of the Denarius' in RW Wallace and EM Harris (eds), *Transitions to Empire: Essays in Greco-Roman History, 360–146 B.C., in Honor of E. Badian* (University of Oklahoma Press 1996) 338.

185 Whitmarsh (n 24) 728.

186 Whitmarsh (n 24) 732.

187 Davies (n 148) 176; Whitmarsh (n 24) 732.

188 Gruen (n 54) 223.

189 E.g. Zoch (n 7) 137; Gruen (n 21) 253–4 citing Dion. Hal. 1.6.2; Cic. *De Div.* 1.43.

190 https://doi.org/10.1093/acrefore/9780199381135.013.2618 accessed 30 November 2024. But cf. Gruen (n 54) 231.

191 Mathisen (n 154) 137.

considerable influence on Rome's arts and sciences.[192] Yet Rome's contact with Greek philosophy must have become more intense with the conquest of all of the Greek colonies in the Italian peninsula and Sicily after the fall of the 'queen of Greater Greece',[193] Syracuse[194] to Roman hands in 212 BC and, most certainly, after representatives of major Greek philosophical schools directly visited Rome and taught philosophy there in 155 BC.[195] Scholars, doctors, educators from the Greek world would form the scientific elite of Rome,[196] as they would form yet again much of the scientific elite of Italy c. 1500 years later, in the 1400s AD, when Constantinople would have fallen into Ottoman hands and scholars from the Greek-speaking world would resort to the Italian peninsula, thereby bringing the arts and sciences of the Eastern Roman Empire to Rome and Italy themselves.

Of course, Rome was traditionally less idealistic[197] and certainly much less philosophical than Greece. 'Intellect, innovation, and imagination were generally not high on the Roman list of virtues',[198] Horace famously stating in his *Epistles* '[h]ad the Greeks held novelty in such disdain as we [Romans], what work of ancient date would now exist?'.[199] The Romans have, thus, been readily described as 'the least curious people in history, as well as the most acquisitive'.[200]

The Greeks were liberals. The Romans were neoliberals. The Greeks were more like modern Europeans. The Romans were more like modern Americans. The Greeks praised and examined nature, the cosmos, the stars and the universe. The Romans mastered the arts of war and administration. The Greeks were philosophers, poets and soldiers. The Romans were soldiers; they were poets too, albeit quite late in the day. The Greeks masterminded the sciences and the arts. The Romans defined the ideas of greed and power. Greece was eternal. Rome was plenipotentiary. Greece was divided and free. Rome was united and disciplined. Greece was humane and divine. Rome was almost always human, all too human. Greece was disperse. Rome was cohesive. Greece grew out of thousands of independent cities all over the Mediterranean, the Black Sea and beyond scattered 'like ants or frogs around a pond'.[201] Republican Rome always perceived itself as the centre of everything in the city, Latium, Italy, the Empire and the then known world. 'The Greek was a sailor at heart, the Roman a landsman'.[202] 'Greece was

192 Gruen (n 54) 224.
193 Davies (n 148) 140.
194 Davies argued that the fall of Syracuse 'created the fashion for Greek artefacts and Greek ideas which henceforth became the norm for all educated Romans': Davies (n 148) 145.
195 JGF Powell, 'The Embassy of the Three Philosophers to Rome in 155 BC' in C Kremmydas and K Tempest (eds), *Hellenistic Oratory: Continuity and Change* (Oxford University Press 2013) 219–48.
196 Cf. Matyszak (n 158) 174.
197 Cf. Mathisen (n 154) 62.
198 Mathisen (n 154) 62.
199 Horace, Ep. 2.1.90–1: 'Quod si tam Graecis novitas invisa fuisset quam nobis, quid nunc esset vetus?' (quote in the English language found in Davies (n 148) 150).
200 Herman (n 15) 110.
201 Plat. Phaedo 109b; cf. Aristot. Pol. 2.1271b.
202 Davies (n 148) 149.

original, Rome derivative. Greece had style, Rome had money. Greece was the inventor, Rome the Research and Development division'.[203] Rome would retain full control over its small colonies; Greece would not be interested in controlling the great cities that would have started as 'colonies'.[204] The Romans were Italic-Hellenistic in their cultural configuration, while the Greeks were not Graeco-oriental but cosmopolitan[205] and Hellenistic in theirs.

Also, one could certainly argue that the overall philosophical approach of the republican Romans to life was generally utilitarian and materialist, not very different to the approach to life which would have been adopted by the uncultured and unruly Roman crowds and masses that would flood the Colosseum from 80 AD onwards. To this day, this materialist and utilitarian approach to life has otherwise prevailed in most of the Western world. Thus, Rome, as a world city, became the utilitarian speculator's dream, already in the final stages of the Republic and, of course, in the years of the Principate, with hundreds of thousands of people from around the Mediterranean and from Europe flooding it for a better future.

This was and continued to be, however, a brash and unsophisticated people as a whole, rightly described by the Roman poet Juvenal as a people that would aspire to 'bread and circuses'.[206] It is the case, however, that republican Rome, especially in the years of the Late Republic, became more philosophy-oriented. These were the times that Rome looked somewhat more like Athens than Sparta. In these years, Rome tended to be and came to be rather eclectic when it came to the philosophical schools that it would embrace; yet, in her eclecticism, the school that Rome mostly embraced was that of Stoicism, with the school of Epicureanism following but being one that was seen with suspicion, as it would conflict Rome's pursuit for glory.[207] Stoicism, on the other hand, literally took Rome by storm.[208] So much so that 'Stoicism was more typical of Rome than of Athens'.[209] In any case, it is only ironic that the predominantly stoic Romans of the last two centuries of the Republic came to realise that even their republican constitution was a good example of a human creation that would ultimately fall,[210] outside the control of those who created and nurtured it, the Roman citizens and Rome's ruling classes, the very fall of the Republic signifying that even a sophisticated constitutional machinery of the kind could ultimately fail and fall.

203 Davies (n 148) 150.

204 Capogrossi Colognesi (n 15) 94.

205 E.g. M Rostovtzeff (n 15) 6.

206 Juvenal, *Satire* 10.77–81.

207 Zoch (n 7) 138.

208 E.g. B Straumann, *The Just State: Greek and Roman Theories of Justice and Their Legacy in Western Thought* (Wiley-Blackwell 2024) 99.

209 Davies (n 148) 150.

210 Cf. Plato, Rep. 8.546a: '[I]t is for a state thus constituted to be shaken and disturbed; but since for everything that has come into being destruction is appointed, not even such a fabric as this will abide for all time, but it shall surely be dissolved, and this is the manner of its dissolution.'

4.8 THE STOIC PHILOSOPHICAL LAYER IN THE ROMAN CHARACTER

Almost all of Rome's establishment recognised Hellenic culture as a mark of an educated Roman and it was the case that eventually the formulation of Roman identity would be one that would have to correspond to Greek ideals.[211] As stated, Rome's true engagement with philosophy commenced from about mid-1st century BC with Cicero and spanned to the death of Seneca after mid-1st century AD.[212] In the Middle Republic and, certainly, in the Late Republic, the educated Romans increasingly looked and behaved like educated Greeks. Cato the Elder had lost: Rome was now a Hellenised city. Latin was the language spoken in Rome but Greek would be a characteristic of the most educated Romans.[213]

Rome also fell in love with Stoicism more than the Greeks of the Hellenistic world, where it was generated; in precise terms, Zeno, the father of Stoicism, was a Cypriot Greek-Phoenician, which, of course, may have to do with the fact that the mainlander Greeks never wholly embraced the particular philosophical system even though many have actually explored it and adopted it in Greece too. In any case, Roman Stoicism, rooted in Platonism,[214] had a positive and a negative impact on Rome: to persevere and fight on *sans peur et sans reproche*, so to speak, and accept as facts of life what one encounters irrespective of pain, was the positive aspect. The whole of the Roman empire might have been built on the stoic idea of absolute Roman resolution and loss without feeling pain against all enemies. However, the negative aspect of Stoicism for the Roman character was its highly conservative nature as to not interfering with the status quo; as to becoming psychologically numb with things that one ought to address and deal with in one's life path. Thus, the conservative Roman character became even more conservative through the largely pro-status quo philosophical system of Stoicism.

Rome's easternisation or Hellenisation led it to decadence according to the erroneous belief of the ultra-conservative doomsters and the Cassandras of Rome,[215] but the Hellenisation of Rome could be partial, misapplied or a more vulgarised type of Hellenicity. In fact, most historians are of the view that Hellenism was not a threat to the conservative Roman society of the Republic.[216] In essence, there was pretension in this, in that the Romans who would accuse Greece of 'luxurious and decadent ways' would plunder and imitate the artistic works of Greeks. They would accuse the Orientals for a luxurious and decadent type of living only for them to lead luxurious lives like wealthy Orientals. Also, the Roman anxieties

[211] Whitmarsh (n 24) 729.
[212] Sedley (n 129) 701.
[213] E.g. Sedley (n 129) 702.
[214] Whitmarsh (n 24) 740.
[215] Cf. Whitmarsh (n 24) 736.
[216] Harris (n 30) 570.

in this respect were not justified,[217] as Greek culture came to (positively) define Roman culture.[218] As an example here, the Hellenisation of Rome supposedly came with luxury[219] and extravagance, when these two traits would not, of course, be necessarily condoned in Greece itself.[220] Beyond this, the Roman accusations against Greek morality and the Greek way of life in the 2nd century BC seem to have been similar to the Greek accusations against Persian morality and the Persian way of life[221] in the 5th century BC.

4.9 THE ROMAN CHARACTER AS IN THE CHARACTER OF BOTH PLEBEIANS AND PATRICIANS

One is to address also the character of the Plebeians and the Patricians in Rome. As stated, the traditional Roman character was about honour, political excellence and moral virtue. This type of character would be praised both by Plebeians and Patricians. Philosophically, however, Rome aspired to Stoicism, that is after Rome started to engage with Greek philosophy. In this respect, because Stoicism was not taught to the masses, it would seem that the stoic character of the Romans would probably emanate from the Stoicism of the educated Romans.

As a society, the Roman society of the Republic was, at least in theory, morally and socially conservative. This social conservatism was relevant both to Patricians and Plebeians, especially through the medium of religion. However, Rome's social conservatism was traditionally about a rather narrow and indoctrinated perception of the world, which, however, started to disappear from the 2nd century BC onwards. Confusion arose amongst the Roman elites, as the continuous Hellenisation of Rome was actually received as a liberal approach to life (as compared to what would seem a more conservative and rustic type of Roman perception of life), when the Greeks would in all probability be more socially conservative than the Romans, even if their culture would be a much more inquisitive one than the Roman one in intellectual terms. Furthermore, it is no accident that the rise of Rome as a world power led to the greater moral degeneracy of the Plebeians and, especially, the Patricians. Polybius mentions as examples of degeneracy Marcellus and Flaminius.[222] Using them as negative examples, his views on this was that Rome from the mid-second century BC was morally debased, when it was an example of political excellence and virtue in the 3rd century BC.[223] Here, however, Polybius might be actually giving 'voice to anti-Roman sentiments among [his]

[217] But cf. Capogrossi Colognesi (n 15) 159.
[218] Wallace-Hadrill (n 135) 91.
[219] Whitmarsh (n 24) 736.
[220] E.g. Hes. WD 694: 'Observe due measure: and proportion is best in all things'. Cf. Plb. 9.10.
[221] Whitmarsh (n 24) 741.
[222] C Champion, 'Historiographic Patterns and Historical Obstacles in Polybius' *Histories*: Marcellus, Flaminius, and the Mamertine Crisis' in B Gibson and T Harrison (eds), *Polybius and his World. Essays in Memory of F. W. Walbank* (Oxford University Press 2013) 146.
[223] Champion (n 222) 146–7.

Greek readership'.[224] Also, whereas Polybius praises 3rd-century Rome, he makes it clear elsewhere that the action of Rome to cross to Sicily in 264 BC was morally reprehensive,[225] thereby effectively contradicting himself. Again, such a stance might be one that showed a man who genuinely believed that the actions of Rome were clearly wrong from the moral point of view or that he did so, not only because he meant his words here but also to satisfy his Greek readership.[226] At other times, Polybius takes a pragmatic approach in justifying Roman expansionism on the grounds of succumbing to the reality of Roman power, even though he recognises the moral imperative behind the independence of smaller states.[227] More generally, the point that Polybius rightly makes is that individuals are the result of a given society and a reflection of this society's cultural practices.[228] However, there was not much space for political innovation on the part of individuals in Rome, in that the conservative Senate, as a collectivity of powerful individuals, would practically set the tone for the Republic. According to Polybius,[229] the opposite is also true but it would seem that the Roman personalities we encounter historically are more the result of their society rather than them affecting the Roman Republic in a dramatic way, especially considering the rather conservative character of the Republic.[230] The rule is not without exception: Sulla, Cicero, Pompey, Julius Caesar and Tiberius Gracchus were actually personalities who attempted to change the Roman state, even if they did not actually achieve this.

4.10 *MOS MAIORUM* AND CORE VALUES

The Roman ethical dogma is a complex composite made out of personal and social virtues. Let us take things from the start though: the Roman character, indeed the character of the constitution of the Republic, was one that was first and foremost based upon the idea of *mos maiorum*. This roughly translates in the English language as 'the ways of the fathers': the traditions, the customs and the established beliefs of life of the forefathers of Rome. Compliance with *leges* (positive instruments of law) and *instituta* (precedent) was also a normal expectation in Rome, as attested by Cicero in the 1st century BC.[231]

The Romans always prided themselves of the superior moral code of their city. Of course, such pride was often more rhetorical than real and in the 1st century BC little of Rome's ethical code was found in the brutal assassinations of

[224] Champion (n 222) 147.
[225] Champion (n 222) 154 citing Polybius 3.26.6.
[226] Champion (n 222) 154.
[227] J-L Ferrary, 'Le Jugement de Polybe sur la Domination Romaine: État de la Question' in Ferrary (n 81) 100 citing AM Eckstein, *Moral Vision in the Histories of Polybius* (University of California Press 1995) 207.
[228] Champion (n 222) 147 citing Polybius 6.47.3–5.
[229] Champion (n 222) 147 citing Polybius 9.23.8–9; cf. 4.2.10–11.
[230] Mommsen (n 16) 332.
[231] TC Brennan, 'Power and Process under the Republican "Constitution"' in Flower (n 5) 21.

thousands of political enemies in the streets of Rome and, of course, in the unashamed imperialistic tendencies of the Republic of the 2nd and 1st century BC. Nor would it be right to upgrade the imperialistic tendencies of the Middle and the Late Republic into a moral approach based on the dogma of 'might is right' or what Thucydides famously put as 'the strong do what they can and the weak suffer what they must'.[232] To do so would be to justify any force of expansionism in the face of human history and, for that matter, the crimes which Rome committed in expanding its empire over the centuries. In any case, Cicero, referring to the Calabrian poet Ennius, states that the Republic is founded firmly 'on ancient customs and men of might'.[233] It is not always clear what the Romans meant by this; perhaps it did not matter what they meant, as long as it could be shown that their acts, decisions and dogmas could be traced back to the ways of their fathers. Equally, even though *mos maiorum* was an abstract and undefined notion, it was about Romanness:[234] a good Roman was one who could display adherence and respect to the ways of the fathers.

4.11 GOOD FAITH AND THE GREED OF THE ROMANS

Finally, good faith played an important role in Rome's military actions. Steel informs us of a position whereby Rome would have established for itself, through *bona fides*, 'a conceptual framework for activity after the end of the war'.[235] Thus,

> These parameters of military success did not necessarily mean the utter destruction of the enemy, though that was a possible outcome; the key point was rather that the enemy should be entirely at the Romans' disposal, who guaranteed in turn the fitness of their own behaviour by an appeal to their *fides*, 'good faith'.[236]

The principle of good faith played a crucial role in the Republic's legal system too; however, it seems that it was in the Late Republic that the development of civil concepts such as good faith occurred.[237]

Greed[238] eventually defined the Roman character and was a key element of Rome's inexorable hunger for growth, wealth and expansion. Rome's expansions, the Roman imperial achievements, were mostly admired by historians throughout

[232] Thuc. 5.89.1.

[233] Cic. Rep. 5.1. Translation as found in the Loeb Classical Library text: DOI: 10.4159/DLCL.marcus_tullius_cicero-de_re_publica.1928.

[234] A Tarwacka, *The Censors as Guardians of Public and Family Life in the Roman Republic* (Routledge 2025) 1.

[235] C Steel, *The End of the Roman Republic, 146 to 44 BC: Conquest and Crisis* (Edinburgh University Press 2013) 69.

[236] Steel (n 235) 68.

[237] Harries (n 15) 642.

[238] E.g. Hoyos (n 14) 1.

the 19th century and at least up until the unravelling of the European colonial empires after 1945.[239] Rome was justified and condoned. So was her greed and, by extension, the greed of modern colonial powers. Nowadays, however, a much more cautious approach is taken as to the imperial 'achievements' of Rome, which came at a very high cost for Rome and, of course, her enemies.[240]

239 Hoyos (n 14) 2.
240 Ibid.

Chapter 5

Lex Hortensia *or How the Roman Republic's Constitution Became More Democratic*

5.1 INTRODUCTION

This chapter explores the significant democratisation of the Republic through the Hortensian Law (287 BC), a crucial point in time in legal and constitutional law terms for Rome, even though the admission that the constitution of the Republic continued to be mostly oligarchic and monarchic in its fundamentals, even after 287 BC, is also made here. Following a contextual approach, the chapter explains the social events and economic factors behind *Lex Hortensia*, the Hortensian Law, and what impact – constitutional, social and political – the particular piece of legislation had on the Republic.

5.2 *LEX HORTENSIA*: TILTING THE REPUBLIC'S CONSTITUTION MARGINALLY CLOSER TO DEMOCRACY

Lex Hortensia had been a major turning point in Rome's history. This was the law that effectively brought an end to the Conflict of the Orders in Rome.[1] As explained in a previous chapter,[2] the Plebeians would through *secessio plebis*, the equivalent of massive popular strikes and absence from socio-economic life, bring Roman society to a standstill. There have been five historically attested such *secessiones* in Roman history (494 BC, 449 BC, 445 BC, 342 BC and 287 BC).

At this point, it is important to note that Rome was a class-based society. Rome's social ordering comprised two different classes of free citizens: the Plebeians and the Patricians. This social dualism seems to be the result of a long development.[3] The division of the Romans into Patricians and Plebeians would run deep in Roman society, with economic, religious[4] and political connotations for Rome and

[1] E.g. RE Mitchell, *Patricians and Plebeians: The Origin of the Roman State* (Cornell University Press 1990) 234. But cf. more recent work from the same author arguing that the conflict of the orders went back to the division of the Romans between Patricians and Plebeians by Romulus: RE Mitchell, 'The Definition of *Patres* and *Plebs*: An End to the Struggle of the Orders' in KA Raaflaub (ed), *Social Struggles in Archaic Rome: New Perspectives on the Conflict of the Orders* (2nd edn, Blackwell Publishing 2005) 128–9.

[2] Chapter 2.

[3] J-C Richard, 'Patricians and Plebeians: The Origin of a Social Dichotomy' in Raaflaub (n 1) 120.

[4] E.g. J Linderski, 'Religious Aspects of the Conflict of the Orders: The Case of *Confarreatio*' in Raaflaub (n 1) 223.

constitution. The Patricians would be descendants of old wealthy and powerful families in Rome, whether of Latin, Etruscan or Sabine descent. Everyone else in Rome was a Plebeian,[5] unless they were a slave. In theory, the Patricians would be the descendants of the original families of Rome, while the Plebeians would be Rome's metics, immigrants that would come to Rome from elsewhere, even though the Patrician *gentes* could not always claim Roman descent, as there were Etruscan and Sabine *gentes* in the Patrician order.

The Plebeians were the poorer free members of society, even though wealthy Plebeians existed. The period between 494 and 287 BC, the Conflict of the Orders in Rome,[6] was a period of major social struggles between the Plebeians and the Patricians, the latter wishing to maintain almost exclusive control over Rome's constitution.[7] Rome was thus a society that was characterised by little social peace and upheaval amongst its orders would be the norm for more than two centuries. The Republic's social struggles would, of course, resurface at other points of time in Rome's history, even after 287 BC, but not to the extent they would occur prior to *Lex Hortensia*. However, the particular law would be responsible for transforming the Republic into a somewhat more democratic constitutional order, even though republican Rome never became a democracy. Through *Lex Hortensia* the constitution of the Republic would have thus ushered in a new era.

In modern terms, *Lex Hortensia* would be a tantamount to a constitutional amendment or revision, tilting the constitution of the Roman Republic a click closer to democracy. *Lex Hortensia* is the constitutional innovation whereby Rome effectively strengthened the powers of the Plebeians. By virtue of *Lex Hortensia*, the Plebeian Council's resolutions (*plebiscita*) would in principle be binding now on the whole of the Republic.[8] This stood for the point in time when Rome (which was never wholly democratic or predominantly democratic in the years of the Republic) started becoming slightly more interested in the idea of democracy. Of course, Rome would be a very late player in this: the Athenians could certainly claim that only a year after the Romans created their republic in 509 BC, a predominantly oligarchic-monarchic mixed constitution for Rome, they were already introducing a democratic constitution for their city in 508/507 BC through the reforms of Cleisthenes.[9] Thus, Athens was becoming more democratic, when

[5] L Capogrossi Colognesi, *Law and Power in the Making of the Roman Commonwealth* (Cambridge University Press 2014) 37.

[6] KA Raaflaub, 'From Protection and Defense to Offense and Participation: Stages in the Conflict of the Orders' in Raaflaub (n 1) 185.

[7] RE Mitchell, *Patricians and Plebeians: The Origin of the Roman State* (Cornell University Press 1990) 18.

[8] E.g. D Hoyos, *Rome Victorious: The Irresistible Rise of the Roman Empire* (Bloomsbury Academic 2019, reprinted 2023) 12. Cf. T Lanfranchi, 'Legislation, Politics and Social Change in the Early Second Century BCE' in M Balbo and F Santangelo (eds), *A Community in Transition: Rome between Hannibal and the Gracchi* (Oxford University Press 2023) 209, making the interesting point that the increase of plebiscites with the concurrent decrease of the involvement of the Consuls in legislative matters in 2nd century BC Rome did not make the Roman constitution more democratic.

[9] J Connolly, 'Political Theory' in A Barchiesi and W Scheidel (eds), *The Oxford Handbook of Roman Studies* (Oxford University Press 2010) 714.

Rome was becoming republican in about the same period of time. In Rome, the rather modest process of 'democratisation' preceded *Lex Hortensia*. Yet, the Plebeians of Rome were not always very successful in this.

Now, Rome would probably not be wholly cognisant of the idea of democracy in most concrete terms, when this idea was already literally taking over Athens at the time Rome was only becoming a republic. Echoes of democracy, however, may well have reached the Romans through trade and their links with the Greeks of southern Italy but that would not necessarily cause any sort of major impact in Rome's constitution. So too, democracy would not be found in the vocabulary of the Latins, practically making the particular notion a foreign one to the Romans in most practical terms. Nonetheless, *Lex Hortensia* proves and substantiates the point that the few educated and powerful Plebeians that pressed ahead with Rome's constitutional reforms towards a somewhat more democratic constitution were aware of the value of the power of the people; they must have been aware of the fact that democracy, whilst not necessarily found in common parlance in Rome, was a goal worth pursuing. Thus, even in the mostly elite-based and elite-run oligarchic-monarchic Rome, the greater power in the hands of the people was an endeavour that the leaders of the Plebeians were willing to fight for and pursue.

5.3 *LEX HORTENSIA* PER SE

The greatest achievement behind *Lex Hortensia* was the fact that, from 287 BC onwards, the laws passed by the Plebeians in assembly would be binding on the whole of the Republic.[10] Practically, the powers of ratification of the Senate were nominally set aside but, in all probability, the grip of the Senate continued to be strong[11] over Plebeian laws throughout the Republic by way of Senate's legal interpretative powers. In theory, already since 449 BC, through the Twelve Tables, Livy reports, 'whatever the people decided last was binding law'[12]. However, even if we take that this was the position of the Republic through the Twelve Tables, the very enactment of *Lex Hortensia* proves that the position of the Roman *populus* was practically rather marginal in the Republic and that the Twelve Tables' wording on this one was hardly respected by Rome's ruling elites, or that, alternatively, laws reached by the Plebeians were not binding on the Republic as a whole but on Plebeians alone. Whereas the Plebeians could in theory now (i.e. post the enactment of the Hortensian Law) press ahead on their own with a law approved by the Plebeian Council, it was not customary in the Roman Republic for a law to come to life without the endorsement of the Senate.[13] *Lex Hortensia* was ultimately about the Senate respecting the will of the Plebeians through consensus.

[10] J Harries, 'Law' in Barchiesi and Scheidel (n 9) 641.

[11] E.g. A Momigliano, *Alien Wisdom: The Limits of Hellenization* (Cambridge University Press 1975) 26.

[12] Mitchell (n 7) 229–30 citing Livy 7.17.12.

[13] J von Ungern-Sternberg, 'The Crisis of the Republic' in HI Flower (ed), *The Cambridge Companion to the Roman Republic* (2nd edn, Cambridge University Press 2014) 79.

However, that consensus was the ultimate prerogative of the Senate even as late as 133 BC.[14]

5.4 THE ROMAN REPUBLIC WAS NEVER A DEMOCRACY

By definition, due to the mixed character of Rome's republican constitution, Rome would not be deemed a democracy. The Athenian Democracy was about popular sovereignty; the Roman Republic was about magistrates, a senate and the people of Rome. As such, Rome of the Republic was never a democracy *stricto sensu*.[15] It would also seem that during the Conflict of the Orders, the leading Plebeian families would not necessarily wish to significantly alter social conditions and/or introduce an Athenian type of democracy at Rome.[16] Indeed, to consider the Roman Republic a democracy in the main would be an imprecise characterisation of her constitution,[17] as Rome was clearly controlled by a rather small number of individuals that would come from a certain number of wealthy families.[18] For instance, until the passing of *Lex Hortensia*, the plebiscites of the Roman people were but a mere formal demand of the Plebeians on the ruling classes and the magistrates of Rome to act and/or make concessions.[19] However, the plebiscites would not be binding. At most, the Plebeian Tribunes could propose and modify the people's demands and Plebeians could be asked to vote on such modified proposals anew.[20] In short, the will of the people would not always be genuinely respected and its plebiscites could practically be rejected through renegotiation between the Tribunes, the magistrates and the Patricians.

Another major democratic deficit in the Republic would be the fact that the Republic's major political and geopolitical decisions would not be based on the majority principle but on the idea of collegiality amongst Rome's senior magistrates (consociation) and the veto powers of certain magistrates, the idea of separation of powers being absent from the constitution.[21] There was division of powers in the constitution but no such thing as a separation of powers in the constitution of the Republic. The classic example here would be the Senate that would concurrently hold executive, military and quasi-judicial powers. In this respect, Rome was not

14 Von Ungern-Sternberg (n 13) 80.

15 E.g. PA Zoch, *Ancient Rome* (Oklahoma University Press 1998) 32.

16 J von Ungern-Sternberg, 'The End of the Conflict of the Orders' in Raaflaub (n 1) 313.

17 Connolly (n 9) 716; but cf. F Millar, *The Crowd in Rome in the Late Republic* (University Michigan Press 1998) 11.

18 Connolly (n 9) 713; the position that Rome was an anocracy, according to which the constitution of Rome would not distinguish between its democratic and autocratic elements (as opposed to it being a republic *per se*), has also been raised: FJ Vervaet, CJ Dart and D Rafferty, 'Reform Unwillingness and the Death of the Roman Republic' in FJ Vervaet, D Rafferty and CJ Dart (eds), *How Republics Die: Creeping Authoritarianism in Ancient Rome and Beyond* (De Gruyter 2025) 105–6.

19 K Von Fritz, *The Theory of the Mixed Constitution in Antiquity: A Critical Analysis of Polybius' Political Ideas* (Columbia University Press 1954) 203, 237.

20 Ibid.

21 Capogrossi Colognesi (n 5) 83.

an Aristotelian state.[22] However, Rome did have a democratic element to it: in theory, the *populus* was powerful; in practice, it was procedurally and technically controlled by Rome's oligarchic and plutocratic elites. Even when 'voting' by units would take place in Rome, such would favour the richer citizens and the ones that would originate from Rome or thereabout rather than citizens from other parts of Latium and Italy.[23] The procedural controls over the popular assemblies of Rome and the fact that magistrates would regulate agenda and law proposals[24] would mean that the idea of democracy was practically a limited one. The democracy that the Plebeians of Rome would enjoy could be described as a managed type of democracy, a poor relative of genuine democracy. Hence, the Republic of Rome could not qualify as a democracy per se. On the contrary, the oligarchic and monarchic elements of the constitution of the Republic would bring Rome closer to a constitution like that of Sparta[25] than that of Athens.

5.5 *LEX HORTENSIA* AS THE BEGINNING OF A GOLDEN CONSTITUTIONAL ERA FOR THE ROMAN REPUBLIC

Lex Hortensia was not just about the partial emancipation of the Plebeians from Rome's ruling elites; it was about a degree of confidence and maturity of the Roman people. These were very interesting times for Rome because it was not just Rome's constitution that was somewhat maturing; it was also its private law that was becoming more sophisticated with such renowned laws as *Lex Aquilia*, Rome's answer to how injuries and damages sustained by one's property as a result of the acts of others could be dealt with legally, that is by way of compensation. A new Rome was clearly on the rise with both *Lex Hortensia* and *Lex Aquilia* having been legislated in pretty much the same year, even though *Lex Hortensia* was probably legislated a short while before *Lex Aquilia*.

Again, it is the case that the Republic did not quite exactly become a democracy through *Lex Hortensia* but the particular law brought Rome closer to democracy. *Lex Hortensia*, thus, enabled the creation of a mixed Patrician-Plebeian 'aristocracy' of magistrates for Rome.[26] *Mutatis mutandis* this was Rome's beginning of a golden constitutional era for it. Did Rome cease to be a mainly stratocratic oligarchy of plutocrats under an otherwise mixed constitution after *Lex Hortensia*? One's response ought to be in the negative here, in that Rome would traditionally institutionalise the different treatment of Plebeians and Patricians in social and economic terms,[27] such institutionalisation of its different societal

[22] Cf. Aristot. Pol. 4.1297b–8a.

[23] HI Flower, 'The Imperial Republic' in Barchiesi and Scheidel (n 9) 524, 519–32.

[24] E.g. N Rosenstein, *Rome and the Mediterranean 290 to 146* BC: *The Imperial Republic* (Edinburgh University Press 2012) 8; B Straumann, *The Just State: Greek and Roman Theories of Justice and Their Legacy in Western Thought* (Wiley-Blackwell 2024) 112.

[25] E.g. Plb. 6.50.14.

[26] Mitchell (n 7) 19.

[27] Connolly (n 9) 713.

segments having had a direct impact on its constitution, its politics and society overall. For instance, it would practically be the nobles and the well-off of Rome that would normally hold top office. In other words, the partial democratisation of Rome in 287 BC did not make it a democracy; nor did the ruling elites of Rome lose any significant power out of it, in that it would be these elites who would steer the Republic in the main until 27 BC and beyond.

Rome's Republic continued to be a divided one even after the Hortensian Law but its previous constitutional fractures and tensions would not show that much any more. As a thought-provoking example here, Rome was traditionally divided between the more Etruscan-oriented Patriciate[28] and the more Greek-oriented Plebs.[29] For instance, the Roman Plebs would show interest in Greek religion and moral outlook.[30] Moreover, aside from the well-known Roman legend that the Romans sent ambassadors to study the legal codes of Athens, Sparta and Gortys prior to drafting the original Ten Tables (subsequently another two tables were added, becoming the Twelve Tables), it is also reported in modern times that the Twelve Tables were not only inspired by Greek legal codes but were imitated from them,[31] the Tables having been drafted on the demand of the Plebeians as the way forward for the Republic's legal system. The spirit, the grammar, the syntax and the words in the Twelve Tables point to Greek influences.[32] Moreover, whereas in the Greek world oligarchic and monarchic systems could certainly be identified in the years of the Roman Republic, the Greek world would come ever closer to more open-ended forms of government, the pinnacle of such being the Athenian Democracy, the other great giant of constitutions of the ancient world. However, the Roman elites (Patriciate) would de facto traditionally prefer the Etruscan approach in respect of government matters, in that the Etruscan forms of government would be monarchic/oligarchic, the Roman Republic following in its constitution a more Etruscan-oriented approach to a certain considerable extent well into the 2nd and 1st century BC. It is not certain whether the Plebeians (i.e. the few rich and educated Plebeians of Rome) would have had contact with the democratic ideas of the Greeks but in all expectation this may well have been the case: the historical memory of the democracy of Pericles, the Golden Age of Athens in the 5th century BC, must have reached the Roman Plebeians in the 4th and the 3rd century BC. And, even though Rome was not interested in the theoretical examination of the concept of democracy in the 3rd century BC, the Plebeians practically acquired a somewhat greater say in the running of the Republic through *Lex Hortensia*.

28 The rule was not without exceptions: see the move of the Fabia *gens* at the end of the 4th century BC from Etruscan culture to Greek culture: Momigliano (n 11) 15.

29 A Momigliano, 'The Rise of the *Plebs* in the Archaic Age of Rome' in Raaflaub (n 1) 179.

30 Momigliano (n 11) 13–14.

31 E.g. Momigliano (n 29) 180; W Eder, 'The Political Significance of the Codification of Law in Archaic Societies: An Unconventional Hypothesis' in Raaflaub (n 1) 246. Cf. Capogrossi Colognesi (n 5) 58.

32 Momigliano (n 29) 180.

Chapter 6

A Constitution in Overdrive Responsible for Building an Empire

> [B]y the peculiar excellence of their political constitution, and the prudence of their counsels, [the Romans] not only recovered their supremacy over Italy, by eventually conquering the Carthaginians, but before very long became masters of the whole world.[1]

> They themselves say that their founders were brought up by the milk of a she-wolf; just so that entire race has hearts of wolves, insatiable of blood, and ever greedy and lusting after power and riches.[2]

6.1 INTRODUCTION

This chapter correlates the sophisticated character of the Roman Republic's constitution, at its best, with the creation of its empire. The chapter departs, however, from a similar point that Polybius made,[3] in that it emphasises the point that it was Rome's overall mixed but predominantly monarchic and oligarchic Republic, a point that Polybius omits, which was mostly responsible for the rise of the Roman empire. A further key point made here is that the constitution of Rome, whilst it was clearly created as a constitution for a city, the city of Rome, effectively enabled Rome to create an empire, even if this was not the original intention of its constitution; even if this came at the expense of transforming Rome from a Republic into a Principate; even if this resulted in the constitution giving way to a more imperial Rome. In this respect, a further point that the chapter makes is that the constitution of the Roman Republic, whilst not one that came with imperial tendencies per se, at least not in much of its constitutional law heyday, actually created the conditions for Rome's imperial ambitions to flourish.

[1] Plb. 3.118.9.

[2] Mithridates of Pontus on the Romans (Justin 38.6.7–8) as cited in KA Raaflaub, 'Born to Be Wolves? Origins of Roman Imperialism' in RW Wallace and EM Harris (eds), *Transitions to Empire: Essays in Greco-Roman History, 360–146* B.C., *in Honor of E. Badian* (University of Oklahoma Press 1996) 273.

[3] Plb. 3.118.9; 3.2.6.

6.2 THE CONSTITUTION OF THE REPUBLIC AS A KEY FACTOR FOR THE RISE OF IMPERIAL ROME

The Republic, its constitution, have defined Rome for centuries until the full retreat of the Republic to the Principate in 27 BC. All of Rome's future achievements and developments, in the years of the Principate and the Dominate, would emanate in one way or another from the Republic.[4] It was the Republic that was responsible for Rome's final embracement of the arts and the letters (initially an area that would be neglected by the Romans), the cultivation of Latin, but also growth in traditional Roman areas such as law through new ideas; the Republic was also responsible for the creation a permanent jury court (the *Quaestio Perpetua*) and, of course, an empire – Rome's republican empire or imperial republic, depending on one's perspective.

Rome thus achieved and attained a number of different things in the years of the Republic, even though it was never a very original or genuine innovator in cultural terms.[5] Yet, what Rome traditionally lacked in the field of the arts and the letters, has been counterbalanced by its traditional inclination for the arts of war and administration, especially because its constitution, the Republic's constitution, would stabilise Rome and actually enable it to eventually expand and prevail. It would also seem that the Roman Republic was initially hegemonic over Italian conquered lands, conventionally until 201 BC, but the hegemonic character of Rome was not unique to it, in that at least Athens and Sparta would have followed similar hegemonic approaches in the past over Greek lands.[6] Of course, the same constitution started to be abused in the Early Republic already but it is the case that until the end of the Middle Republic, Rome's enabling machine was its constitution. More interestingly, whereas the constitution of the Republic would practically retreat in the final century of the Republic, the Republic would still actually base its imperial ambition on that constitution, which in many respects was stratocratic (military-based).

It was the Republic that, from an insignificant polity of desperadoes and opportunists[7] in central Italy, became a full-blown empire in the 2nd and 1st century BC. The greatest legal achievement of the Republic was not its Twelve Tables, otherwise a magnificent collection of civil law[8] provisions mostly; nor its empire.

4 HI Flower, 'The Imperial Republic' in A Barchiesi and W Scheidel (eds), *The Oxford Handbook of Roman Studies* (Oxford University Press 2010) 519.

5 Flower (n 4) 519, citing TJ Cornell, *The Beginnings of Rome: Italy and Rome from the Bronze Age to the Punic Wars (c. 1000–264 BC)* (Routledge 1995).

6 On a comparison between the Roman empire and previous Greek hegemonies, see e.g. J-L Ferrary, 'L'Empire de Rome et Les Hégémonies de Cités Grecques chez Polybe' in J-L Ferrary (ed), *Rome et Le Monde Grec* (Les Belles Lettres 2017) 85–92.

7 D Hoyos, *Rome Victorious: The Irresistible Rise of the Roman Empire* (Bloomsbury Academic 2019, reprinted 2023) 1.

8 E.g. PA Zoch, *Ancient Rome* (Oklahoma University Press 1998) 55; L Capogrossi Colognesi, *Law and Power in the Making of the Roman Commonwealth* (Cambridge University Press 2014) 60.

The Republic's greatest achievement has been its mostly silent and stealthy constitution,[9] a constitution that would be particularly abstract, as in indistinct, and, for this reason, particularly flexible,[10] a constitution that would allow the Republic to steer through most perilous times with relative ease for the greatest part of its history. Eventually, Rome's constitution would also directly or indirectly affect in one way or another almost all of the world's republican (mixed) constitutions. The Constitution of the United States, in particular, would be the leading example as to how a modern constitution has drawn certain significant information from the Roman Republic's constitution in a number of different ways,[11] even though the democratic element in the modern constitution of the United States of America is by all means much more significant and powerful than Rome's democratic element ever was.

Quintessentially, the constitution of the Roman Republic is responsible for three things: first, the overall stability it offered to Rome in the first place; second, prosperity, a prosperity which it offered to the Roman *imperium*; and, third, Roman growth and expansion. Prosperity in Rome drove the constitution of the Republic and its growth, but the other way around too: the Republic's constitution was also strongly affected, if not manipulated, at the later stages of the Republic by Rome's ruling and wealthy classes (see Sulla's Reforms between 82 and 80 BC as the leading example in this respect).

6.3 THE RISE OF ROME AS AN IMPERIAL POWER FROM THE 3RD CENTURY BC

Appetite can grow stronger by mere tasting. Republican Rome did not start as an imperial power but became one over time. Mommsen was, thus, wrong[12] to deny[13] Roman aggression, even though equally there was no such thing as a Roman plan to grow an empire originally. Even at the late stages of the Early Republic, it was not yet absolutely clear whether Roman ambitions would span beyond central Italy. The constitution of the Republic was thus not originally designed and configured with a future empire in mind. However, Rome stands for a *locus classicus*[14] when it comes to an empire,[15] eventually becoming a key geopolitical paragon

[9] Cf. L Capogrossi Colognesi (n 8) 97, placing his emphasis on the policies of the Roman Senate rather than constitution as a whole.

[10] E.g. Capogrossi Colognesi (n 8) 193.

[11] Flower (n 4) 519, citing MNS Sellers, 'The Roman Republic and the French and American Revolutions' in HI Flower (ed), *The Cambridge Companion to the Roman Republic* (Cambridge University Press 2004) 347–64.

[12] E.g. ES Gruen, *The Hellenistic World and the Coming of Rome* (University of California Press 1984, reprinted 1986) 282.

[13] Gruen (n 12) 5, citing T Mommsen, *Römische Gesichte* I (Berlin, 1903, first published 1854).

[14] Plb. 21.32.2: *«ὁ δῆμος ὁ τῶν Αἰτωλῶν τὴν ἀρχὴν καὶ τὴν δυναστείαν τοῦ δήμου τῶν Ῥωμαίων»* ('The Aetolians to respect the empire and the majesty of the Romans') – Treaty of Rome with Aetolia in 189 BC.

[15] Hoyos (n 7) 1.

of balancing in the Hellenistic world.[16] Rome's imperial rise ran a parallel road with Rome's constitutional rise. The constitution of the Republic fed into and supported Rome's imperial ambition. Also, as has been shown, Rome from 287 BC onwards became slightly more democratic with the passing of *Lex Hortensia*. The Middle Republic, Rome's constitutional law heyday, happens to also be the era in which the Republic became imperial. That came at a cost: the Republic's constitution would be in the process of retreating, as it could not sustain the weight of the empire it had created. Moreover, in the Late Republic the constitution was just disregarded by powerful Roman personalities. Historically, there seem to be three reasons for Rome's expansion, especially in the East: (i) the anxiety of the Romans for the Macedonians and the Seleucids who could threaten Roman control of revered Greek cities and Hellenistic states and kingdoms such as Athens and Egypt respectively; (ii) Roman greed; and (iii) Rome's attempt to restabilise the Hellenistic world.[17]

The situation in southern Italy was otherwise changing in favour of Rome: King Pyrrhus had left the Italian peninsula in 275 BC and the Romans were then left literally unchecked to expand there as they wished, except for one formidable competitor of theirs: the Carthaginian Empire. Nonetheless, by 270 BC all of peninsular Italy, south of Cisalpine Gaul, was under Roman control.[18] Eventually, the Etruscans too came under the full control of the Romans in the North in 264 BC, when the last pocket of Etruscan resistance was eliminated. It was still not clear whether Rome would wish to expand beyond this, that is whether it would wish to conquer Sicily. For instance, the Roman Senate did not wish in 264 BC to proceed with the invasion of Sicily by dispatching Roman troops against Carthaginian forces. Polybius reports that it was the Roman people that pressed ahead with this decision because they 'wanted some means of repairing the losses which they had sustained in every department'[19] from Rome's previous wars. With the exception of free Syracuse, Sicily would become Rome's first overseas territory in 241 BC after it would come out victorious against Carthage in the First Punic War. Rome would then expand its *imperium* to Corsica and Sardinia in 237 BC; in 212 BC Syracuse too would fall in Roman hands,[20] and by 201 BC, with the end of the Second Punic War, Rome would have also conquered parts of Illyria and Iberia, while Carthage's sphere of influence would have been significantly reduced in the Western Mediterranean. It was now all too clear that the ambition of Rome spanned well beyond the Italian peninsula. It was now absolutely clear that Rome's ambition was to become a major geopolitical power, an imperial power.

The internal stabilisation that Rome's largely unwritten republican constitution offered to the city was a key reason for Rome's military projection to the world.

[16] J-L Ferrary, 'Le Monde Hellénistique, Rome et La Notion d' Équilibre International' in Ferrary (n 6) 109–18 citing *inter alia* Plb. 1.83.2–4 and 30.5.6–8.

[17] Hoyos (n 7) 24–5.

[18] Hoyos (n 7) 18.

[19] Plb. 1.11.2.

[20] Zoch gives a 211 BC date for the fall of Syracuse: Zoch (n 8) 112.

The mixed character of the constitution, as in its oligarchic-monarchic character with strong military characteristics, was the reason behind Rome's imperial success. Rome was now ahead of its competitors in the Greek world in constitutional terms as it was not any more a pale and insignificant kingdom somewhere in central Italy but a thriving imperial Republic. It had matured in both constitutional and military terms to the point that it could confidently expand its sphere of influence and territory in the centuries that followed. Polybius, however, alarmed by the fact of Rome's defeat in 216 BC at the Battle of Cannae, implied that Rome's constitution was in need of reviewing.[21] The alarm that he raised was more moral than real, to please the conservative elites of Rome, as Rome by 146 BC was the sole undisputed power in the then known world.

6.4 ROME'S MIXED BUT MOSTLY OLIGARCHIC CONSTITUTION AND POLITICS AS THE ENGINE FOR THE RISE OF ITS EMPIRE

The success of Rome's constitutional and political ordering resulted in Rome's imperial expansion. Polybius confirms the point in Book 6 of his *Histories*.[22] This success 'can be measured in terms of Rome's victories in war'[23]. These victories were the result of Rome's powerful constitution. This was a constitution 'constituted for obtaining power'[24]. Furthermore, if the Romans had reason to believe in the overall well-being of their political system and the constitution of the Republic prior to Rome's expansion in most of the Italian peninsula, Sicily, Corsica, Sardinia, Iberia and Illyria, their continuous victories over kings and oligarchies must have only increased their sense of pride and confidence in their republic.[25] In this respect, the role of the Senate, as a key constitutional player in Rome, was crucial. Of course, the Roman Senate would often merely react to what was happening beyond the strict borders of the Republic; however, despite the absence of a coherent geopolitical policy for expansion in the 4th century BC, the military successes and expansion of Rome during the Middle Republic can also be put down to Senate's mostly right decisions in strategic and geopolitical matters. Effectively, Rome's military direction would be mostly decided in the Senate and by the Republic's magistrates, something which Polybius omits. Thus, it was not the mixed constitution of Rome that allowed Rome to rise: it was the mixed constitution of Rome with its mostly oligarchic/monarchic characteristics that would allow it to do so. This concentrated degree of power in the hands of the

[21] Plb. 6.11; also, E Dench, *From Barbarians to New Men: Greek, Roman, and Modern Perceptions of Peoples of the Central Apennines* (Oxford University Press 1995) 80, 83.

[22] Plb. 6.50.4. Also, F Walbank, 'A Greek Looks at Rome: Polybius VI Revisited' (1998) 17 *Scripta Classica Israelica* 45, 45–6.

[23] Flower (n 4) 527, citing K-J Hölkeskamp, 'Conquest, Competition, and Consensus: Roman Expansion in Italy and the Rise of the *Nobilitas*' (1993) 42 *Historia* 12–39.

[24] Plb. 6.50.4.

[25] Cf. Flower (n 4) 527.

oligarchic Roman elites must have enabled, in turn, the Roman military to move and act swiftly at the times of the Middle Republic.

On the other hand, in the interests of historical accuracy, Rome's constitutional pride often transformed into military arrogance, the peak of its historical arrogance being the destruction of Corinth and Carthage on the indirect or direct orders of the Senate respectively. In this respect, Cicero would inform us that he regretted the destruction of Corinth.[26] Whether the Romans (Cicero included) were genuine about their regret for the destruction of Corinth 102 years afterwards, when Cicero's mentions his regret about this in *De Officiis* (On Duties), is open to debate, but the fact that the proud imperial Republic of Rome would have reached hybris[27] in geopolitical terms on certain occasions in its military past has clearly started entering geopolitical Roman discourse. There were no imperial brakes in Rome's constitution. This was, in fact, an element in the Republic's constitution that the Romans did not cultivate: when to stop. Thus, the Republic's constitution was one of checks and balances for the internal running of the state, as in the Roman core of the state, but it did not have in place such checks and balances for Rome's foreign policy. In any case, it was the internal degree of stability that Rome achieved through its constitution and political system that allowed it to maintain its power, endure geopolitical casualties and prevail over the ones it had defeated. Furthermore, Rome would invent, so to speak, new forms of organisation to rule over foreign peoples and lands.[28]

6.5 THE CONSTITUTION OF ROME AS AN ENABLING DEVICE FOR ROME'S MILITARY EXPANSION

The Romans would not have designed their constitution with military expansion in mind.[29] In the first steps of the Republic, the concerns of the ruling classes of Rome would be the mere survival of Rome against its Italic enemies and relative stability for Rome, which might have actually looked more like a town than a city at the time. Of course, the main raison d'être of Rome's constitution was the guarantees that it offered to Rome's ruling elites and people. By all means, the constitution of the Republic, as it matured in the span of hundreds of years, since the conventional year of 509 BC (establishment of the Republic), has been the cornerstone of Rome's overall internal stability. Two important points are worthy of note here: the first point is that the maturing of the Republic in military terms took more than two centuries since the original conception of its constitution; the second point relates to the first point, that is to say that the long span of the

26 Cic. Off. 3.46.

27 E.g. Dench (n 21) 81.

28 Cf. WV Harris, 'Power' in Barchiesi and Scheidel (n 4) 566–7 citing M Mann, *The Sources of Social Power*, I (Cambridge University Press 1986) 3.

29 Cf. T Whitmarsh, 'Hellenism' in Barchiesi and Scheidel (n 4) 730, citing ES Gruen, *The Hellenistic World and the Coming of Rome* (1984 University of California Press), who makes a similar point, that the Roman empire was not part of a strategic plan.

Republic (509–27 BC) was one that came with multiple transformations to Rome's constitution and, by extension, with changes to its military organisation (e.g. in the second half of the 3rd century, Rome's military was reorganised). Crucially, however, the military aspects of the constitution were of central importance in Rome's rise to the status of empire. It would, therefore, seem that, while the constitution of the Republic was not created with an empire in mind, it was created for the purposes of enabling its military.

PART III

A MIXED POLITY OF MONARCHIC, OLIGARCHIC, ARISTOCRATIC AND DEMOCRATIC ELEMENTS

Chapter 7

The Roman Republic as a Mixed Polity

7.1 INTRODUCTION

This chapter explains why Rome was a mixed reality in the first place and how this resulted in a mixed constitution for it, a republic, a polity. From its humble and obscure beginnings in the years of the Monarchy to its transformation into a world city in the years of the Republic, Rome was always a place where diverse cultures, peoples and ideas came together. From Rome's mythical founding, to the composition of her population, to the historical fact that Rome's culture operated in the orbit of the more established cultures of Greece and Etruria and to the mixed elements of her constitution, one observes that spirit of mixity in almost every aspect of Rome and the Roman Republic. Furthermore, this chapter offers an explanation as to Rome's mixed constitution by also presenting the overall constitutional law outlook of the Republic, it combining monarchic, oligarchic, aristocratic and democratic elements.

7.2 ROME AS A MONGREL

> *Nos sumus Romani qui fuimus ante Rudini.*[1]

> We act in a manner similar to the people of Pæstum who dwell in the Tyrrhenian Gulf; for it happened to them, though they were originally Greeks, ... becoming Tyrrhenians or Romans, and to have changed their language, and all the rest of their national habits.[2]

As the Romans would openly admit, the eternal city was what one would call a historical mongrel. So much so, that certain Romans, in the apogee of their Republic, would wish to forget the well-known (amongst the Roman people) legend of the she-wolf and the random beginnings of Rome; they would wish to cast away from memory the very fact that the synoecism of villages that Rome once was, was nothing less, nothing more, nothing else than a random concentration of Italic populations in the orbit of greater civilisations such as the Etruscan[3] and the Greek civilisation. In any case, Rome, in historical terms, has been traditionally

[1] Cicero probably referring to Ennius on the latter acquiring Roman citizenship: Cic. de Orat. 3.168: 'We, who once were Rudians, are now Romans'.

[2] Ath. 14.31.

[3] E.g. L Capogrossi Colognesi, *Law and Power in the Making of the Roman Commonwealth* (Cambridge University Press 2014) 37.

seen as a new kid in the Mediterranean block. The 'eternal city' would thus not compare well with the likes and the longer historical paths of much more established cities in the Mediterranean world such as Mycenae, Troy, Athens, Tyre or even its own Alba Longa.[4] Of course, the area where Rome was conventionally established in 753 BC was settled prior to the particular year, which seems to be more of a symbolic year as to the unification of settlements there. Rome, however, represents one of the best examples in human history of how a civilisation, which has not been particularly original in its configuration, has actually somehow grown to succeed in what it set out to achieve. Roman culture has traditionally been a mixed one, combining Latin, Etruscan, Sabine and Greek cultural characteristics.[5] As for Rome itself, what once was a moderate settlement of farmers spread out in a series of villages on its Seven Hills, rose to a citizenry of a quarter of a million[6] in the fourth century BC and a citizenry of more than four million in the time of Augustus.[7] Rome, thus, eventually came to be a great mother city of diverse influences, but it is the case that there is little Roman in ancient Rome except perhaps the legend that made Rome Roman. Rome, as we know it, was more what it came to be (i.e. republican and imperial), not what it originally was (i.e. monarchic and rustic).

Indeed, by common assent, Rome was originally but a moderately sized settlement of relatively backward peasants somewhere in central Latium; close to the sea, east of a river, Tiber, its residents being mostly engaged with farming. Its trade was mostly one-sided when it came to industrial goods and art, Rome importing from the Etruscan Italian North and the Greek Italian South products, art and artefacts on a considerable scale. These trade imports led to powerful cultural imports from Greece and Etruria into Rome. The first Roman coins were based on the Campanian Greek didrachms, the Roman composite order was a fusion of the Corinthian and the Ionic order, Greek statues and art were imitated in Rome as a matter of course; the Roman toga, certain Roman religious rituals and Rome's hydraulic engineering originated from the Etruscans and so on. Roman culture *mutatis mutandis*, if one could raise the idea that such a thing as Roman culture existed per se in the strict sense, is something that one observes much later in

[4] See Addendum III.

[5] But cf. T Mommsen, *The History of Rome*, vol. 1 (W Purdie Dickson tr, Macmillan & Co. 1901) 54–5.

[6] In 224 BC, a census showed 273,000 Romans and another half a million Latins and allies of Rome: D Hoyos, *Rome Victorious: The Irresistible Rise of the Roman Empire* (Bloomsbury Academic 2019, reprinted 2023) 10 citing Polybius.

[7] W Eder, 'Republicans and Sinners: The Decline of the Roman Republic and the End of a Provisional Arrangement' in RW Wallace and EM Harris (eds), *Transitions to Empire: Essays in Greco-Roman History, 360–146 B.C., in Honor of E. Badian* (University of Oklahoma Press 1996) 441; S Hin, 'Population' in HI Flower, *The Cambridge Companion to the Roman Republic* (2nd edn, Cambridge University Press 2014) 150; HI Flower, 'The Imperial Republic' in A Barchiesi and W Scheidel (eds), *The Oxford Handbook of Roman Studies* (Oxford University Press 2010) 522. In her 2010 chapter, Flower also mentions a figure of 12 million citizens at the end of the Republic (as a new hypothesis).

Rome's existence. In any case, Rome and the Romans, in their original configuration, were mostly Latin, Sabine and Etruscan of predominant rustic stock[8] in formal terms, or 'barbarians'[9] in Greek terms, or what one would call agrarian peasants, greatly unaffected and untouched by any sort of intellectual enquiry. Rome, as the she-wolf legend reminds us, started rather wild, primitive and violent.

In any case, the Romans themselves would report that after Rhea Silvia was raped by the God of War, Mars, becoming impregnated as a result of the rape, she conceived and gave birth to twins, Romulus and Remus. Rhea Silvia was then imprisoned by her uncle, Amulius, the new King of Alba Longa, who had previously removed her father, Numitor, from the throne. Amulius also ordered the drowning of her new-born twins in the river Tiber, as they could pose a threat to his reign. The river was swollen and the servants that were to throw the infants into it could not approach it. Another version of the legend suggests that the servants were actually successful in putting the twins in a trough, which eventually came out on one of Tiber's banks. The legend also has it that the first stepmother of Rome to find and nurture her twins, as in Rhea Silvia's twins, was a passing she-wolf, a *lupa*. In formal Latin, the term *lupa* literally means she-wolf. Metaphorically, however, the Latins would colloquially use the same term for prostitute. Rome, the fierce, semi-barbaric[10] daughter of the Mediterranean world, stepchild of Etruria and Greece, the then 'mistress of the world', as she was personified into Rhea Silvia's two exposed and deserted-under-a-fig-tree infants, Romulus and Remus, somewhere in the Palatine Hill, was thus initially nurtured either by a wild beast or a prostitute. Romulus and Remus were offspring of war. Rome was offspring of war. War was the father of Rome. Rome, as in Romulus and Remus, never saw their true mother ever again, after her imprisonment and death, despite Antho's attempt, the daughter of Amulius, to have Rhea Silvia's life spared. Rhea Silvia threw herself into the river Tiber, thereby committing suicide. Upon adulthood, Romulus and Remus removed Amulius from the throne and killed him to avenge their mother's death.

Myths, of course, are about powerful symbolisms. Either way, whether Rome was nurtured by a she-wolf or a prostitute, one cannot escape the thought that

8 The well-known punishment of Mettius on the orders of King Tullus Hostilius, a 7th BC Roman king, offers indicative but cogent evidence of the barbaric state in which Rome was for many centuries after its conventional founding in 753 BC. Mettius' body was ordered to be torn apart after it had been tied up to two opposing chariots, the horses of which were lashed to disjoint his body with force. Livy (Liv. 1 28), in apparent embarrassment, many centuries later called this 'the first and last punishment of a type so heedless of human laws occurred among us Romans' (translated by Zoch: PA Zoch, *Ancient Rome* (University of Oklahoma Press 1998) 19). Nonetheless, Rome's inhuman treatment of gladiators in the Colosseum speaks volumes to the fact that Rome's bloodthirsty vices and retributive sense of justice of the 7th century BC continued for long and went well into the 1st and the 2nd centuries AD. Also, Lucretia's Rape, historical or not, stands for another didactic story full of symbols as to the primitive, despotic and tyrannical ways that Roman kings would deploy against their subjects and so on.

9 Plin. Nat. 29: '*[N]os quoque dictitant barbaros et spurcius nos quam alios Ὀπικῶν appellatione foedant*'.

10 Cf. T Whitmarsh, 'Hellenism' in Barchiesi and Scheidel (n 7) 736.

the legend tells us that Rome's beginnings were humble, mysterious and profoundly dark. All we know effectively is that War was the father of Rome, her mother being a raped woman of Trojan descent somewhere in Latium, her first stepmother, as in the first stepmother of Romulus and Remus, being a *lupa*. The conception of Rome, thus, symbolises its forced, ferocious and dark beginnings. It also symbolises its mixed and obscure beginnings. The she-wolf that nourished Silvia Rhea's children initially, Romulus and Remus, symbolises the eternal and immutable forces of nature; the she-wolf is the mother figure representing the forces of fertility, good fortune, strength, confidence and protection, such forces becoming synonymous to the rise of Rome and Roman power. The subsequent killing of one brother by the other, the killing of Remus by Romulus, the founder of Rome, signifies Rome's internal conflicts and clashes[11] between similar but diverging elements of its population.

Who would have thought, however, that Rome, the future mistress of the world, would have been initially nurtured, at least in her mythological and symbolic dimension, through her offspring, Romulus and Remus, by some wild beast or, even more alarmingly, by some prostitute, i.e. after her infant twins would have been deserted in the nature of Latium? Thereafter, a shepherd, Faustulus, would take the infants away from the she-wolf and would raise them with his wife, Acca Larentia, who others claim (due to her alleged promiscuity) symbolised the she-wolf prostitute.[12]

7.3 THE SPIRIT OF MIXITY AS A UNIVERSAL IN ROME AND ITS CONSTITUTION

This spirit of mixity is found everywhere in Rome's history and myths. The Romans – mainly Latino-Sabines by ethnic configuration, Etruscans through foreign occupation and infiltration, Greeks by education – have been perceived as a composite collective traditionally. Indeed, over its history, Rome was governed by rather diverse networks. Thus, '"[f]oreign" kings, senators, and consuls are only explainable if we see Rome as a vehicle commandeered in turns by different supra-ethnic aristocratic networks'.[13] Moreover, as will be seen below, Rome in the years of the Republic, the Monarchy and Rome prior to the Monarchy, came in contact and has been affected by four ethno-cultural circles: the Latin circle, the Etruscan circle, the Greek circle, and the Sabino-Samnite[14] circle (see Figure 7.1).

[11] Cf. Mommsen (n 5) 69–70.

[12] E.g. A Fraschetti, *The Foundation of Rome* (Marian Hill and Kevin Windle (trs), Edinburgh University Press 2005) 3.

[13] N Terrenato, 'Early Rome' in Barchiesi and Scheidel (n 7) 515.

[14] The term 'Sabino-Samnite' would better reflect this ethno-cultural circle. For more on the close relationship of Rome with these people, the peoples of the Apennines, see e.g. E Dench, *From Barbarians to New Men: Greek, Roman, and Modern Perceptions of Peoples of the Central Apennines* (Oxford University Press 1995) 1–2, 3.

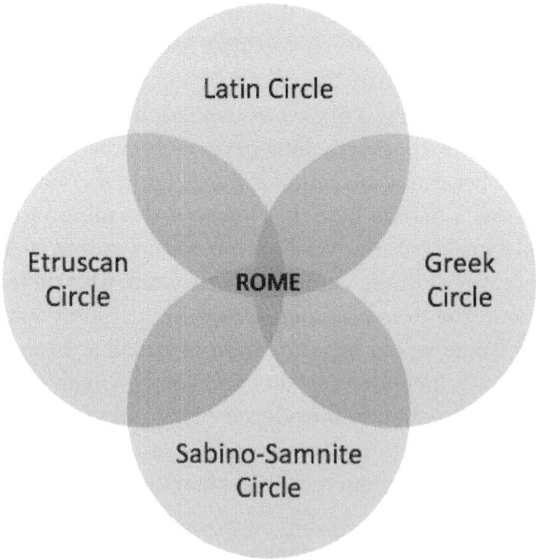

Figure 7.1 The ethno-cultural circles that have affected ancient Rome

We also find this spirit of mixity in the Republic's constitution. Polybius, for instance, considered the mixed character of the constitution as the Roman Republic's greatest characteristic, in that it created, according to him, the best form of constitution.[15] The Romans themselves otherwise revealed their mixed beginnings through the legends they devised. Thus, when Romulus killed Remus, one of the first things that Romulus did was to offer asylum to persecuted persons and fugitives for Rome to create a permanent population.[16] That spirit of Rome's mixed character was also apparent in the Abduction (Rape) of the Sabine women by the Romans, these women being 'necessary' for Rome to acquire a female population. The Romans who would have been the result of rape would now be the rapists. The Sabines came to make peace with the Romans eventually, when the Sabine women stepped in between their fathers and what were now their Roman husbands, and Sabines were integrated into Rome. However, there are powerful hints as to the importance of Sabine culture and, by extension, foreign cultures, on Roman culture per se.

First comes the historical fact that there would be Patrician families in Rome that would draw descent from the Sabines. Second, the Rape of the Sabine women effectively relates to the fact that there must have once been certain significant admixture of Latins and Sabines in Rome.[17] Third, the intrusion of

[15] Plb. 6.3.

[16] E.g. E Dench, 'Roman Identity' in Barchiesi and Scheidel (n 7) 272; M Beard, *SPQR: A History of Ancient Rome* (Liveright Publishing 2015) 66; G Bradley, *Early Rome to 290 BC* (Edinburgh University Press 2020) 107.

[17] Bradley (n 16) 104, 107. Cf. Capogrossi Colognesi (n 3) 12.

Sabine forces into the Citadel of the Roman Capitol and its capture by them[18] is another way for Roman legend to tell us that Sabines could enter, or may have entered, key elements of Roman life, albeit by force or trickery (for the use of trickery by the Sabines, see e.g. Tarpeia's assassination by them after she betrayed her fellow Romans). Fourth, the reaching of peace between Romans and Sabines resulted in the latter becoming citizens of Rome.[19] Fifth, the second king of Rome, Numa Pompilius, was a Sabine himself. However, the more profound influence by Etruscan[20] and Greek cultures on Rome is also apparent in Roman legends already. Thus, a number of Rome's kings were Etruscan, while at least one of them was of Greek descent, the Romans otherwise openly attesting that the first settler of Palatine Hill in Rome would be a Greek from Arcadia, Evander. His mother, Carmenta or Nicostrate, amended certain letters of the Greek alphabet into Latin letters and Evander subsequently introduced his mother's alphabet into Latium and so on. These legends often coincide with scientific findings: e.g. the Latin alphabet seems to have arisen from the Chalcidian/Cumaean version of the Greek alphabet and so on.[21]

The point that this monograph makes in constitutional law terms echoes Rome's mixed and obscure beginnings: she who was wild and free came to be orderly and mature. She who was tremulous and meek came to be confident and powerful. The young Republic, wild and free from the shackles of the monarchy in 509 BC, was initially quite primitive and embryonic in constitutional and developmental terms but came to set an example in world history, in its constitutional apex, the period between 287 and 133 BC, which this monograph explores in detail and when she was in the process of creating, through her constitution, an empire. The wild daughter would have created a magnificent constitution over the centuries. She who had mixed roots came to crystallise them into Rome's mixed constitution, balancing the old with the new, the Plebeians with the Patricians, the different cultural and ethnic influences, Latin, Sabine, Etruscan and Greek that would compose and inform Rome into one; the forces of monarchy, oligarchy, aristocracy and democracy into a concrete whole.

As for the Republic's constitution, there are at least three different ways according to which one observes its mixed character: (i) the Republic was a polity in Aristotelian terms, i.e. a mixed form of governance combining monarchic, aristocratic, oligarchic and democratic elements; (ii) in the Republic's constitution one observes not only the three classic constitutional powers as per Aristotle and Montesquieu's separation of powers (Executive, Legislature and Judiciary) but also a fourth one, which was crucial to the Roman Republic – Rome's Military (see Figure 7.2); and (iii) to make things more interesting, even Rome's offices and

[18] Zoch (n 8) 13.

[19] Zoch (n 8) 13; Beard (n 15) 64.

[20] E.g. M Crawford, *The Roman Republic* (2nd edn, Fontana Press 1992) 32.

[21] E.g. R Wallace, 'The Latin Alphabet and Orthography' in J Clarkson (ed), *A Companion to the Latin Language* (Wiley-Black 2011) 9–10.

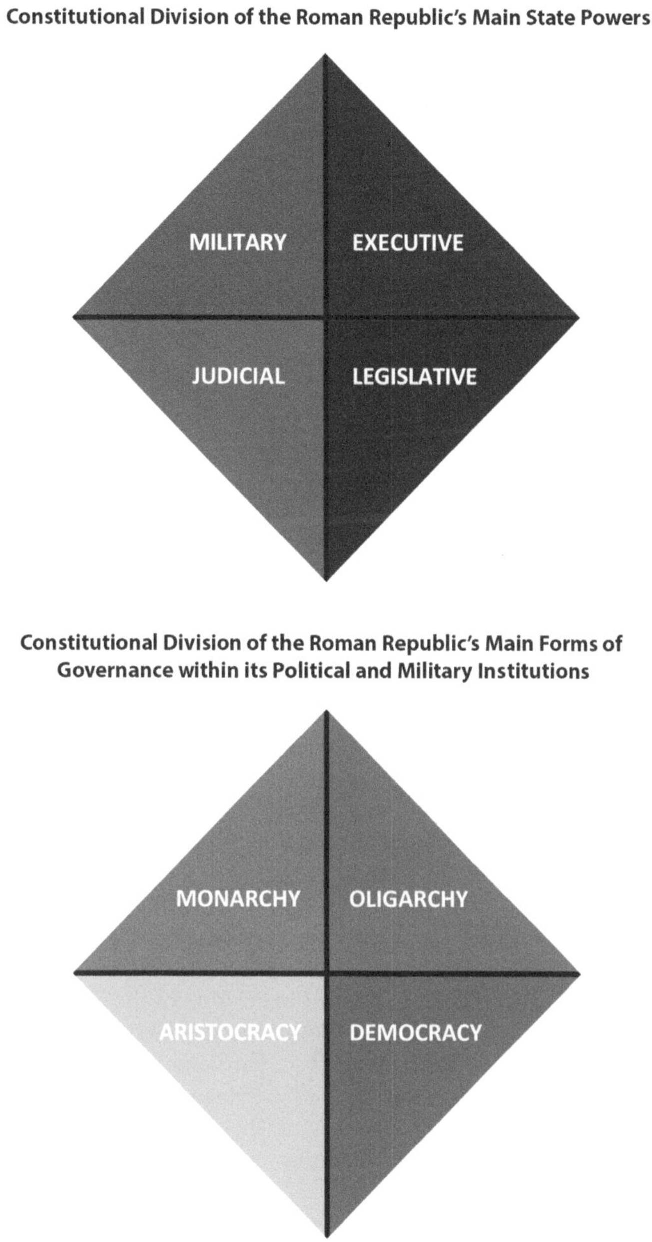

Figure 7.2 The Republic – The Senate and the Roman People: constitutional division of the Roman Republic's main state powers; constitutional division of the Roman Republic's main forms of governance within its political and military institutions

magistrates, its top officials, often came with functions that would move beyond one form of constitutional power. The clearest example of a body of mixed powers in Rome was the Senate. It would combine in its operations quasi-legislative, executive and military powers. The Senatus was Rome's constitutional centre: not only would it offer direction for Rome's laws, for example by reference to *mos maiorum* (the customs and traditions of Rome's ancestors), but it would also order and execute constitutional *ultima* in cases of emergency for the Republic, often for the wrong reasons, informally since 133 BC (order to kill Tiberius Gracchus) and formally from 121 BC (order to kill the brother of Tiberius, Gaius Gracchus). Indeed, it would be the Senate that would offer direct guidance to Rome's Consuls as to whether war operations would be the preferable option to peace.

7.4 THE REPUBLIC WAS NOT A DEMOCRACY: ROME WAS A MIXED POLITY COMBINING MONARCHIC, OLIGARCHIC, ARISTOCRATIC AND DEMOCRATIC ELEMENTS

For all analytical intents and purposes, a point that has to be first made in this chapter, from the constitutional law point of view, is that the Roman Republic was not a democracy.[22] The Roman Republic was neither a democracy, nor an oligarchy, a monarchy or an aristocracy. It was actually a combination of these systems of governance. Indeed, it was readily apparent in the 3rd and 2nd centuries BC that the Republic was clearly a combination of democratic, aristocratic, monarchic and oligarchic elements. The picture is less clear with the Roman Republic of the 5th century BC, the sources of which operate on the borderline between legend and reality. The Roman Republic of the 5th century BC seems to have been much less developed and its precise nature is obscured between legend and narratives that do not always hold the credibility of concrete and attested historical subject matter. The period between 509 and 494 BC, for instance, has been described as 'transitional',[23] whilst the period between 494 and 451/0 BC has been described as a 'proto-republican' one.[24] The idea that the Republican period proper commences in c. 450/449 BC with the creation of the Twelve Tables has also been put forward,[25] even though the historical conventional beginning of the Roman Republic would be that of 509 BC. Furthermore, due to the apparent lack of scientific historical interest[26] amongst Romans for the developments of their time or for older Roman history – it should be remembered that the Romans started composing their own history, on their own, only as late as late

[22] E.g. Zoch (n 8) 32. For a similar point, see section 5.4 of the analysis further above. But cf. F Millar, *The Roman Republic in Political Thought* (University Press of New England 2002) 6.

[23] HI Flower, *Roman Republics* (Princeton University Press 2010) 33.

[24] Flower (n 23) 33, 48.

[25] Flower (n 23) 33, 48.

[26] Cf. Flower (n 23) 39.

3rd century BC[27] – the constitutional picture seems to be somewhat vague and ambiguous in relation to the Republic of the 5th and 4th centuries BC. Finally, it should be maintained that, whilst ancient sources, such as Polybius, did not describe all of Rome's constitution in a very scientific way, Polybius was certainly right to the extent that the constitution of the Republic was a mixed one to the point that not even the Romans themselves were able to categorise it.[28] However, Polybius, as will be explained below, deliberately presented the constitution of the Republic in a certain way by silencing certain aspects thereof. For instance, whilst he posited that it combined monarchic, aristocratic and democratic elements, he omitted from his analysis the strong oligarchic elements that characterised and defined the Roman Republic.

7.5 ROMAN REPUBLICAN HISTORY AND THE MIXED AND CONSERVATIVE CHARACTER OF THE REPUBLIC

Roman republican history has otherwise been written by Greek 'outsiders' mostly such as Dionysius of Halicarnassus, Polybius, Posidonius and Plutarch with the exception of Livy,[29] who was not a Roman either *stricto sensu*, but a Roman citizen descending from north-east Italy. Of course, the name of Fabius Pictor, a Roman by descent, should also be mentioned here as the first Roman historian who dealt with the Republic but also Roman history as a whole, even though his work does not survive. In any case, it would be important to reiterate that the constitution of the Roman Republic was a mixed one. Rome was a mixed polity. Republican Rome in its constitutional apogee was a polity of mixed constitutional characteristics. Historically, Rome's constitution was not fixed and it would change according to the needs of its citizens.[30] Etymologically, the term 'republic' emanates from Latin '*res publica*'. Ontologically, 'the term *res publica* suggests the unity of all citizens in a shared civic community that transcends the social divisions of class, neighbourhood, or family'.[31] Sociologically, however, the Roman Republic was a rather conservative republic,[32] Rome's system of *clientela* (protection of certain Plebeians by certain Patrician patrons) being by far the best illustration of a reciprocal responsibility system, unique to Roman society, designed 'to maintain the status quo and to preserve the privileges of the [wealthy] Patricians'.[33] Also, the

27 Flower (n 23) 38, stating that '[h]istorical writing in both prose and in verse … grew out of the context of the Second Punic War'.

28 Plb. 6.11.

29 Flower (n 23) 41; Bradley (n 16) 16, 17, 21–2, 23, 82.

30 A Lintott, *The Constitution of the Roman Republic* (Clarendon Press 1999) 28.

31 Flower (n 23) 12.

32 Cf. Flower (n 23) 45: 'Roman society appear[s] highly traditional and slow to change, even under intense pressure from external enemies and from internal social tensions'.

33 RW Mathisen, *Ancient Roman Civilization: History and Sources* (Oxford University Press 2019) 65. For more on Rome's patrons and *clientela*'s system, see N Davies, *Europe: A History* (Pimlico 1996, reprinted with corrections 1997) 170.

'way of the ancestors' (*mos maiorum*), an idea that was often invoked by Rome's Censors and the Senate, was, of course, responsible for this state of affairs and many other of Rome's conservative social and family norms.

7.6 THE REPUBLIC'S MONARCHIC AND OLIGARCHIC ELEMENTS TRADITIONAL PREVALENCE OVER ITS ARISTOCRATIC AND DEMOCRATIC ELEMENTS

Furthermore, the Republic's monarchic and oligarchic elements were traditionally stronger and more powerful than its democratic and aristocratic ones. In respect of the fact that the Roman elites were sceptical of the rule of the masses,[34] the constitution of the Roman Republic was partially Platonic. Whereas the Roman elites would comprehend and appreciate quite late in the day the value of philosophy or indeed the idea of (a) philosopher king(s), they would, at the very least, imply that the Roman masses would be better served and controlled by Rome's plutocrats, which in principle would be more and better educated than the Roman Plebeians. Furthermore, the will of the Roman people was normally null and void in practical terms without consent (*auctoritas patrum*) by the Senate.[35] Overall, the Roman Republic concentrated most of its powers in the hands of hundreds of wealthy Roman citizens and magistrates.[36] This is unlike most Western modern republics, which, at least in theory, are more democratic in their constituent characteristics. Republican Rome was mostly oligarchic.[37] Modern republics tend to be mostly democratic. In Aristotelian terms, however, the point remains: the Roman Republic was a polity, a mixed polity. As such, in the Aristotelian perception of the world, the Roman Republic was one of these mixed[38] constitutions, a polity.[39] However, it was not a perfect mixed polity, in that it also combined monarchic elements, which a classic Aristotelian polity (mixed constitution) would not necessarily tolerate. Moreover, it was self-interest and fear that kept the institutions of the Republic interdependent to one another.[40] It was self-interest and fear that gave birth to the Roman Republic; it was exactly self-interest and fear that signalled its fall. The Republic, as it was generated and developed over the centuries, was more the result of reactive politics than a proactive type of constitutional design. Aristotle

[34] Cf. A Herman, *The Cave and the Light: Plato Versus Aristotle and the Struggle for the Soul of Western Civilization* (Random House 2014) 27–8.

[35] H Mouritzen, *Politics in the Roman Republic* (Cambridge University Press 2017) 20–1.

[36] E.g. Mouritzen (n 35) 23.

[37] Cf. Crawford (n 20) 1.

[38] Cf. Lintott (n 30) 192.

[39] Cf. Mouritzen (n 35) 11.

[40] Mouritzen (n 35) 11, citing Lintott 1997: 'The theory of the mixed constitution at Rome' in *Philosophia Togata II: Plato and Aristotle at Rome*, ed. J. Barnes and M. Griffin (Oxford) 70–9 at 79; Asmis, E. 2005. 'A new kind of Model. Cicero's Roman constitution in De republica', AJPh 126: 376–416 at 380.

had otherwise compared the constitutions of 153[41]/158[42] city states but one would not be aware, for certain, whether he or his students would have had the chance to examine that of the Roman Republic, as only fragments of his examination of the Athenian constitution have come down to us.[43] Considering that Aristotle lived in the 4th century BC, it would be highly probable, however, that he and his students must have at least become aware of the existence of a rather small but constitutionally interesting – albeit otherwise remote and mostly insignificant at the time – republic in the Italian peninsula, called the Roman Republic with its own mixed constitution, structures and traditions. So too, they must have become aware of the fact that certain Tyrrhenian and Greek kings ruled the Roman kingdom before it became a republic.[44] Whether their awareness of the Roman Republic would have led them to research the Republic's constitution remains a mystery,[45] in that Rome did not belong to Greek city states,[46] at least not *stricto sensu*.[47]

7.7 ROMAN MAGISTRATES' DUTIES REINFORCING THE MIXED CHARACTER OF THE REPUBLIC

A point that is often missed about the Roman Republic's mixed character is the fact that its magistrates would also come with mixed duties and functions. Thus, the mixed character of the Republic emanated also from the fact that a single Roman magistrate could concurrently hold political, military and religious powers. For instance, a Praetor, who was an *ex officio* member of the Roman Senate

[41] K Zweigert and H Kötz, *An Introduction to Comparative Law* (Tony Weir (tr), 3rd edn, Oxford University Press) 49.

[42] Millar (n 22) 15 citing Aristotle, *Fragmenta*, V. Rose (ed) (Leipzig 1886) 258f. Also, G Verhasselt, 'Heraclides' Epitome of Aristotle's *Constitutions* and *Barbarian Customs*: Two Neglected Fragments' (2020) 69 *The Classical Quarterly* 672, 672; Herman (n 34) 70.

[43] Zweigert and Kötz (n 41) 49.

[44] Roman King Lucius Tarquinius Priscus belonged to the Etruscan line kings of Rome; his father, however, Demaratus, was of Greek descent, a Corinthian. Of clearly Etruscan roots was the second King of the Etruscan dynasty of Roman kings, Servius Tullius. The third and final Etruscan king of Rome was Lucius Tarquinius Superbus but it would not be perfectly clear whether he would belong to the bloodline of Lucius Tarquinius Priscus as the grandson or the son of the latter. It would be practically impossible to be his son though. As such, if there was a relationship between Lucius Tarquinius Priscus and Lucius Tarquinius, this must have been one between grandfather and grandson.

[45] Cf. Millar (n 22) 158.

[46] This is the view that Millar supports: Millar (n 22) 16, 158.

[47] Cf. Millar (n 22) 13, referring and citing the 4th century BC writer Heraclides' view that Rome was a Greek *polis*: Heraclides Ponticus, Frag. 102, in F. Wehrli, *Die Schule des Aristotles 7: Herakleides Pontikos* (2nd edn, Basel 1969), quoted from Plutarch, *Life of Camillus* 22.2. Millar goes on to say that such a view would go too far, as the language of the inhabitants of early Rome was Latin. Raaflaub mentions that 'Rome was [neither] a Greek city nor that it was exactly like a Greek city … in structure and early development Rome and many archaic Greek cities were closely comparable': KA Raaflaub, 'The Conflict of the Orders in Archaic Rome: A Comprehensive and Comparative Approach' in KA Raaflaub (ed), *Social Struggles in Archaic Rome: New Perspectives on the Conflict of the Orders* (2nd edn, Blackwell Publishing 2005) 27.

(i.e. a political figure), could also be the commander of a Roman military unit, whilst also being a religious Pontiff acting for life.[48] Furthermore, the Aediles, aside from their administrative functions, were also magistrates who would exercise, among other functions, low ranked judicial duties (e.g. for sales transactions and could issue in this respect an *edictum aedilicium*), whilst they could also exercise forum policing powers and so on.[49]

7.8 ROME AFFECTED BY GREECE AND ETRURIA – A MIXED CULTURE THAT RESULTED IN A MIXED CONSTITUTION

Rome was not falling *stricto sensu* in the Greek circle; it spoke a 'barbaric' language, Latin, and, while it was clearly affected in cultural terms by Greece and Etruria, it was not a Greek city, when in all likelihood it was once under Etruscan rule. Romans would not be allowed to participate in the Olympic Games, as they would be non-Greek, and it would be only in 80 BC, many years after Rome conquered mainland Greece, that Sulla would move the games to Rome, thereby practically allowing Romans to participate in the games. Yet that was not a choice of the originators of the games but a thing imposed by the Roman conqueror on the Games. Therefore, for so many real reasons, Rome was a 'barbaric', a foreign, city in the main, at least in the Greek mindset, albeit of certain considerable interest to Greek intellectuals such as Aristotle, Polybius, Plutarch and others. Also, one ought to consider here the thought-provoking example of the Macedonians as 'barbarians'. Thus, even the Macedonians were considered 'barbarians' in 4th century BC by the most 'nationalist' Athenian circles who would, of course, oppose the relentless rise of Macedonia almost all over Greece. Macedonians were, of course, speakers of a Doric Greek dialect, being a Greek race with certain ideological influences from the Thracians when it came to their model of kingship, and yet they were considered 'barbarians' by these circles. As a matter of fact, Athenians would not call the Macedonians barbarians because they were, or because the Greek Doric tribes of Macedonia would be more ferocious and warlike than the Athenians. They would call them barbarians because it actually suited them to do so. Also, the Macedonians would be monarchic when the Athenians would be democratic. Rome, on the other hand, if known to the same circles, must have clearly been wholly 'barbarian' to them, considering that it did not simply speak a different Greek dialect, like the Macedonians did, but, as stated, a different language altogether – Latin.[50]

[48] E.g. IE Τζαμτζής, *Ο Μεσογειακός Κόσμος* (*Εκδόσεις Σάκκουλα* 2014, *ανατύπωση* 2018) 96–7.

[49] Τζαμτζής (n 48) 94.

[50] But cf. Dionysius of Halicarnassus view that Latin was a semi-barbaric Greek language of Aeolian descent infiltrated with many words from barbaric languages because of the Romans' promiscuity with other languages, this resulting in them not being able to pronounce all of their sounds properly. See Dionysius of Halicarnassus, *Roman Antiquities* 1.90.1 (*Ῥωμαῖοι δὲ φωνὴν μὲν οὔτ' ἄκρως βάρβαρον οὔτ' ἀπηρτισμένως Ἑλλάδα φθέγγονται, μικτὴν δέ τινα ἐξ ἀμφοῖν, ἧς ἐστιν ἡ πλείων Αἰολίς, τοῦτο μόνον ἀπολαύσαντες ἐκ τῶν πολλῶν ἐπιμιξιῶν, τὸ μὴ πᾶσι τοῖς φθόγγοις ὀρθοεπεῖν*).

Nevertheless, Rome of the 4th century BC could be fitted quite readily 'into Greek conceptions of a *polis*'.[51] Plutarch otherwise reports that Aristotle accurately gathered information about the capture of the city of Rome[52] by the Gauls in 390 BC, an event that deeply marked both the Republic and the Roman psyche. Furthermore, despite Rome's constant and traditional efforts to show certain links with the Greeks and the Greek world (the myths of Evander, the Pallantines of Arcadia being the first settlers of Rome's Palatine Hill and the story of the Roman commission to Greek city states in preparation of the Twelve Tables are indicative in this respect), Rome was fundamentally a city of 'barbarians' for the Greeks. In fact, both the Greeks and the Romans themselves would coincide in their assessment of Roman people and culture as rustic and barbaric. For instance, the Roman propaganda mechanisms, also taking the form of poetry lines from the leading lyric Samnite Roman poet Horace, would openly call Latium 'rustic'[53] and the Romans 'savage winners'[54] with reference to the looting of Corinth in 146 BC. This famous quote otherwise reveals the fact that, whilst Rome was superior to Greece by the 2nd century BC in military terms, it was still – by common assent between Romans and Greeks, aside from Cato the Elder – a culturally inferior barbaric 'relative' of Greece.[55] It should also be remembered that the overwhelming majority of Romans in the years of the Monarchy and for the greater part in the years of the Republic were effectively agrarian peasants,[56] a people with little to no education, devoid of any intellectual endeavours or an interest in the arts, as in creating novel, inspirational, original forms of art.

Even Sparta, with its legislator Lycurgus and its famous poets Cinaethon, Tyrtaeus and Alcman, must have looked like an intellectual giant when compared to rustic Rome, at least for the greatest part of her republican era. And yet, despite Rome's humble cultural beginnings and its agrarian ways, one must make the admission that Rome was not a barbaric city but a city of partially diverse semi-barbaric people(s) for most of its life in the years of the Republic. Equally, Aristotle, despite the Greek world's reluctance to examine the laws and constitutions of 'barbarians',[57] would not necessarily confine his comparative constitutional research to the Greek city states only, as we know for a fact that in his *Politics* he considered the constitution of Carthage.[58] Reverting to the point made about the 'barbaric' Romans, the Carthaginians too would qualify by Greek standards as 'barbarians'. However, Aristotle, unlike Plato who dismissed the Carthaginians

Also, on the awareness of the ancients (the Romans included) of their mixed languages, see B Stevens, 'Aeolism: Latin as a Dialect of Greek' (2006/7) 102 *The Classical Journal* 115.

[51] Millar (n 22) 2.

[52] Plut. Cam. 22.3.

[53] Hor. Ep. 2.1, verses 156–7: *Graecia capta ferum victorem cepit et artis intulit agresti Latio.*

[54] Ibid.

[55] Cf. MT Boatwright, *Peoples of the Roman World* (Cambridge University Press 2012) 66–7.

[56] Cf. Crawford (n 20) 29.

[57] Mathisen (n 33) 18.

[58] Aristot. Pol. 2.1272b.

as 'hopeless barbarians',[59] clearly considered them civil enough to include them in his treatises. Of course, for the Greeks, Carthage was a politically exotic place, as was Rome. What must have made the Carthaginian constitution even more interesting to the Greeks, though, was the fact that behind it one would find in the 6th century BC the most prosperous city in the then known world,[60] whilst as of early 3rd century BC it was the strongest state in the Western Mediterranean[61] with an empire of its own. A major difference also between Carthage and Rome in the 4th century BC, the time Aristotle wrote his works, was that Carthage ruled an extensive empire in the Western Mediterranean, whilst Rome was but a relatively backward republic with a limited jurisdiction to it, controlling only parts of Latium, northern Campania and certain areas of Central Italy. Rome as Carthage, however, had links with the Greek world (as well as with the Etruscan world) but would that be enough to compare its laws with those of the Greek city states?

Finally, with regard to the influence of the Etruscans over Rome, we know from the Roman myths that a number of Roman kings would be of Etruscan descent. Even if these Etruscans kings never existed, the Roman myths effectively reveal to us the powerful influence of the Etruscans over Rome. Furthermore, certain Patrician families in Rome would descend from Etruscans. Indeed, Rome was under the direct or indirect influence of the Etruscans at least up until 5th century BC. More interestingly, the idea that it was the Etruscans who have actually transformed the settlement of villages east of Tiber into the city of Rome has also been raised.[62] Also, when the Roman Monarchy was in the process of transforming itself from an Etruscan monarchy into the Roman Republic, one of the arguments was that the Senate would better represent the Latin, the Sabine and the Etruscan patrician families of Rome (as opposed to having an absolute Etruscan king running Rome).[63] Rome started reacting more aggressively against the Etruscans from the 4th century BC. Eventually, Rome would not only extinguish the last Etruscan resistance in Italy (i.e. by 264 BC) but the Etruscan language would disappear under Roman rule by 1st century AD. Despite this, many of Rome's customs, religious practices and systems could be traced back to Etruscan influences.[64]

59 Herman (n 34) 81.

60 Mathisen (n 33) 16.

61 Mathisen (n 33) 19.

62 LS Cunningham and JJ Reich, *Culture and Values: A Survey of the Humanities* (7th edn, Thompson/Wadsworth 2006) 88.

63 Cf. TJ Cornell, *The Beginnings of Rome: Italy and Rome from the Bronze Age to the Punic Wars (c. 1000–264 BC)* (Routledge 1995) 114, citing P Willems, *Le sénat de la république romaine* I (Louvain 1885) 22, G Devoto, *Atheneum* 31 (1953), 335–43, U von Lübtow, *Das römische Volk* (Frankfurt 1955) 39–40 and A Bernardi, *Nomen Latinum* (Pavia 1973) 17–18.

64 On archaeological evidence on the influence of the Etruscans in Rome, see A Momigliano, 'The Rise of the Plebs in the Archaic Age of Rome' in KA Raaflaub (ed), *Social Struggles in Archaic Rome: New Perspectives on the Conflict of the Orders* (2nd edn, Blackwell Publishing 2005) 171.

7.9 SOPHISTICATION OF THE ROMAN REPUBLIC'S MIXED CONSTITUTION – THE ROMAN POLITY'S PREDOMINANT CHARACTERISTICS

One thing is certain: despite the Greek categorisation of the Romans into barbarians mostly by implication, the Roman Republic came to eventually develop a sophisticated constitution and system of governance that would compare well even with the more sophisticated constitutions of the Greek world. For a barbaric or semi-barbaric people, the Romans actually developed a particularly sophisticated constitutional engine in the form of their Republic. It was not perfect, of course, but it worked mostly well. The predominant oligarchic and timocratic tendencies of the Roman Republic did not make this a less developed constitution, for example as compared to the democratic Athenian constitution at the Golden Age of Pericles. One must compare like for like. Thus, it might well be the case that the Athenian constitution was, by far, the most sophisticated democratic constitution of its time. Equally, Rome's republic might well have stood for the most sophisticated mixed-oligarchic constitution in the world in much of its existence, and so on. One must, thus, examine a constitution through the lens of its achievements contemporary to that constitution. All else would be anachronistic. Having said that, one could still draw valid indicative comparisons *mutatis mutandis* between elements of the constitution of the Roman Republic and modern republics. So too, despite the fact that the constitution of the Roman Republic happened to be mostly oligarchic, this does not make it of lesser value in one's constitutional law analysis, and lessons could be learnt through the examination of the constitution of the Roman Republic for modern republics.

7.10 INITIAL TAXONOMISATION OF THE ROMAN REPUBLIC'S BODIES AND OFFICES BY WAY OF THEIR CONSTITUTIONAL NATURE

The Republic's bodies and offices by way of their constitutional nature can be summarised as follows (see also Figure 7.3):

Magistrates and Offices of Monarchic Nature

- **Consuls × 2**: Executive + Legislative + Limited Judicial + Occasional Military Function
- **Proconsul(s)**: these had similar powers to those of Consuls at Provinces level (from 2nd century BC onwards)
- **Dictator – *Magister Populi/Praetor Maximus***: Military Function + Executive Function + (Legislative Power under Sulla's reforms)
- **Interrex**: this was a caretaker magistrate and his office occurred during *interregnum* 'when no consuls, praetors, or dictator remained in office'[65]

[65] Lintott (n 30) 28.

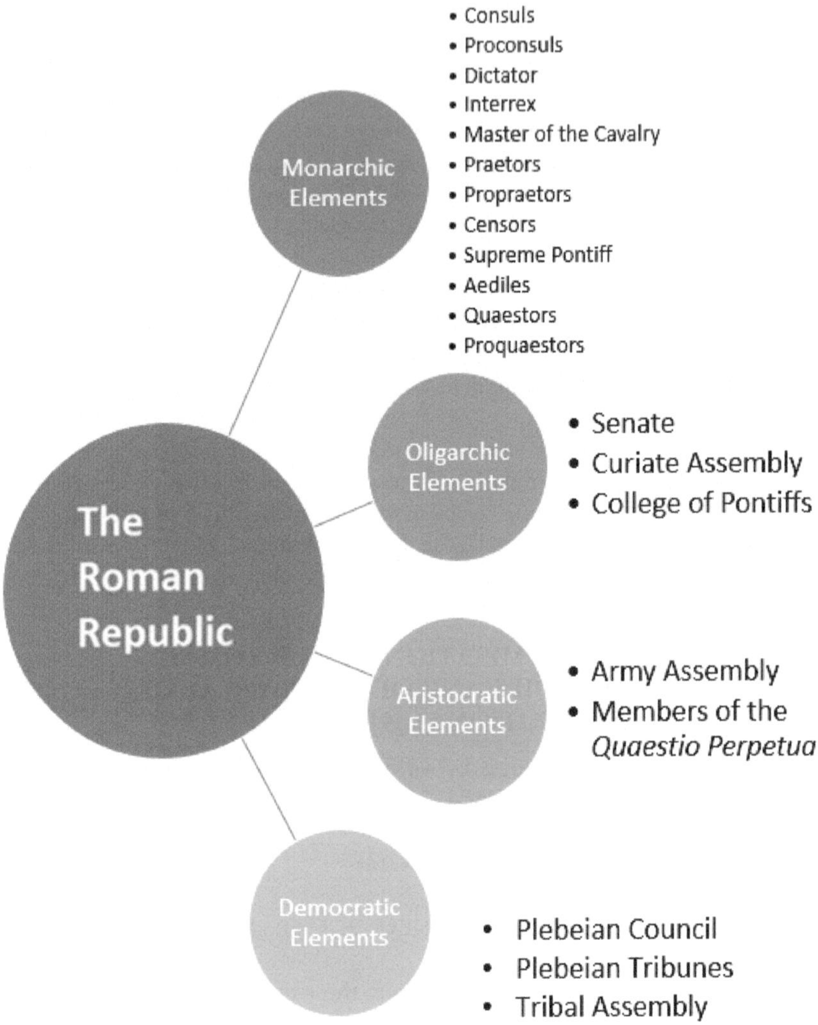

Figure 7.3 Constitutional architecture of the Roman Republic

- **Master of the Cavalry – *Magister Equitum***: Military + Executive Function (this was the lieutenant officer of the Dictator)
- **Praetors**: Judicial + Military Function
- **Propraetor(s)**: these were magistrates who would act in the place of Praetors
- **Censors × 2**: Executive/Administrative Function
- **Supreme Pontiff – *Pontifex Maximus***: Religious + Executive Functions
- **Aediles**: Executive/Administrative Functions
- **Quaestors**: Executive + Military Function
- **Proquaestors:** these were magistrates who would act in the place of Quaestors

Magistrates and Offices of Oligarchic Nature

- **Senate – *Senatus***: Legislative Function + Executive Function (directs all magistrates except Tribunes) + Military Function as to deployment of Roman forces
- **Curiate Assembly – *Comitia Curiata***: Legislative + Judicial Functions
- **College of Pontiffs**: Executive + Religious Functions

Magistrates and Offices of Aristocratic Nature

- **Army Assembly/Centuriate Assembly – *Comitia Centuriata***: Military Function + Executive Function + Limited Judicial Function
- **Permanent Jury Court – *Quaestio Perpetua***: Judicial Function

Officials and Bodies of Democratic Nature

- **Plebeian Council – *Concilium Plebis***: Legislative Function
- **Plebeian Tribunes**: Legislative + Executive Function
- **Tribal Assembly – *Comitia Tributa***: Legislative Function

Chapters 10, 11, 12 and 13 will elaborate on the above. Chapter 9 will first introduce the reader to the Republic's constitution per se.

Chapter 8

The Social and Economic Forces behind the Republic's Constitution

[S]alus populi suprema lex esto[1]

8.1 INTRODUCTION

This chapter proceeds on the thesis that the constitution of the Republic was the result of considerable socio-economic engineering over the centuries in which the Republic grew and matured, and, of course, the result of relevant forces, mainly ones that emanated from Rome's ruling classes. Judging from the fact that to its finals days the Republic was predominantly controlled by oligarchic elites, the Plebeians of Rome did not always seem to have the great role they ought to have in the building of Rome's republican constitution. The Roman *populus* never acquired the degree of consolidated sovereign power that the Athenian *demos* in the heyday of Athens' classical democracy acquired, even though Thucydides would warn us that even in Athens the *demos* could actually be controlled by the authority of a single man.[2] In this respect, while the Roman people would also play a certain role in the evolution of the constitution, their say and their effect on the constitution would traditionally be technically and procedurally more limited than the say and the effect that the Roman elites would have on it. Yet, it would be a mistake to underestimate the power of the Roman *populus* in crucial moments for the Republic. For instance, in the early Middle Republic already, the turning point in favour of Rome's invasion of Sicily was the decision of the Roman people[3] to invade it rather than the decision of the Senate or the elites of Rome per se, Rome's Senate and oligarchic elites being reluctant to invade Sicily. So too, in the Middle Republic, almost all of Rome's offices would become open to Plebeians, even though, equally, such offices would be mostly controlled and manned by members of Rome's ruling elites until the end of the Republic.

1 Cic. Leg. 3.8: 'Let the welfare of the [Roman] people be [Rome's] supreme law'. Translation made by the author.

2 Thuc. 2.65.9: 'In short, what was nominally a democracy became in his hands government by the first citizen'.

3 Plb. 1.11.

8.2 ROME AS A GREAT SOCIO-ECONOMIC LABORATORY

Close to Rome's mixed constitutional reality, it being a mixed polity *par excellence*, came the fact that Rome has actually been one of history's greatest socio-economic laboratories. The Roman Republic's economic history commences, according to Polybius, with Rome's first treaty with Carthage in 509/507 BC.[4] From its transformation from a rustic kingdom in central Italy into an imperial Mediterranean republic and from the expansion of Roman citizenship to Italic peoples to the fact that Rome engaged with world trade, Rome socio-economic engineering was more than significant. One might pose the question here 'how could this be, if the ruling oligarchic elites of Rome held a firm grip on the Republic for centuries'?

One's answer in this respect would be found in the fact that the starting point of these poor souls,[5] the Plebeians of Rome, was so low, that any minor tweak of the Republic's social and, by extension, constitutional 'code', would amount to social innovation of considerable value, despite the reactionary, conservative[6] and pro-status quo policies and tendencies of the Patriciate and the plutocratic elites of Rome. Of course, if the Plebeians were a generally marginalised amorphous[7] element in the Republic's constitutional core of free citizens, the position of Rome's slaves could be described as wholly marginalised, in that these individuals enjoyed no legal personality, were considered possessions (*mancipia*) and were generally found at the lower end of Roman society. Plebeians were, thus, free but slaves were not; yet both of these elements of Roman society would be Rome's subaltern populations. Rome's oppressed, however, in the form of the Plebeians, did manage to bring occasional reform to Roman society and, by extension, to Rome's constitution. Alarmingly, however, even where reform would be initiated, such would occasionally either be subsequently practically reversed or suffocated and silenced by the controlling and manipulative ways and tactics of Roman elites. The ruling elites of Rome could, thus, be so reactionary that proposals of mere political opponents would be taken to be proposals of enemies, who would be worthy of assassination. In this respect, one notes the fact that Rome's history is rife with assassinations and massive proscriptions of political enemies, especially in the Late Republic.

Rome's social and economic beginnings were otherwise humble. Mommsen makes a related point in this respect: the Roman state was based on the Roman

[4] Plb. 3.22–3; J-J Aubert, 'The Republican Economy and Roman Law: Regulation, Promotion, or Reflection?' in HI Flower, *The Cambridge Companion to the Roman Republic* (2nd edn, Cambridge University Press 2014) 170.

[5] On the appalling conditions for most of the Plebeians in Rome, see e.g. K Bowes, 'Roman Agriculture from Above and Below: Words and Things' in C Courrier and JC Magalhães de Oliveira (eds), *Ancient History from Below: Subaltern Experiences and Actions in Context* (Routledge 2023) 134. The reader would be reminded that exceptionally one could find wealthy Plebeians in the years of the Republic but, equally, most of the Plebeians were leading sub-standard lives.

[6] T Mommsen, *The History of Rome*, vol. 1 (W Purdie Dickson (tr), Macmillan & Co. 1901) 332.

[7] M Beard, *SPQR: A History of Ancient Rome* (Liveright Publishing 2015) 36.

family, Roman families coming in the form of *gentes* (clans); these *gentes* constituted the Roman community in the first place.[8] Rome of the Monarchy and at least until the end of the fourth century BC has been traditionally described as a typical example of a society and culture the socio-economic characteristics of which could be reduced into an agricultural environment of peasants mostly.[9] Initially, the poorest of Rome's Plebeians would be called *proletarii* from which, of course, classic Marxist theory has produced the term proletariat. These *proletarii*, persons with little property or no property, would be called as such because all they could offer to Rome was their *proles*, their children.[10] The Roman constitution would be particularly harsh on this Plebeian segment: whereas they could vote in the Centuriate Assembly, they would vote last, if at all.

For all analytical intents and purposes, an exploration of the Roman socio-constitutional reality here would be about Rome's history from below;[11] the more uncomfortable aspect of Rome's constitutional history, one that reveals the more sinister and grave aspects of her constitution. We are in the world of socio-economic context here and, most certainly, rightly so: Rome's greatest constitutional victories (e.g. its move towards democratisation through *Lex Hortensia*) were as a matter of fact the result of this socio-economic context. Even then, Rome's conservative and oligarchic circles and elites would wish to suffocate the will of the *populus*, which at least in their eyes must have looked like a mob.

A political economic perspective could also be relevant in our assessment of the Republic's constitution, the idea here being that the Roman people in their totality would be what the lawyers call the Principal and the Agent, with the *populus* being the principal and the magistrates being the agents,[12] even though one could take alternative perspectives on this.[13] Rome's social forces would not allow the Republic's constitution not to keep government agents, in the form of elected and appointed officials, in check, even if they would come mostly from the wealthy and the noble classes. The Republic would do so in three ways: first, by seeking qualifications behind its government officials; second, by electing many of them; and, third, by the moral control that the Censors would in any case exercise over magistrates.[14]

[8] Mommsen (n 6) 80.

[9] E.g. M Rostovtzeff, *The Social and Economic History of the Roman Empire* (Oxford University Press 1926) 13–14.

[10] Beard (n 7) 144.

[11] E.g. JC Magalhães de Oliveira and C Courrier, 'Ancient History from below: An Introduction' in Courrier and Magalhães de Oliveira (n 5) 3–5, citing *inter alia* EP Thompson, *The Making of the English Working Class* (Vintage Books 1963) 12–13.

[12] EA Posner, 'The Constitution of the Roman Republic' in G Dari-Mattiacci and DP Kehoe (eds), *Roman Law and Economics: Institutions and Organizations Volume I* (Oxford University Press 2020) 35.

[13] Posner (n 12) 39–40.

[14] Posner (n 12) 41.

8.3 PROVISIONAL ALLIANCE BETWEEN THE PATRICIANS AND THE PLEBEIANS TO REMOVE THE TARQUINS

What is also fascinating is that, before the rise of the Republic, two otherwise conflicting social forces in Rome, the nobles and the people, would temporarily unite to overthrow the Tarquins and, by extension, the Monarchy.[15] This was an uneasy compromise but one that was effective, even though the conflict of the Plebeians and the Patricians would become fierce during the first two centuries of the Republic and until 287 BC. There is a slightly different reading to this alliance: the story of the rape of Lucretia (which means wealth in Latin), was the plutocratic elites of Rome's symbolic way to say that the Monarchy, under the supposedly tyrannical Tarquins, would turn against the wealth of Rome. This, in turn, must have triggered the old noble families of Rome to mobilise the people of Rome in their efforts to bring down the Monarchy.

8.4 THE DISTURBING AND UNCOMFORTABLE DIVISIONS WITHIN ROMAN SOCIETY

In theory, the constitution of Rome would be about SPQR (*Senatus Populusque Romanus*), the Senate *and* the people of Rome. It would be about a harmonious consensus between Rome's elites and the people. In practice, the history of the Republic was not always a particularly pleasant one or a comfortable reality for Rome's order of the Plebeians. The social struggles of Rome, the Roman constitution frequently reflecting these, were quite remarkable in the face of human history. In fact, the divisions between the Plebeians and the Patricians in the first steps of the young Roman Republic were running so deep that Livy reports that '[t]wo states had been created out of one: each faction had its own magistrates, its own laws'.[16]

As such, for the first half of the 5th century BC, the Roman Republic effectively came with two separate 'constitutions' (hence the reactionary but convenient rhetoric of the Middle Republic and Late Republic elite Romans about Rome's social consensus and the harmonious whole of their state). Perhaps the social conflicts in Athens would come close to those of Rome but in Rome the situation was probably even more problematic as social peace was not often the case. Indeed, from about 578 BC, when the second Etruscan noble of the Tarquins would rise to the throne as Rome's sixth *Rex*, that is without the approval of the Roman people, to the sidelining of the Plebeians in the running of the Republic until 287 BC, when *Lex Hortensia* came about, Rome was a reality where social peace was simply not the case. A further disturbing reality behind the Roman Republic from 509 BC onwards was the fact that the Plebeians would be originally sidelined, as in excluded from Rome's magistracies altogether. Moreover, it is a disturbing fact of Roman history that before

[15] Mommsen (n 6) 332.
[16] Liv. 2 44.

Lex Canuleia in c. 445 BC,[17] Plebeians could not marry Patricians. Finally, even more alarming would be the fact that, even after the Roman magistracies would open to the Plebeians, the old monarchic-oligarchic grip of the Roman elites would practically still be there for centuries, and the Roman oligarchies of the Republic would control the boat of the Republic to a much greater extent than the Plebs. This is how the Roman elites controlled the Republic until its final demise: whereas all of the offices would eventually open to Plebeians, most of the offices would be manned by members of the oligarchic and plutocratic elites of Rome. Wealthy Plebeians would join the ranks of these elites but they would mostly align themselves with the old Patrician families. Finally, the status quo would be reinforced by these old and new elites because most of the magistrates would emanate from these elites, elites that had agenda-setting[18] powers over the people and the Republic.

8.5 ROME AS A GENERALLY CONSERVATIVE SOCIO-ECONOMIC REALITY

Roman society was a generally conservative society originally but also for the most part of the Republic; so was its silent and stealthy constitution, which would be based on *mos maiorum* and the normally continuous preservation of old laws of constitutional significance. As an example here, one would mention the fact that Rome's laws would never be abolished unless explicitly abolished.[19] Practically, Rome's constitution was added legal and legislative layers over time, but these layers were difficult to remove. Technically, most of them continued to exist, even if their application would be limited or zero. However, as Rome was opening itself to the world, through its expansions and its Hellenisation, the same Roman elites that would in theory uphold *mos maiorum* would start subscribing to the worldviews and cultural elements of others.[20] In this respect, the supposed old fidelity of the Roman elites to *mos maiorum* and, by extension, to an 'originalist' interpretation of the constitution, would come under question, in that 'new' Rome (e.g. of the 2nd and the 1st century BC) might apply the constitution in different ways to 'old' Rome (e.g. of the 3rd and the 4th century BC). Practically, much of the 'formal' constitution would fundamentally remain the same but its interpretation could change over time, even if it would make references to traditional devices such as *mos maiorum*. Finally, the conservative tendencies of Rome's elites, as these were found in the Republic's constitution, can be explained from the mere fact that the Roman society was hierarchical[21] and patriarchal.

[17] Liv. 4 6.

[18] Posner (n 12) 46.

[19] E.g. JS Richardson, 'Old Statutes Never Die: A Brief History of Abrogation' in M Austin, J Harries and C Smith (eds), *Modus Operandi: Essays in Honour of Geoffrey Rickman* (Institute of Classical Studies – School of Advanced Study, University of London 1998) 56.

[20] ES Gruen, *Culture and National Identity in Republican Rome* (Cornell University Press 1992) 1.

[21] Cf. K Vlassopoulos, 'Subaltern Community Formation in Antiquity: Some Methodological Reflections' in Courrier and Magalhães de Oliveira (n 5) 45.

8.6 DEMOCRATIC SOCIAL FORCES VERSUS OLIGARCHIC SOCIAL FORCES

Rome's oligarchic elites would traditionally have the upper hand in the Republic. This 'Roman' position seems to reflect the situation over in neighbouring Etruria, which seems to have traditionally favoured strong monarchic/oligarchic constitutional models. The imposition of Etruscan tyrants for about two generations in the era of the Roman Monarchy was, thus, a rather natural model for the Etruscans. Equally, while the Romans opposed such form of government eventually, they maintained many of the Etruscan *syncentrotic* forms of government. This meant that the oligarchic and the monarchic offices of Rome would practically hold more power in the Republic's constitution than its more open-ended democratic and aristocratic elements. The effect of Greece and, by extension, the effect of the idea of democracy on the Plebeian leaders, while theoretically significant from the beginning of the Republic, never reached the point that would make the constitutional reality of Rome move from a mixed form of government to a more-democratic-than-not form of government.

A related point would be that it was not just Rome's constitution *stricto sensu* but also Rome's constitution *lato sensu* that has been directly affected by Rome's socio-economic forces, especially Rome's wealthy oligarchic elites. Rome's constitution *lato sensu* eventually went, of course, to her imperial ambition. In this respect, Rostovtzeff gives the thought-provoking example of Rome's capitalists and class of landowners wishing to destroy Carthage because Carthage as an economic competitor would immediately disappear.[22]

[22] Rostovtzeff (n 9) 21.

Chapter 9

The Roman Constitution Per Se and Methodological Considerations

9.1 INTRODUCTION

This chapter explores the constitution of the Roman Republic per se. It posits in agreement with the bibliography that the Roman Republic operated under a sophisticated constitutional framework that came with advanced features of balancing, even if the constitution of the Romans would be a constitution that would not be anywhere near wholly codified or written. Indeed, one of the finest features of the constitution of the Roman Republic was its fixity and conservative nature, on the one hand, and its stealthy and flexible character, on the other hand.

9.2 METHODOLOGICAL CONSIDERATIONS

Whereas the chapter follows a legal approach in the main, it would be practically inevitable for our analysis to be a composite one, as in an interdisciplinary one. By all means, aside from legal matter per se, the grasping of the constitution of the Roman Republic, especially as it flourished after 287 BC, would have to take legal historical, comparative, and political science matter into consideration. So too, in addition to the socio-economic analysis of the previous chapter, certain of the social forces of Rome, as they have affected her constitution, will also be highlighted in this chapter too. Of course, it would also be important to note here that the constitutional law exercise ought not to take a legal historical approach alone. Moreover, to explain the emergence of Roman constitutional thought, one should not reduce relevant constitutional ideas to their historical context.[1] Historical context is, thus, of great significance; nevertheless, our constitutional law analysis would have to take into account both legal historical context and modern constitutional law matter into account.

A key methodological point to be made is that such concepts as 'constitution' and 'state' were alien to the Romans.[2] Indeed, as will be seen, the Roman perception of their *res publica* was rather monolithic. Not only did the Romans not have the concepts to explain the phenomenon of their constitutional order but they also traditionally lacked the interest and the tools to do so. Rome was a highly

[1] B Straumann, *Crisis and Constitutionalism: Roman Political Thought from the Fall of the Republic to the Age of Revolution* (Oxford University Press 2016) 13.

[2] L Capogrossi Colognesi, *Law and Power in the Making of the Roman Commonwealth* (Cambridge University Press 2014) xxii.

utilitarian society and, by extension, a highly utilitarian constitutional reality; so were the persons who devised her constitution over the centuries. The modern legal scholar ought to note that Rome's constitution was also a stealthy and agile one, while at other times a purposefully silent one. With the reader in mind, the term 'constitution' for the legal-political phenomenon, which has clearly been the case in the years of the Republic in the form of the public law reality called the *res publica*, should be the preferable term methodologically. The reason for this is that such a term would make greater sense to the moderns and would also come close[3] as a term to the more precise term which the ancient Greeks would use and which they call *politeia* (*πολιτεία*) or *politeuma* (*πολίτευμα*).[4] Moreover, whereas this monograph pays due recognition to the centrality of the Twelve Tables in the Republic's overall legal system and civil law, it also recognises that the Tables were not part of Rome's public law and constitution per se.[5] Having said that, it would also be important to appreciate that the Twelve Tables actually included *mutatis mutandis* constitutional/political rights: for example, the fact that the execution of a Roman could not occur without trial.[6]

The Republic's constitution could be further divided into the constitution per se or the constitution *stricto sensu*, which, of course, was directly applicable within Rome's *pomoerium*, and the Republic's constitution *lato sensu*, which could be taken to be the constitution as a legal-political stabilising factor for the city of Rome to the point that this enabled Rome's geopolitical ambition and expansion beyond Rome, Latium and Italy. The focus of this chapter is on the former but in other chapters of this monograph the idea of Rome's constitution *lato sensu* is explored for the benefit of the reader.

9.3 A COMPLEX 'CONSTITUTION' FOR THE ROMAN REPUBLIC

The Romans did not have a constitution with a capital 'C' but a constitution with a small 'c'.[7] The Romans of the Republic did not practically have a written[8] or a codified constitution, even though elements of constitutional law could be found in various areas of Roman Law: from very limited constitutional law aspects of the Twelve Tables, to *Lex Hortensia*, *Lex Villia Annalis*, and so on. In other words, the constitution of the Romans was scattered and could be found in various places

[3] E.g. P Pasquino, 'Classifying Constitutions: Preliminary Conceptual Analysis' (2013) 34(3) *Cardozo Law Review* 999, 1009.

[4] But cf. Capogrossi Colognesi (n 2) xiii who prefers the term 'commonwealth'.

[5] E.g. Capogrossi Colognesi (n 2) 61.

[6] E.g. EA Posner, 'The Constitution of the Roman Republic' in G Dari-Mattiacci and DP Kehoe (eds), *Roman Law and Economics: Institutions and Organizations Volume I* (Oxford University Press 2020) 38 citing A Lintott, *The Constitution of the Roman Republic* (Clarendon Press 1999) 149.

[7] Cf. Straumann (n 1) 17.

[8] TC Brennan, 'Power and Process under the Republican "Constitution"' in HI Flower (ed), *The Cambridge Companion to the Roman Republic* (2nd edn, Cambridge University Press 2014) 19.

of Roman law, a bit like the constitutions of modern Britain and Israel. The fact that Rome's republican constitution was not to be found in a single place did not make her constitution unsophisticated or soft. The fact that the constitution of the Republic was scattered did not mean that the Romans were not well-aware of its remit and the precise positioning of Rome's institutions, magistrates and bodies in the Republic. On the contrary, the constitution of the Roman Republic was mostly stable and effectively constituted hard law as it was institution-based with fixed terms and an extensive list of checks and balances. However, the same constitution allowed for significant flexibility, through interpretative devices such as *mos maiorum*. Thus, the constitution of the Roman Republic was a flexibly stable constitution, a balancing constitution rather like wood floating on water,[9] always moving, always balancing, always trying to stay afloat until its final decay. Rome's constitutional powerhouse, the Senate, would make sure that the proper interpretation of the constitution would be the case, for it was the Senate that was Rome's ultimate interpreter of her constitution, even though the Senate was not a constitutional court in the modern sense. A final critical point to be made is that the Roman constitution has been traditionally perceived as a complex[10] and mixed[11] one.

9.4 WAS THERE A CONSTITUTION IN THE ROMAN REPUBLIC?

The fact that a constitution in a given legal space is largely unwritten or is not wholly codified does not mean that such a space lacks a constitution. This was the case of the Roman Republic's constitution. The constitution of the Roman Republic was everywhere and nowhere. It both existed and did not exist. It was to be found everywhere in Rome's institutions and the checks and balances which Rome has developed over the centuries. It was not to be found anywhere as it was not codified. And yet, there were *leges* of constitutional significance such as *Lex Hortensia* and *Lex Villia Annalis*.

Thus, the best response here, by far, would be the one that would suggest that there was no such thing as a Constitution in Rome in the modern sense of the term (normally a codified, central and formal piece of legislation with more than considerable impact on the organisation and the overall running of the state). '[T]he Romans never dreamed of a creating a definitive constitutional charter, much less of setting it down in writing.'[12] Nonetheless, as was the case almost all over the then known ancient world (with the obvious exceptions of Lycurgus' Grand Rhetra in Sparta and the Solonian constitution in Athens, *mutatis mutandis*

[9] Cf. Ł Perlikowski, 'How Does One Understand the Stability of Political Regimes from a Theoretical Point of View?' (2019) 6 (63) *Politeja* 111, 112, 118–19 referring to Hume.

[10] Plb. 6.3.7: '*πολιτείαν τὴν ἐκ πάντων τῶν προειρημένων ἰδιωμάτων συνεστῶσαν*'.

[11] Plb. 6.3.3: '*περὶ δὲ τῆς Ῥωμαίων οὐδ' ὅλως εὐχερὲς οὔτε περὶ τῶν παρόντων ἐξηγήσασθαι διὰ τὴν ποικιλίαν τῆς πολιτείας*'.

[12] Capogrossi Colognesi (n 2) xxi. Cf. R Syme, *The Roman Revolution* (Clarendon Press 1939) 15.

'codified' constitutional texts), the Romans did have a constitution, that is a polity that, even though it would not be anywhere near a wholly codified reality, would still stand for a constitution. The magnificent institutional layout of Rome's constitution would actually prove not only its existence but also its very organised character. As contextual information here, Aristotle has been reported to have compared the constitutions of 158 city states (Carthage, a foreign city, being included in such comparisons). According to current sources, however, there would not be cogent evidence as to whether he would have also examined the constitution of Rome, even though we are aware of the fact that he was quite familiar with Roman history through the well-known story of Rome's capture by the Gauls in 4th century BC.[13] Thus, the point to be made is that it was possible from ancient times already to compare, in principle, constitutions of different city states, whether these would be 'codified' or 'non-codified'. One of these constitutions was that of Rome, even though the first person to have done so, at least according to current sources, was not Aristotle but Polybius.

In modernity, very interestingly, the British constitution is one that would come relatively close to the overall situation that one would encounter in republican Rome: as in the case of the British constitution, the overall constitutional layout of the Roman Republic would comprise conventions and traditions (*mos maiorum*) with positive instruments (*leges*) affecting it at various points in Rome's history. At other times, established constitutional practices and rights such as *provocatio* (right to appeal against severe punishment), as was enacted through the Valerian Law and as such a right was solidified through the Porcian Laws, would be part and parcel of Rome's wider constitution, as would the right to annul laws later in Rome's history, from 98 BC onwards, when the *Lex Caecilia Didia* came into effect. The British constitution could, thus, be perceived as broadly similar to what one would encounter in republican Rome in constitutional terms in at least two ways: the British constitution, as Rome's republican constitution, recognises constitutional conventions; as Rome's republican constitution, the British constitution has laws of constitutional significance too which have not been codified under a single consolidated instrument called the Constitution.

Reverting to the constitutional situation of republican Rome, Rome's constitutional conventions (frequently by inducing the idea of *mos maiorum*, i.e. 'the ways of the fathers of Rome'), as these would be frequently brought to the fore by Rome's top magistrates and Senators, would practically rule the day in the running of the republic. To make things more interesting, the 'fuzzy' and obscure nature of the constitution of the Republic, to use Brennan's terminology,[14] also had connotations for the Republic's central institution, the Senate: the Senate, even though it did not have a constitutional charter to its (executive and quasi-legislative) powers, was by all means Rome's constitutional engine. This was a 'fuzzy' constitution with a 'fuzzy' constitutional engine at its heart, the Senate.

[13] Plut. Cam. 22.3.

[14] Brennan (n 8) 19.

However, the constitutional theorist cannot but pinpoint the fact that, whilst Rome's normative constitution was not wholly settled and was rather indistinct, the constitutional-institutional layout of the Republic was almost perfectly settled and established, especially in the Middle Republic, in that the Romans knew or would have reason to know 'who was doing what' in their republic when it would come to the operations of the Republic's magistrates, institutions and bodies.

Equally, the fact that Rome and so many other cities of the ancient world would be run on constitutional conventions and constitutional traditions would not mean that these would come with no constitutions or constitutional frameworks to them. Thus, the best approach in the area would probably be to observe and examine the constituent elements of the Roman Republic through the lens of the ancient world. This lens would then clearly allow us to observe a fully blown constitutional reality in the Roman Republic, albeit one that would be different to our modern constitutions.

Finally, it should be noted at this initial stage of our analysis in this chapter, that the republic became a wholly imperial one, effectively Rome post the Treaty of Apamea in 188 BC,[15] when the Seleucid Empire would be kept at bay and the Eastern Mediterranean would indirectly come under Rome's sphere of influence. The Republic would then steadily and increasingly become one of personalities[16] and this is another point that will be made in this monograph, especially when it comes to explaining the demise of the Republic and, of course, its constitution. Furthermore, the Plebeians would eventually serve more in positions of magistrates, which would previously be mostly reserved for Patricians. To conclude, there was indeed a constitution in the Republic, the republic manifesting itself as a polity, with the Roman constitution comprising magistrates, conventions (*mos maiorum*) and laws (*leges*), it also having been greatly influenced eventually by leading political and military figures, Rome's social and economic classes, and so on.

9.5 OVERALL COLLECTIVE CONSENSUS BEHIND THE CONSTITUTION OF THE REPUBLIC

Moreover, the Roman constitution, unlike the constitutions of many Greek city states, could not point to the genius of a single person or a single driving spirit behind it in the way many leading Greek *poleis* would entrust their constitutional designs to a single personality: for example, Lycurgus, Draco, Solon, Minos or Cleisthenes. That was not the point of the constitutional exercise in Rome and Rome would take pride from the fact that hers was a constitution that 'did

[15] Another candidate for Rome's transformation into an imperial Republic is 201 BC, when Rome came out victorious from the Second Punic War.

[16] Capogrossi Colognesi (n 2) xxi–xxii.

not derive from a single conception at a specific time but owed its evolution to multiple contributors over a span of generations and centuries'.[17]

Polybius also confirms the point that the Roman constitution was not about abstract reasoning [abstract and obscure as it was on purpose] but the result of 'continually adopting reforms from knowledge gained in disaster'.[18] The reluctance of the Romans to allow over the centuries the 'drafting' of their constitution to a single central personality must also be related to the traditional fear and reluctance of the Romans to rely on a single military figure or charismatic leader for long, unlike the Greeks would, for example in the case of Alexander the Great.[19]

The Romans would not only find the idea of a single man in charge of their Republic abhorrent but would also actually push their thesis a step further in this respect: not only would the idea of a single man running the Republic cause great anxiety to them and, of course, the elites of the Republic, but also Rome's constitution would actually be an amalgam of historical efforts, accidents and personalities – no single man would take credit for Rome's great constitution but Roman history itself and the former generations of Romans. Cato was mostly right on this one, except for one thing: the oligarchic elites would wish to hide the fact that its members (e.g. Patricians and wealthy Senators) were actually mostly responsible for the design of the Republic traditionally. Thus, the Catonian position was correct overall, with the note that the general 'anonymisation' of the designers of Rome's constitution over the centuries was done on purpose.

Beyond this, one should recall that every organised legal system is about a certain degree of abstraction.[20] The constitution of the Romans in the years of the Republic was a particularly abstract one and, for that reason, a fuzzy one. Its degree of abstraction, as in its indistinct character, predominantly emanated from the fact that this was a constitution that was practically silent in a number of areas where modern constitutions would not be silent: for example, in the area of separation of powers. Furthermore, with the exception of a certain number of major pieces of constitutional *leges* and constitutional *plebiscita*, and the mostly clear-cut terms and functions of the offices of senior and junior magistrates of the Republic, much of Rome's constitution was practically left in the hands of the Senate to devise and interpret. The interesting device of *patres maiorum* as the Republic's constitutional *ultima ratio* (i.e. the customs and traditions of the forefathers of Rome) would frequently be invoked by the Roman Senate, especially when it came to the interpretation of the Republic's constitution. The particular constitutional device can be characterised as a masterpiece of the ruling oligarchic elites of Rome in Machiavellian and Goebbelsian terms: it could mean a number of different things to different Romans and Senators but what ultimately mattered was what the

17 ES Gruen, *Culture and National Identity in Republican Rome* (Cornell University Press 1992) 83 citing Cic. *De Rep*. 2.1–2.

18 Plb. 6.10.13–14.

19 M Beard, *SPQR: A History of Ancient Rome* (Liveright Publishing 2015) 161.

20 Cf. WV Harris, 'Power' in A Barchiesi and W Scheidel (eds), *The Oxford Handbook of Roman Studies* (Oxford University Press 2010) 565.

Senate collectively would consider *patres maiorum*, so that the Senate would guide the Roman masses towards the path it would consider best for the interests of Rome's ruling classes and, by extension, for the interests of the Republic. The interests of the *populus* were, of course, a consideration but the oligarchic character of the Senate would mean that the interests of Rome's Patrician elite would come first and foremost in their constitutional considerations.

Theoretically, at least under Cicero who defined the *res publica* 'as the people's concern but ... the people are an assemblage of multitudes associated to one another under the law',[21] the collective consensus of Rome was denominated by Rome's people as they were united under the law. Practically, however, the Senate would steer the Republic and much of her constitution as it wished,[22] on the basis that the Senate's interpretation and *consulta* would not go beyond to upset or cause uproar amongst the Roman people. As the masses of Rome, the Plebeians, were largely illiterate and not quite exactly the best-equipped people in the world to consider, grasp and appreciate high notions or legal concepts which the Senate would consider, even the slightest interpretative tweak of the Senate would streamline the masses of Rome in the 'right' direction, the way a shepherd does by leading one of their sheep so that the rest of the sheep follow suit. Yet, more interestingly what has started as an 'abstract' Republic became over the centuries an increasingly legalistic one: by 1st century BC legal experts and influential politicians would be a key characteristic of the Republic,[23] as would, of course, powerful personalities. In any case, Rome's republican constitution was a constitution that the ruling elites would use to promote their interests mainly, which practically stood for the greater economic interests of the Republic, as the Plebeians would traditionally be poor and would have fewer economic interests in the Republic than Rome's wealthy families and elites. Having said that, being Plebeian did not automatically make one poor.[24] One was not a Patrician if one were a Plebeian but rich Plebeians could also be found in Rome.[25]

Importantly, whereas the Romans would naturally extend their empire through their expansions to new lands and territories, the constitution of the city of Rome per se did not seem to apply directly there. Territorial *imperium* ought not to be confused with the Roman Republic's precise remit of its constitution. Roman law was not a territorially based legal system during the Republic. It was a personality-based one. The Roman government per se would fully extend to Rome itself, with the Romans being otherwise reluctant to create a new separate or additional constitutional order and administration in their conquered territories for lack of political will and personnel.[26] Equally, the Republic's constitutional

[21] Cic. Rep. 1.39.

[22] Cf. Capogrossi Colognesi (n 2) 82.

[23] Cf. Harris (n 20) 565.

[24] D Hoyos, *Rome Victorious: The Irresistible Rise of the Roman Empire* (Bloomsbury Academic 2019, reprinted 2023) 13.

[25] Ibid.

[26] E.g. PA Zoch, *Ancient Rome* (University of Oklahoma Press 1998) 131.

extensions (e.g. through the operations of Proconsuls and Propraetors in the provinces) would allow one to maintain that the Republic's constitution *lato sensu* also applied in the provinces and beyond Rome. Moreover, in the years of the late Early to Middle Republic, the Roman strategy as to conquered Italian lands and peoples would gradually change by concentrating on the creation of Roman and Latin colonies, i.e. between the end of the Second Latin War in 338 BC and the beginning of the First Punic War in 264 BC.[27] And it was the Senate that took the lead in developing such a new strategy.[28]

Although Roman law, beyond the constitution *stricto sensu*, as this applied in the city of Rome, could apply in new territories, it is to be noted that the distinction of private and public law in Roman law in the years of the Middle Republic was not crucial as it became later in the development of Roman law.[29] Roman citizens used Roman law. However, Italy was in the process of becoming Romanised through *civitas sine suffragio* from the second half of the 3rd century BC, Roman law extending in this way to new citizens living outside Rome vis-à-vis Roman citizens found in Rome or elsewhere.[30]

Clearly, the march of Roman law in the Italian peninsula was not as powerful as the march of Rome's legions but it was by all means as effective. The Latins could take advantage of Roman Law protection even before Rome's territorial acquisitions through such legal devices as *commercium*,[31] the Romans leaving the constitutional frameworks of the Latin cities, which they would have conquered, unaffected.[32] At other times, the 'translation' of Roman law devices into Latin territories (e.g. in private land law matters) would not be perfect and the laws there would resemble Roman law but would not be exactly the same.[33] In the conquered territories, local customs and laws would be respected, unless they would conflict with Roman law interests and policies, the Romans constantly promoting the self-governance[34] of their conquered peoples.

Historical exceptions to this have been the almost total suffocation of Capua in 211 BC[35] and the annihilation of Corinth and Carthage in 146 BC. Collaborators of Rome ('*amici*') in foreign lands and protectorate states of Rome would enjoy great

[27] ST Roselaar, 'The Grand Strategy? Spoils and Colonization in the Fourth and Third Centuries BCE' in M Helm and ST Roselaar (eds), *Spoils in the Roman Republic: Boon and Bane* (Franz Steiner Verlag 2023) 177–80.

[28] Roselaar (n 27) 177.

[29] E.g. G Hamza, 'The Classification (divisio) into "Branches" of Modern Legal Systems (Orders) and Roman Law Traditions' [2006] *European Journal of Law Reform* 361, 361.

[30] Capogrossi Colognesi (n 2) 102.

[31] Cf. ST Roselaar, 'The Concept of *Commercium* in the Roman Republic' (2013) 66 *Phoenix* 381, 381, 388. Also, in respect of *conubium* (the right to marriage between Romans and non-Romans) see ST Roselaar, 'The Concept of *Conubium* in the Roman Republic' in PJ du Plessis (ed), *New Frontiers: Law and Society in the Roman World* (Edinburgh University Press 2013) 102–22.

[32] Capogrossi Colognesi (n 2) 101.

[33] Ibid.

[34] Zoch (n 26) 131.

[35] Capogrossi Colognesi (n 2) 104–5.

privileges (e.g. no taxation) as compared to Rome's average conquered territory which would have previously resisted and would have to pay taxes to Rome.[36] So would the federated states to Rome, which would be independent of Roman state officials.[37] Federated states to Rome without a treaty would also enjoy privileges but Rome could revoke their status.[38] The conquered Roman provinces were governed by a Roman, either a Proconsul or a Propraetor, who with the support of armed forces would run the province without interfering with any previous social aspects and customs of the province. However, the provinces would be liable to a stipend to Rome.[39]

9.6 MONOLITHIC DIMENSION OF THE *RES PUBLICA* IN THE ROMAN MIND

More interestingly, the Romans would not split into two the meaning of their *res publica*: in other words, the *res publica*, translated as the 'public matter',[40] would concurrently mean both the constitution of Rome and Rome's system of political governance.[41] This monolithic dimension of the concept of *res publica* seems to have had rather wide-ranging implications for the understanding of the Romans vis-à-vis both their constitution and their political system. The Romans not distinguishing between form and content[42] in the Republic's layout meant that they had a fused perception of the 'public matter', their *res publica*. This singular perception of their republic was one that would indistinguishably incorporate both constitutional rules and the way it was politically run. In a sense, this was both a strength and a weakness.[43] For instance, this unitary approach could be a strength for Roman elites to control the Roman masses through a rather obscure constitutional-political nexus of rules that the average person in Rome would not comprehend. However, this would be a weakness because that obscure spirit of the Roman Republic's layout could not be one that would ultimately withhold the rise of the Principate. Finally, most interestingly, whereas the Greeks would normally academically distinguish between constitutional system and political content in their societies, when the Romans would not, both Greeks and, by extension, Romans would perceive state and society as fused[44] in their *poleis*. Due to the singular perception of the *res publica*, such a fusion of state and society too must have been automatic in Rome and Roman thinking.

[36] Zoch (n 26) 131.
[37] Ibid.
[38] Ibid.
[39] Zoch (n 26) 132.
[40] HI Flower, 'The Imperial Republic' in Barchiesi and Scheidel (n 20) 519.
[41] Cf. Flower (n 40) 519–20.
[42] E.g. Flower (n 40) 520.
[43] Flower (n 40) 520.
[44] Cf. M Herman Hansen, 'Was Sparta a Normal or Exceptional Polis?' in S Hodkinson (ed), *Sparta: Comparative Approaches* (The Classical Press of Wales 2009) 396–7.

9.7 A DEVELOPED CONSTITUTION THAT LACKED CONCEPTS DUE TO OLD LATIN'S LACK OF CULTIVATION – INDIFFERENCE OF THE ROMANS TOWARDS CONSTITUTIONAL CONCEPTUALITY AT LEAST UNTIL THE TIMES OF POLYBIUS

Latin is a beautiful language. However, it was not very developed in the times of Old Latin and works of philology were not exactly Latium's forte for many centuries in the years of the Roman Monarchy and the Republic. The affection held by most of us for Latin tends to be one that arises out of the cultivation of the Latin language in its classical era. Beyond this, it would seem that the apparent lack of cultivation of Latin in the years of Old Latin has had considerable connotations *inter alia* for the lack of development of the theoretical disciplines in Rome.

Even more interestingly, old Latin, the Latin that was spoken for 400 plus years in the period of the Republic, at least until c. 75 BC, did not seem to have a concept of *politeia*, or what would literally translate as 'a state [of citizens]' from Greek into the English language.[45] Beyond the rather late cultivation of the Latin language in the Late Republic into what came to be known as classical Latin, the more sophisticated and refined version of the Latin language, as cultivated by such personalities as Cicero, there was also profound lack of concepts (let alone constitutional concepts) in the Latin language[46] to the point that even the educated Romans would have effectively developed a singular conception of the 'public matter', that is their Republic (*res publica*). Thus, old Latin did have the term *civis* but not *civitas* as in state,[47] as *civitas* traditionally meant citizenship;[48] *quantus* but not *quantitas*; *qualis* but not *qualitas*, and so on. It was a language with a more than significant lack of concepts and, when Greek concepts were taught in Rome, many of these would be simply left untranslated by mere reason of the fact that there were no Latin equivalents[49] or because this 'code-switching',[50] as linguists would call the direct use of Greek into Latin, would be a sign of intellectual cultivation.[51] Cogent evidence to this is, of course, the very fact that even one of Rome's leading legal minds, Cicero, was highly constrained by the Old Latin language's limitations.[52] Cicero would have otherwise attempted to posit that Latin

[45] Capogrossi Colognesi (n 2) xxiii: 'It is well known that the Romans did not have a word to refer to their political system comparable to the one so familiar to us: "the state".'

[46] Cf. Flower (n 40) 520.

[47] E.g. Capogrossi Colognesi (n 2) xxiii.

[48] Cf. C Ando, *Roman Social Imaginaries: Language and Thought in the Context of Empire* (University of Toronto Press 2015) 7.

[49] D Sedley, 'Philosophy' in Barchiesi and Scheidel (n 20) 702.

[50] T Whitmarsh, 'Hellenism' in Barchiesi and Scheidel (n 20) 733.

[51] Whitmarsh (n 50) 733, citing S Swain, 'Bilingualism in Cicero? The Evidence of Code-switching' in JN Adams, M Janse and S Swain (eds), *Bilingualism in Ancient Society: Language Contact and the Written Text* (Oxford University Press 2002).

[52] E.g. J Gregory, 'Cicero and Plato on Democracy: a Translation and its Source' (1991) 50(3) *Latomus*, 639, 639.

was superior to Greek but this may have been more of a genuine concern rather than a genuine position, as in the Rome of his time there was a serious prospect that Greek could imminently and totally become the predominant language in the field of culture over Latin.[53]

Indeed, the closest classical Latin came to the term *politeia* was when Cicero defined the Latin term *civitas* as *concilium coetusque hominum jure sociati*:[54] that is, a state would be defined as an 'assembly of the people united by law'.[55] Even the genius (that Cicero clearly was) found himself at great pains to define the term *civitas* for the Romans because he did indeed have to use basic Latin terms in so doing.[56] Thus, whereas the Latin term '*civis*' would be used amongst the Romans,[57] there was no widely known Latin word in his time for *polites* (citizen of a city in Greek), so instead he used the everyday term 'homo' (human in Latin) to come up with his definition of *civitas*. Cicero thus reaches the point to define *civitas* by the dry, commonplace and less-than-constitutionally-precise term 'homo', which merely stands for human being. Thus, in agreement with a point made for Polybius as to the Romans being 'rational barbarians',[58] the Romans were running a highly sophisticated and rational constitution for their state, but one that was not examined scientifically or systematically except by outsiders at least until the years of the Late Republic, when the Romans themselves started to do so.

This monolithic dimension of the Republic in the Roman mind seems to, therefore, be the result, amongst others, of old Latin,[59] a language which was not particularly cultivated in the way classical Latin,[60] the more refined and beautiful version of ancient Latin, was cultivated in the Late Republic. Wittgenstein also reminds us that 'the limits of [one's] language are the limits of [one's] world'.[61] Thus, the Romans did not seem to even have the words, and for that matter the very concepts, to express the proper distinction between constitutional aspects of

[53] N Petrochilos, *Roman Attitudes to the Greeks* (National and Capodistrian University of Athens 1974) 30.

[54] Cic. Rep. 6.13.

[55] Translation by the author of this monograph.

[56] Cf. Whitmarsh (n 50) 731 where he makes the point that, according to Cicero, Greek was better suited as a language to explain the greatness of the Roman Empire, citing Cic. Arch. 23. Cicero was right that Greek was Rome's *lingua franca* for so many reasons; centuries after Cicero, the Eastern Romans too would predominantly speak Greek for most of the existence of the Eastern Roman Empire.

[57] '*Romanus sum civis*' was the oral declaration that the citizens of Rome would make to signify their status and the rights and duties that came with such status. Legend has it that at least as early as the years of the Early Roman Republic the Romans would be aware of their *civis* status. See e.g. the famous exclamation of Gaius Mucius Scaevola before the Etruscan King Porsena: 'I am a Roman citizen, men call me C. Mucius' (Liv. 2 12).

[58] A Erskine, 'Polybios and Barbarian Rome' (2000) 3 *Mediterraneo Antico* 165, 182.

[59] Cf. Flower (n 40) 520.

[60] Classical Latin too did not always have words or concepts readily found in Greek. See e.g. Suet. Tib. 71.

[61] L Wittgenstein, *Tractatus Logico-Philosophicus* (Kegan Paul, Trench, Trubner & Co. 1922) 74 at 5.6 and 5.62.

their Republic and the political system behind it. One of the greatest paradoxes behind Rome's magnificent constitution, has, thus, been the fact that the constitution of the Roman Republic was a rational and well-functioning constitution, highly abstract and purposefully fuzzy, but one that could otherwise lack constitutional concepts or terms per se.

The Republic was an institutions-based republic. The Republic's constitution was an institutions-based constitution. The Republic, at its core, was one of magistrates and institutions that resulted in a highly effective constitution, especially in the Middle Republic and a few decades before that, through multiple checks and balances, without such a constitution coming though with the very conceptual constitutional terms that other ancient and, of course, modern constitutions would come. To the defence of the Romans comes the fact that the Spartans were not particularly interested in the conceptual exploration of their constitution either. Of course, Lycurgus, the legendary father of Sparta's Great Rhetra, must have dealt with and explored concepts of constitutional law but we would not have written monuments that he would have done so in a scientific way. Thus, the Romans and the Spartans would have developed their constitutions in rather similar ways, both the Romans and the Spartans being interested in good government but not necessarily in the conceptual and scientific exploration of their constitutions.

This was thus an abstract and fuzzy constitution comprising monarchic, oligarchic, aristocratic and democratic features without the Romans being even remotely interested in these categorisations of its institutions until the times of Polybius. Or to put it otherwise, we have no Latin or ancient sources prior to Polybius that would show an interest in Rome's constitutional layout, as in a conceptual framework or in constitutional terms and concepts, beyond the historical references to the offices of Rome's magistrates. There do not seem to be any sources that would discuss the Roman Republic's mixed constitutional character prior to him.

Rome's constitution with the Senate at its driving seat was driven rather smoothly without even the ruling classes of Rome (let alone the Plebeians) being interested in the conceptuality behind the frameworks and the institutions of their state. This can be explained in at least three different ways, which can also be combined. The lack of interest on the part of the Romans to scientifically examine their Republic until the Late Republic could be down to the traditional negligence of the Romans for the letters, the arts and the sciences. Indeed, when it comes to the cultivation of the Roman constitution, the Romans have shown indifference to cultivating and formalising their public law,[62] let alone the constitutional core thereof. In the ideology of the Roman Republic, all matter was public until the point that state would withdraw its interests and claims from such matter.[63] Second, one can put this down to the fact that many of Rome's institutions seem

[62] Brennan (n 8) 20.
[63] Ando (n 48) 93.

to have been inspired, if not imitated or duplicated, from elsewhere: for example, the two Consuls of Rome or the Roman Senate were not unique to Rome (see, for instance, Sparta's two Kings and *Gerousia* or the two Suphetes and the Council of the Elders in Carthage, which, at least in the former case, the case of Sparta, seem to be institutions older than the institutions of the Consuls and the Senate in Rome). Nonetheless, there could be a third more sinister explanation as to why Roman constitutional law vocabulary and concepts were so poor: if concepts such as democracy or oligarchy would have entered the Latin language or if such concepts would have been formalised in a written and codified constitution, such would be understood and circulate widely in the streets of republican Rome – a destabilising factor for the Republic and the Patriciate altogether. The prerogatives of Rome's establishment would be at risk.[64] Who in the right mind, amongst the members of the elites of Rome, would want the Romans to realise that the Senate was but a de facto hereditary oligarchy of the same old families of Rome, while democracy in Rome was limited at best and procedurally manipulated at worst? Who from Rome's establishment would wish to put constitutional concepts in writing in the form of a formal constitution? Rome's constitution was practically a constitution without constitutional lawyers and conceptual frameworks, until the Late Republic effectively, when things like the *ultimum consultum* and Rome's mixed constitution would become more well-known and slightly more studied, for example, by personalities such as Cicero. However, by the time such concepts and 'lawyers', mostly in the form of orators, came into the Republic's life, the Republic was dead.

9.8 FUZZY, COMPOSITE, AT OTHER TIMES ABSTRACT, ELSEWHERE SPECIFIC BUT MOSTLY EFFECTIVE

Fuzzy,[65] indistinct, vague but also complex would be the best words to describe the constitution of the Roman Republic. Rome's constitution was fuzzy because almost anything in the Republic, spanning from Rome's political structures to the Senate's constitutional interpretative powers, could be taken to be constitutional matter. It was indistinct because, as explained, as per monolithic perception of the Roman mind of the *res publica*, one could not identify where precisely it would begin and end. Also, it was vague because it was abstract and it was abstract because it was vague. This was a largely unwritten, uncodified, customary, institutions-and-magistrates-centred constitution that was not found in a single place. The constitution was quite specific when it came to the terms of office of magistrates. Even more so, the Republic would come with a full institutional-constitutional layout which would speak volumes of the sophistication of the constitution of the Republic (Figure 9.1). In Rome, one could also move from one position to another but one could not stay more than a certain period of

[64] Brennan (n 8) 20.

[65] Brennan (n 8) 19.

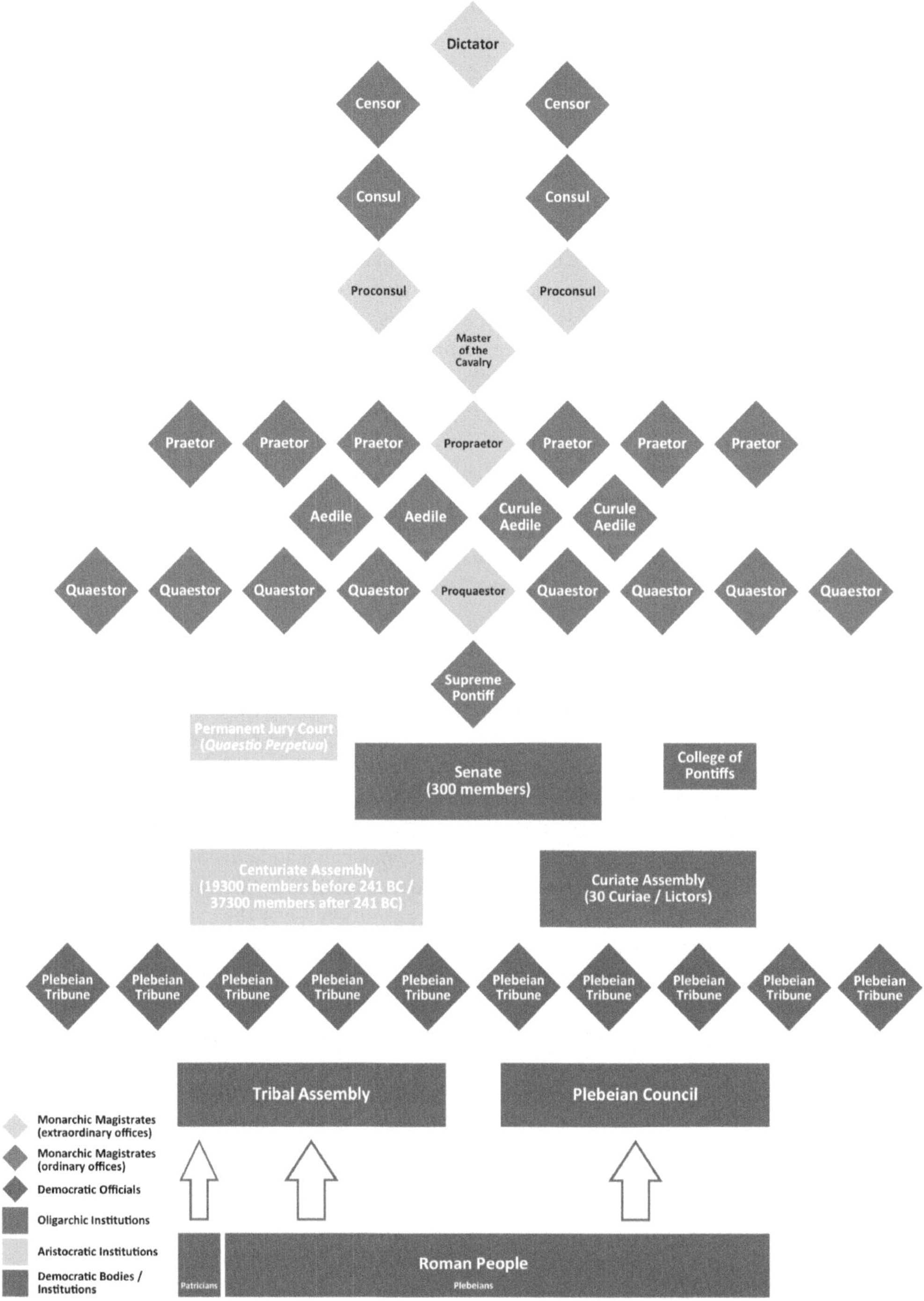

Figure 9.1 The constitution of the Roman Republic (c. 133 BC) – magistrates, institutions and bodies of the Republic

time in a position. Concurrently, the constitution of the Roman Republic would largely differ from one's average modern constitution, in that it was not codified per se. From the modern world, the constitutions that would morphologically come closest to that of the Roman Republic would be those of the State of Israel and the United Kingdom. Both the constitution of the Republic and those of Israel and the United Kingdom would be largely uncodified, even though laws of constitutional significance could be found in all three of them. Customary constitutional practices play a significant role in the United Kingdom as they do in the State of Israel. This was, of course, the case throughout the Roman Republic for matters that would be interpreted under the device of *patres maiorum* and so on. However, from the modern world, the constitution that would conceptually come closest to that of the Roman Republic would be that of the United States of America.

The fuzzy nature of Rome's constitution went well with the Romans' traditional reluctance to define the concept of law.[66] The Romans traditionally never wished to wholly engage with the conceptuality of 'law', even though they actually excelled in their mastering of the law in the private law sphere to a more than significant extent. This changed in the 1st century BC with Cicero. Before that, the lack of conceptualisation of Rome's constitutional matter was more than apparent, if not suspicious. Moreover, the preciseness of Rome's Twelve Tables, being a fundamentally private law type of legislation (with the exception of Table IX), was nowhere to be found in Rome's constitution except in the terms of offices and the functions of the magistrates and institutions of Rome, and in certain laws of constitutional significance. Other than that, the constitution of Rome was a largely undefined reality. Of course, that lack of conceptuality did not hinder the operations of Rome's peculiar but powerful constitution. In fact, its silent and stealthy characteristics in places made it highly agile, malleable and effective.

The Roman Republic also clearly started as a rather indistinct and highly developmental republican construct, a mixed constitution. Over the centuries, despite its overall abstraction and indistinct character, Rome's republican constitution became somewhat clearer. For instance, the Republic between 287 and 133 BC was a much more stable, a much more coherent republic than the Roman republic(s) in the first stages of Rome's republican history. The conservative and relatively stable character of the Republic in the 3rd and 2nd centuries BC (or what Flower called the 'Republics of the *Nobiles*') substantiates the point. Thus, the Republic was 'fuzzy' but still relatively stable and effective in constitutional terms. Finally, the Republic between 287 and 133 BC compares well with the chaotic state of affairs in the Republic between 133 and 27 BC (Late Republic), when the Republic was a republic but in name only.

[66] On the Roman lack of a definition of law, see e.g. J Harries, 'Law' in Barchiesi and Scheidel (n 20) 638.

9.9 *IUS PUBLICUM* AND LACK OF DEFINITION THEREOF

As stated, there was reluctance in Rome to deal with the cultivation of the concept of law per se. Again, the Romans would have excelled in law but the conceptuality of the sophisticated system of law, which they would have developed in the form of the Roman Republic, was not most apparent as it had not been traditionally cultivated. For instance, *ius publicum* was part and parcel of Rome's legal system, as was the Republic. However, there does not seem to be a clear definition of such during the years of the Middle Republic and law would be something that would broadly relate to the community.[67] In the sphere of public law, aside from republican Rome's *leges*, one would also find criminal law and procedural laws about guardianship and other family matters.[68] Moreover, the interpretation and the application of the aforementioned was entrusted in the Senate, Rome's courts of justice and the *comitia*.[69]

9.10 *IUS PUBLICUM* PER SE

The situation in the Roman Republic was particularly interesting when it came to its public law. On the one hand, one clearly notices the absence of a consolidated, codified, written constitution. On the other hand, while there was no constitution in written form or in a single place, there were at least in the times of Polybius a great deal of laws of constitutional significance.[70] Here one notes on an indicative basis the following laws: the Hortensian Law of 287 BC (on the power of the Roman Plebeians to create laws for the Republic); the Claudian Law of 218 BC (on the restriction of business activities of the Senators and their offspring); the Cincian Law of 204 BC (on the limitation of value of gifts received and offered and on the restriction of gifts in exchange for public services); the First Porcian Law of 199 BC extending the *provocatio ad populum* (right to appeal to the people of Rome); the Orchian Law of 181 BC (against luxury); the Villian Law of 180 BC (on the sequence of offices in the Republic and minimum ages for one to attain a magisterial office); the Calpurnian Law of 149 BC (establishing the first permanent jury courts), and so on. Thus, one observes a particularly sophisticated and extensive nexus of constitutional laws in the Republic, even if these would be scattered in Roman *ius publicum*. The fragmented nature of Rome's *ius publicum* compares well with the consolidated and codified nature of the Twelve Tables of 449 BC, Rome's law that was primarily concerned with private law matters.

Ius publicum at Rome was about magistrates, institutions and laws of constitutional significance. The latter's importance in public law matters is self-explanatory

67 Cf. Harries (n 66) 639. In relation to the Late Republic's position of *ius publicum* as a source of constitutional norms in Rome, see Straumann (n 1) 54–62.

68 Harries (n 66) 639–40.

69 Harries (n 66) 640.

70 K Von Fritz, *The Theory of the Mixed Constitution in Antiquity: A Critical Analysis of Polybius' Political Ideas* (Columbia University Press 1954) 174.

as is the significance of institutions. For instance, the Senate was at the very heart of almost all public law-related matters in one way or another. More interesting than the Senate's importance in public law matters was the role of the magistracies in such matters. A major characteristic of the magistrates was the fact that the offices of higher magistrates came with *imperium*, full constitutional power in designated military and civil areas. These were magistracies that would be 'considered as autonomous, self-sufficient realities, deriving their powers and legitimacy from a long line of investitures'.[71]

Finally, the pinnacle of the constitutional-institutional ordering of the Roman republican *ius publicum* was found in the fact that, in the absence of a written constitutional *rhetra*, a written codified constitution, it was a well-known fact amongst the Romans that the constitution of the Republic was governed by principles: the principle of collegiality (e.g. amongst magistrates of the same office); the principle of certain magistrates being able to veto one another (e.g. in the case of dyarchic offices such as Consuls and Censors); and the principle of annuity of the majority of constitutional offices, when it came to their normal fixed terms, and so on.

9.11 FOUR DIMENSIONS IN THE CONSTITUTION OF THE ROMAN REPUBLIC, NOT THREE

The Roman Republic was a monarchy-oligarchy-aristocracy-democracy. The Republic was not a monarchy-aristocracy-democracy (as advocated by Polybius[72] and Cicero[73]) (Figure 9.2). For instance, Polybius posited that the Consuls of Rome were representative of the monarchic element in the constitution, the Senate was representative of its aristocratic element, while the people's assemblies were representative of its democratic element.[74] Nevertheless, the Senate, the constitutional heart of the Roman Republic, was not an aristocratic body according to the idealistic Ciceronian and the rather rounded Polybian picture of the world, but rather an oligarchic body according to Aristotelian doctrine, it being a body of 'few and wealthy',[75] exactly as Aristotle defined an oligarchy.

[71] C Nicolet, *The World of the Citizen in Republican Rome* (PS Falla (tr), University of California 1980) 207.

[72] Plb. 6.3; 6.13.

[73] Cic. Rep. 2.41; 2.56.

[74] E.g. Von Fritz (n 70) 8.

[75] Aristot. Pol. 3.1279b: 'The argument therefore seems to make it clear that for few or many to have power is an accidental feature of oligarchies in the one case and democracies in the other, due to the fact that the rich are few and the poor are many everywhere (so that it is not really the case that the points mentioned constitute a specific difference), but that the real thing in which democracy and oligarchy differ from each other is poverty and wealth' / '*ἔοικε τοίνυν ὁ* [35] *λόγος ποιεῖν δῆλον ὅτι τὸ μὲν ὀλίγους ἢ πολλοὺς εἶναι κυρίους συμβεβηκός ἐστιν, τὸ μὲν ταῖς ὀλιγαρχίαις τὸ δὲ ταῖς δημοκρατίαις, διὰ τὸ τοὺς μὲν εὐπόρους ὀλίγους, πολλοὺς δ' εἶναι τοὺς ἀπόρους πανταχοῦ (διὸ καὶ οὐ συμβαίνει τὰς ῥηθείσας αἰτίας αἰτίας γίνεσθαι διαφορᾶς), ᾧ δὲ διαφέρουσιν ἥ τε* [40] *δημοκρατία καὶ ἡ ὀλιγαρχία ἀλλήλων πενία καὶ πλοῦτός ἐστιν*'.

Polybian / Ciceronian thesis
in relation to the Constitution of the Roman Republic

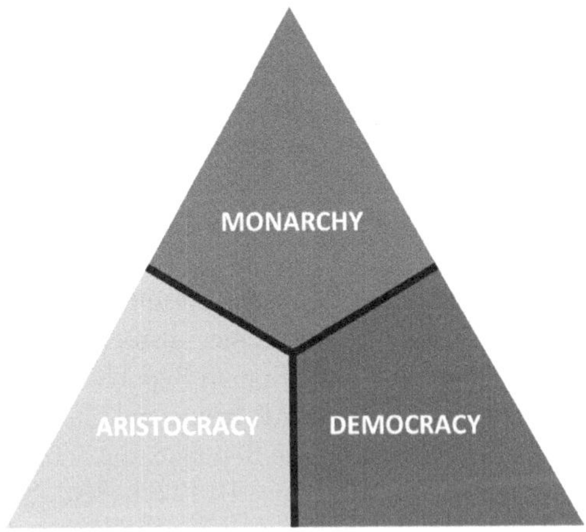

Monograph's thesis
in relation to the Constitution of the Roman Republic

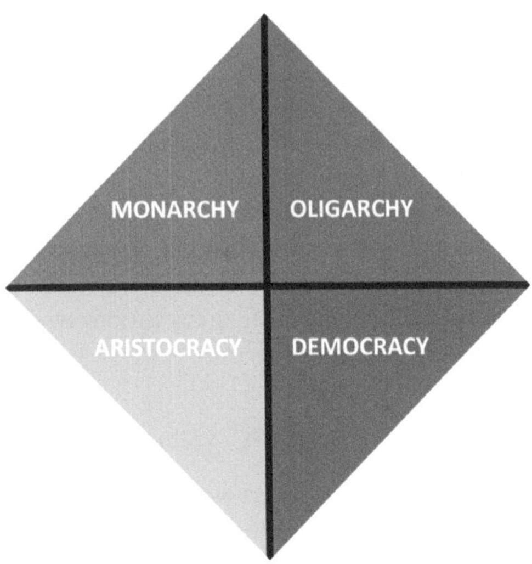

Figure 9.2 Polybian/Ciceronian thesis in relation to the constitution of the Roman Republic – monograph's thesis in relation to the constitution of the Roman Republic

The book's proposed four-part division of powers otherwise created a powerful constitutional engine for the Roman Republic, allowing it to flourish in legal, political and geopolitical terms. The Roman Republic's constitution is responsible for creating an empire and, of course, for maintaining order in Rome to a considerable extent for most of the period between 287 and 133 BC, historically Rome's constitutional and political apogee in the Republican era. However, the Republic's constitutional engine went into overdrive in the 3rd and much of the 2nd centuries BC. It effectively burnt out in the later part of the 2nd century BC because, even though it was originally conceived as a constitution for the city of Rome, it was now the constitution of an empire, which it created but could no longer support.

The constitutional composite of Rome thus resulted in a mixed polity, effectively a polity combining monarchic, oligarchic, aristocratic and democratic features into one under the umbrella of the Roman Republic. Moreover, contrary to the rounded and idealised perceptions of Polybius and Cicero about the Senate being an 'aristocracy', a central body in the Republic, the Senate was an oligarchy in Aristotelian terms (agreement with *Politics* III 1279b–80a). So too, whereas the constitution of the Republic was mixed as a whole, the Roman Republic was one of oligarchic and monarchic tendencies mainly. The aristocratic elements in Rome were rather limited: the Centuriate Assembly *mutatis mutandis* and the members of the *Quaestio Perpetua*. The role of the *populus*, Rome's democratic element, while generally important, should not be exaggerated as its role was clearly procedurally controlled by Rome's elites. In short, Rome in the more mature period of its republican existence was practically a mixed polity with strong oligarchic (predominantly) and monarchic (to a lesser extent) tendencies, combining also a limited number of democratic and aristocratic features. Nor was the Republic a polity/politeia *stricto sensu* under Aristotle's classification of constitutions, but a mixed polity with extra features beyond the Aristotelian perception of a polity – this was a republic combining four elements (not three under Aristotle's original Polity model).[76] Thus, the constitution of the Roman Republic was an Aristotelian polity+ or an Aristotelian polity with an asterisk (as will be seen in Chapter 14), the obvious asterisk being that it would also additionally incorporate Monarchic (e.g. the Dictator) and Dyarchic (e.g. the Consuls and Censors) elements in it, when Aristotle's polity model about mixed constitutions would combine aristocratic, oligarchic and democratic elements only.

9.12 A CONSTITUTION OF HOPE AND FEAR

> *Omnium primum avidum novae libertatis populum, ne postmodum flecti precibus aut donis regiis posset, iure iurando adegit neminem Romae passuros regnare.*[77]

[76] See Pasquino's analysis in this respect: P Pasquino, 'Machiavelli and Aristotle: The Anatomies of the City' (2009) 35 *History of European Ideas* 397, 399–400.

[77] Liv. 2 1.

The first and most characteristic element in the constitution of the Republic was its staunch resistance to the rule of a single man. Fear of a tyranny thus dictated the Roman mind and, by extension, the constitution of Rome. A single man would pose grave dangers to the Roman community[78] and the Republic ought to safeguard against the rise of a single man to absolute power. The constitutional fear of the Romans was, thus, also their constitutional hope in this respect. The Romans from the years of the last *Rex* realised that an unchecked Kingship, as in an absolute monarchy, could quickly deteriorate into a tyranny. The idea of a single person running the Republic for long would thus be met with fierce resistance in Rome's ruling elites. The only exception to this would be the office of the Dictator but this was an office that was designed to be effected in certain extraordinary times for the Republic and would only operate for very limited periods of time, the Senate occasionally giving its constitutional blessings to an appointed-by-a-Consul Dictator, whom it would still oversee as a whole.

9.13 CHECKS AND BALANCES EVERYWHERE IN THE CONSTITUTION

Coextensively, for the same fear of returning to the primitive tyrannical monarchic years of the Late Monarchy, something which Polybius identifies as a problem of Kingships,[79] an extensive system of checks and balances, an embryonic concept of the Rule of Law relating to fixed office terms, and a normal expectation that all Roman citizens, including magistrates, comply with the law, could be observed in Rome's republican constitution.[80] For Polybius a mixed constitution, such as the constitution of Sparta and the constitution of the Roman Republic, was about a system of checks and balances.[81] A major exception here would be the virtual absence of anything near a perfect separation of powers in the Roman Republic, even though John Adams would have impliedly praised[82] the separation of powers in Rome: the fact of the matter is that, if the US Constitution has one of the clearest separations of power in the world, the Republic of Rome had one which was blurry at best. Magistrates and institutions in the Roman Republic could exercise supervisory authority over other specific magistrates and institutions in a similar manner to the way the Seven Hills of Rome oversee one another, but such authority was both complementary and collegiate; it was about whether these magistrates and institutions would be acting *intra vires* or *ultra vires*. Through its extensive system of checks and balances, the Rome of the Republic clearly prioritised law

[78] E.g. Flower (n 40) 520.

[79] Plb. 6.7. as a whole and, in particular, Plb. 6.7.7–8.

[80] E.g. Capogrossi Colognesi (n 2) 71–2; K Morrell, 'Enabling Laws, Rule of Law, and the Transformation of the Roman Republic' in FJ Vervaet, D Rafferty and CJ Dart (eds), *How Republics Die: Creeping Authoritarianism in Ancient Rome and Beyond* (De Gruyter 2025) 197–8.

[81] E.g. Von Fritz (n 70) 184, 306.

[82] J Adams, *A Defence of the Constitutions of Government of the United States of America*, I (John Stockdale 1794) 175–6.

over individuals but equally it was powerful individuals that brought the end of the Republic.[83]

9.14 OVERALL DIVISION OF POWERS BUT LACK OF PURE SEPARATION OF POWERS

Additionally, whereas the Roman Republic was effectively an Aristotelian polity+[84] and certainly one that would be characterised by a full set of checks and balances – especially when it would come to terms of office and the supervisory authority of magistrates and institutions against one another – the Roman Republic would not practically comply with a pure separation of powers model.[85] Classic examples here would be the fact that executive and legislative offices would be mixed: for example, the Senate would hold both extensive executive powers and 'legislate' through interpretation, whilst the Roman military's interference with the more civil side of Rome's constitution would make such separation of powers even blurrier.

Thus, one observes a certain departure from the classic Aristotelian doctrine of separation of powers. One would be reminded here that the Aristotelian-Montesquian doctrine of separation of powers would relate to three powers: the Executive, the Legislative and the Judiciary. Such a division could, in theory, be scientifically plausible in the case of the Roman Republic's division of powers. However, the more pragmatic division of the Roman Republic's powers would not allow us to divide all of its powers on the Aristotelian-Montesquian model raw, as this would actually neglect the powerful military element in the running of the Roman Republic as well as in the expansion of such. It would neglect the fact that the civil side of the constitution and the military side of the constitution were mixed. The Consuls, for instance, were both the Republic's top magistrates in times of civil peace but also Rome's top military generals. Rome's military power was thus a constitutional and political power. For instance, scholars such as Lintott, who argued this point, would base arguments on ancient sources.[86] To pretend otherwise would be scientifically perilous. It is, therefore, proposed that such a power ought to be referred to as republican Rome's 'stratocratic element' (rule of the military) or Rome's fourth power, the militocratic power.[87] Of course, the Roman Republic traditionally was never quite exactly a military junta in the modern sense. Yet, there were occurrences of the military power clearly taking control over the rest of Rome's powers even in the years of the Republic, albeit for brief periods of time mostly. The Roman Republic's established office of the Dictator would be the best illustration in this respect. So too, it has to

83 Cf. Von Fritz (n 70) 323.

84 See Chapter 14 for more on this.

85 Aristot. Pol. 4.1297b–8a.

86 E.g. A Lintott, *The Constitution of the Roman Republic* (Clarendon Press 1999) 1–2.

87 Connolly speaks of Rome as a 'militaristic oligarchy': J Connolly, 'Political Theory' in Barchiesi and Scheidel (n 20) 713.

be noted here that military experience counted considerably in one's attainment of high political ranks in Rome, the clearest example in this respect being the office of Consuls, which would normally have to be filled by experienced soldiers. Generally, under the Servian Constitution (already in existence since the years of the Monarchy), a military and social organisation constitution for Rome's classes and soldiers, which lasted up until 241 BC and which was resurrected for a brief period of time between 82 and 80 BC, the Roman Republic was highly militocratic. The effect of this type of social and military arrangement clearly waned in the 2nd and 1st centuries BC while these arrangements were only briefly resurrected in the Late Republic. In any case, unlike the stricter Aristotelian-Montesquian doctrine of separation of powers, the exposition herein proceeded on the three well-known constitutional powers plus the power of the military (stratocratic power) to better explain the full layout of the Roman Republic's constitution.

9.15 AN IDEALISED IMAGE OF CONSENSUS IN ROME

The Republic was one that had deliberative politics in its heart.[88] In theory, a sort of idealised image of consensus was one that ran in Rome's political and, by extension, constitutional veins, already from the years of the Monarchy, when the *Rex* would seek the advice of the Senate for important matters affecting the community.[89] In practice, during the Republic, it was the wealthier oligarchic elites of Rome that had the final say in given matters, as such an elite would be crystallised in the Republic's most powerful body, the Senate. The compromises reached in political matters in Rome were based on an idealised perception of Rome, as in the creation of a unitary community.[90] This pendulum of compromises first started to become apparent with the so-called Conflict of the Orders.[91]

9.16 MOSTLY STABLE BUT DYNAMIC OCCASIONALLY IN THE YEARS OF THE MIDDLE REPUBLIC

Equally, the grip of the old Patrician families on the constitution of the Republic was beyond question. In fact, deliberately using archaic language, the Republic's old laws of constitutional essence were drafted in such a way that would make Rome's constitution a cryptic type of constitution.[92] This would often be a constitution open to interpretation and interpretation most certainly favoured the ruling class of the Patricians, the Senate and so on, as the constitutional interpreters would come from Rome's nobility. Moreover, one would be reminded, as

[88] Flower (n 40) 522.
[89] Capogrossi Colognesi (n 2) 21.
[90] Flower (n 40) 522–3, citing C Nicolet, *The World of the Citizen in Republican Rome* (University of California Press 1980).
[91] Flower (n 40) 523, citing C Nicolet, *The World of the Citizen in Republican Rome* (University of California Press 1980).
[92] Capogrossi Colognesi (n 2) 71.

per Flower's thesis, that the Middle Republic would be the republics of the *nobiles*, that is to say republics wherein the nobles of Rome would exercise significant control. The constitutional law scholar would, thus, have to maintain that many of the key aspects of the constitution would be political, in that they would be open to the political interpretation of Rome's ruling classes.[93] This being the case, the monarchic/oligarchic tendencies of the Republic's constitution were fundamentally down to the fact that these old Patrician families controlled and wished to continue to control the greatest part of Rome's wealth and political power. As a result, the Republic's constitution was mostly a stable and a conservative one, but it would occasionally display the characteristics of a dynamic one, when there would be need for the constitution to stabilise state, or when an apparent social dynamic would be existent and would need to be taken into account.[94] Nonetheless, one notes here another valid point made by Flower: the fact that the period between 509 and 27 BC was not a reality in which there was a sort of uniform political pattern with no changes to it.[95] On the contrary, as explained earlier in the analysis,[96] the division of the Roman republican period into a number of republics holds considerable validity, even though such terms as Early Republic, Middle Republic and Late Republic are used as the more traditional terms for the benefit and the convenience of the reader. Equally, however, the constitutional phenomenon of the Republic (as opposed to the very distinct political republics that comprised the phenomenon of the Roman Republic) was mostly unitary, in that the Roman antipathy towards the rule of a single person over Rome was mostly upheld throughout the Republic's history (with the obvious exceptions in the 1st century BC). So too, historically and constitutionally, the institutions of Rome would change relatively little from the beginning to the end of the Republic and changes would mostly be nominal ones (e.g. Consuls would be named to Consular Tribunes and then Consular Tribunes would be named Consuls anew; the emergency constitutional powers of the Dictator would somewhat transform into Senatorial constitutional powers in the form of *senatus ultima consulta*, despite the fact that the office of the Dictator would not have been abolished, and so on).

9.17 AN ELITIST AND PLUTOCRATIC CONSTITUTION IN THE MAIN: CORE INSTITUTIONS AND MAGISTRATES IN THE REPUBLIC

The Republic was a mixed constitution, run by officials, as in magistrates that would hold office for a limited period of time and would be supervised by other magistrates, as would Rome itself by the city's constitutional core and most powerful institution, the Senate. A move from one magistratorial position to another

93 Ibid.

94 But cf. Flower (n 40) 520.

95 Flower (n 40) 520.

96 As in Chapter 3 herein.

was normally allowed but the tenure in given positions was limited in time. Rome's republican constitution was practically mostly elitist, despite the opening of magistratorial offices to Plebeians. In addition to the wealthy class of Patricians holding a key role in manning the Republic's offices and institutions, poor Plebeians were excluded from acquiring office, thereby allowing us to also maintain that the constitution of the Roman Republic would also come with a clear plutocratic inclination. Also, Rome was not as explicitly plutocratic as Carthage was, but plutocratic[97] it was. Indeed, had Rome not been plutocratic, it would never have been imperial. Rome's imperialism also supported its plutocratic circles. The same could be said of Carthage and its great empire. A major difference, however, between the constitution of the Roman Republic and the constitution of the Carthaginian Empire has been the fact that the Carthaginian Empire was mostly plutocratic, whilst the Roman Republic was mostly oligarchic. Authors have traditionally called the plutocratic elements of Carthage[98] and the oligarchic elements of Rome such as the Senate[99] 'aristocratic' but this would not accurately reflect the constitutional picture of these two major Mediterranean states.

Rome grew ever greedier, however, as it gradually acquired more land in the Italian peninsula, Europe and around the Mediterranean. Accordingly, it must have been clearly realised (e.g. in the 3rd century BC) already that the more Rome would expand its *imperium*, the more this would come to the benefit and the satisfaction of its ruling classes. The Roman game became a Latin game then. The Latin game became an Italian game thereafter. The Italian game became a Mediterranean game, and so on. Thus, Rome's imperial dream was clearly not for the sake of her *imperium* per se but for the sake of satisfying the ever-growing greed of its ruling classes and elites for resources, wealth, power and control. Roman expansionism was profoundly devoid of any attempt to impose Roman culture on locals (the only exception being the Romanisation of the Italian populations by the Romans). Roman colonisers would establish temples to Greek and Roman gods, in the new areas which they would colonise, but their cultural expansionism was one of cultural paraphernalia that these colonisers would bring with them for themselves; these cultural paraphernalia would not necessarily be used to assimilate the locals into Roman culture.

Roman expansionism was as dry and utilitarian as Rome itself was as a city, and as dry as the Roman plutocrats and the Romans themselves were as a people.

97 Cf. RE Mitchell, 'The Aristocracy of the Roman Republic' in R Howarth (ed), *Hearsay, History, and Heresy: Collected Essays on the Roman Republic by Richard E. Mitchell* (Gorgias Press 2010) 127: 'The [Roman] aristocracy developed naturally out of primitive society's reliance upon wealthy, powerful men'.

98 E.g. Aristot. Pol. 2.1273a where Aristotle makes the point that Carthage has an aristocratic system with divergences to oligarchy and democracy. However, Aristotle also openly states that 'the rulers [in Carthage] should be chosen not only for their merit but also for their wealth, as it is not possible for a poor man to govern well or to have leisure for his duties'. He peculiarly states, however, the election by wealth as 'oligarchic' (when one could readily speak of a plutocratic approach).

99 E.g. Plb. 6.11.12.

It would be paradoxical if the semi-barbaric republican Romans would have any pursuits of cultural assimilation of others through their conquests, when they themselves were one of the least cultural people in the Mediterranean world. As such, Rome was a disinterested conqueror in destroying local cultures and communities except in rare circumstances, as in the cases of Carthage and Corinth. Thus, Rome as a conqueror chose, after it conquered, to become one of history's greatest tax collectors, it being almost completely disinterested in the assimilation of locals to Roman traditions, ideas and culture. Rome, as a conquering force, was dry, pragmatic and devoid of any cultural plans of assimilation of the conquered. Its ruling plutocratic oligarchy would make sure that it would remain faithful to such a cause.

When it comes to the elitist spirit of Rome's constitution, one notes the way and the timing of opening public offices to Plebeians and the overall running of the state by Patricians and wealthy oligarchies that made the Republic's constitution elitist. Even though *Lex Hortensia* made the Republic more 'democratic', it did not turn the tide of the Republic into a democracy, as the Senate and, by extension, the Patricians continued to exert more than considerable control over the Republic.

9.18 FACTIONLESS CONSTITUTION AND THE PREVALENCE OF THE SENATE OVER THE ROMAN PEOPLE

Rome did not have political factions in most of its republican existence. Political parties were unknown in Rome. In fact, the supposed unity of the Roman community was based on the idea that a divided society is a weak society.[100] Thus, Rome of the Republic, especially in the Middle Republic, was to do all it could to avoid one-man states and factions within Rome.[101] The Late Republic, however, proves that neither of these goals was achieved.

9.19 THE SEQUENCE OF OFFICES IN THE REPUBLIC (*CURSUS HONORUM*)

In the Roman Republic, one ought to normally first complete military service and become Military Tribune before proceeding with the other political-military offices in the traditional *cursus honorum* and it would seem that at least until the 3rd century BC, a Military Tribune could be either appointed or elected.[102] Through *Lex Villia* of 180 BC, the sequence of offices in the constitution of the Republic became clearer.[103] From lower to higher office, this was Rome's sequence of offices

[100] Cf. Flower (n 40) 523, citing C Nicolet, *The World of the Citizen in Republican Rome* (University of California Press 1980).

[101] Ibid.

[102] E.g. JH Clark, 'Were Tribuni Militum First Elected in 362 or 311 BCE?' (2016) 63 *Historia: Zeitschrift für Alte Geschichte* 275, 290–1; P Freeman, *Julius Caesar* (Simon & Schuster 2008) 47.

[103] IE Τζαμτζής, *Ο Μεσογειακός Κόσμος* (Εκδόσεις Σάκκουλα 2014, ανατύπωση 2018) 89.

under *Lex Villia*: Plebeian Tribune, Quaestor, Aedile (whether Curule or Plebeian), Praetor and Consul.[104] Exceptionally, a Plebeian Tribune (i.e. in the case of a Plebeian citizen wishing to proceed with a magisterial office per se after the office of Plebeian Tribune) could notionally and hierarchically stand in between Quaestors and Aediles in the *cursus*, thereby being able to become a Plebeian Aedile or even Praetor without becoming a Quaestor previously. In theory, a Plebeian Tribune could become Quaestor but one need not be a Plebeian Tribune as a precondition to becoming a Quaestor. However, a person who had become a Quaestor could certainly move to the office of Plebeian Tribune and Tiberius Gracchus seems to have followed this path. The significance of the *cursus honorum* was two-fold: first, on the constitutional side of things, the persons attaining Consul status would be deemed the most successful citizens of the Republic. It is also noted at this point that persons in the Roman Republic who acquired considerable political and social recognition in their life for their political and military achievements could also reach the status of Censor, one of Rome's highest offices, even if such office operated outside the *cursus honorum*.[105] Second, on the administrative side of things, the sequence of offices was about a fully regulated, institutional republic, the offices of which came with a certain hierarchical sequence, status, fixed terms and confined roles (see Figure 10.3 for more on the Roman *cursus*).

9.20 ESSENTIAL BACKGROUND INFORMATION FOR APPRECIATING NATURE OF AND ACCESS TO REPUBLICAN ROME'S OFFICES

It is deemed appropriate at this point to offer readers certain background information before making their way through the following four chapters on Rome's monarchic, oligarchic, aristocratic and democratic institutions. The magisterial offices of Republican Rome effectively started as offices that would almost exclusively be manned by members of the old noble families of Rome (Patricians). Plebeians, especially, from wealthy Plebeian families, could also eventually find their way into magistratorial positions, albeit to a lesser extent than Patricians. Indeed, a number of offices in republican Rome were mostly manned by personnel belonging to the Patrician class, even after such offices, in principle, became open to both Plebeians and Patricians. In any case, with the development of the Republic, 'a joint [P]atrician-[P]lebeian aristocracy developed, the tribunate, the source of power the [P]lebeians used earlier to gain parity with the [P]atricians, becoming little more than another "establishment" office'.[106] Nonetheless, the Patricians continued to hold their significant share of Rome's leading positions for some time, even after the Plebeians holding offices would have increased in

[104] Ibid.
[105] Ibid.
[106] Mitchell (n 97) 108.

number.[107] It would otherwise seem that the '[t]he Roman nobility was always of great vitality and ever in search of talent. Its attitude was not one of vigorous exclusion of outsiders but of carefully controlled inclusion'.[108]

In any case, wealth was a condition precedent for accessing the Republic's public offices and vice versa. Indeed, the elites of Rome, whether on the Patrician side of things or on the Plebeian side, were characterised by one thing: wealth. 'Ancient sources associate riches with aristocratic status'.[109] Wealth meant nobility and nobility meant access to power. Additionally, a wealthy Plebeian was a significantly different sub-species of citizen to a mere poor Plebeian one: more respectable and one to whom the Republic's state offices would much more readily open their doors, when it came to engaging oneself with politics and administration. To all this, one is reminded that, as compared to wealth, education did not traditionally matter greatly to republican Romans, especially at the humble beginnings of their agrarian and rustic republic. Rome did not start as a major intellectual power. For many centuries of the Republic, philosophers did not roam the streets of Rome and were forbidden to enter Rome or were even expelled from it. Poetry was not cultivated. The arts were imported from the Greeks and the Etruscans, and so on. The well-known myth of the she-wolf nurturing Romulus and Remus speaks volumes, in symbolic terms, of Rome's wild beginnings. Education was, thus, something that the wealthy could afford to their offspring but not a condition precedent to acquiring public office. The fact that eventually wealth signified that one had received certain considerable education did not make education a *sine qua non* to acquiring office in Rome. In Rome, one's bloodline traditionally mattered more than one's education, albeit not always and not necessarily. Education otherwise started to become a 'trend' in Rome much later in the 3rd and 2nd centuries BC, when there was a major influx of Greek scholars in the city, who were used as teaching personnel for Roman youth, especially youth of noble descent.

Eventually, the Republic opened the doors of its administrative and magistratorial offices to people from classes below the Patrician class. These persons were called 'new men' (*novi homines*). They started taking office in Rome's offices, as the Republic developed. Rome was at this time still a mid-sized republic, the territorial reach of which was limited to Latium and central Italy; however, it would subsequently be in the process of becoming an empire. Therefore, despite initial attempts of the Patricians to restrict the number of privileged families,[110] Rome's changes in its citizenry, territory, prosperity and the complexity of its society meant that more men of sophistication, albeit of less noble background than the background of the Patrician class, were required to take office to run their empire. Apparently, the continued efforts of the Roman nobility to maintain its privileges and hegemony were actually the single most important factor for upward mobility

107 Mitchell (n 97) 109.
108 DC Earl, *The Moral and Political Tradition of Rome* (Cornell University Press 1967) 13.
109 Mitchell (n 97) 131.
110 Mitchell (n 97) 127.

in Roman society and politics.[111] Rome's nobles 'were both the guardians of the walls of privilege and the traitors who opened the gates'.[112] They eventually had to open the doors of certain of Rome's offices in order for them to maintain their grip on the consulship, the censorship and the priesthoods.[113] In this respect, it is to be noted that such doors were not widely opened and the office of the Consul, for instance, has been manned only on a certain number of occasions by four 'new men': by Flaminius in 224 BC; by Cato the Elder in 195 BC; by Marius on seven occasions between 106 and 88 BC; and by Cicero in 63 BC.[114]

111 Ibid.
112 Ibid.
113 Ibid.
114 Τζαμτζής (n 89) 140.

Chapter 10

Monarchic Elements

10.1 INTRODUCTION

The abolition of the Roman Monarchy did not signify the wholesale abolition of monarchic elements from the constitution of the new Roman Republic. On the contrary, while the Republic abolished the *Rex*, it established and came with a number of offices of monarchic and dyarchic essence. The Republic thus hid well, close to its constitutional heart, the Senate, an oligarchic body, monarchic and dyarchic offices, as Rome's top executive administrative and military magistrates, even though these would not be as powerful as the collective will of the Senate. The *Rex* ruled in the years of the Monarchy but the Senate ruled for most of the Republic, steering Consuls and normally advising Consuls on the appointment of a Dictator, even though this was not always necessary. In any case, the dyarchic office of the elected Censors, the dyarchic office of the elected Consuls, and the monarchic office of an appointed Dictator would stand for the Roman Republic's highest offices, in normal times in the case of the former two, and in extraordinary times in the case of the Dictator. Nevertheless, the Consuls, certainly, and the Dictator, indirectly, would be steered by the collective will of the Senate.

The Roman Monarchy, on the other hand, was traditionally an absolute type of Kingship vested with powers, in theory, from the people and the Senate of Rome. According to ancient sources such as Dionysius of Halicarnassus, Rome's *Rex* and the symbols of monarchic power came from Etruria.[1] For most of the Monarchy's existence, the *Rex*, who would stand at the top of the Monarchy, would invite his 100 Senators, the *Patres* of Rome, and work together with them, but legend has it that the Monarchy eventually retreated into a tyranny under Lucius Tarquinius Superbus, the last *Rex* of Rome. The tyranny of the last three decades of the Roman Kingdom was conventionally abolished in 509 BC with the rise of the Republic, but the Romans wished to retain limited-in-term but powerful in authority monarchic/dyarchic elements in their Republic's constitution up until 27 BC. Of course, with the rise of the Principate in the same year and the abolition of the Republic, extraordinary powers would again be in the hands of a single man, the first Roman emperor, Octavian, who simultaneously enjoyed both Tribunician and Consular powers. In theory, he could be vetoed but in practice none would stand in his way. A puppet Senate would declare him the Risen

[1] E.g. TC Brennan, *The Fasces: A History of Ancient Rome's Most Dangerous Political Symbol* (Oxford University Press 2023) 11.

(*Augustus*), while he himself would, in all probability, take also the title of First Citizen/Prince (*Princeps*) of Rome. The monarchic elements of Rome divided and fragmented in the years of the Republic would be very reminiscent of certain of the key powers of the old *Rex* (Figure 10.1) under the Monarchy, especially the powers that came with the normal office of the two Censors, the normal office of the two Consuls, the normal office of the Praetors and the extraordinary office of the Dictator, as these four types of magistrates would have in their hands many of the old powers of the *Rex*, albeit for very limited periods of time (one year for Consuls and Praetors normally, six months, in all probability, for Dictators, and eighteen months for Censors). Also, major distinguishing characteristics of Rome's monarchic/dyarchic offices was normally their *imperium* and the fact that Lictors would escort these top Roman officials. However, it should be noted that the fact that a Roman magistrate would not have *imperium* would not mean that their office could not be of monarchic/dyarchic nature.

10.2 *IMPERIUM*

Imperium was the classic quality that certain of the offices of the Roman Republic enjoyed for such to exercise monarchic or *mutatis mutandis* monarchic powers. However, not all Roman magistrates had *imperium*, only Rome's top magistrates: these were the Consuls, the Dictator, the Master of the Cavalry, the Praetors, the Proconsuls, the Propraetors, the Curule Aediles and the Interrex. As will be seen, the Censors and the Supreme Pontiff did not have *imperium* and yet their office was still of monarchic/dyarchic nature. *Imperium* effectively stood for an office's governmental and/or military plenipotentiary power(s). It was command of the highest order, whether in civil or military terms, and it was hierarchical. Thus, the *imperium* of a Consul in military matters was considered higher than the *imperium* of a Praetor; the *imperium* of the Dictator was higher than the *imperium* of his lieutenant officer, the Master of the Cavalry, and so on.

In the Roman Republic, institutions that enjoyed *imperium* (full monarchic powers in designated areas of responsibility) would stand for Rome's highest offices, a major exception being the office of the Censors, the status of which was one of the highest in Rome, even if Censors did not hold *imperium*. For practical but also for highly symbolic reasons, the Roman magistrates holding *imperium* would all be followed by Lictors (attendant guardians – see Figure 10.2). Four institutions in the Roman Republic enjoyed monarchic powers without them holding *imperium*: (i) the Supreme Pontiff, the religious leader of Rome, advising on ceremonial matters and Rome's Senate on related matters; (ii) the Censors; (iii) the Quaestors; and (iv) the Plebeian Aediles (as opposed to the Curule Aediles who actually held *imperium*). None of these four magistrates had *imperium*, yet the Supreme Pontiff had monarchic powers over the College of Pontiffs, while the Censors' powers were absolute in their area of responsibility, with only future Censors being able to overturn a previous Censor's decision. Quaestors and Aediles too also had considerable autonomy in their operations, making their offices of monarchic essence

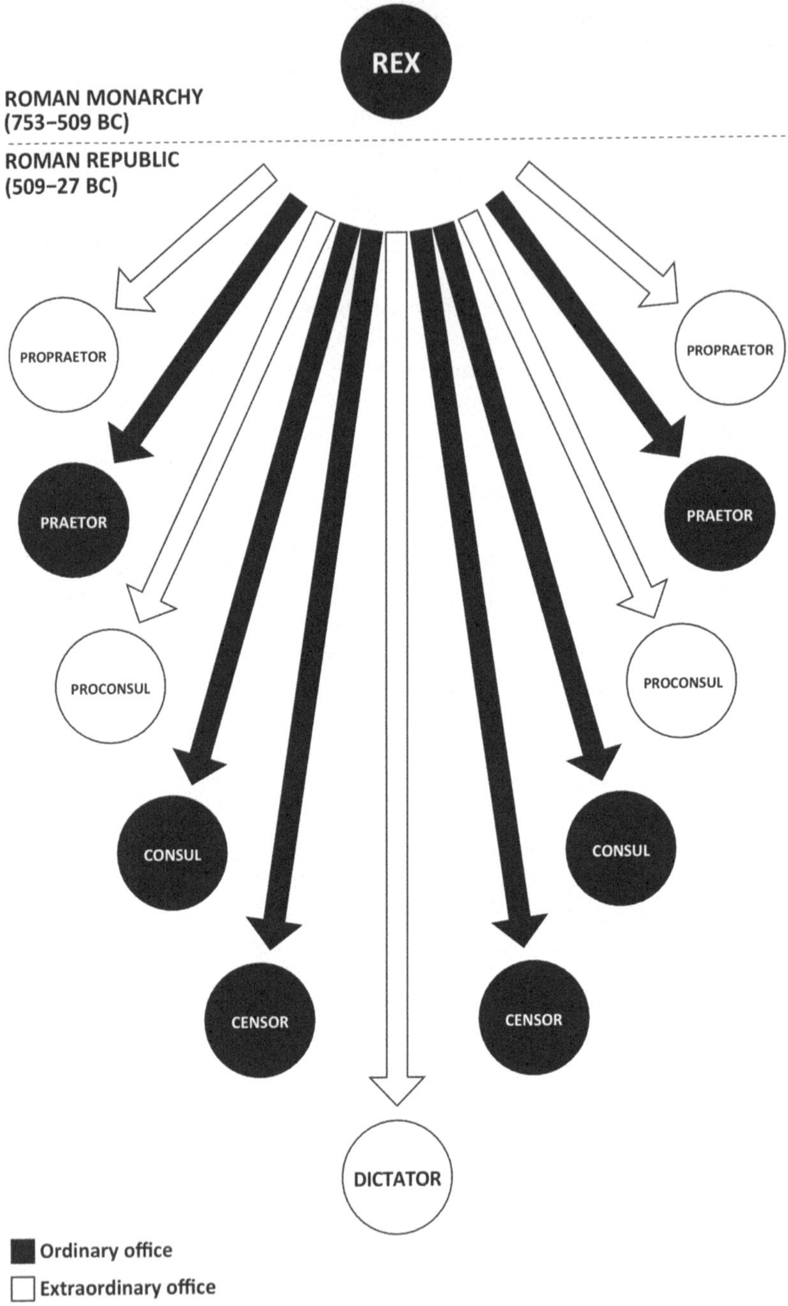

Figure 10.1 Conceptual fragmentation of the *Rex*'s powers into offices of monarchic and dyarchic nature in the years of the Republic

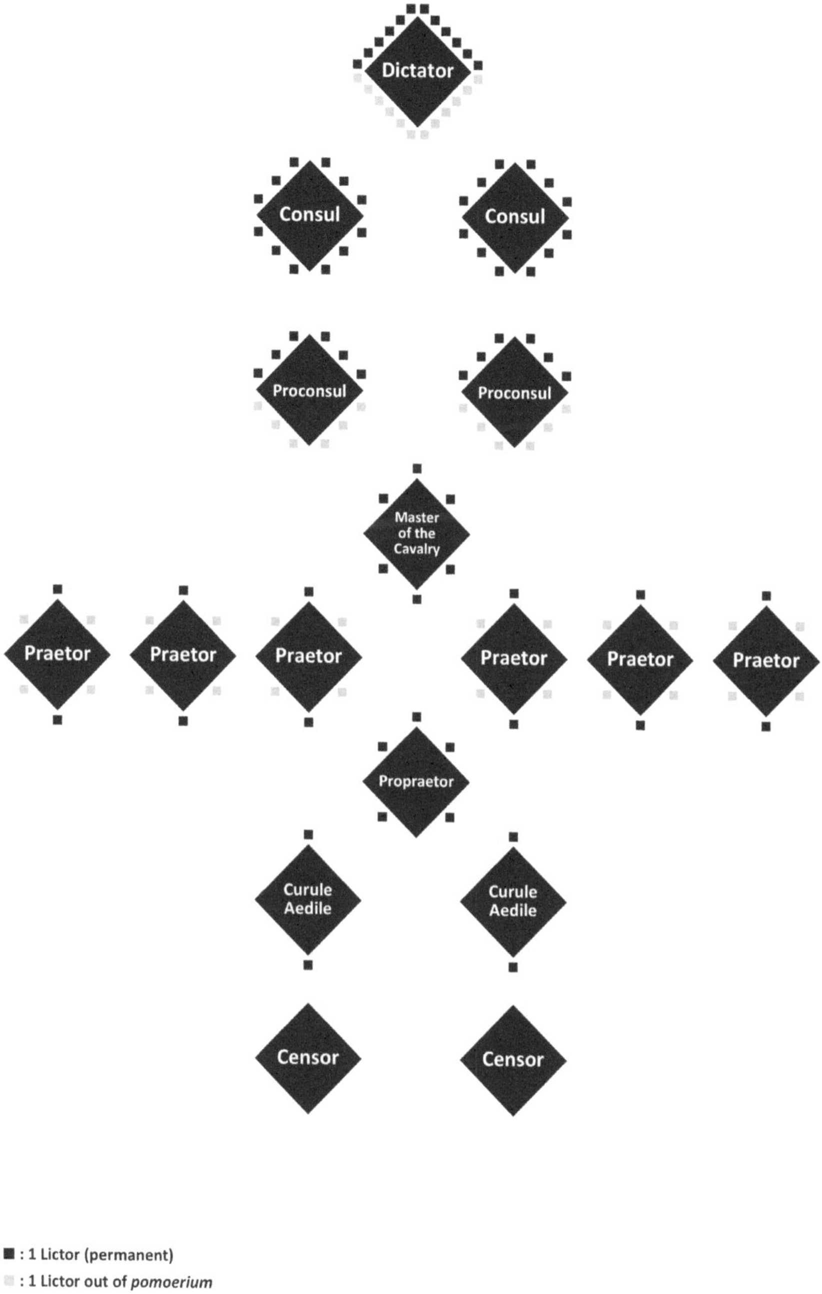

Figure 10.2 The significance and ranking of the Roman Republic's monarchic and dyarchic elements based on their number of lictors

effectively. As stated, *imperium* in the Roman Republic was the highest form of command and authority. The offices that came with such would be particularly prestigious and would be sought after by Rome's ambitious politicians and military officers; however, the monarchic office of the Supreme Pontiff and the dyarchic office of the Censors proves the point that the prestige of a Roman office in the Republic would not be solely dependent on *imperium*.

A relatively little-known but distinguishing and interesting fact about Rome's monarchic/dyarchic officers with *imperium* is the fact that all such officers were followed by an appropriate number of Lictors depending on office, when Rome's other magistrates were not followed by such.[2] Lictors in Rome's republican constitution were guardians and attendant officers of Rome's top monarchic officials and tradition has it that the axes (*fasces*) which they would carry with them originally emanated, as a practice and a symbol of power, from Etruria.[3] These *fasces* in the hands of the Lictors had a dual function: to protect Rome's top magistrates and to serve as powerful symbols (insignia)[4] of power. As already maintained in the previous chapter, the Romans had a relatively coherent system and sequence of honours. One ought to normally follow a certain career path prior to reaching the higher or, indeed, the highest offices of the Republic. The path included a military element, and a civil-military element, post military element. The Romans have called this sequence of offices *cursus honorum* (see Figure 10.3 for a full exposition of the Roman *cursus*). Finally, it is important to note that, whereas the highest offices of the Republic would eventually open to Plebeians, one's rise in the *cursus* was also dependent on one's financial power.[5]

10.3 THE CONSULS

Reminiscent of Sparta's dual kingship and Carthage's two Sufetes system were the two Consuls of the Roman Republic, who would effectively be the closest one would get to the old king(s) of Rome in times of constitutional peace. Constitutional duality in Rome, constitutional dyarchy in most precise terms, occurred not only in the case of the Consuls but also in the case of Rome's two Censors, the two Curile Aediles, the two Aediles and the *Duumviri Navales*. The fascination of the Romans with constitutional duality[6] and the existence of the dual office of Consuls in Rome could in fact relate to the Roman twins of Romulus and Remus,[7] the twins who were Rome's first leaders, when the fascination of the Spartans with constitutional duality and the existence of the dual office of Kings in Sparta could relate to the Spartan twins of Castor and Pollux.

[2] Livy states that in the case of a college of ten Interreges in office in Roman regal times, only one would carry the insignia of *imperium* and would be followed by Lictors: Liv. 1 17 5–6.

[3] Brennan (n 1) 9.

[4] Ibid.

[5] I Shatzman, *Senatorial Wealth and Politics* (Latomus 1975) 233.

[6] Cf. M Beard, *SPQR: A History of Ancient Rome* (Liveright Publishing 2015) 64.

[7] Beard (n 6) 64.

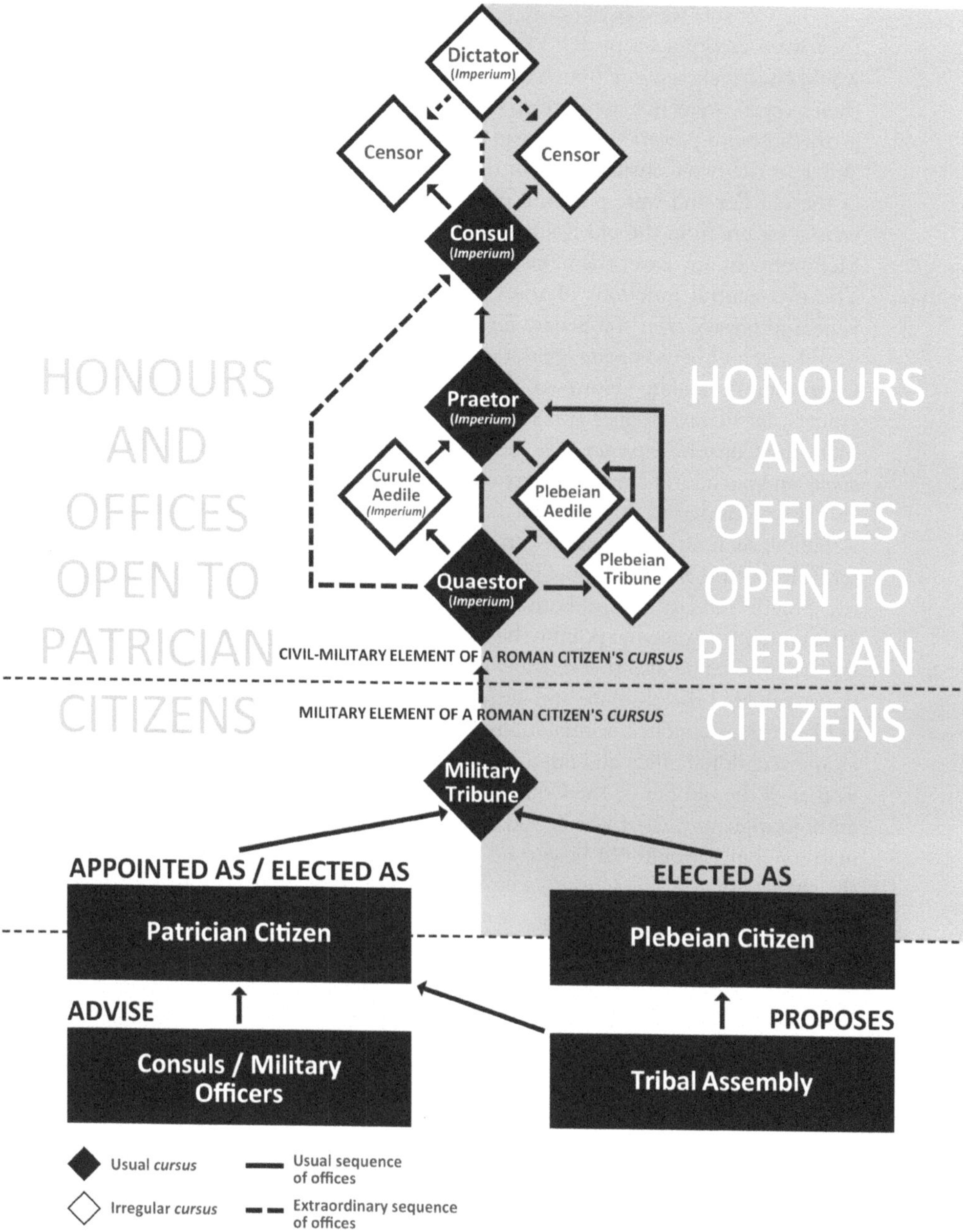

Figure 10.3 *Cursus Honorum* – sequence of offices in the constitution of the Roman Republic – Roman course of honours (3rd and 2nd century BC)

The Consuls were periphrastically usually known as 'the Twelve Fasces',[8] as they were escorted by twelve Lictors.[9] They were Rome's top magistrates and would effectively 'assume [much of] the king's position and authority'.[10] However, their powers were not absolute *stricto sensu*, or more precisely, not as absolute as the absolute powers of the *Rex* in the final century of the Roman Monarchy. Whereas the two Consuls stood for the office that assumed many of the powers[11] of the old *Rex* and were powerful political figures in the Roman Republic, they were a far cry from the old Roman *Reges* (kings) in the years of the late Roman Monarchy. In any case, the Consuls were practically constitutional monarchs.[12] The two central functions of the Consuls within Rome would be (i) to convene and preside over the Senate for important matters of policy, on which they would act, and (ii) to create legislation and appoint new magistrates through the Centuriate Assembly.[13] However, the Consuls would also be Rome's top military officers; let us say, Rome's two Field Marshals or top two military Generals. As such, the Consuls' *imperium* was subdivided into home civil command (*imperium domi*) and outside-of-Rome military command (*imperium militiae*).[14]

Also, considering that the office of Consuls arose in the times of the Roman Republic, such an office was historically preceded in comparative constitutional terms by both the office of dual kingship in Sparta and, probably, the office of the two Sufetes in Carthage, as both of these offices seem to go back to at least the 7th century BC. A further point to be made here would be that, whilst the office of the Dictator could also theoretically be used as the Roman Republic's institution that resembled the absolute and authoritarian ways of most of the old monarchs of Rome, the Republic's normal intent behind the particular office was for it to act as an exceptional office and not as an office of continuous conventional *imperium* as that of the old *Rex* or the Consuls. Whilst Dictators could normally act in an authoritarian way, the Consuls too could give orders like a monarch in military matters[15] but it would not be certain that they could act in a similar way within the city of Rome.[16] The Consuls were proposed by the Senate and the Centuriate Assembly would appoint them.[17] A major limitation to their office was the fact that it was normally a one-year[18] office. A feature that Consuls shared with the

8 Brennan (n 1) 1.
9 Brennan (n 1) 1, 50.
10 PA Zoch, *Ancient Rome* (University of Oklahoma Press 1998) 33.
11 Cf. Zoch (n 10) 33.
12 R Seager, 'Polybius' Distortions of the Roman 'Constitution': A Simpl(istic) Explanation' in R Gibson and T Harrison (eds), *Polybius and his World. Essays in Memory of F. W. Walbank* (Oxford University Press 2013) 249.
13 L Capogrossi Colognesi, *Law and Power in the Making of the Roman Commonwealth* (Cambridge University Press 2014) 73.
14 Ibid.
15 N Davies, *Europe: A History* (Pimlico 1996, reprinted with corrections 1997) 171.
16 A Lintott, *The Constitution of the Roman Republic* (Clarendon Press 1999) 18.
17 Davies (n 15) 171.
18 Zoch (n 10) 33.

office of the Dictator was the fact that Consuls would be holders of *imperium*, as would be the office of the Dictator.

In any case, these two Roman magistrates, the Consuls, largely held monarchic powers (as opposed to such powers being concentrated in the hands of a single official).[19] The paradox of monarchic powers in the hands of two officials is not unique to Rome in historical terms and must have practically arisen and/or practically been justified by Republican Rome's reluctance to concentrate too many powers (monarchic or not) in the hands of a single official[20] (major exception to this being the office of the Dictator, whose exercise of powers normally would be even more time-limited than the exercise of powers of the Consuls). In fact, the idea that the office of the Consuls was created out of fear and hatred for the monarchy could be plausibly raised.[21]

The Roman political and constitutional genius in the creation of such an office has been found in the fact that this new office did not merely replace the old *Rex*. It both replaced the *Rex* and actually created two '*Reges*' (taking the form of Consuls),[22] each one controlling the other. Strategically, the constitution of the Roman Republic also limited their term in the office to one year,[23] even though there were exceptional occasions when Consuls were re-appointed. Also, it must be noted that two Consuls could veto each other's decisions, whereas in Sparta the expectation was that the two Kings would not consider vetoing one another. The spirit of collegiality between the two Kings of Sparta was higher than that between the two Consuls of Rome. Equally, the Consuls of Rome could readily keep each other in check but that could bring the Republic to a constitutional standstill: if one of the two Consuls exercised his veto against his colleague.

Thus, republican Rome's clear reluctance to concentrate many powers in the hands of a single individual was already apparent in the office of the two Consuls who could effectively veto one another. In most precise terms, one would, therefore, speak in the times of the Republic of a constitutional dyarchy, two persons effectively having and sharing monarchic powers. Very reminiscent of the powers of the old Roman kings has also been the fact that the Consuls could appoint Senators (as would the Roman king(s) in the first two centuries of the Monarchy) up until the Ovinian Plebiscite in late 4th century BC when such power was transferred to the Censors. Under the new law, any magistrates would also become Senators *ex officio*. From 367 BC one of the Consuls would normally have to be a Plebeian.[24] However, the more finalised version of the office of the Consuls must have occurred as late as 300 BC.

19 But cf. H Mouritzen, *Politics in the Roman Republic* (Cambridge University Press 2017) 10, disagreeing with the Polybian view that the Consuls of Rome were of monarchic essence.

20 E.g. Zoch (n 10) 15.

21 Zoch (n 10) 33.

22 E.g. Capogrossi Colognesi (n 13) 52.

23 TC Brennan, *The Praetorship in the Roman Republic*, vol 1 (Oxford University Press 2000) 13; Capogrossi Colognesi (n 13) 72.

24 A Kamm, *The Romans* (Routledge 2006) 13. But cf. A Lintott (n 16) 37, 105. He states that it was in 342 BC that a law came into effect to allow Plebeians to stand for the office of Consul.

The Consuls were the second most prestigious office in republican Rome after the Censors. Yet their military campaigns would have to come with the Centuriate Assembly's final seal of approval before they commence operations[25] and the Senate would thereafter still supervise their campaigns.[26] Also, besides their military functions, amongst their civil functions were religious functions and presiding over Roman games, the latter being the case on the basis that the celebration took place while they were still in Rome.[27] The Consuls were also Rome's top diplomatic representatives, receiving ambassadors of other states and speaking on the part of the Senate to them.[28] While in Rome, they would also act as intermediaries between the Senate and the people of Rome and would also enjoy legislative initiative in the popular assemblies.[29] Originally, their office was indistinct from the office of the Praetors. Up until 367/6 BC the offices of the Consuls and of all other magistrates in Rome was filled by Patricians only.[30] 'By 342 the battle was essentially won, with the admission of [P]lebeians to the consulate; the most important consequence [being] the creation of a mixed [P]atrician-[P]lebeian nobility'.[31] In 172 BC, for the first time in the Republic's history, both Consuls came from the Plebeian class.[32] The Consuls effectively concentrated in their hands significant political, military and administrative powers. And yet they would not effectively reign supreme over Rome without any constraints by any other body or office in the Republic in the way the late King(s) of Rome would reign supreme over the city. In practical terms, the Consuls would be responsible for Rome's politics, be in command of large Roman military concentrations (armies) and would also, occasionally, be in direct control of Rome's most important conquered provinces. Being the supreme commanders of the Roman army and the highest judicial authorities in the Republic, the only bodies that could impose effective limitations in the exercise of their powers would be the Senate and the Plebeian Council. As such, to revert to modernity, in certain respects (aside from the judicial function of the Consuls), the office of the US President seems to be coming *mutatis mutandis* quite close to certain of the powers of Rome's Consuls.

Also, W Eder, 'Republicans and Sinners: The Decline of the Roman Republic and the End of a Provisional Arrangement' in RW Wallace and EM Harris (eds), *Transitions to Empire: Essays in Greco-Roman History, 360–146 B.C., in Honor of E. Badian* (University of Oklahoma Press 1996) 451 where he states that the year Plebeians were allowed to become Consuls was 366 BC.

25 Capogrossi Colognesi (n 13) 73.

26 Ibid.

27 E.g. F Pina Polo, *The Consul at Rome: The Civil Functions of the Consuls in the Roman Republic* (Cambridge University Press 2011) 57.

28 Plb. 6.12; Pina Polo (n 27) 81.

29 Plb. 6.12; Pina Polo (n 27) 98, 99.

30 RE Mitchell, *Patricians and Plebeians: The Origin of the Roman State* (Cornell University Press 1990) 14; HI Flower, *Roman Republics* (Princeton University Press 2010) 45; Capogrossi Colognesi (n 13) 53.

31 M Crawford, *The Roman Republic* (2nd edn, Fontana Press 1992) 25.

32 RE Mitchell, 'The Aristocracy of the Roman Republic' in R Howarth (ed), *Hearsay, History, and Heresy: Collected Essays on the Roman Republic by Richard E. Mitchell* (Gorgias Press 2010) 111.

10.4 THE PROCONSULS

These high-ranked officers of Rome would normally be drawn from the classes of previous Consuls, their tenure as Proconsuls being one year long.[33] Roman provinces were otherwise run by Proconsuls and Praetors.[34] Proconsuls seem to have been wholly integrated in the Republic's constitutional machinery from the 2nd century BC onwards when Republican Rome would be more of a republican empire.[35] However, the first Proconsul seems to have been Quintus Publilius Philo who was given by the Senate *pro consule*[36] powers in 327 BC. Thus, a Consul in head of a military campaign could be extended his office as Proconsul for another year by the Senate.[37] His powers as Proconsul at the time were quite different to the powers of Proconsuls from the 2nd century BC onwards. Finally, whereas Proconsuls in the Roman Empire would have the same *imperium* as Consuls, such would be limited to a province's level. At such level, Proconsuls could issue laws and delegate their authority and *imperium* to certain of their inferior officers.[38] The Proconsuls were followed by a small team of administrators comprising a Quaestor and a few Legates.[39]

10.5 THE PRAETORS

Of lower status to the status of Consuls eventually,[40] the Praetors were officers with largely monarchic powers who performed either administrative judicial or military functions.[41] Their periphrastic name was the 'Six Axes'[42] (the *Hexapelekeis* and the *Sexfascales* in Greek and Latin respectively), as they were followed by six Lictors. However, from the 2nd century BC onwards the number of permanent Lictors following them seems to have been reduced down to two.[43] Whereas the powers of Consuls of Rome would come closest to certain of the main supreme powers of the old kings of Rome, it should be stated at this point that the Praetors too, even after the office of Praetors became separated from the office of Consuls, had authority (*imperium*) which was not legally distinct from that of the Consuls.[44]

[33] RW Mathisen, *Ancient Roman Civilization: History and Sources* (Oxford University Press 2019) 134.
[34] Ibid.
[35] E.g. D Hoyos, *Rome Victorious: The Irresistible Rise of the Roman Empire* (Bloomsbury Academic 2019, reprinted 2023) 12.
[36] Powers in the place of a Consul, that is.
[37] Hoyos (n 35) 12.
[38] Mathisen (n 33) 134.
[39] Ibid.
[40] Cf. Brennan (n 23) 1, 29; FK Drogula, *Commanders & Command in the Roman Republic and Early Empire* (University of North Carolina Press 2015) 41, 188–9.
[41] Zoch (n 10) 35.
[42] Brennan (n 1) 1, 34, 52.
[43] Brennan (n 1) 54.
[44] Drogula (n 40) 192.

However, when it came to their jurisdiction,[45] it would seem that this was somewhat autonomous to that of the Consuls despite the fact that one could still launch an appeal against them to a Consul or the Tribunes. Equally, their lower status to Consuls was symbolised by the fact that each Praetor would traditionally be followed by 6 Lictors, unlike Consuls who would, of course, be followed by 12 Lictors[46] each.

Moreover, the *imperium* of the Praetors was lesser than the *imperium* of the Consuls.[47] Apparently, however, the traditional office of the praetor was one with military characteristics *inter alia* and 'virtually identical in authority and capacity to the consulship'[48] (hence the monarchic and military essence of the Praetorship). One of the key functions of Praetors was that they could also be the governors of provinces. Former Consuls and former Praetors would normally be used in the running of provinces.[49] Special forms of Praetors were the Urban Praetor (*Praetor Urbanus*) and the Peregrine Praetor (*Praetor Peregrinus*). The former was responsible for the administration of justice[50] and private law cases in Rome, whilst the latter heard cases relating to foreigners.[51] The institutionalisation of praetors occurred in 366 BC, the first Plebeian Praetor otherwise assuming office in 337 BC.[52] Of course, the opening of the institution to Plebeians would not make it less monarchic in its outlook or its functions than was originally conceived. The particular institution thus remained a largely monarchic one in its fundamental characteristics despite its opening to commoners. Up until 242 BC the Roman Republic had a single Praetor. After this year, a second Praetor was instituted so that the judicial workload of Rome's other Praetor would be lightened.[53] In 228 BC the number of Praetors reached four,[54] while their number was increased to six after 197 BC.[55] In the Late Republic, with Sulla's reforms, post his dictatorship, the number of Praetors increased to eight.[56] Praetors were elected by the Centuriate Assembly.[57]

45 Lintott (n 16) 18.
46 Zoch (n 10) 33; Brennan (n 1) 50.
47 TC Brennan, 'Power and Process under the Republican "Constitution"' in HI Flower (ed), *The Cambridge Companion to the Roman Republic* (2nd edn, Cambridge University Press 2014) 27.
48 Drogula (n 40) 184.
49 Kamm (n 24) 16.
50 E.g. Zoch (n 10) 35.
51 Mathisen (n 33) 87.
52 Kamm (n 24) 16; Mathisen (n 33) 86. Mitchell gives a 336 BC date: Mitchell (n 30) 14.
53 IE Τζαμτζής, *Ο Μεσογειακός Κόσμος* (Εκδόσεις Σάκκουλα 2014, ανατύπωση 2018) 92.
54 Brennan (n 47) 27.
55 Brennan (n 47) 27; Brennan (n 1) 34.
56 Τζαμτζής (n 53) 92.
57 E.g. Hoyos (n 35) 9.

10.6 THE PROPRAETORS

In 327 BC the office of the Propraetors was generated.[58] These Roman officers with *imperium* and of monarchic outlook in their operations were extended their praetorial powers for a year through the process of prorogation[59] and acted *pro praetore*, that is in the place of a Praetor.[60] The office developed over time and from 197 BC onwards the Propraetors could regularly be conferred the *imperium* of a Consul (i.e. in operations beyond Rome).[61]

10.7 THE SUPREME PONTIFF (*PONTIFEX MAXIMUS*)

Presiding over the College of Pontiffs, Rome's top religious collective body, was the *Pontifex Maximus*.[62] Despite the fact that the key functions of the Supreme Pontiff were mainly religious and ceremonial, he also had powers over public moral order. Additionally, the Supreme Pontiff also had 'disciplinary powers over the priestly classes'.[63] A Supreme Pontiff was appointed for life.[64] Somewhat revealing of the fact that this was a religious magistrate of monarchic essence was the fact that the state-owned house in which he resided would be called the 'Regia'.[65] The office of the Supreme Pontiff and other religious offices would otherwise open to Plebeians in 300 BC.[66] Finally, the monarchic character of the office of the Supreme Pontiff can be attested from the fact that in old Latium there seems to have been an office of priest-kings.[67] In that the Supreme Pontiff was Rome's head of state religion,[68] a comparable office to Rome's Supreme Pontiff was an old monarchic remnant in the Athenian Democracy, the *Archon Basileus*, but the possibility of that Athenian office being comparable to Rome's *Rex Sacrorum*[69] cannot be excluded. The *Rex Sacrorum* was an office of monarchic essence that fell into disuse by the end of the Republic: it may have ranked as a religious office higher than that of the Supreme Pontiff, as would the Priests of Jupiter, Mars and Quirinus,[70] but it would seem that the Supreme Pontiff would appoint the *Rex Sacrorum* in the first place.[71]

58 Brennan (n 47) 28.
59 Ibid.
60 Ibid.
61 Ibid.
62 Capogrossi Colognesi (n 13) 29.
63 Kamm (n 24) 13.
64 Capogrossi Colognesi (n 13) 29.
65 E.g. Zoch (n 10) 39.
66 Mitchell (n 30) 14.
67 Capogrossi Colognesi (n 13) 17, 18.
68 E.g. Brennan (n 1) 26, 78.
69 The *rex sacrorum* seems to have been a regal institutional remnant in the years of the Republic: Capogrossi Colognesi (n 13) 72.
70 E.g. G Forsythe, *A Critical History of Early Rome* (University of California Press 2006) 136, citing Festus, 198L s.v. *ordo sacerdotum*.
71 E.g. Liv. 40 42.

10.8 THE CENSORS

A further institution of monarchic essence was that of the Censors, first formally instituted in 444/443 BC[72] in the form of a dyarchy, as in the case of the Consuls. The two Censors held registrar functions and also acted as financial and tax officers.[73] Their most important function was the census.[74] To protect Rome's morality (*regimen morum*)[75] by supervising compliance and respect for the customs of the ancestors (*mores maiorum*), even within Roman households,[76] was their second most important function. However, the morality of women was excluded from a censor's sanctioning,[77] and women's morality was reserved for their fathers and husbands to supervise.[78] As in the case of Consuls, the Censors could veto one another. However, except for this limitation in their role, they would not be subject to any other Roman officer's *intercessio*.[79] Furthermore, they would be directly responsible for inspecting public works and would set guidelines for Rome's public morality.[80] Due to the nature of their role, they could, of course, directly reproach members of the Senate for their actions or inactions through the so-called *nota censoria* (censorial mark)[81]. In this respect, their powers would extend to powers of removal of members of the Senate, especially if they felt that the morality of individual Senators was not up to standard.[82] The censorial mark, whether on Senators or any other free Roman male citizens, would signify stigma, loss of honour, a tarnished name (*ignominia*)[83] and potential further sanctioning.[84] The office of Censors opened to Plebeians in 351 BC.[85] From 318 BC the Censors would also make the list of Senators.[86] The Censor was the most prestigious ordinary office

[72] Cf. Mitchell (n 30) 21, Lintott (n 16) 35 and W Kunkel and R Wittmann, *Staasordnung und Staatspraxis der römischen Republik: Die Magistratur* (C.H. Beck 1995) 391. They state that the first censors were elected in 443 BC. Also, Capogrossi Colognesi (n 13) 78 who gives a 442 BC date. Others put the institution of the office as late as 366 BC: see A Tarwacka, *The Censors as Guardians of Public and Family Life in the Roman Republic* (Routledge 2025) 10–11 for a review of dates.

[73] Kamm (n 24) 14.

[74] Tarwacka (n 72) 90.

[75] E.g. AE Astin, 'Regimen Morum' (1988) 87 *The Journal of Roman Studies* 14–34; Tarwacka (n 72) 8.

[76] On comparing the Athenian and Spartan approaches in such matters with that of Rome, see D.H. 20.13.2–3.

[77] Tarwacka (n 72) 106.

[78] Tarwacka (n 72) 106–7.

[79] Τζαμτζής (n 53) 93.

[80] Kamm (n 24) 14.

[81] Τζαμτζής (n 53) 93.

[82] Capogrossi Colognesi (n 13) 79.

[83] Tarwacka (n 72) 7.

[84] Tarwacka (n 72) 210.

[85] Mitchell (n 30) 14; Mathisen (n 33) 86. But cf. Lintott (n 16) 37. Lintott states that in 339 BC Publilius Philo, who was a Plebeian Dictator, brought a law into effect allowing Plebeians to become Censors.

[86] Tarwacka (n 72) 90.

in the Roman Republic, ranking even higher than that of Consuls[87] but, equally, it was not included in the ordinary *cursus honorum*.[88] In the Republic, only the extraordinary office of the Dictator held a higher status than the ordinary office of the Censors. Coming initially, up until 434 BC, with a five-year term, their term in office would thereafter extend to a maximum of eighteen months,[89] when no executive office in Rome would normally come with a term greater than a year.[90] Re-election to the office of Censor was not possible[91] and, despite the Censors' powerful position in the Republic, they had no *imperium*[92] and no Lictors escorted them.[93] Therefore, unlike Consuls and Praetors, who had *imperium*, Censors were magistrates *sine imperio* (without *imperium*).[94] Their powers instead took the form of *potestas*.[95] And yet the two Censors, as leading magistrates, offered systemic stability to the Republic.[96] Elections for Censors[97] took place once every five years[98] and they were elected by the Centuriate Assembly.

10.9 THE DICTATOR

Of clear monarchic essence in republican Rome was the office of the Dictator. This was an extraordinary office[99] and was the Republic's traditional 'wild card' to situations of great need and emergency, the Roman Dictator being a man of more-than-considerable-but-not-necessarily-wholly-absolute[100] powers who would be called to 'turn the Republic's ship around'. The Republic's era commenced in 509 BC and it seems that the Republic's first appointed dictator was Larcius who took office as Dictator either in 501 or in 498 BC (rather than a second person named Valerius by Livy).[101] Dictators could act in an authoritarian way even within the city of Rome, although opinion is divided as to the rationale behind this.[102] The office of the Dictator, when invoked, was in constitutional

87 Capogrossi Colognesi (n 13) 80.
88 Τζαμτζής (n 53) 93; Tarwacka (n 72) 7.
89 E.g. Zoch (n 10) 35; cf. Tarwacka (n 72) 12, 14, 208.
90 WV Harris, 'Power' in A Barchiesi and W Scheidel (eds), *The Oxford Handbook of Roman Studies* (Oxford University Press 2010) 570.
91 Τζαμτζής (n 53) 93; Tarwacka (n 72) 7.
92 Zoch (n 10) 34.
93 E.g. Tarwacka (n 72) 20.
94 Τζαμτζής (n 53) 93; Tarwacka (n 72) 8.
95 Ibid.
96 Tarwacka (n 72) 7, 208.
97 E.g. Hoyos (n 35) 14.
98 Capogrossi Colognesi (n 13) 80; Τζαμτζής (n 53) 93.
99 Kunkel and R Wittmann (n 72) 666.
100 Cf. M Wilson, *Dictator: The Evolution of the Roman Dictatorship* (University of Michigan Press 2021) 87.
101 RT Ridley, 'The Origin of the Roman Dictatorship: An Overlooked Opinion' (1979) 122 *Rheinisches Museum für Philologie* 303, 303.
102 Lintott (n 16) 18, citing Dionysius of Halicarnassus (Ar 5, 707) emphasising the point that a dictator was an officer who would repress civil unrest, Cicero (Rep. 1. 63, 2.56) stating that his job was

terms 'a [temporary and brief] restoration of the old Roman kingship'[103] during the times of the Republic but the use of this office did not alter the constitutional form of the Republic, in that the Republic itself would name a Dictator and tolerate such an extraordinary office for limited periods of time only. This was Rome's office of what the Greeks called an *αἱρετὴ τυραννίς*,[104] an elective tyranny,[105] or the office of the *Aisymnetai* (*Αἰσυμνῆται*),[106] extraordinary magistrates of extraordinary powers normally for definite[107] terms. The overall purview of the Dictator was that of a Consul,[108] only that he would act largely unchecked and on his own. One did not have to be a former Consul to be appointed as Dictator.[109] However, in the Republic's history most of the Dictators were former Consuls or Consular Tribunes.[110] As stated, when it was used, the office of the Dictator seems to have been largely unchecked. However, after 300 BC the right to veto or appeal a dictatorial decision seems to have been won.[111] The Dictator would also be called *Praetor Maximus*[112] (Supreme Magistrate of the Republic) or *Magister Populi*[113] (Master of the People or Master of the Army[114] so that his office would be distinguishable from the office of his lieutenant officer, the *Magister Equitum* (Master of the Cavalry)).

In any case, for the dictatorial card to be played on the Roman Republic's constitutional table, the appointment of a Dictator by a single Consul would suffice.[115] The Senate could be involved in the process of appointing a Dictator but its involvement does not seem to have been strictly necessary.[116] However, a law by the Centuriate Assembly was issued for a Dictator's proper and full installation in the Republic's top office in extraordinary times, normally up until the point that the nominating-of the-Dictator Consul's legal term would expire[117] and for a maximum term of six months[118] but it is not perfectly clear whether this six months term was always or occasionally upheld even in the period before the

to provide a single commander in war times and Livy (2.18 ff) who thought that the office of the dictator was there to inspire fear in the Plebeians.

103 Hoyos (n 35) 13.

104 D.H. 5.73.3.

105 Wilson translates this form of tyranny as a 'chosen' form of tyranny: Wilson (n 100) 265.

106 Aristot. Pol. 3.1285a; D.H. 5.73.3 citing Threophrastus.

107 D.H. 5.73.3. But cf. Aristot. Pol. 3.1285a where it is stated that certain *Aisymnetai* would hold office for life, when other office-holders of the kind would hold office only for fixed periods of time.

108 Wilson (n 100) 87.

109 Wilson (n 100) 101.

110 Ibid.

111 Zoch (n 10) 34. Cf. L Capogrossi Colognesi (n 13) 75.

112 Liv. 7 3 [5].

113 Ridley (n 101) 303, 303.

114 E.g. T Mommsen, *The History of Rome*, vol 1 (W Purdie Dickson (tr), Macmillan & Co. 1901) 325.

115 Wilson (n 100) 6, 95, 100, 124; Pina Polo (n 27) 188.

116 Wilson (n 100) 6, 71, 103–4, 107, 108, 111–19, 120, 127, 130, 131, 137, 139, 144, 153. But cf. Pina Polo (n 27) 188, arguing that 'the designation of a dictator was always decided by the senate'.

117 Mommsen (n 114) 325.

118 Mommsen (n 114) 325; Zoch (n 10) 34.

Late Republic. It is to be noted that in the Late Republic the term of office of the Dictator could span to years.

The Dictator would not, technically speaking, extinguish the *imperium* of other Roman magistrates; yet the actions of other magistrates would be subject to the Dictator's will. For instance, the Consuls too, if and when a Dictator were appointed, would succumb to his will and could not veto him, especially considering that one of the two Consuls would have nominated the Dictator in the first place.[119] Also, unlike the Consuls who would have to co-ordinate with other magistrates, the Dictator was under no such obligation.[120] Furthermore, the Dictator's *imperium* would be greater than the *imperium* of the Consuls.[121] It is also the case that, unlike Consuls, who were followed by 12 Lictors each, the Dictator was followed by 24 Lictors.[122] There is powerful symbolism behind this: whereas in the Roman mind the Consuls were the highest and most prestigious office in times of civil peace, the Dictator was actually in extraordinary times, times of military emergency and civil unrest, the most powerful out of the two offices, effectively assuming and exercising the powers of both Consuls. The Dictator's authority would, thus, be tantamount to the combined authority of the two Consuls: Rome was run by two Consuls in times of civil peace or by one Dictator in times of great civil unrest and military emergencies. Polybius informs us that the Dictator, unlike the Consuls, was followed by 24 Lictors.[123] The position that the Dictator was followed by 12 Lictors within *pomoerium* but 24 Lictors outside *pomoerium* has also been raised and seems rather reasonable so that the Polybian approach and a later approach maintained in the bibliography could be reconciled.[124]

As stated, it is not perfectly clear whether the office of the Dictator was normally limited to a standard six-month period.[125] It would be ideal if it did. The hypothetical six months' duration of the office would otherwise seem to reflect the six-month notional length of a military campaign.[126] The Dictator's office was used quite frequently in the Early Republic, especially in the 4th century BC.[127] The office, however, was excessively used during the Second Punic War, which led the Romans to use it less for many decades after 201 BC.[128] While the office was merely constitutionally overused during this specific timeframe of the Middle Republic, the office came to be constitutionally abused in the Late Republic.

119 E.g. Brennan (n 1) 21.

120 EA Posner, 'The Constitution of the Roman Republic' in G Dari-Mattiacci and DP Kehoe (eds), *Roman Law and Economics: Institutions and Organizations Volume I* (Oxford University Press 2020) 43.

121 Kunkel and Wittmann (n 72) 665; Capogrossi Colognesi (n 13) 75.

122 E.g. Zoch (n 10) 34.

123 Plb. 3.87.7–8. Also, D.H. 10.24; Plut. Fab. 4.2. Cf. App. BC 1.11.100; Dion. Cass. 54.1.3.

124 Brennan (n 1) 20.

125 But cf. TJ Cornell, *The Beginnings of Rome: Italy and Rome from the Bronze Age to the Punic Wars (c. 1000–264 BC)* (Routledge 1995) 227, Zoch (n 10) 34, Capogrossi Colognesi (n 13) 75 and Mathisen (n 33) 80, all four of them stating that the office was limited to six months.

126 Capogrossi Colognesi (n 13) 75; Brennan (n 1) 20.

127 Brennan (n 1) 20.

128 Ibid.

For instance, the office clearly deteriorated into an absolutist type of office in and during Sulla's dictatorship and, of course, the same has been the case in the times of Julius Caesar, when he declared himself *dictator perpetuo* (dictator in perpetuity) in 44 BC: he was assassinated by certain Senators a few months after he did so. Prior to this, Julius Caesar was already Dictator for at least four years.

Finally, the first Plebeian Dictator was appointed in 356 BC,[129] whilst the more absolute version of the Dictator's office (as in his powers not being subject to veto or appeal) came to an end in 300 BC. The moderated version of the Dictator's office lasted until 82/81 BC, when Sulla not only assumed the office as constitutional and legislative dictator but also acquired the office without a set limit to his term, even though his term as dictator practically came to an end in 80/79 BC. The absolute office of Dictator would be re-enacted by Julius Caesar on at least four occasions between 49 and 44 BC, this being both a cause and a symptom behind the collapse of the Roman Republic and it would be no coincidence that many of the best years of the Republic were years in which the moderated version of the office of the Dictator operated. One could argue that simply because Rome was undergoing highly turbulent times after 133 BC, the office of the absolute Dictator became necessary. Equally, one could certainly *a contrario* argue that Rome's Republic was already in a terminal state and even the re-enactment of the more absolute version of the office of the Dictator would not reverse the Republic's fortunes. In fact, the opposite seems to have been the case: the re-enactment of the absolute office of the Dictator eventually added pressure to the Republic, such pressure being yet another cause of its eventual demise in 27 BC.

10.10 THE MASTER OF THE CAVALRY

The deputy officer of a Dictator would be the Master of the Cavalry (*Magister Equitum*),[130] another office of monarchic essence. As the name of this office suggests, the Master of the Cavalry was the head of Rome's cavalry and held *imperium*.[131] He was guarded and followed by six Lictors.[132]

10.11 THE INTERREX

In the absence of Consuls, Praetors or Consuls in office, a caretaker governor[133] of the Republic was normally temporarily appointed: the Interrex. This extraordinary office[134] existed in the years of the Monarchy but continued with the same

[129] Lintott (n 16) 37; Mathisen (n 33) 86. Mitchell gives a 357 BC date: Mitchell (n 30) 14.
[130] Mommsen (n 114) 325–6.
[131] Zoch (n 10) 34.
[132] But cf. Zoch (n 10) 34 stating that the Master of the Cavalry was followed by twelve Lictors.
[133] E.g. Mitchell (n 30) 26.
[134] A Koptev, 'The Five-Day Interregnum in the Roman Republic' (2016) 66 *The Classical Quarterly* 205, 205, 212.

name and the same functions in the years of the Republic.[135] The period in which this caretaker official, the Interrex, exercised his authority was called *interregnum*. The Interrex was a Patrician Senator[136] with largely monarchic powers. He was responsible for the restoration of power and the normal handover of such to the newly elected magistrates. As stated, the office of the Interrex seems to have existed in Rome's regal times too. For instance, after Romulus died, an Interrex, in the form of a Senator, was responsible for running Rome for five days[137] and then passed the *interregnum* to another Senator[138] until the next king was finally and formally appointed. Rome's first *interregnum* allegedly lasted for one year up until the enthronement of Numa Pompilius, Rome's second king.

10.12 THE AEDILES

These were mid-rank officials who supervised public works, religious buildings, markets and public spectacles.[139] Additionally, they had agoranomic and road traffic overseeing functions: for example, they could supervise weight and measurements, fine traders for breaking the law, supervise road traffic regulation, and so on.[140] Amongst other duties, they were responsible for the supply of wheat and potable water to Rome and the running of public games in the city such as *ludi Romani* and *ludi plebei*.[141] They were four after 366 BC, two of whom were Plebeians. The additional two Aediles, post 366 BC reform, would be called Curules.[142] Aediles per se were elected by the Plebeian Council, whereas Curules (Curule Aediles) were elected by the Tribal Assembly.[143] The powers of the Aediles were of monarchic essence, albeit of lesser significance than the powers of other officials of republican Rome. Finally, whereas the functions of Plebeian Aediles were similar to those of Curule Aediles, the former did not hold *imperium* but the latter did.

10.13 THE QUAESTORS

These were relatively low-rank officials assisting other Roman magistrates, especially the Consuls.[144] Of Western Mediterranean Dorian Greek origin,[145] the

135 Crawford (n 31) 22.
136 Mouritzen (n 19) 23.
137 Zoch (n 10) 15.
138 Ibid.
139 Kamm (n 24) 16.
140 E.g. Zoch (n 10) 36.
141 Τζαμτζής (n 53) 94.
142 Ibid.
143 Ibid.
144 E.g. Pina Polo (n 27) 3.
145 E.g. F Pina Polo and A Díaz Fernández, *The Quaestorship in the Roman Republic* (De Gruyter 2019) 9. Cf. K Latte, 'The Origin of the Roman Quaestorship' (1936) 67 *Transactions and Proceedings of the American Philological Association* 24, 28.

Roman office of Quaestors (searchers)[146] has been an imitation[147] of the Greek office of *Mastroi/Masteres* (*μαστροί/μαστῆρες*), acting as treasurers[148] and official investigators/administrators of financial matters eventually (*quaestores aerarii*) in the Republic. The classic office of *quaestores aerarii* ought to be distinguished from the older office of *quaestores parricidii*, the latter office having had semi-judicial investigatory functions. The office of Quaestors was instituted in 446 BC;[149] it opened to Plebeians in 421 BC[150] and it was in 409 BC that the first Plebeians were elected to the particular office.[151] After 80 BC, if one became a Quaestor, one would also automatically become a Senator.[152] The powers of Quaestors could be largely described as monarchic, in that not only would they promote the monarchic office of Consuls but they would also hold a certain degree of autonomy[153] to take their own decisions. Their main functions were: control the military or be responsible for a civic treasury (*aerarium*) and keep official records.[154] They numbered four after 421 BC, eight after 267 BC and twenty from Sulla's reforms onwards.[155] In the years of Julius Caesar, their number increased to forty.[156] As stated, Quaestors could also serve administrative military or military functions: during war, they 'had the duty of paying the troops and procuring supplies for the general. During the battle itself, the [Q]uaestor might command a wing of the cavalry'.[157] Finally, Proquaestors were magistrates who acted in place of Quaestors.

146 Latte (n 145) 29.
147 Latte (n 145) 33.
148 Latte (n 145) 28.
149 Lintott (n 16) 35; cf. Pina Polo and Díaz Fernández (n 145) 41, 65, giving respectively a 447 BC and a 446 BC date and 76 where both dates are given.
150 Pina Polo and Díaz Fernández (n 145) 50.
151 Pina Polo and Díaz Fernández (n 145) 46, 76.
152 Zoch (n 10) 35.
153 Pina Polo and Díaz Fernández (n 145) 52.
154 Kamm (n 24) 16.
155 Kamm (n 24) 16.
156 Τζαμτζής (n 53) 94.
157 Zoch (n 10) 35.

Chapter 11

Oligarchic Elements

11.1 INTRODUCTION

The oligarchic elements in the constitution of the Roman Republic such as the Senate, the Curiate Assembly and the College of the Pontiffs are explored, taxonomised and analysed in this chapter. The chapter, in agreement with Aristotelian doctrine, discards the idealised Ciceronian and rather rounded Polybian view that the Senate was an aristocracy, as it was actually more of a closed oligarchic elite of wealthy male Roman individuals, mostly emanating from Rome's Patrician families, the Senators being appointed for life on hereditary privilege and wealth as opposed to them being elected and democratically legitimised.

11.2 THE OLIGARCHIC ESSENCE OF THE ROMAN REPUBLIC

The Roman Republic was characterised by powerful oligarchic elites. This was a republic wherein its monarchic and oligarchic elements traditionally prevailed over its aristocratic and democratic elements.[1] For instance, the Senate, a body with strong oligarchic credentials, was at the centre of the Roman Republic's constitution. Rome's deep state comprised its magistrates; yet the constant core of Rome's deep state was the Senate. The Senate, as we shall see, was neither an aristocracy in the Aristotelian sense, nor an exclusively plutocratic body. In this respect, the main criticism against Polybius' picture of Rome's constitution is the fact that he did not most accurately present it when he could. Thus, he seems to carefully omit from his analysis the fact that the Roman Republic was more of an oligarchy,[2] controlled by the Senate,[3] despite the overall mixed character of the Republic. However, the Senate was a body combining both plutocratic and oligarchic features, thereby coming very close to Aristotle's definition of oligarchy.

The Senate was most powerful in the years of the Republic. The soul of the Republic was not found in the Senate. It was the Senate itself. The Ciceronian and the Polybian views as to the aristocratic essence of the Senate are otherwise

[1] E.g. K Von Fritz, *The Theory of the Mixed Constitution in Antiquity: A Critical Analysis of Polybius' Political Ideas* (Columbia University Press 1954) 133–4; R Seager, 'Polybius' Distortions of the Roman "Constitution": A Simpl(istic) Explanation' in R Gibson and T Harrison (eds), *Polybius and his World. Essays in Memory of F. W. Walbank* (Oxford University Press 2013) 247.

[2] Cf. C Nicolet, *The World of the Citizen in Republican Rome* (PS Falla (tr), University of California 1980) 1.

[3] Seager (n 1) 252.

discarded as rather rounded, idealistic and political. So is the Late Republic's coined term '*optimates*' (which is, of course, the Latin translation of the Greek term 'aristocrats', i.e. the 'best men'). These pro-aristocratic narratives and adjectives were narratives and adjectives that the ruling oligarchic elites of Rome would use for institutions such as the Senate and persons such as the *optimates* to fully justify the otherwise oligarchic tendencies and nature thereof. Calling oneself an aristocrat always sounds better than calling oneself an oligarch. This was the approach taken by Rome's elites.

Another body of oligarchic features in republican Rome was the College of Pontiffs, a religious body of head priests, but its ceremonial and advisory powers would come nowhere near the powers of the Senate, which could be described as the constitutional heart of the Republic. Finally, the Curiate Assembly, a relic of the Roman Monarchy in the years of the Republic, was a body of oligarchic features but its powers came to be significantly reduced in practical terms, as these were eventually taken over by other bodies of the Republic. Also, all of these oligarchic elements were elements that were traditionally made out of Rome's nobles. However, Plebeians too would eventually be allowed to take office in these bodies but the overall composition of such bodies would still be mostly made out of nobles. Additionally, it is to be noted that 'aristocratic equality did not exist even among the nobles'[4].

To make things more interesting, Rome's nobility also comprised wealthy members of the public who would hold leading office, such as a position in the Senate, and members of the public who would be wealthy in themselves such as the *Equites* (knights), who would also make for an upper class of Roman citizens, but would not actually stand for the highest class of Roman citizens, as Patricians would.[5] Rome's division of nobility into sub-classes went as far as ranking Praetorian families lower than Consular families, and so on.[6]

The leading nobles in Rome, as in the majority of Patricians, it has been argued, 'must have [descended from] citizens of Rome by the beginning of the Republic'.[7] These were Rome's old families who effectively steered the Republic, especially through the Senate. For instance, the control of the popular assemblies over the Senate was more theoretical than practical.[8] So strong was the grip of Rome's oligarchic elements and elites on the Republic that even in 'instances of popular sovereignty [these would be] limited to special occasions, and [would be] in any case much undermined by the socio-economic structuring and procedural rules of the popular assemblies'.[9] The roots of the Patricians, as a class of nobles, seem to relate to the appointed-by-the-King council of elder advisers

[4] RE Mitchell, 'The Aristocracy of the Roman Republic' in R Howarth (ed), *Hearsay, History, and Heresy: Collected Essays on the Roman Republic by Richard E. Mitchell* (Gorgias Press 2010) 102.

[5] Cf. Mitchell (n 4) 121–2.

[6] Mitchell (n 4) 121.

[7] Mitchell (n 4) 104.

[8] Seager (n 1) 250.

[9] Seager (n 1) 251.

in the years of the Monarchy, which was something like[10] a senate, before the Republic's Senate.[11] Its composition was made out of the *patres* (the fathers) 'of the most prosperous and powerful *gentes*',[12] *gentes* being groups of relatives (clans) that would claim descent from a common ancestor in the male line. The nobles of the Monarchy (except Rome's last King lineage, the line of the Tarquins, who were expelled from the city) continued to be nobles in the years of the Republic, whilst the Patricians in the years of the Monarchy were also Patricians in the years of the Republic.[13] Equally, it would be a mistake to think that the Patrician families of Rome descended only from the original citizens of Rome or 'that they made up the complete Roman aristocracy [as in Roman nobility]'.[14]

11.3 THE SENATE

For most of its history, the Senate was, in the essence of the matter, an oligarchic body of plutocrats who would normally base their membership in the Senate on hereditary right and privilege. As its name suggests, this was Rome's Council of Elders, a sort of a *Gerousia* Roman style, and one of its key functions was to advise the Consuls.[15] This was Rome's principal policymaking body, its State Council;[16] Rome's politburo, ministry of foreign affairs, finance, religion and defence;[17] comprising mostly Patricians. Practically, this was also the Roman nobility's constant watchdog[18] over the Republic. The Senate did not represent Rome's establishment; it was Rome's establishment. It was effectively the Roman Republic's undisputed constitutional champion for centuries until its demise.[19] It is not perfectly clear how old one ought to be to become a Senator. Once one became a Senator, however, one held office for life, unless removed by a Censor. Removal from a senatorial position was rare and it was the death of Senators that would potentially change their overall number[20] but also initiate the procedure for their replacement.

10 RE Mitchell, *Patricians and Plebeians: The Origin of the Roman State* (Cornell University Press 1990) 17.
11 E.g. Mitchell (n 10) 2, 17.
12 Mitchell (n 4) 104.
13 E.g. Mitchell (n 4) 104.
14 Mitchell (n 4) 105.
15 H Mouritzen, *Politics in the Roman Republic* (Cambridge University Press 2017) 20.
16 T Mommsen, *The History of Rome*, vol 1 (W Purdie Dickson (tr), Macmillan & Co. 1901) 330.
17 Cf. L Capogrossi Colognesi, *Law and Power in the Making of the Roman Commonwealth* (Cambridge University Press 2014) 81.
18 E.g. Mitchell (n 10) 64.
19 K-J Hölkeskamp, *Rekonstruktionen einer Republik: die politische Kultur des antiken Rom und die Forschung der letzten Jahrzehnte* (Oldenbourg Wissenschaftsverlag 2004, reprinted 2014) 34.
20 C Steel, *The End of the Roman Republic, 146 to 44* BC: *Conquest and Crisis* (Edinburgh University Press 2013) 4.

The Senate traditionally enjoyed great respect in Rome.[21] It was Rome's driving political and legal engine, the Roman Republic's guarantor and supervisor. To the Greeks, the Roman Senators resembled an assemblage of kings and Mommsen is illuminating in this, in that the Roman Senators traditionally enjoyed royal powers not in practice but in prerogative within the Roman community.[22] The approval of the Senate (*auctoritas patrum*) of the decisions of Rome's popular assembly seems to have originally (as in the early Republic) been a right[23] of the Patricians and then a requirement[24] on them but this may have eventually become a formality in Rome's republican mixed constitution.[25] Additionally, the Senate was de facto characterised by hereditary[26] and nepocratic tendencies.[27] A hereditary monarchy is, of course, still a monarchy. So too, a fundamentally hereditary oligarchy, as was the Senate, is, of course, still an oligarchy. It is not an aristocracy. Even though Roman nobles (to whom Senators belonged), as the wealthiest citizens of Rome, tended to receive the best education[28] in Rome, the education of the Senators did not quite exactly make Senators an aristocratic body per se, especially by virtue of their collectivity, for the traditional emphasis of membership in the Senate was on hereditary right, wealth[29] and family origin. Indeed, membership to the Senate was by birth or status originally, to the point that only Patricians could become Senators.[30] As such, for most of its history, '[t]he Senate and its magistrates were dominated by the [P]atricians'.[31] Also, in the early Roman Republic, 'the [P]atricians held virtually all the social, political, and economic privileges'.[32] The early Republic seems to have been one wherein 'the [P]atricians held all the political and religious offices [something that] suggests a hereditary system of executive power quite different from the later republican political culture'.[33] As such, in the first century of the Republic there was practically no distinction between the Patriciate and the class of Senators: they were one and the same.[34] From the late 4th century BC 'all citizens might have been eligible [to become Senators] but the poor were, of course, never considered'.[35] It is not perfectly clear when exactly in

21 E.g. D Hoyos, *Rome Victorious: The Irresistible Rise of the Roman Empire* (Bloomsbury Academic 2019, reprinted 2023) 11.
22 Mommsen (n 16) 98–100.
23 Mitchell (n 4) 135.
24 Ibid.
25 Mouritzen (n 15) 20.
26 E.g. Mouritzen (n 15) 21.
27 Cf. F Millar, *The Roman Republic in Political Thought* (University Press of New England 2002) 170.
28 Mitchell (n 4) 101–2.
29 Cf. Capogrossi Colognesi (n 17) 40.
30 E.g. RW Mathisen, *Ancient Roman Civilization: History and Sources* (Oxford University Press 2019) 80. But cf. TJ Cornell, *The Beginnings of Rome: Italy and Rome from the Bronze Age to the Punic Wars (c. 1000–264 BC)* (Routledge 1995) 247–51.
31 PA Zoch, *Ancient Rome* (University of Oklahoma Press 1998) 32.
32 Mathisen (n 30) 81. Cf. Mitchell (n 4) 105–6.
33 HI Flower, *Roman Republics* (Princeton University Press 2010) 24.
34 L Capogrossi Colognesi (n 17) 81.
35 Mouritzen (n 15) 36.

the years of the Roman Republic magistratorial experience would allow a former Roman magistrate to become a member of the Senate by mere virtue of such experience. However, from 318 BC (or from 313/312 BC), *Lex Ovinia*, or more precisely, the *Plebiscitum Ovinium*, made it preferable for Censors to appoint magistrates, Aediles and Curules to the Senate; up until that point Censors had perfect discretion on who to appoint in the Senate.[36] However, this does not affect the argument that the Senate was an oligarchic body, in that the Roman magistrates, for most intents and purposes and for most of the Republic's history, came from the higher classes and the wealthier families of Rome.

However, a paradox occurred with the fall of the Roman monarchy: those who opposed the hereditary character of the last three Kings of Rome, the Patricians, continued to base their membership to the Senate on hereditary right.[37] Thus, the Senate in the years of the Republic was mainly composed of members of the old noble families of Rome. The Senate not only retained its previous powers under the Monarchy but it actually extended them with the rise of the Republic.[38] The Senate's oligarchic credentials were already re-emphasised at the very beginning of the Republic, that is from the establishment of the Republic in 509 BC until 494 BC, when the Senate would be the sole governing body of Rome. Thus, for the period of the first fifteen years after the abolition of monarchy, the Republic was controlled by the Senate only, comprising Patricians only. It is opined that the rise of the Republic and the sole governing role of the Senate in the first years of the Republic was (i) a reaction to the last three hereditary Kings of Rome who practically disregarded the Senate's initial power to appoint the King of Rome;[39] (ii) a reaction to the fact that for more than a 100 years (616–509 BC) Etruscan or Greek kings would govern Rome, when the Senate would actually better represent the Latin, Sabine and Etruscan patrician families of Rome and elements of Roman society;[40] and (iii) a reaction altogether to the absolute and tyrannical rule of the final stages of the monarchy.

The alleged rape of Lucretia by Tarquin, if Lucretia ever existed,[41] must have been but an excuse to overthrow the monarchy, as the alleged abduction of Helen by Paris was but an excuse for the Greeks to attack and eventually conquer and

[36] IE Τζαμτζής, *Ο Μεσογειακός Κόσμος* (Εκδόσεις Σάκκουλα 2014, ανατύπωση 2018) 97–8.

[37] There is controversy, however, as to whether the class of Patricians was existent in the years of the Roman Monarchy or whether such class actually arose in the very early stages of the Republic. See e.g. Mathisen (n 30) 81.

[38] Mommsen (n 16) 329.

[39] FF Abbott, *A History and Description of Roman Political Institutions* (Ginn & Company 1901, rev. edn 1907) 10.

[40] Cf. Cornell (n 30) 114, citing P Willems, *Le sénat de la république romaine* I (Louvain 1885) 22; G Devoto, *Atheneum* 31 (1953), 335–43; U von Lübtow, *Das römische Volk* (Frankfurt 1955) 39–40; and A Bernardi, *Nomen Latinum* (Pavia 1973) 17–18. On the three ancient tribes of Rome and how such defined the Roman *populus*, see also Mathisen (n 30) 80. Both Cornell and Mathisen coincide in stating that the Roman people were made out of three tribes: Ramnes (descending from Romulus), Tities (descending from Titius Tatius) and Luceres (from Etruscan *lucumo*).

[41] M Beard, *SPQR: A History of Ancient Rome* (Liveright Publishing 2015) 121.

destroy Troy. Nonetheless, the causes of resentment against the monarchy must have been running deep into the minds and the veins of the Roman oligarchic elites in the 7th and 6th centuries BC. To the Roman mind, a few leaders would be better than one leader. A powerful senate, as in the Senate in the years of the Republic, would be better geared towards the running of Rome than a despotic and tyrannical King would be. Beyond this, with regard to the Senate's initial composition, Livy informs us that the first 100 Senators in the times of the Roman Kingdom were the progenitors of Patrician families.[42] As a body, it does not seem to have exceeded 300 Senators in the years of the Republic up until 81 BC, when Sulla increased the number of Senators to 600.[43] As stated, a Senator would normally hold office for life, unless removed.[44] In the years of the Monarchy the appointment of senators would be made by the King himself. Appointments to the Senate during the years of the Republic were initially made by the Consuls, whilst after 350 BC or after 312 BC, depending on one's sources, it would be the Censors who would appoint senators.[45] However, the Senate was a largely oligarchic body even in the Middle and the Late Republic, as it would still predominantly comprise oligarchic Patricians,[46] albeit with important distinctions within their class now (*gentes maiores*, *nobiles* and knights).[47] For instance, the politics of the Late Republic have been described as 'a conflict between a dominant oligarchy drawn from a set of powerful families, and their opponents; … the senate [was] governed by virtue of its *auctoritas* and was ruled by a clique of *nobiles* … who also controlled access to the consulate'.[48]

One could, of course, argue that the Senate was an aristocracy, as Polybius did,[49] but it was not an aristocracy *stricto sensu*, at least not in the original Greek Platonic-Aristotelian sense of the word, as in the rule of the best.[50] The Platonic-Aristotelian perception of aristocracy would come much closer to what people in the English-speaking world would call a system of meritocracy, even though

42 Liv. 1 8.

43 Τζαμτζής (n 36) 98.

44 Ibid.

45 A Kamm, *The Romans* (Routledge 2006) 16; Mitchell (n 4) 133. The former author gives an approximate 350 BC date, whilst the latter author gives a 312 BC date, i.e. when it would come to the appointment of Senators by Censors.

46 Cf. Steel (n 20) 3, who speaks of censors appointing to the Senate members 'of distinguished families'.

47 N Davies, *Europe: A History* (Pimlico 1996, reprinted with corrections 1997) 165.

48 MA Robb, *Beyond Populares and Optimates: Political Language in the Late Republic* (Franz Steiner Verlag 2010) 19, citing *inter alia* M Gelzer, *Die Nobilität der Römischen Republik* (Berlin 1912) 22–32 and R Syme, *The Roman Revolution* (Oxford 1939) 18.

49 A Lintott, *The Constitution of the Roman Republic* (Clarendon Press 1999) 65.

50 Polybius in *Histories* 6.13.8, who would not always perceive the Republic in strict scientific terms (as in constitutional law terms), chose his words carefully in this part of his work: 'one would imagine the constitution to be a complete aristocracy', the emphasis being on the word 'imagine'. The Greek original text speaks of a constitution that 'looked like' an aristocracy – as opposed to it being an aristocracy ('*ἐξ ὧν πάλιν ὁπότε τις ἐπιδημήσαι μὴ παρόντος ὑπάτου, τελείως ἀριστοκρατικὴ φαίνεθ᾽ ἡ πολιτεία.*')

aristocracy and meritocracy should not be used as perfect synonyms to one another. For Plato and Aristotle, wealth was not quite exactly a condition precedent for someone to become or to be considered to be the best in their field, even though, equally, the offspring of the wealthy could also be considered for being the best in a given field upon merit and merit alone. To take the Roman Republic's Senate as an aristocracy, however, would thus be departing from Platonic-Aristotelian doctrine: at an extreme, it would mean that simply because Patricians formed the overwhelming majority of the Senate, subjectively considering themselves the best element of Roman society, the Senate too was, by extension, aristocratic. However, one could not automatically assume so on the subjective beliefs of Patricians about themselves, for the Senators would occasionally get it wrong or very wrong and would be responsible for certain dramatic twists and turns in the history of the Republic. The Senate was not an aristocracy. In the essence of the matter, it was an oligarchy of plutocrats, originating mostly from the old wealthy families of the Republic. The meaning of aristocracy, as in the rule of the highest classes of society, is a much later one and not one that would be a synonym to the Aristotelian term of 'aristocracy'.[51] It is only if we considered the Patricians the highest class of Roman society (as they clearly were), in the modern sense of the term, that the adjective 'aristocratic' could be a fitting one for the Senate. However, that would be anachronistic, that is we would view the Roman Republic through the lens of the modern term of 'aristocracy' (as opposed to taking the classic Aristotelian view in the matter). As such, the point certainly remains: the Senate was an oligarchy of plutocrats.

According to Aristotelian doctrine, there would be at least two different ways to support the view that the Senate was an oligarchy rather than an aristocracy. First, Aristotle's definition of oligarchy combines the characteristics of both oligarchy *and* plutocracy, these two characteristics being the two key features of Rome's senatorial class. Indeed, the class of Senators would historically first and foremost preserve its own privileges and rights, its own vested interests rather than the interests of Rome *stricto sensu*, even if in theory it was the Senate that was overseeing key aspects of the Republic as a whole. The Senators, in their collectivity, the Senate as an institution, were thus more of an oligarchy than an aristocracy per se, even if we went as far as suggesting that the best citizens of Rome, by upbringing, would be its senators; even if we went as far as suggesting that the main interests of the Patrician class represented the main interests of Rome. The prevalent characteristics of a Roman Senator would be his wealth and the fact that he would, much more often than not, belong to the limited class of Patricians, the interests of whom he would have to uphold. Yet under the Aristotelian typology of constitutions, a body such as the Senate would stand for an oligarchy rather than an aristocracy, for aristocracy is first and foremost about the common good of a given society. The powerful interests, which the senatorial class would preserve (its own interests primarily included), would thus make the Senate more of an

[51] Millar (n 27), 170.

oligarchy than an aristocracy in the Aristotelian sense.[52] Of course, such were the interests of the powerful Patricians and, by extension, the interests of Senators, that the interests of the Republic would largely coincide with the interests of the Patricians and the Senators (and vice versa). In this respect, one is reminded that the Patricians controlled most of Rome's wealth and resources and, by extension, their vested interests in Rome and its republic practically represented most of Rome's interests in absolute terms. To perceive the Senate as an aristocratic body, however, would be either naïve at worst or idealistic at best.[53] Cicero's positioning of the Senate into aristocracy can thus be discredited as an idealistic approach, if not a biased one, considering that he himself was a cog of the Roman constitutional engine and establishment. As for Polybius, one can reasonably assume that his attempt to somewhat misrepresent[54] the constitution of the Roman Republic was deliberate,[55] in attempting to minimise 'the predominance of the senate over magistrates and people'.[56] He seems to have done so, as he considered the Roman Republic's mixed constitutional characteristics as acting as a sort of constitutional brakes to Rome's democratic elements and masses, Polybius not exactly being a great friend of democracy in Athens and Thebes.[57] More interestingly, his work might have been designed in such a way so that his Roman supervisors would use it as a justificatory point of reference for controlling Rome's masses. Even more interestingly, it has also been argued that Polybius may have drafted his work in the way he did because he was trying to explain to his fellow Greeks the 'savagely unfathomable monster [that Rome was, a monster] that had come out of the west and turned their world upside down'.[58] Thus, his idealisation of the Roman constitution, a constitution that allowed Rome to rise to the status of an empire according to him, was an indirect reminder to his fellow Greeks that Rome was the superior partner now in the relationship between Greece and Rome, and that Rome had to be respected.

This brings us to our second point as to how a body such as the Roman Senate would be deemed an oligarchy rather than an aristocracy under Aristotelian doctrine: Aristotle, particularly wary of the term *ὀλιγαρχία*, alerts us also to the fact that the few tend to be the rich and the many [in Rome these were the Plebeians] tend to be the poor,[59] so much so that 'wherever the rulers owe their power to wealth, whether they be a minority or a majority, this is an oligarchy, and when the poor rule, it is a democracy'.[60] For Aristotle, oligarchy stands for an oligarchy of

[52] For more, see Aristotle's *Politics* II, III and IV.
[53] Cf. Millar (n 27) 51–2.
[54] Seager (n 1) 254.
[55] Seager (n 1) 248–9.
[56] Seager (n 1) 252.
[57] Seager (n 1) 252–3.
[58] Seager (n 1) 254.
[59] Aristot. Pol. 3.1279b.
[60] Aristot. Pol. 3.1280a.

wealthy individuals[61] looking after their own interests, as exactly was the case with the overwhelming majority of Roman Senators. As Winters successfully argued, '[for ancient Greek philosophy] oligarchy always refers to the nexus between wealth and power'.[62]

The Senate was by all means a body with extensive explicit and expansive implicit powers. Peculiarly but purposefully, it was a religious body too and its high moral standing would be signified by theoretical ethical authority, its *auctoritas*.[63] Moreover, whereas the Roman Republic did not have a codified constitution, the Senate effectively was Rome's constitutional heart in the years of the Republic. '[T]he Senate was the focal point of intersection where [Roman] institutions and conventions met, where conventions were adapted to situations, and where decisions were made about how to use the fixed institutions according to changing conventions.'[64] No other body, no person in Rome, not even the people of Rome, would actually enjoy the degree of power that the Senate would enjoy. And yet, remarkably, the Senate, despite its strong oligarchic nature, represented 'the Roman community's collected political wisdom'.[65] Over the centuries, it would somewhat change in its composition and membership but, as will be seen, this was a conservative political body that would occasionally base its decisions 'on the ways of the ancestors' (or, at least, on what it would perceive as the ways of the ancestors). Changes would be brought to the Senate composition and internal structures, it otherwise remaining intact as the Republic's constitutional engine. From about 275 BC the *princeps senatus* would informally lead the Senate,[66] the office acquiring certain significant procedural powers in the running of the Senate up until 80 BC when Sulla reformed/removed it.

The *princeps senatus*, 'invariably a Patrician',[67] was a person of considerable political and moral gravitas, in that he would have previously held the offices of Consulship and Censorship (i.e. prior to becoming the leader of the Senate).[68] It would seem, however, that, under Sulla's constitution, the office of the *princeps senatus* was removed, the particular official 'shap[ing] debate and mediat[ing] conflicts in earlier times'.[69] Furthermore, despite the Senate's membership being relatively extensive, i.e. it would comprise 300 to 600 Senators in the times of the Republic,[70] this was not exactly a political forum open to all, nor a political forum

[61] Ibid. Also, R Syme, *The Roman Revolution* (Clarendon Press 1939) 10, 17–18.

[62] JA Winters, *Oligarchy* (Cambridge University Press 2011) 27. Cf. Mouritzen (n 15) 9, reminding us that in the Aristotelian worldview oligarchy was 'the rule of the well-to-do'.

[63] Hoyos (n 21) 15.

[64] W Eder, 'Republicans and Sinners: The Decline of the Roman Republic and the End of a Provisional Arrangement' in RW Wallace and EM Harris (eds), *Transitions to Empire: Essays in Greco-Roman History, 360–146 B.C., in Honor of E. Badian* (University of Oklahoma Press 1996) 449.

[65] Zoch (n 31) 37.

[66] FX Ryan, *Rank and Participation in the Republican Senate* (Franz Steiner Verlag 1998) 170.

[67] Steel (n 20) 4.

[68] Τζαμτζής (n 36) 101.

[69] Flower (n 33) 121.

[70] Davies (n 47) 170.

that would represent Patricians and Plebeians proportionately. As a matter of fact, even when the Senate was partially 'democratised' in 444 BC (allowing Plebeians to become Senators), such a reform related to wealthy Plebeians[71] (as opposed to all Plebeians) and so on. One could also consider that the 'opening up' of the Senate to the Plebeians would not make the senate more democratic *stricto sensu*, in that this was invariably an oligarchic-plutocratic body. However, one could argue that the Senate was the core of a new patrician-plebeian plutocracy.[72] Its partial 'democratisation' was more of a plutocratisation, as in wealthy Plebeians being able to become Senators. After all, the class of Senators was a class of proprietors.[73] The senatorial class was a caste apart[74] from the rest of the Roman classes and it could not accept anyone in its ranks. Nor should one neglect the fact that the Senate's powerful oligarchic tendencies would be readily apparent from the fact that the Patrician patrons of Rome could influence their clients to vote in a certain way in Rome's popular assemblies.[75] It was the Patricians (who traditionally comprised the overwhelming majority of the Senators) who tended to influence the masses of Rome in their popular assemblies through *clientela* and not the masses of Rome who affected the Patricians and, by extension, the Senators. An exception here was the pressure that Rome's masses exercised upon a reluctant and divided Senate in 264 BC, when the Senate succumbed to the will of the Roman people to invade Sicily.

In most precise terms, the Senate was an oligarchy of mainly Patricians for most of the Roman Republic's history (as opposed to it being democratised in any sort of significant way or it having a democratic essence to it, unless the acceptance of a limited number of wealthy Plebeians could be taken to amount to a sort of limited democratisation of the particular body). The Senate, thus, stood for an oligarchic body of plutocrats, most of whom were, of course, offspring of noble Roman families. Livy has also indirectly informed us of the fact that, at least from 300 BC, the Roman Republic was clearly one that would support the powerful interests of the few over the many: 'I think that the reason for renewing [this law] so often was solely the fact that the excessive power exercised by a few men was dangerous to the liberties of the plebs'.[76] All in all, the Senatus was mainly supported in the final stages of the Republic by what Cicero would call *Optimates*,[77] 'aristocrats', but one notes here that these *Optimates* were generally drawn from the wealthy circles of the Roman patricians (as opposed to the same persons representing the 'best' parts of Roman society in an objective way in the Aristotelian sense).

71 Mommsen (n 16) 339–40. Cf. Mitchell (n 4) 107: 'At Rome it would always be possible for some non-aristocrats to translate their wealth into social status, influence, and political office'.
72 Cf. Von Fritz (n 1) 208–9, 228.
73 E.g. I Shatzman, *Senatorial Wealth and Politics* (Latomus 1975) 11–46.
74 Shatzman (n 73) 109.
75 Mathisen (n 30) 80.
76 Liv. 10 9 4.
77 Cic. Sest. 45.

The Senate was a not a parliament in the modern sense either, even though it would share certain characteristics of a modern parliament. 'Senators were not elected and had no constituents …'.[78] Rather the Senate would more plausibly be seen as an oligarchic consultative body with interpretative and executive powers that would set the tone of Rome's overall direction in legal and political matters. Lintott rightly suggests that it would make little sense to '[seek] to distinguish between [the Senate's] *de iure* and *de facto* powers'.[79] Equally, the Senate never acquired the characteristics of a supreme legislative body.[80] Polybius must, therefore, have been right at least in this: the Senate was not about sovereignty; it was about management of day-to-day matters in Rome and empire.[81] Indeed, the consultative and directive tone that the Senate would set for Rome's ambitions would become clearest in the case of it managing the actions of Consuls in military operations. The Senate was Rome's strategic mastermind in war matters. The Consuls, on the other hand, were Rome's military heads both in strategic and tactical war matters. Nevertheless, the Senate could even cancel the Consuls' plans by reacting or obstructing them.[82] Interestingly, it would be Consuls who would appoint Senators in the first place, that is up until late 4th century BC. By 100 BC, however, such power had already been enjoyed by the Censors of the Republic for more than 200 years. Furthermore, during *interregna*, in the absence of curule magistrates (consuls, praetors or dictators), the *patres* of the Senate[83] were responsible for the running of the Republic, occasionally together with the *interreges*, caretaker officials, between an old consuls regime and a new consuls regime.

Nor was the Roman Senatus a representative body of elected officials the way a modern senate (e.g. the American Senate after 1913 or the Japanese House of Councillors after 1983) would be. As stated, Roman Senators were appointed, originally by the Consuls and afterwards by the Censors. Indeed, the Senate seems to have started as the Roman King's advisory oligarchic court that would otherwise be appointed by the King himself. The senators would collectively appoint future kings and so on. However, in the later stages of the Monarchy, such a power must have been taken away from them. Generally, to become a Senator one normally needed to have considerable wealth or originate from a Patrician family, even at the more democratic times of the Republic (287–133 BC). Alternatively, even Plebeians could be admitted to it on the basis that they had at least served as high-ranking government officials (magistrates).[84] As such, in the years of the Republic, this originally royal institution (as in one that effectively served as the Roman king's court), the Senate, would have been salvaged, its composition having been made out of Patricians only initially. From the 4th century BC onwards

[78] Zoch (n 31) 37.
[79] Lintott (n 49) 86.
[80] Lintott (n 49) 87.
[81] Lintott (n 49) 65.
[82] Τζαμτζής (n 36) 117, citing Plb. 6.15.
[83] Lintott (n 49) 67.
[84] Kamm (n 45) 16.

it conditionally allowed Plebeians to become Senators. Eventually, all males of political power would be able to become Senators. Thus, in the Senate one could find, aside from Patricians per se, 'former [C]onsuls, [C]ensors, [P]raetors, [T]ribunes, [A]ediles and even [Q]uaestors'.[85]

One could, therefore, certainly argue that the Roman Senate of the Republican period was a sort of indirectly 'elected' plutocratic oligarchy but from a limited pool of wealthy and powerful individuals; as stated, its membership was originally decided by Consuls but after the Ovinian Plebiscite in late 4th century BC by the Censors. The Senate would comprise mostly Patricians originally and after a certain point *ex officio* magistrates too.

The Senate was almost always in the years of the Monarchy and the Republic an exclusive political club: its exclusive character made it a political club controlled by a few hundred wealthy male individuals. 'It was the core of a self-perpetuating élite'.[86] Even when the Senate expanded in numbers, it was still a rather exclusive club: Rome had an empire to run now and the effective powers which the Senators held in their hands were quite considerable, especially considering the vast geopolitical space that Rome would now control. Sulla increased the numbers of the Senators to 600 but he did not do so by opening the Senate further to the Plebeians, but by allowing *Equites* (the class of Roman knights, the second class of nobles in Rome after the Senatorial class) and nobles from other Italian cities.[87] Julius Caesar increased the Senators to 900 but Augustus reduced their number to 600.[88]

Whoever controlled the Roman Senate controlled the Roman Republic.[89] 'In formal terms, it was the popular assemblies which appointed the chief officials, and the officials who appointed the Senate. In reality, it was the Senators who made all the institutions function to their advantage'.[90] Thus, the role of the Roman people was potentially quite significant; so too, elite leadership was always required to articulate the wishes of the public.[91] The Senate also exercised considerable influence on legislative matters in Rome, albeit indirectly. Indeed, the control of the Senate extended to 'both electoral and legislative assemblies'[92] in Rome. It was not Rome's *de jure* legislative engine; it was Rome's *de facto* legislative engine. For instance, Consuls and Tribunes had to receive approval by the Senate prior to putting forward a legislative proposal to an assembly.[93] Furthermore, the Senate would issue decrees (*consulta*) or, let us say, in the more modern sense, come up

85 Zoch (n 31) 37.
86 Davies (n 47) 170.
87 Flower (n 33) 121, 128.
88 Zoch (n 31) 38.
89 Davies (n 47) 170; Mathisen (n 30) 87.
90 Davies (n 47) 170.
91 Steel (n 20) 49.
92 WV Harris, 'Power' in A Barchiesi and W Scheidel (eds), *The Oxford Handbook of Roman Studies* (Oxford University Press 2010) 571.
93 Mathisen (n 30) 87.

with directive guiding resolutions of overall legal nature, which would otherwise be generally obeyed. As such, the Senate would not, technically speaking, create Roman law *stricto sensu*; it would do something more important than that: it would interpret it.[94] It was the guardian of the law rather than its creator.[95] Thus, in formal terms, its *consulta* would not create Roman law. In practical terms, however, its positions about the law, as these were directed to the popular assemblies, would influence the creation and development of Roman law. A related point here would be that the consultative nature of the Senate from the years of the Monarchy was salvaged and strengthened in the Republic. However, the Senate, whilst still a consultative body as a whole, now had considerable legal powers. This was effectively Rome's hidden constitutional law engine. Furthermore, the Senate would not only have a powerful advisory role in relation to the Republic's laws but it would also invalidate legislation.[96] As a matter of fact, it abused its powers in this respect in the Late Republic with catastrophic consequences.[97]

A most interesting moral tool of the Senate with legal connotations to it, however, was the *Senatus Consultum Ultimum*. Using this tool, the Senate would morally authorise the full use of executive powers by certain affected Roman magistrates *and* their disregard of the law for certain designated matters to save the Republic altogether. In modern legal terms, the *Senatus Consultum Ultimum* effectively amounted to emergency legislation that actually authorised its recipients to exercise extraordinary executive powers in perceived challenging times for the Republic. It amounted to a wild political and legal card, if the Republic did not necessarily wish to appoint, through a Consul, a Dictator. This was, thus, not about the effective suspension of the constitution under the leadership of a Consul, which could otherwise occur by way of appointing a Dictator.[98] Rather the *Senatus Consultum Ultimum* was a mechanism activated in times of constitutional emergency, the Senate exercising its quasi-legal powers to authorise certain persons with full executive powers. The *Consultum Ultimum* was normally drafted in general and imprecise terms,[99] the reason being that the details of such would be filled in by the person(s) authorised to act under it.[100] Such a tool would in all probability have been devised in the 2nd century BC. Traditionally, the particular tool was used against the dissidents of the Senate's conservative wing.[101] Highly unfortunate, through the use of the *Senatus Consultum Ultimum*, was the fact that this would arm the hands of the Roman mobs to execute the wishes of the Senate, as in putting to death the Senate's enemies without popular trial, when the law

94 Mathisen (n 30) 87.
95 Mommsen (n 16) 100.
96 M Crawford, *The Roman Republic* (2nd edn, Fontana Press 1992) 26–7, citing Cicero, *de legibus* II, 13–14, cf. 31.
97 Crawford (n 96) 26.
98 Cf. Flower (n 33) 85–6.
99 Cf. Flower (n 33) 86.
100 Lintott (n 49) 87–8.
101 Τζαμτζής (n 36) 100.

expected otherwise.[102] Before Rome started, through the Senate, to use such a type of *consultum*, it normally appointed a Dictator up until 202 BC,[103] the first *consultum ultimum* having been formally used in 121 BC against Gaius Gracchus and Flaccus.[104] However, de facto use of such was first made against the brother of Gaius Gracchus, Tiberius Gracchus, in 133 BC. This was an extraordinary 'constitutional' tool, which has been used a total of thirteen times[105] in the 2nd and the 1st century BC. The frequency of use of such a tool by the Senate, with the parallel rise of dictators in Rome in the 1st century BC, meant that the Republic's old stability would be lost forever.[106] Together with the loss of political and constitutional stability, the Republic would give way to the Principate. The commencement of the use of the particular tool effectively signified the beginning of the end of the Republic, whilst the last time this tool was used was against Julius Caesar.

The Senate also enjoyed certain executive powers. For instance, a lesser known function of the Senate was the power it exercised in controlling how public money was spent.[107] Further senatorial powers included security and the administration of Italy.[108] It was also responsible for Rome's foreign policy.[109] For instance, the orders for the destruction of Carthage in 146 BC came from the Senate itself. We do not have precise historical data as to whether the destruction of Corinth in 146 BC was directly ordered by the Senate but the initial deployment of Lucius Mummius, a Roman army and a fleet against the Achaean League in the same year was authorised by the Senate itself.[110]

Furthermore, it was the Senate that would originally appoint a Dictator in times of crisis for the Republic. Thus, the Senate would initially appoint the dictators too, officials with extraordinary powers in times of crisis. The Senate appointed its last dictator in 202 BC. At this point, one is reminded that the nomination of the Dictator would normally be made by a Consul. However, the Senate could still have a say in this, even though this does not seem to have been a strict requirement on the nominating Consul. Sulla brought the office of the Dictator

[102] Ibid.

[103] MB Wilson, *Dictator: The Evolution of the Roman Dictatorship* (University of Michigan Press 2021) 267.

[104] E.g. Flower (n 33) 85.

[105] In 121 BC (against Gaius Gracchus and Flaccus); in 100 BC (against Saturninus and Glaucia); in 83 BC (against Sulla); in 77 BC (against Lepidus); in 63 BC (against Catilina and his alleged conspirators); in 62 BC (against Quintus Caecilius Metellus Nepos and Julius Caesar); in 52 BC (against Milo and Clodius); in 49 BC (again against Julius Caesar); in 48 BC (against Caelius and again against Milo); in 47 BC (against Dolabella); in February 43 BC (against Antony); in the Summer of 43 BC (against Octavian) and in 40 BC (against Salvidienus).

[106] Cf. Mouritsen (n 15) 169: 'Political violence ... was a symptom of political instability as well as one of its causes, at the same time expressing and escalating underlying conflicts'.

[107] Crawford (n 96) 26; Seager (n 1) 250, citing Polybius 6.13.1–3, cf. 6.14.2; Mathisen (n 30) 87.

[108] Crawford (n 96) 26; Seager (n 1) 250, citing Polybius 6.13.4–5.

[109] Crawford (n 96) 26; Mathisen (n 30) 87.

[110] ES Gruen, 'The Origins of the Achaean War' (1976) 96 *The Journal of Hellenic Studies* 46, 66. But cf. J-L Ferrary, *Philhellénisme et Impérialisme* (BEFAR 1988) 3, making the point that the order for the destruction of Corinth came from the Senate.

back for a few years in the 1st century BC, becoming a dictator himself. Of course, the last person to hold the office of Dictator for a number of years during the Republic, before he was murdered, was Julius Caesar, again in the 1st century BC.

Traditionally, one found in the Senatus the most experienced politicians of Rome. 'Experienced politician' here ought not to be taken as a synonym for 'virtuous politician' in the Aristotelian sense. However, in this respect, the Senatus was remotely, but only remotely, an aristocratic body. Equally, the oligarchic and mostly hereditary credentials of the Senate would tilt it closer to an oligarchic semi-hereditary[111] structure. The wealth of a designated number of Romans, the Senators, the closed character of the Senate for most of its Republican life, and the leading role of the Patricians within it would effectively justify the oligarchic nature thereof. Furthermore, as Rome was expanding its empire in the Mediterranean, so were the political ambitions of Senators.

The Senatus in the times of the Republic, especially from the 3rd century BC onwards, resembled ever more a wasp nest of imperialists and fascists alike. Conspiracies and intrigues were now rife in the Senatus. The greedier the senatorial circles became, the greedier the Roman Republic would be. The ever-growing greed of Rome for resources, taxes, wealth and power was only a reflection of its Senatorial class for the same. In theory, the Senatorial class would strive for the glory of Rome. In practice, especially in the later stages of the Republic, the Senators would often trample underfoot Rome's glory and ambitions by prioritising personal interest and greed. In so doing, they would not hesitate to sacrifice human lives, whether Roman or foreign. It would be the Senatus that would decide how much bloodshed would be necessary and where. Yet the loss of human life would not mean much for the Senate. Occasionally hypocritical to the core, Roman nobles after 100 BC[112] would have reached political hybris by accusing the many devices of Odysseus' spirit only for them to have excelled in political trickery, conspiracies, corruption and proscribing political opponents. The detail that Roman propaganda was selectively silencing was that Odysseus used many of his devices to return to Ithaca, to survive, to meet his family, when Senators would be using political trickery much worse than Odysseus' to strengthen their political position, maintain their benefits and expand their wealth. In any case, when compared to the Senatorial class's trickery and devious ways, Odysseus must have resembled an angel. Of course, Odysseus has traditionally been idealised, but, unlike idealised-by-Homer Odysseus, the aims of the Senators did not always justify the means. In the 1st century BC, the Roman Senators were fighting political 'ghosts', being frequently engaged in political witch-hunting.

Thus, Rome's mechanisms of propaganda would detest the 'dishonourable' ways of Odysseus only for them to use very similar, if not 'superior', tactics to the survival tactics and opportunistic ways of Odysseus, a mythological ghost.

111 Cf. Steel (n 20) 5–6, rightly noting that the office of the Senator was not hereditary but the tools to become a Senator were.

112 E.g. see Virgil's Aeneid in this respect.

So perverse was the position of Roman propaganda in the 1st century BC that Aeneas, the Odysseus of Rome *mutatis mutandis*, would be facing similar challenges to Odysseus but would have been sanctified simply because he was deemed to be a Roman mythical hero with roots in Troy, one of the many original cities that Rome claimed as a place of origin for itself (the other being Pallantium in Arcadia and Alba Longa in Latium, the relevant mythological figures being Evander and Romulus respectively). According to the Romans themselves,[113] and, as seen in a previous chapter,[114] Rome must have been a mongrel of a city with 'origins' ranging from Troy to Arcadia, Etruria and Latium.

In any case, the teeth of the oligarchy that the Senate was, were shown in 133 BC, when the Senators gave lessons of political 'tact' for all posterity: it was Senators, 'acting as a mob in defense of their privilege',[115] that beat to death with wooden chairs Tiberius Gracchus and many of his followers,[116] Gracchus' 'crime' being that he was attempting to redistribute land in favour of the poor landless Plebeians and was seeking a second term as Tribune. It is the case, however, that Tiberius made three tactical mistakes in his attempt to reform the distribution of land amongst Romans: (i) he convinced the Plebeian Council to remove from office his Co-Tribune, Marcus Octavius, for attempting to veto him; (ii) he attempted to be elected Tribune for a second time in a row, that is after the expiration of his year in office as Tribune, when this was not provided for in the Republic's practices; and (iii) above all, his reform triumvirate, the team that would be responsible for overseeing his land reform, composed of himself and two members of his family.[117] Yet the political mistakes of this promising young man would by all means not justify in any possible way his assassination. Furthermore, between 133 BC and 85 BC, when the Republic was closing in on its final relatively democratic days, before its deterioration to the more autocratic period before its very end (85 to 27 BC), seven Consuls and four Tribunes were murdered in the streets of Rome,[118] many of whom on the direct instigation of the Senate itself. In 52 BC, the Senate's building was burnt and Pompey would become the sole Consul of Rome.[119]

The Senate would now be but a shadow of the old oligarchic body that would stand at the heart of Republican Rome. From an oligarchy of wealthy individuals it would steadily transform itself into an oligarchic tyranny of criminals. Rome's

113 Cf. Cornell (n 30) 60–1, citing H Strasburger, *Zur Sage von der Gründung Roms* (Heidelberg 1968), who maintained that the story of Romulus might not have been an indigenous legend but rather anti-Roman propaganda from Magna Grecia in the late 4th century BC. Cornell, however, immediately rejects this theory.

114 Chapter 7.

115 Mitchell (n 4) 143.

116 Mathisen (n 30) 142–3.

117 Τζαμτζής (n 36) 166.

118 A Herman, *The Cave and the Light: Plato Versus Aristotle and the Struggle for the Soul of Western Civilization* (Random House New York 2014) 117, citing JFVD Balsdon (ed), *Roman Civilization* (Harmondsworth: Penguin, 1965) 39.

119 Flower (n 33) 31.

Republic was in its death throes because its constitutional heart, the Senate, was sick. Furthermore, as has been rightly suggested in the bibliography, '[t]he willingness of the senators to violate the principle of *sacrosanctitas*, which made the persons of the Tribunes inviolate, demonstrates the degree to which they were prepared to violate past traditions in pursuit of their agendas'.[120] In early 1st century BC, the Senators reached new political lows: killing opponents and stealing land were certain of their greatest 'achievements' in this period. In 44 BC the Senate was looking more like a closed mafia club comprising gangs of murderers and thugs, disguised as nobles, than anything that would resemble a learned consultative body of elders for the Republic: a number of Senators[121] would have planned and performed the execution of Julius Caesar, other Senators watching in apathy and horror. Three hours after the soulless corpse of Julius Caesar was removed from the scene of the assassination, chaos ensued in Rome and the Republic would soon but collapse altogether. Caesar's disregard for the Senate and its oligarchic interests, the belief of the conspirators that he would eventually become king of Rome (the exact same accusation having being coined against Tiberius Gracchus 89 years before the assassination of Caesar) and other personal vengeance reasons might well have armed the hands of his murderers, mostly members of a rather decadent elite of oligarchs in the form of Senators. Perhaps in the minds of the Senators that organised Caesar's murder was the fact that they saw themselves as acting as the guardians and protectors of a twisted version of Rome's republican constitution, or whatever was left of it anyway. Through that, they might have also felt that it was not just their office and their interests which they were guarding and protecting but also, co-extensively, the Roman Republic and its empire. Caesar's murderers, in the form of Senators, were, of course, historically wrong in their political calculations in thinking that they would save the Republic,[122] as the fall of the Republic after Julius Caesar's death was but a historical necessity with the Principate replacing the Republic in full glory in 27 BC.

A year after Caesar's assassination, in 43 BC, it was the Senators who were on the receiving end of the highly violent atmosphere they had created for many decades: the proscription of the Second Triumvirate resulted in the assassination of at least 300 Senators and 2,000 *Equites* (Knights).[123] One of the proscribed deceased was Cicero. The Republic was falling and falling, and the Senate's steady deterioration at least since the assassination of Tiberius Gracchus in 133 BC, after which date extensive violence would be Rome's new 'normality', was a key reason for the Republic's eventual collapse. So much for Polybius' 'aristocrats' of Rome, Senators, Patricians and other nobles. The Late Roman 'Republic' of

[120] Mathisen (n 30) 143.

[121] As many as 60 senators might have been conspirators to Julius Caesar's murder: DF Epstein, 'Caesar's Personal Enemies on the Ides of March' (1987) 46 *Latomus* 566, 566.

[122] Mathisen (n 30) 181.

[123] Davies (n 47) 179.

c. 1st century BC would be replaced by an autocratic emperor with 'old institutions [such as the Senate] … obliged to work in a new way'.[124]

To conclude, whereas the Senate was originally a by and large republican conservative oligarchy, the Senate, in the final days of the Republic (see 1st century BC), became but a shadow of the body that had been mostly responsible for the rise of the Roman Republic and, by extension, the rise of its empire. What was the oligarchic heart of the Republic became the cancer that led to its eventual demise.

11.4 THE CURIATE ASSEMBLY

In the years of the Republic, the Curiate Assembly was an oligarchic legislative and judicial body from the times of the Monarchy. Originally, even in the years of the Republic, it comprised 30 Curiae (wards), which were then replaced by 30 Lictors of Patrician descent. In the first steps of the Republic, the functions of this body must not have differed from its functions under the Monarchy. In the times of the Republic, however, probably from the 3rd century BC onwards, the Curiate Assembly fell into decline. However, whilst it was eventually reduced to a rubber-stamping type of institution in the years of the Republic,[125] formally approving certain of the Senate's actions, it was never abolished in the same years and actually retained certain powers as a body even after the fall of the Republic. It would otherwise seem that most of its powers may have already been transferred to the Tribal Assembly with *Lex Publilia* (Publilian Rogation) in 471 BC. Another view holds that the powers of the Curiate Assembly passed to the Centuriate Assembly in the 4th century BC.[126] In any case, this body originally represented the 30 Curiae of Rome (ten wards for each of the three original tribes[127] of Rome) and was an only-largely-representative-of-the-people body in the times of the Monarchy but with no democratic powers to it, as the only persons that could vote in it were Patricians. In the times of the Republic, this body gave formal approval to the election of Consuls and would act as a judicial body. However, one's conclusion here would be that the Curiate Assembly led a rather strange life of almost non-existence and non-significance, the institution 'retain[ing] ghostly existence … until the end of the Republic'.[128] The Curiate Assembly stands, from the institutional historical point of a view, as one of the better historical examples of a largely useless and formalistic type of body that stood the test of time, outsurviving the Republic. Its retainment related to the preservation of traditional institutions[129] (occasionally unnecessary ones or ones that were mere relics of the past in the years of the Republic and the years of the Principate).

124 Davies (n 47) 182.
125 G Bradley, *Early Rome to 290 BC* (Edinburgh University Press 2020) 106.
126 Kamm (n 45) 17.
127 Ramnes (descending from Roman Romulus), Tities (descending from Sabine Titius Tatius) and Luceres (from Etruscan *lucumo*).
128 Cornell (n 30) 25.
129 Ibid.

11.5 THE COLLEGE OF PONTIFFS

A final institution of oligarchic essence would be the College of Pontiffs. This was a collective body of the highest-ranking religious leaders of Rome. We do not know much about the precise nature of the College of Pontiffs except for the fact that this was a college of the head-priests of Rome, its head, *Pontifex Maximus*, wielding certain considerable political power as Rome's religious leader in the years of the Republic. Initially, only Patricians could be appointed to the College. However, after 300 BC, Plebeians could, by virtue of the *Lex Ogulnia*, also be admitted to mixed priestly colleges.[130] It is not certain, however, whether these colleges comprised significant numbers of Plebeian head-priests. The first Plebeian *Pontifex Maximus* (Head of the College of Pontiffs) was Tiberius Coruncanius, his appointment having been made in 254 BC. In the years of the Republic, the College comprised a maximum of 15 Pontiffs. The office, due its confined character and unchecked character by other bodies of the Republic, was largely oligarchic in essence.

[130] Eder (n 64) 451.

Chapter 12

Aristocratic Elements

12.1 INTRODUCTION

The aristocratic elements in the constitution of the Roman Republic, namely the Army Assembly (also known as the Centuriate Assembly) and the members of the *Quaestio Perpetua*, a sort of permanent jury court, are explored, taxonomised and analysed in this chapter. As has been explained above, the Republic, contrary to the views of Polybius and Cicero, actually came with very limited aristocratic features and the Senate would actually be an oligarchic body rather than an aristocratic one.

12.2 THE CONSTITUTION OF THE ROMAN REPUBLIC CAME WITH LIMITED ARISTOCRATIC FEATURES

Rome's tendency towards aristocratic elements of governance (as in the rule of the best[1] or the rule of philosopher kings[2]) was traditionally limited. Indeed, Rome traditionally hovered as a whole between monarchy, plutocracy and oligarchy. The aristocratic and democratic elements were traditionally more limited than the monarchic and oligarchic elements in the Republic's constitution. The democratic elements became stronger (but not decisively stronger) only in the second half of the Roman Republic's era as per classic periodisation. Unlike Plato's *Republic*, the aristocratic elements of the Roman Republic's constitution were very limited, albeit not absent. Nevertheless, while the Republic did not come close to strict Platonic doctrine, its overall constitutional machinery was magistratorial and, by extension, *mutatis mutandis* broadly aristocratic. Also, as has been shown elsewhere in the analysis, Cicero's and Polybius' views on the Senate, supporting the idea that it was an aristocratic body, are discarded as idealistic[3] in the case of the former and as rounded in the case of the latter. Aristotle's definition of an oligarchy[4] would better match the character of Rome's Senate. Effectively, the only two bodies that could be given the aristocratic tag in the years of the Roman

[1] Aristot. Pol. 3.1279a; 4.1293b.

[2] Plat. Rep. 5.473c–d.

[3] TC Brennan, 'Power and Process under the Republican "Constitution"' in HI Flower (ed), *The Cambridge Companion to the Roman Republic* (2nd edn, Cambridge University Press 2014) 19–20.

[4] Aristot., Pol. 3.1280a.

Republic before 133 BC would be that of the Centuriate Assembly remotely, and the *Quaestio Perpetua* somewhat more readily.

12.3 THE CENTURIATE ASSEMBLY (ARMY ASSEMBLY)

The Centuriate Assembly (also known as the Army Assembly) was an aristocratic[5] representative body of soldiers, coming with military, executive and limited judicial powers. In this, one would find the best and the finest of Rome's soldiers and military officers. This was Rome's military heart and it was mostly one that would promote the best for Rome's imperial ambitions. However, it would also be right to maintain that the voting rights of its members were based on plutocratic/timocratic[6] considerations (e.g. its richer members would vote before its poorer members).[7] Beyond this, the Centuriate Assembly's key duties ranged from electing the highest state officials (Consuls, Praetors and Censors) to declaring war, establishing peace arrangements and approving certain legislation that would be binding upon all Roman people.

The Army Assembly also came with certain judicial functions. These were mainly concerned with *perduellio* (high treason) cases. The principle behind the Centuriate Assembly's military-judicial functions was practically the fact that Rome's soldiers and military officers were by definition the best people to judge military offences such as treason. Judicial cases could be brought directly to the Army Assembly or by referring the matter to the people through *provocatio ad populum*.[8] The body was almost wholly timocratic under the so-called Servian Constitution of the Roman Republic (509–241 BC). Between 241 and 27 BC, however, the body became slightly less timocratic by opening its membership to greater numbers of soldiers. Unlike the Centuriate Assembly under the Servian Constitution, the reorganised Centuriate Assembly after 241 BC allowed even more classes of centuries (military units comprising 100 men) to play a decisive role in its voting. Under the old Servian Constitution, the class of officers and the first class of centuries alone could vote and decide matters. Exception to the reorganised Centuriate Assembly between 241 and 27 BC was Dictator Sulla's reforms that effectively resurrected the old almost fully meritocratic character of the particular body for the period between 82 and 70 BC.

The Centuriate Assembly, a military body in principle, was constitutionally powerful: as stated, it would actually choose Consuls, Censors and Praetors,[9] making it a central constitutional military body behind Rome's more civil constitutional engine, that of the Senate. Nevertheless, while the two were flip sides

[5] E.g. RE Mitchell, *Patricians and Plebeians: The Origin of the Roman State* (Cornell University Press 1990) 60.

[6] PA Zoch, *Ancient Rome* (University of Oklahoma Press 1998) 38.

[7] Zoch (n 6) 38.

[8] E.g. IE Τζαμτζής, *Ο Μεσογειακός Κόσμος* (Εκδόσεις Σάκκουλα 2014, ανατύπωση 2018) 110.

[9] D Hoyos, *Rome Victorious: The Irresistible Rise of the Roman Empire* (Bloomsbury Academic 2019, reprinted 2023) 14.

of Rome's constitution (civil and military), they were not wholly separated. The more plausible thesis would be to perceive Senate and Centuriate Assembly as relatively auxiliary bodies to one another. For instance, while the Consuls would emanate from the Centuriate Assembly and would amount to Rome's top military leaders or generals, they could convene[10] and preside[11] over the Senate, and so on.

12.4 THE *QUAESTIO PERPETUA*

Another *mutatis mutandis* aristocratic body in Rome was the *Quaestio Perpetua*, Rome's permanent jury court. Thus, from 149 BC onwards, this would probably be the best expression of a genuinely aristocratic body in the Roman Republic. *Lex Calpurnia de repetundis*, the Calpurnian Law against Embezzlement for the Recovery of Property, was the landmark legislation that established permanent courts in the Rome of the Republic. Apparently, this law did not abrogate previous legislation and it was a new piece of legislation altogether.[12] Also, while these new courts dealt with matters which would go into the criminal law sphere as a whole, albeit under established civil law procedure apparently,[13] the insertion of theirs into Rome's overall constitutional machinery in conjunction with the selective choosing of the judges of these courts meant that the Republic's constitution was practically strengthened on its more aristocratic side. In any case, through this enabling piece of legislation, legal action for embezzlement could be brought at any time (as opposed to a senior Roman magistrate putting a question of the kind to a popular body or the matter being decided on an *ad hoc* basis). The misappropriation of public funds whether in Rome or, eventually, in its provinces would now be directly actionable. Rome was not just confident but its legal system too was constantly strengthening. The body's jury composition originally comprised Senators only (i.e. up until the mid-120s BC) and this seems to have been the result of a selective approach, as a Praetor would first create a pool of jurors from the Senate which would not necessarily include all Senators. In subsequent decades and in the Late Republic, the composition of the *Quaestio Perpetua* changed every ten to twenty years or so, hovering from a body made out of *equites* only to a body of mixed panel jurors; to a body of Senators once again; to a body of jurors that came from the tribes, and so on.

[10] Zoch (n 6) 33.
[11] Zoch (n 6) 38.
[12] JS Richardson, 'Old Statutes Never Die: A Brief History of Abrogation' in M Austin, J Harries and C Smith (eds), *Modus Operandi: Essays in Honour of Geoffrey Rickman* (Institute of Classical Studies – School of Advanced Study, University of London 1998) 56.
[13] E.g. Richardson (n 12) 59.

Chapter 13

Democratic Elements

13.1 INTRODUCTION

The democratic elements in the Roman Republic such as the Plebeian Council, the Plebeian Tribunes and the Tribal Assembly are explored, taxonomised and analysed in this chapter. The chapter does so by exploring the democratic essence of relevant institutions, especially by considering their correspondence and their respect to the will of the Roman people.

13.2 DEMOCRATIC ELEMENTS IN THE CONSTITUTION OF THE ROMAN REPUBLIC

Rome was never a democracy, for example, in the way classical Athens would be a democracy or in the Greek sense of the term.[1] Rome in the times of the Republic was by all means a mixed polity.[2] The Athenians, on the other hand, unlike the Romans, would have set their almost-perfect-for-its-time but imperfect-in-the-modern-sense democracy as the crown jewel in the political and constitutional development of their city state, despite the fact that even the Athenian constitution would not have actually done away with the totality of old monarchic or aristocratic elements from pre-classical era. And yet the constitution of classical Athens would be deemed as highly democratic as it clearly was.

Equally, whereas the Roman republican constitution may have grown over the centuries to eventually become more sophisticated than the Athenian one, it never made that decisive step that would make itself more democratic than not. The Roman Republic's constitution grew to become a more sophisticated system of governance than the Athenian one but democratic *stricto sensu* it was not. It did manifest democratic characteristics and it was partially democratised in the later stages of the Republic but one could not characterise it as a more democratic constitution than not. Athens would be the clear winner in this respect and Rome would come a distant second.

Of course, the Roman Republic's constitution did not have to be democratic as the ruling classes of Rome effectively wished to retain continuous control of the Roman state over a span of five republican centuries and even after that in the years of the Principate. The Athenian constitution, however, would have made

[1] E.g. A Kamm, *The Romans* (Routledge 2006) 13. Cf. Thuc. 2.37.

[2] E.g. Plb. 6.11–13.

that decisive step to move away from oligarchic or monarchic forms of power. An explanation for the more conservative republican constitution of Rome might be the stringent class system and the very legal system of Rome, a generally conservative system of well-established vested interests. Another possible explanation is that the republican Romans, while ready and willing to move away from the more Etruscan-oriented type of monarchy which they once had, did not wish to wholly abolish all monarchic elements from their Republic's constitution. Rome's traditional republican affection for an orderly and law-based system must have also played a role in the creation of a mixed government in the city of Rome, combining monarchic, oligarchic, aristocratic and democratic elements under the same constitutional packaging.

Moreover, Rome's more open imperial aspirations, especially from the 3rd century BC onwards, would have practically strengthened and entrenched further the republican constitution's less-than-predominantly-democratic core, despite attempts to partially democratise the constitution. The core of the Roman Republic thus remained monarchic-oligarchic until the final days of the republic. Or to put it otherwise, Rome was both politically and morally conservative and *syncentrotic* (centralising), when Athens was only morally conservative as a society (e.g. evidence of this is the condemnation of Socrates to death for introducing new *daemonia* amongst the Athenian youth). Had Athens been politically conservative too, or, at least, as conservative as Rome would be, the chances are it would not have generated the system of democracy it cultivated in Pericles' Golden Age. By all means, Rome's degree of political conservatism was not as prevalent in Athens, to the point that by the beginning and the fall of the Republic the same two classes – the Senators and the *equites* (knights) – would be the upper classes that would dominate system and state.[3] Rome's republican constitution did have, however, democratic elements in it, albeit not ones that would make it a democratic constitution. Even in Rome, however, opposing the people was not a good idea. The Tribunes of Rome would have to take into account and respect the will of the Roman people as a guiding principle of the Republic.[4] Even the Senate would occasionally have to do so, even though the wealthy class of Patricians that it mostly consisted of would manipulate the Roman *populus* through procedural legal and socio-political means (e.g. *clientela*). In theory, the *populus* was powerful.[5] In practice, however, it was easily manipulated and controlled by Rome's elites. Rome's popular assemblies were thus procedurally controlled by magistrates and the *populus* could not debate except in informal meetings (*contiones*).[6] So too bills were initiated on the advice of a magistrate, and so on.[7]

[3] Kamm (n 1) 13.

[4] A Lintott, *The Constitution of the Roman Republic* (Clarendon Press 1999) 128, citing Polybius (6.16. 4–5).

[5] Cf. N Rosenstein, *Rome and the Mediterranean 290 to 146 BC: The Imperial Republic* (Edinburgh University Press 2012) 8.

[6] Rosenstein (n 5) 8.

[7] Ibid.

Democracy is, of course, not assessed only by the way a state is run in constitutional terms. It is also assessed by observing whether all social classes in a given state can acquire office on equality and merit. Again, in theory, Plebeians could be admitted 'as partners [to Patricians] in virtually all state positions by the end of the fourth century'.[8] In practice, however, '[P]atricians continued to hold their share of the highest and most prestigious positions for some time despite a decrease in their numbers'.[9] Thus, the democratic access of Plebeians to state positions started relatively late and was relatively limited for much of the Republic's life. It would also seem that even when more Plebeians were allowed to hold state office, most of the control of the Republic, when it came to who could acquire and run state office, was still in the hands of Roman nobles. Yet, Rome did actually have certain democratic institutions and did aspire to democracy as a whole.

13.3 SO WAS POLYBIUS WRONG ABOUT THE STRENGTH OF ROME'S DEMOCRATIC ELEMENT?

Polybius famously claimed that in the constitution of the Roman Republic the most important element was that of the people (*οὐ μὴν ἀλλὰ καταλείπεται μερὶς καὶ τῷ δήμῳ, καὶ καταλείπεταί γε βαρυτάτη*) and that its constitution was a democracy (*καὶ δημοκρατικόν ἐστι τὸ πολίτευμα*).[10] As Polybius makes direct use of the term 'demos' (*τῷ δήμῳ*) in the original Greek text, we could *mutatis mutandis* conclude that he effectively refers to Rome's democratic element, the Roman *populus*. Nonetheless, the point he makes is peculiar, if not suspicious. What did Polybius really mean here and what was his intention for Roman and Greek readers? There are three analytical paths one could follow here. First, if one took things literally, one would conclude that the Rome of the Republic in the 2nd century BC had the democratic element as the most important element out of the three (sic) elements Polybius maintained for Rome's constitution: the democratic element was the most important one amongst the monarchic, the democratic and oligarchic elements in Rome's constitution according to him. However, there is a second interpretation to be also kept in mind: considering that the Roman people were effectively controlled in so many respects by Rome's plutocratic elites (i.e. by its top magistrates and the Senate), Polybius may have meant that the democratic element in Rome is the most important one *in theory*, this effectively justifying the *populus* element in Rome's SPQR constitutional designation. However, the order in Rome's SPQR abbreviation, an order which would rarely change,[11] would place the Senate first and the *populus* second. Finally, the reader should recall that

[8] RE Mitchell, 'The Aristocracy of the Roman Republic' in R Howarth (ed), *Hearsay, History, and Heresy: Collected Essays on the Roman Republic* by Richard E. Mitchell (Gorgias Press 2010) 109.

[9] Ibid.

[10] Plb. 6.14.

[11] D Hoyos, *Rome Victorious: The Irresistible Rise of the Roman Empire* (Bloomsbury Academic 2019, reprinted 2023) 11.

Polybius was not exactly a great supporter of the idea of democracy.[12] Democracy was not considered by him an ideal constitutional form. Thus, Polybius could be sending, between the lines, warning signals to the Roman elites as to the fact that Rome's democratic element was becoming stronger: 'the democratic element in Rome is the most important one' would equate to 'the democratic element in Rome is so strong that it should be kept under control by Rome's magistrates and its oligarchic elites, if Rome is not to decline'. To conclude, the literal interpretation here would not be appropriate considering that the mobs of Rome were traditionally highly manipulated by Rome's constitutional establishment. Polybius must have meant that Rome's strengthening of the democratic element should be kept in check and that it would cause problems to Rome's constitutional stability, if it became stronger than it already was.

13.4 THE PLEBEIAN TRIBUNES

A democratic office observed in the Roman Republic was that of the Plebeian Tribunes, an executive office in the main. The Tribunes were the leaders of Rome's Plebeians. They were not, however, magistrates of the Republic *stricto sensu*.[13] In fact, their role was 'to protect [Plebeians] from abuses of power'[14] of the Senate and the Republic's other magistrates. As compared to the Consuls, the Tribunes had negative powers when the Consuls had positive powers.[15] The Plebeian Tribunes seem to have arisen from the office of the Military Tribunes but other than that there does not seem to be any constitutional connection between the two offices.[16] The office of the Plebeian Tribunes was sacrosanct[17] and their functions instrumental in the running of the Republic's popular element (Plebeians). Tribunes could act individually (i.e. not in agreement with other Tribunes) and, therefore, potentially lead themselves into conflict with other Tribunes.[18] Tribunes in the years of the Republic could go as far as challenging the policies and the decisions of the Senate.[19] By extension, their functions were also quite instrumental for the running of the Republic as a whole. However, whereas they would hold considerable powers, they would still be accountable

[12] E.g. K Von Fritz, *The Theory of the Mixed Constitution in Antiquity: A Critical Analysis of Polybius' Political Ideas* (Columbia University Press 1954) 85.

[13] T Mommsen, *The History of Rome*, vol 1 (W Purdie Dickson (tr), Macmillan & Co. 1901) 355; PA Zoch, *Ancient Rome* (Oklahoma University Press 1998) 36.

[14] Zoch (n 13) 36. Also, EA Posner, 'The Constitution of the Roman Republic' in G Dari-Mattiacci and DP Kehoe (eds), *Roman Law and Economics: Institutions and Organizations Volume I* (Oxford University Press 2020) 37.

[15] Mommsen (n 13) 355.

[16] Mommsen (n 13) 354.

[17] E.g. C Steel, *The End of the Roman Republic, 146 to 44* BC: *Conquest and Crisis* (Edinburgh University Press 2013) 2; Hoyos (n 11) 12.

[18] Steel (n 17), 3 citing L Thommen, *Das Volkstribunat der späten römischen Republik* (Steiner 1989).

[19] E.g. ES Gruen, 'Augustus and the Making of the Principate' in K Galinsky (ed), *The Cambridge Companion to the Age of Augustus* (Cambridge University Press 2005) 39–40.

to the Tribal Assembly.[20] The tool of *intercessio* was the Tribunes' most powerful legal and political tool: the exercise of which would practically mean that, on occasion, the Republic's actions and measures, as in the actions of its formal magistrates, could be brought to a standstill. This was thus a form of veto. That veto could be exercised against any of Rome's magistrates except the Censors.[21] The Plebeian Council would elect Tribunes annually[22] and it would elect ten of them every year.[23] From 149 BC, Tribunes would *ex officio* also be members of the Roman Senate.[24] The specific form of *potestas* that Tribunes would enjoy was called *tribunicia potestas* within the *pomoerium*; this was not, of course, *imperium* but the sacrosanct nature of this *potestas* in this designated area was the rough equivalent of the powers with which *imperium* came.[25] Finally, whereas the powers of the Tribunes were quite extensive, they would often be targeted politically by Rome's oligarchic elites. Indeed, there have been many historical examples of the brutal assassination of Tribunes, as actioned, requested or instigated by the Senate, a Dictator or powerful statesmen.[26]

13.5 THE TRIBAL ASSEMBLY

One of Rome's well-known bodies of democratic essence in the years of the Republic would, of course, be the Tribal Assembly. This was a legislative body, organised in tribes,[27] the Tribal Assembly being the body of free males in republican Rome that would come as a body somewhat close to the *Ecclesia* of the Athenian *demos*. However, the powers of the Tribal Assembly would clearly not be as extensive as those of the *Ecclesia* in the Athenian Democracy. Also, unlike the Plebeian Council, which was a body for Plebeians only, both Patricians and Plebeians could participate and vote in the Tribal Assembly. The Tribal Assembly issued laws (*leges*), whilst the Plebeian Council would issue resolutions (*plebiscita*). The Tribal Assembly was responsible for the election of Quaestors, Curule Aediles and certain Military Tribunes.[28]

20 WV Harris, 'Power' in A Barchiesi and W Scheidel (eds), *The Oxford Handbook of Roman Studies* (Oxford University Press 2010) 571.
21 IE Τζαμτζής, *Ο Μεσογειακός Κόσμος* (Εκδόσεις Σάκκουλα 2014, ανατύπωση 2018) 95.
22 Zoch (n 13) 36.
23 Τζαμτζής (n 21) 95.
24 Zoch (n 13) 36.
25 Τζαμτζής (n 21) 95.
26 Harris (n 20) 572.
27 A Kamm (n 1) 17.
28 Cf. C Nicolet, *The World of the Citizen in Republican Rome* (PS Falla (tr), University of California 1980) 224, 228.

13.6 THE PLEBEIAN COUNCIL

Let us now turn to the final democratic element in the Roman Republic's constitution, the Plebeian Council. This was practically the closest that the Plebeians of republican Rome would come to their own 'people's parliament'. As its name suggests, the Plebeians would be the only element represented in this otherwise democratic body, and Patricians would be excluded. The fourth legendary King of Rome, Ancus Marcius, was a Plebeian king who constituted the order of the Plebeians from imported captives[29] in late 7th century BC, probably Latins, Sabines and Veientes (Etruscans). The Council passed laws that would apply to itself and, by extension, to the Plebeians until 287 BC when it was accepted through *Lex Hortensia* that the resolutions (plebiscites) of the Plebeian Council would be binding on both Plebeians and Patricians alike, that is on the whole of the State without approval from Senate.[30] The particular law (*Lex Hortensia*) would practically equalise the effect of *plebiscita* to *leges*, making the former binding on the whole of the Roman people (Patricians included).[31] *Plebiscita* and *leges*, resolutions and laws, would now come with the same constitutional effect in principle. Also, up until 339 BC, the *auctoritas patrum* was given by the Senate to the Plebeian Council after the latter would have voted for a law; after 339 BC, however, the *auctoritas patrum* was expected to be given before the Plebeian Council would have voted for a law.[32] Furthermore, *Lex Maenia* would require, sometime between 291 and 219 BC, the Senate to approve through *auctoritas patrum* Plebeian-approved bills.[33] The dictatorial Republic of Sulla, however, in the years of the Late Republic, took away almost all of the powers from the Plebeian Council from 88 BC and for a certain period of time. Other functions of the Plebeian Council related to the election of *Aediles Plebis*[34] and the adjudication of cases that came with high fines.[35] The office of the Tribune of the Plebeians was created in 494 BC. This official was responsible for convening the Plebeian Council and could take grievances to the Senate or the Consuls on behalf of the Plebeians. As has been explained further above, the powers of the Tribunes were quite extensive, in that they could veto state decisions including Senate's decrees.

[29] N Davies, *Europe: A History* (Pimlico 1996, reprinted with corrections 1997) 151.

[30] RW Mathisen, *Ancient Roman Civilization: History and Sources* (Oxford University Press 2019) 86.

[31] Τζαμτζής (n 21) 111–12.

[32] Τζαμτζής (n 21) 100.

[33] FK Drogula, 'Plebeian Tribunes and the Government of Early Rome' (2017) 51 *Antichthon* 101, 117–18.

[34] Τζαμτζής (n 21) 111.

[35] Τζαμτζής (n 21) 112.

Chapter 14

A Unique Constitutional Blend

14.1 INTRODUCTION

Every constitution is unique, in that, even if it is emulated, its implementation might differ significantly from source constitution.[1] However, this chapter makes the point that the constitution of the Roman Republic was genuinely unique for a number of reasons, but above all because of its amalgamation of diverse elements. The chapter also recaps and assesses certain of the findings in this part of the monograph, and posits the uniqueness of Rome's republican constitution, as this has affected political thought and constitutions over the centuries. Finally, indicative comparisons are drawn between Rome's constitution and other constitutions from the ancient world and modernity.

14.2 WHAT MAKES A CONSTITUTION UNIQUE?

For us to appreciate the uniqueness of the constitution of the Roman Republic, it would be important to establish what makes a constitution genuinely unique in the first place. Of course, constitutions are traditionally geared towards a locality but that alone does not necessarily make them unique in themselves or ones that would come with genuine features of their own. The Spartan constitution, for instance, has been previously deemed 'unique' because, even though Sparta's institutions were not always unique in themselves, the combination of these institutions was quite unique.[2] In this respect, Rome was no different to Sparta: it is highly unlikely that all of her institutions would have been the pure creation of local genius but rather that certain of them would have been taken from elsewhere (e.g. the office of the Quaestors). Nonetheless, Rome's constitutional mix has been truly impressive. Rome, in the years of the Republic, practically generated a most sophisticated constitutional machinery which to this day is the cause of admiration. By all means, whereas older constitutions to the Roman Republic's

[1] A classic example in this respect would be the constitutions of Hong Kong and Macau: AHY Chen and PY Lo, 'The Constitutional Orders of "One Country, Two Systems": A Comparative Study of the Visible and Invisible Bases of Constitutional Review and Proportionality Analysis in the Chinese Special Administrative Regions of Hong Kong and Macau' in R Dixon and A Stone (eds), *The Invisible Constitution in Comparative Perspective* (Cambridge University Press 2018) 230, 231, 265 and 266–67.

[2] S Hodkinson, 'Introduction' in S Hodkinson (ed), *Sparta: Comparative Approaches* (The Classical Press of Wales 2009) xvii.

constitution would come with many of the characteristics that Rome chose for its own constitution, the magnificent entwining and interweaving of so many ideas into one is the Republic's greatest achievement: the combination of a unique system of checks and balances; vetoing; terms of office; the powers of Rome's Censors to impeach; and regular elections all stand for Rome's great constitutional legacy, which is still very relevant to us in modernity.

The uniqueness of a constitution can also be attested by its endurance in time. One reasonably ought not to expect that the Republic's constitution in 509 BC was exactly the same as the Republic's constitution after 133 BC or in 27 BC. Indeed, that would be neglectful of republican Rome's ever-increasing sophistication in political and legal terms over the centuries. Nonetheless, the core of Rome's constitution in the 5th century BC was not all that different to Rome's constitution in the 2nd century BC. If the Roman idea of fear of the rule of one man for too long was an archetypal idea for the constitution of the Roman Republic in 509 BC, this idea was kept practically intact over the Republic's path until its final days. That is not to say that Rome did not deteriorate into abusive dictatorships beyond the normal office of the Dictator in its c. 500 years of continuous existence. It clearly did in the 1st century BC when it was still a republic in principle. However, the antibodies that the Republic had created were so powerful that the Romans would reach the point of killing the enemies or potential enemies of the Republic, even though economic interests were also a key cause behind the assassinations of presumed or real enemies of the Republic.

Moreover, characteristics unique to a constitution can be attested by the successes of a constitution when it comes to the prosperity and the well-being of the people it serves but, also, more thought-provokingly, by whether or not its territorial remit can be solidified. It would seem that the constitution of the Republic has been successful in increasing the prosperity of Rome as a whole, its ruling elites acquiring the lion's share in this respect. When it comes to Rome's constitution solidifying its *territorium*, this clearly has been the case as Rome defended its lands, eventually becoming, however, an imperial republic from the 3rd century BC onwards.

14.3 CONCEALMENT OF THE CONSTITUTIONAL DRAFTERS OF ROME AND THE ORIGINS OF THE ROMAN REPUBLIC'S CONSTITUTION

The Romans have taken great pains to conceal who were the persons behind the Roman Republic's original and subsequent configuration. As per current sources, one would, therefore, be almost wholly aware of the constituent elements of the Republic but not the roots or the authors behind Rome's constitution. In fact, the Romans took pride of the fact that theirs was a constitution that could not identify a single personality behind it: the *res publica* was so perfect in the thinking of the Romans of the Republic due to the purported fact that it was the constitutional distillate of the collective Roman genius, the result of the collective wisdom of the Romans.[3] There was no single personality in Rome's history who could claim intellectual fatherhood of the Republic's constitution.[4] However, we are aware of the fact that already, from the years of the Monarchy, the Roman constitution was often externally inspired. Even Mommsen, who committed an error of historical judgement about Roman constitutional law, claiming that it was the result of pure local genius by reason of the fact that its ideas were named in Latin,[5] gives out elsewhere that the Servian military constitution was fundamentally Hellenic.[6] Of course, the fact that Rome's military constitution was of foreign inspiration does not make Rome's constitution of foreign inspiration; but to reach the conclusion that all Roman constitutional law was Roman-inspired would be missing the point. The Etruscans and the Greeks must have affected Rome's constitution. However, this was not a weakness for Rome's constitution but a strength, for it was the Romans themselves who perfected the constitutional mix behind their Republic.

14.4 AMALGAMATION OF IDEAS IN THE REPUBLIC'S CONSTITUTION AS THE RESULT OF ROMAN GENIUS

Even if the Romans attempted to conceal the origins and the authors behind the Roman constitution, as they clearly have, one thing is certain: the amalgamation of ideas, whether foreign or local, was theirs and they should be the ones to be credited with the very uniqueness of the constitutional mix that one observes in the Roman Republic's configuration. So should they be credited for what was once Rome's new building, the *Regia*, and its architectural style which according to Mommsen was the equivalent of a *Prytaneion*.[7] In other words, whereas one finds common constitutional elements in Rome with those in other ancient constitutions (e.g. the Spartan one or the Carthaginian one), the Romans seem to be responsible for the final configuration of their constitution.

[3] ES Gruen, *Culture and National Identity in Republican Rome* (Cornell University Press 1992) 83, citing Cic. *De Rep.* 2.1–2. Cf. the idea of collective wisdom of the Romans with the unity principle for the city of the Greeks. On the latter, see B Straumann, *Crisis and Constitutionalism: Roman Political Thought from the Fall of the Republic to the Age of Revolution* (Oxford University Press 2016) 194–5, citing M Schofield, *Plato* (Oxford University Press 2006) 216–17.

[4] E.g. V Arena, 'Varro, the Name-Givers, and the Lawgivers: The Case of the Consuls' (2021) 38 *Polis* 588, 588–9 citing Cic. *Rep.* 2.1–3. Cf. the approach in the Greek world, where the Spartans and the Athenians would ascribe excellence to named lawgivers, Lycurgus and Solon respectively: J Harries, 'Roman Law Codes and the Roman Legal Tradition' in JW Cairns and PJ du Plessis (eds), *Beyond Dogmatics: Law and Society in the Roman World* (Edinburgh University Press 2007) 86–7.

[5] T Mommsen, *The History of Rome*, vol. 1 (W Purdie Dickson (tr), Macmillan & Co. 1901) 105.

[6] Mommsen (n 5) 123, 142.

[7] Mommsen (n 5) 142

14.5 FULL CONSTITUTIONAL POWERS TO THE *RES PUBLICA* – LIMITATION OF THE POWERS OF THE MAGISTRATES

Part of the success and the uniqueness of the Roman Republic's constitution was that it came with a magnificent aspiration: the full enabling of the *res publica* through the limitation of the powers of the magistrates behind the *res publica*. This, of course, is related to the fact that the Romans of the Republic would traditionally be most reluctant to allow the powers of a single man to extend for long unchecked. The constitutional enabling of the Republic was directly related to the limitations imposed on Roman magistrates.[8] In Roman thinking, the limitations and the checks on the magistrates of Rome would practically amount to the flourishing of the constitution and, by extension, the state.

14.6 UNIQUE IN SPACE – UNIQUE IN TIME

Yet, the greatest element for the uniqueness behind the Roman Republic's constitution was the fact that its final configuration was not just unique in the geographical space of the then known ancient world but also unique in time to the point that it has affected future constitutions, even in modernity. The *locus classicus* of a modern constitution that has been affected in a number of ways by the constitution of the Roman Republic has been the Constitution of the United States of America.[9] Of course, the Americans did not embrace *holus bolus* the constitution of the Roman Republic and it is the case that they actually rejected many parts thereof.[10] For instance, the drafters of the American constitution significantly departed from it, in that they chose to create a federal Republic based on the 'representative' principle,[11] a principle which was not, of course, the case in the Roman Republic. Equally, one could state here that the Constitution of the USA with its thorough system of checks and balances is one which is a distant descendant of the so-called mixed or balanced constitution,[12] which one would also observe in the constitution of the Roman Republic. However, a major American constitutional innovation on the Roman Republic's constitution, so to speak, was the fact that the Founding Fathers created fewer suffocating checks and balances for their once young federal republic and a much stronger, a single,

[8] Mommsen (n 5) 313.

[9] EA Posner, 'The Constitution of the Roman Republic' in G Dari-Mattiacci and DP Kehoe (eds), *Roman Law and Economics: Institutions and Organizations Volume I* (Oxford University Press 2020) 35, 48.

[10] Posner (n 9) 35.

[11] MNS Sellers, 'The Roman Republic and the French and the American Revolutions' in HI Flower (ed), *The Cambridge Companion to the Roman Republic* (2nd edn, Cambridge University Press 2014) 405–6.

[12] N Rosenstein, *Rome and the Mediterranean 290 to 146* BC: *The Imperial Republic* (Edinburgh University Press 2012) 5.

unified executive branch.[13] The Americans have, thus, simplified and modernised the Roman republican model considerably by rejecting[14] the Roman checks and balances model by generating their own model. So too, the United States of America, as a constitutional-political construct, would, by all means, be deemed far more democratic than the Roman Republic was even after 287 BC. Democracy was further embraced in the US Constitution in 1913 through Amendment XVII when the election of the American Senators was directly left in the hands of the American people. The US Constitution became even more democratic than it was previously configured and, of course, much more democratic than that of the Roman Republic. In France too, the world's other great example of republican constitutions, the French have built constitutions that would come ever closer to the institutions of the Roman Republic, especially closer to the end of the 18th century,[15] while the modern French Republic could certainly show through its republican tradition significant affiliation with central aspects and institutions of republican Rome.

14.7 THE REPUBLIC AS AN ARISTOTELIAN POLITY+

Polybius effectively presented the constitution of the Republic as an Aristotelian polity.[16] Did Rome have the genuine characteristics of an Aristotelian *politeia* though? The first thing to mentioned here is that the Roman Republic was a mixed polity with strong oligarchic and monarchic tendencies, unlike the rounded and idealised perceptions of Polybius and Cicero about the Senate being an 'aristocracy',[17] a central body in the Republic, it being an oligarchy in Aristotelian terms (that is in perfect agreement with *Politics* III 1279b–1280a). The aristocratic elements in Rome's constitution were rather limited: the Centuriate Assembly *mutatis mutandis* and the *Quaestio Perpetua*. In short, Rome in the more mature period of her republican existence was practically a mixed polity with strong oligarchic (predominantly) and monarchic (to a lesser extent) tendencies, combining also a limited number of democratic and aristocratic features. Nor was the Roman Republic a polity/politeia *stricto sensu* under Aristotle's classification of constitutions, but a mixed polity – this was a republic combining four elements – not three under Aristotle's original polity model (in this respect, see, for instance, Pasquino's designation of constitutions on the Aristotelian classification of constitutions).[18] Thus, the Constitution of the Roman Republic was an Aristotelian

[13] Posner (n 9) 35.

[14] Posner (n 9) 48, citing RM Gummere, *The American Colonial Mind and the Classical Tradition* (Harvard University Press 1963) 176.

[15] MNS Sellers (n 11) 410.

[16] J Connolly, 'Political Theory' in A Barchiesi and W Scheidel (eds), *The Oxford Handbook of Roman Studies* (Oxford University Press 2010) 713.

[17] Plb. 6.3; 6.13. Cic. Rep. 2.41; 2.56.

[18] P Pasquino, 'Machiavelli and Aristotle: The Anatomies of the City' (2009) 35 *History of European Ideas* 397, 399–401.

polity+ or an Aristotelian polity with an asterisk, the obvious asterisk being that it would also additionally incorporate monarchic (Dictator) and dyarchic (Consuls and Censors) elements in it, when Aristotle's polity model (mixed constitution) would combine aristocratic, oligarchic and democratic elements only (see Figure 14.1 for a comparative illustration of the classic Aristotelian designation of constitutions, the Polybian/Ciceronian approach and the actual model of the Roman Republic as an Aristotelian polity+). However, Aristotle would applaud the highly mixed character of the Roman Republic's constitution, as for him the combination of more than two types of constitutional government would be superior to the combination of just two forms of constitutional government.[19] In the case of the Roman Republic, Aristotle would in all probability have found the existence of four forms of constitutional government into one particularly appealing.

14.8 MACROCOMPARISON OF THE ROMAN REPUBLIC'S CONSTITUTION WITH LEADING ANCIENT CONSTITUTIONS

The Roman Republic, of course, both differed and resembled other ancient constitutions. The Republic will be compared here with leading ancient constitutions; such macrocomparison will be made on the principle of functionality[20] of comparisons. Historical and socio-legal context under comparative law's contextuality[21] principle will also be taken into account as appropriate. Furthermore, in comparative law, the classic thesis, which this monograph follows, is that 'like has to be compared with like' (*similia similibus*).[22] It would be correct, however, to maintain that, while Rome was not a democracy, the limited democratic component of its Republic (e.g. its popular assemblies) could be compared with the preceding democratic realities found elsewhere in the ancient world (e.g. in Athens). Comparisons of ancient constitutions otherwise become ever more common in the bibliography: for example, Straumann compares Athens and Rome as well as Greek and Roman constitutional thought;[23] Mouritzen compares the Athenian *demos* and *Ecclesia* with Rome's popular assemblies;[24] Capogrossi Colognesi readily assumes that 'the history of Rome is firmly tied to the world we associate with

19 Aristot. Pol. 2.1266a; 4.1294a.

20 E.g. K Zweigert and H Kötz, *An Introduction to Comparative Law* (Tony Weir (tr), 3rd edn, Oxford University Press 1998) 34; M Graziadei, 'The Functionalist Heritage' in P Legrand and R Munday (eds), *Comparative Legal Studies: Traditions and Transitions* (Cambridge University Press 2003) 100–31; E Örücü, *The Enigma of Comparative Law: Variations on a Theme for the Twenty-First Century* (Brill Academic Publishers 2004) 20.

21 E.g. P Legrand, 'The Same and the Different' in Legrand and Munday (n 16) 240–311; J Husa, 'The Comparatist and Plato's Cave' in L Siliquini-Cinelli, D Gianti and M Balestrieri (eds), *The Grand Strategy of Comparative Law: Themes, Methods, Developments* (Routledge 2024) 55–66.

22 Örücü (n 20) 20.

23 Straumann (n 3) 191–237.

24 H Mouritzen, *Politics in the Roman Republic* (Cambridge University Press 2017) 16–18.

I. Classification of Constitutions under Aristotle's *Politics* III

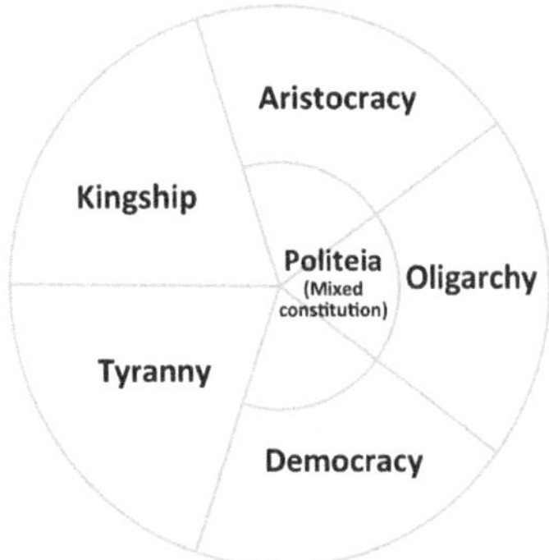

II. Polybian / Ciceronian Positioning of the Roman Republic under Aristotle's *Politics*
(N.B. Polybian / Ciceronian perception of the Senate in conflict with *Politics* III 1279b–1280a)

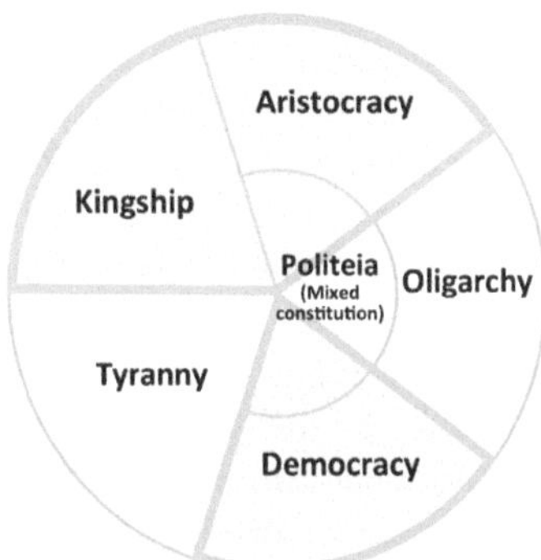

III. Monograph's Thesis on the Constitution of the Roman Republic under Aristotle's *Politics*
(positioning of the Senate in agreement with *Politics* III 1279b–1280a)

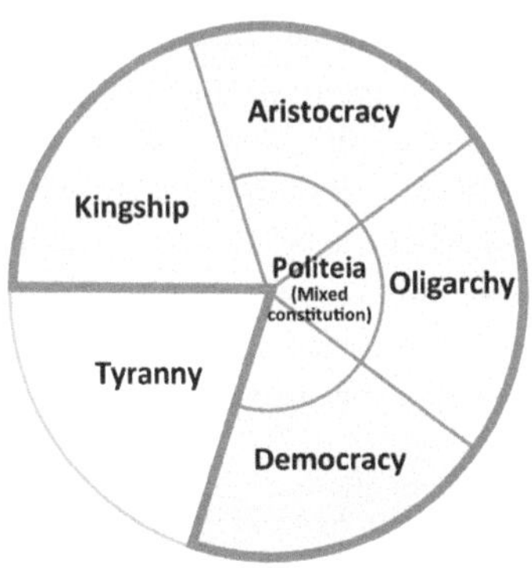

Figure 14.1 The Roman Republic as an Aristotelian polity+

"classical antiquity," that of the Greek *poleis* and of Rome itself'[25] while he finds the comparison of Etruscan kings and Greek tyrants convincing;[26] elsewhere, the Greek tyrant has been compared with the Roman dictator;[27] and so on. In our macrocomparison of ancient constitutions, we shall examine, on an indicative basis, those of Sparta of the 5th century BC, Athens of 460–431 BC, Carthage of 4th century BC and Rome of 3rd and 2nd century BC.

When it comes to form of government, Rome presents us with overall similarity to the constitutions of Sparta and Carthage: all these three constitutions would be deemed mixed ones,[28] the Carthaginian one tilting closer to plutocracy but Rome too could be perceived as a relatively plutocratic constitutional reality throughout the Republic, as the oldest and wealthiest families of Rome would be 'represented' in the Senate, which was Rome's central co-ordinating body in constitutional terms. The Roman Republic also dramatically differs from the Athenian Democracy, in that it was a republican, a mixed system, when the form of government in Athens was democratic. The core of Rome's constitution was oligarchic-democratic, as was the case in the Spartan constitution. The core of the Athenian constitution was democratic, while the core of the Carthaginian constitution was oligarchic-plutocratic.

The constitutional centre of the Roman Republic was, of course, the Senate, while the five Ephors were the constitutional centre of Sparta. Rome was similar in that respect to Carthage, as the Council of the Elders in Carthage seemed to be the Carthaginian Empire's constitutional centre. Athens differed to Rome in this respect, however, as the *Ecclesia* was practically supreme over the rest of the Athenian institutions. In Rome, the *populus*, the Tribal Assembly and the Plebeian Council were not constitutionally emancipated to the point that they would be deemed the Republic's constitutional centre, even after *Lex Hortensia*. Relevant bodies, it has been explained,[29] were practically procedurally controlled by Rome's magistrates.

Moreover, the Roman Republic, Sparta and Carthage were oligarchic constitutions as a whole. When it comes to the most powerful individuals in the Spartan constitution, these were Sparta's Senators/Elders (*Γερουσιασταί*) and its Ephors (*Έφοροι*). In Athens, the most powerful individuals were practically its free Athenian male citizens (*Εκκλησιασταί* or *Εκκλησιάζοντες*). In Carthage, the two individuals holding most power in their hands were the two Suphetes, *mutatis mutandis* the Kings of Carthage, together, probably, with the Elders of Carthage (*Γερόντιον* or *Παλαιοί*), while in the Rome of the Republic it would practically be the two Censors and the two Consuls in normal times and the Dictator in

[25] L Capogrossi Colognesi, *Law and Power in the Making of the Roman Commonwealth* (Cambridge University Press 2014) xxxii.

[26] Capogrossi Colognesi (n 25) 38–9.

[27] A Kalyvas, 'The Tyranny of Dictatorship: When the Greek Tyrant Met the Roman Dictator' (2007) 35 *Political Theory* 412.

[28] On Sparta's mixed constitution, see e.g. Plat. Laws 3.693d–e; Aristot. Pol. 2.1265b.

[29] Refer to Chapter 13 herein.

extraordinary times who would hold the most constitutional power in their hands as individuals. A distinction to be drawn here is that between the Consuls and the Dictator, on the one hand, and the Censors, on the other hand: technically, the former two held *imperium*, when the latter did not. However, the Censors were constitutionally formidable, in that their powers of removal, appointment and supervision over the Republic were extensive and significant.[30]

All four constitutions compared had from limited to extensive monarchic elements to them but in the case of Athens this was symbolic. For instance, the role of the *Archon Basileus* (*Ἄρχων Βασιλεύς*), democratic Athens' Magistrate King, was just one of the few monarchic remnants in the Athenian constitution, a relic from the past, the powers of the particular officer being mainly religious. All four came with democratic elements. Three of them, with the exception of Athens, came with oligarchic elements. The same three, with the exception of Athens again, came with aristocratic elements but such elements were limited. Plutocratic elements were not part and parcel of Athens' and Sparta's[31] constitutions but in Rome and Carthage the plutocratic elites significantly affected the system of government at crucial points of time. The same three constitutions came with gerontocratic elements, whereas the Athenian constitution was not defined by such elements. Finally, the Athenian constitution came with an institution that somewhat remotely resembled a modern parliament: the *Boule* (*Βουλή*). The close and oligarchic character of the senates in Sparta, Rome and Carthage would not otherwise come close to the democratic parliaments of contemporaneity.

For fear of the rule of one man, the Rome of the Republic also aspired to dyarchies, as did Sparta and Carthage to some extent. The two Consuls and the two Censors would be classic offices of monarchic powers in the form of dyarchies.[32] It is not clear whether it was only the Roman fear of the rise of a tyrant that made dyarchy a central choice in Rome's constitution or whether the Romans were inspired by dyarchies in older[33] constitutions to theirs (e.g. that of Sparta's dual kingship),[34] or both. Of course, the Consuls and the Censors of Rome were not hereditary offices, unlike the Kings of Sparta (*ἀρχαγέται*[35] or *βασιλεῖς*[36]) that would be hereditary[37] offices. Furthermore, one notes that the five Ephors of Sparta would change after one year, as would the Consuls and Praetors in Rome. What is

30 Refer to Chapter 10 herein.

31 On Sparta's animosity towards the possession of silver and gold in late 5th century BC, see e.g. M Herman Hansen, 'Was Sparta a Normal or Exceptional Polis?' in Hodkinson (n 2) 402, citing Plut. Lys. 17.1–6; Xen. Const. Lac. 7.6.

32 On the use of the term 'monarchic' for dyarchic offices, see e.g. Aristot. Pol. 2.1265b.

33 E.g. in the wider Greek world, beyond Sparta's dual kingship, dyarchies, rare as they were, existed in the Heroic Ages Lycia and Messenia: see Herman Hansen (n 31) 403, citing Hom. Il. 6.192 (sic) and Paus. 4.4.4.

34 On Sparta's dyarchy, see e.g. E Millender, 'The Spartan Dyarchy: A Comparative Perspective' in Hodkinson (n 2) 1–67.

35 Plut. Lyc. 6.2.

36 Tyrtaeus 4.3 and 5.1 as cited in Herman Hansen (n 31) 403.

37 Millender (n 34) 40.

Table 14.1 Macrocomparative chart of the world's leading ancient constitutions

Relevant Subject Area of Comparison	THE SPARTAN CONSTITUTION (5th century BC)	THE ATHENIAN CONSTITUTION (PERICLEAN DEMOCRACY c. 460–431 BC)	THE CONSTITUTION OF CARTHAGE (c. 4th century BC)	THE CONSTITUTION OF ROME (3rd and 2nd century BC)
Form of Government	Mixed Constitution (Republic/Polity)	Democracy	Mixed Constitution (Republic/Polity)	Mixed Constitution (Republic/Polity)
Constitutional Core of the State	Oligarchic-Monarchic – Limited Democratic	Democratic	Plutocratic-Oligarchic with the Election of the Suphetes being Democratic	Oligarchic-Monarchic – Limited Democratic
Constitutional Centre	The Ephors	The *Ecclesia*	The Council of the Elders	The Senate
Nature of Constitutional Centre	Oligarchic	Democratic	Oligarchic	Oligarchic
Credentials of Constitutional Centre's Legitimacy	Democratic	Democratic	Oligarchic-Plutocratic	Oligarchic
Government's Co-ordinating Force(s)/ Person(s)/Group	The Ephors and the *Gerousia*	The *Ecclesia*	The Suphetes and the Council of the Elders	The Senate
Most Powerful Individual(s) Constitutionally	The Ephors	The Citizens	The Suphetes/the Elders	The Two Consuls and the Two Censors/The Dictator (in relation to fixed term offices) and the Senators (in relation to their normally life term office)
Unitary/Federal	Unitary	Unitary	Unitary	Unitary
Form of Control over Associated/ Conquered/ Colonised States and Lands	Hegemonic	Hegemonic until 454 BC; imperial thereafter	Imperial	Hegemonic over Italian territories mostly until 201 BC; imperial thereafter
Term of Citizens/ Magistrates within Constitutional Centre	1 year	For life	N/A	Senators were for life, unless removed, which was rare
Monarchic Elements in the Constitution	Yes	Yes but most limited in the form of the Three *Archontes*	Yes	Yes
Oligarchic Elements in the Constitution	Yes	No	Yes	Yes

Table 14.1 (*cont.*)

Relevant Subject Area of Comparison	THE SPARTAN CONSTITUTION (5th century BC)	THE ATHENIAN CONSTITUTION (PERICLEAN DEMOCRACY c. 460–431 BC)	THE CONSTITUTION OF CARTHAGE (c. 4th century BC)	THE CONSTITUTION OF ROME (3rd and 2nd century BC)
Aristocratic Elements in the Constitution	Yes (partially)	Yes (partially)	Yes (partially)	Yes (partially)
Democratic Elements in the Constitution	Yes	Yes	Yes	Yes
Plutocratic Elements in the Constitution	No	No	Yes	Yes
Gerontocratic Elements in the Constitution	Yes	No	Yes	Yes
Democratic Parliament	No	Yes (*Βουλή* of 500)	No	No
Free Male Citizens Only in the Constitutional Machinery	Yes	Yes	In all probability, yes	Yes, but women too could attend the *Contiones*
Single King	No	Yes, the *Archon Basileus*, but limited to religious and certain judicial functions	No	No
Dyarchy of Kings	Yes	No	Yes	Yes
System that the City would impose on Conquered/ Defeated Territories	Oligarchies	Mostly democracies; also, *cleruchies* (estates system)	In all probability, the subject areas of Carthage held similar systems of government to the metropolis (Carthage)	System of garrisons and, occasionally, cleruchies; oligarchies, especially in Greece
Checks and Balances	Yes	Yes	Yes	Yes
Vetoing	Yes, e.g. the *Gerousia* could veto the *Apella*	No, since the 462/461 BC reforms	N/A	Yes, e.g. a Consul could veto the other Consul
Fixed Terms	Partially	Yes	Partially	Yes, for elected and appointed magistrates and officials. Senators were for life, unless removed
Power to Impeach	Yes	Yes, especially through ostracism	N/A	Yes, the Censors had the power to remove Senators
Regular Voting	Yes	Yes	Yes	Yes

also clear is that the two Spartan Kings' office was collegiate,[38] whereas the office of the two Roman Consuls' office, whilst collegiate,[39] allowed one Consul to veto the actions of the other Consul, to prevent abuse of power. Also, it is to be noted that another leading constitution of the ancient world, that of Carthage, came with a dyarchy in the form of the two Suphetes (*Šoupheṭim*).[40] These would be the two *Kritai* of Carthage, nominally its two 'Judges' but, practically, its two Kings. In Rome too an old name for the Consuls seems to have been that of *iudices*.[41] Livy informs us also that Carthage's two Suphetes enjoyed the same *imperium* as Rome's two Consuls.[42] However, Seneca seems to go a step further: for him the Consuls and the Suphetes would 'administer'[43] the Roman Republic and the Carthaginian Empire respectively, even though he gives no further information than that except for the fact that he cites in his reference the old office of *Ceryx* (*Κῆρυξ*) and the office of *Prytan(is)* (*Πρύτανις*), impliedly in Athens. Polybius also mentions that the Roman Republic was very similar to Sparta and Carthage, in that the Carthaginians had Kings and an 'aristocracy', a Senate, the *Gerontion* (*Γερόντιον*),[44] as he calls it.[45] It goes without saying that all three constitutions of Sparta, Rome and Carthage came with a senate to them. The Spartan Senate (*Γερουσία*) was the smallest one of the three with 30 members (28 Senators per se plus the two Kings of Sparta) to it but Sparta was in all probability the smallest city[46] among the cities of Sparta, Carthage and Rome (e.g. in the 3rd century BC). Rome's classical Senate, the one from the beginning of the Republic to 133 BC, was an institution in the region of 300 members.[47] The number of Carthaginian Senators cannot be adduced according to current sources.[48] Table 14.1 illustrates the above in addition to offering certain other macrocomparative elements in relation to these four ancient constitutions.

14.9 MACROCOMPARISON OF THE ROMAN REPUBLIC WITH LEADING MODERN CONSTITUTIONS

It would take a new separate volume to compare the Roman Republic's constitutions with modern constitutions. Of course, from modern constitutions it is the

38 Millender (n 34) 11.
39 Capogrossi Colognesi (n 25) 74.
40 On Carthage's dyarchy, see IE Τζαμτζής, *Carthago Καρχηδών* (Εκδόσεις Σάκκουλα 2023) 29–57.
41 Arena (n 4) 593.
42 Liv. 30 7 5.
43 Sen. Tranq. 9.4.5.
44 Plb. 6.51.2.
45 For more on the comparison between Carthage and Rome, see Τζαμτζής (n 40) 29–30.
46 On the oliganthropy of Sparta, see e.g. Herman Hansen (n 31) 393–6 and S Hodkinson, 'Was Sparta an Exceptional Polis?' in Hodkinson (n 2) 432–42.
47 E.g. RE Mitchell, *Patricians and Plebeians: The Origin of the Roman State* (Cornell University Press 1990) 2; D Hoyos, *Rome Victorious: The Irresistible Rise of the Roman Empire* (Bloomsbury Academic 2019, reprinted 2023) 11.
48 E.g. Τζαμτζής (n 40) 63–5.

constitution of the USA that comes closest to the overall spirit of the constitution of the Roman Republic. However, relevant macrocomparative headings for a brief macrocomparison between the Roman Republic's constitution and the British constitution, the US Constitution, the Italian Constitution, the German Basic Law and the French Constitution would include the following at the very least: mixed form of government (even in the UK, which is a Constitutional Monarchy), checks and balances; veto powers; terms of office;[49] impeachment powers, regular elections and constitutional emergency powers. To this list one can add the selection of officials;[50] and the overall (but not anywhere near perfect in the case of the Roman Republic) division of powers.[51] The claim, of course, is not that the above would be found in modern constitutions in a very similar way to the constitution of the Roman Republic but rather, more subtly, that the Republic's core constitutional characteristics are very much still with us in the world of modern democracies through different means and constitutional devices. For instance, there is no such thing as an extraordinary office of the Dictator in the world's modern and developed Republics but there is such thing as emergency constitutional powers, distant constitutional echoes of the Republic's *senatus consulta ultima*, and so on.[52] Table 14.2 is submitted for the benefit of the reader as a macrocomparative chart between the constitution of the Roman Republic and certain of the world's modern constitutions.

49 Posner (n 9) 43–4.
50 Posner (n 9) 41.
51 Posner (n 9) 42–3.
52 On Rome's emergency and extraordinary powers and regimes, see Straumann (n 3) 64–74 (office of the Dictatorship), 74–88 (Decemvirates (Ten-Man Commissions) and the dictatorial republics of Sulla and Julius Caesar), 88–100 (*Senatus ultima consulta*) and 100–17 (extraordinary orders).

Table 14.2 Macrocomparative chart of the constitution of the Roman Republic and certain modern constitutions

Relevant Subject Area of Comparison	THE CONSTITUTION OF ROME (3rd and 2nd century BC)	THE CONSTITUTION OF THE UK (1215 to date)	THE CONSTITUTION OF THE USA (1787/89 to date)	THE ITALIAN CONSTITUTION (1947/48 to date)	THE GERMAN BASIC LAW (1949 to date)	THE FRENCH CONSTITUTION (1958 to date)
Form of Government	Mixed Constitution (Republic/Polity)	Constitutional Monarchy	Mixed Constitution (Republic/Polity)	Mixed Constitution (Republic/Polity)	Mixed Constitution (Republic/Polity)	Mixed Constitution (Republic/Polity)
Constitutional Core of the State	Oligarchic-Monarchic	Democratic	Democratic	Democratic	Democratic	Democratic
Constitutional Centre	The Senate	The House of Commons (as opposed to the Parliament as a whole)	The President and the Congress	The Parliament	The National Federal Diet	The President and the Parliament
Nature of Constitutional Centre	Oligarchic	Democratic	Monarchic (President)/ Democratic (Congress)	Democratic	Democratic	Monarchic (President)/ Democratic (Parliament)
Credentials of Constitutional Centre's Legitimacy	Oligarchic	Democratic	Democratic	Democratic	Democratic	Democratic
Government's Co-ordinating Force/ Person	The Senators as a collective	The Prime Minister	The President	The Prime Minister	The Chancellor	The Prime Minister
Most Powerful Individual(s) Constitutionally	The Censors and the Consuls/the Dictator (when it came to fixed term magistrates) but also the Senators as officials for life	The Prime Minister	The President	The Prime Minister	The Chancellor	The President
Unitary/Federal	Unitary	Unitary – Greater devolution to Scotland, Northern Ireland and Wales since 1921, 1998, 2006, 2012, 2014, 2016 and 2017	Federal	Unitary but certain autonomy has been granted to 5 out of 20 Italian Regions	Federal	Unitary

Separation of Powers	Partial and limited; more of a division of powers in offices occasionally having mixed powers in themselves	Yes	Yes	Yes	Yes	Yes
Term of Citizens/ Magistrates/Officials within Constitutional Centre	Senators were for life, unless removed, which was rare	Indefinite five-year terms for the Members of the House of Commons on democratic mandate	Indefinite two-year terms for Representatives and indefinite six-year terms for Senators on democratic mandate; two four-year terms maximum for the same person holding Presidential Office	Indefinite number of terms for the elected members of the Assembly and the elected Senators on democratic mandate; however, five Senators are for life	Indefinite number of terms for Members of the Lower and the Upper House of the Diet on democratic mandate	Indefinite number of terms for members of the National Assembly and the Senate on democratic mandate; two five-year consecutive terms maximum for the President
Monarchic Elements in the Constitution	Yes (multiple)	Yes (the British Monarch)	Yes (the American President)	Yes (the President of the Republic)	Yes (the Federal President of the Republic)	Yes (the President of the Republic)
Oligarchic Elements in the Constitution	Yes	Partially – see hereditary peers and appointees in the House of Lords	No, especially after 1913, when Senators started to be elected directly by the US people throughout the federation	No, with the exception of the very few Senators appointed for life or becoming senators of the kind *ex officio*	No	No
Aristocratic Elements in the Constitution	Yes	Yes	Yes	Yes	Yes	Yes
Democratic Elements in the Constitution	Yes	Yes	Yes	Yes	Yes	Yes
Plutocratic Elements in the Constitution	Yes, in that the Senate was traditionally controlled by Rome's wealthiest families	Yes *lato sensu*, especially through lobbyism	Yes *lato sensu*, especially through lobbyism	Yes *lato sensu*, especially through lobbyism	Yes *lato sensu*, especially through lobbyism	Yes *lato sensu*, especially through lobbyism
Monarch or 'Monarch' or Monarchic Elements with Executive Powers	Yes	No; limited, mostly formal, executive powers	Yes	No; limited, mostly formal, executive powers	No; limited, mostly formal, executive powers	Yes

Table 14.2 (*cont.*)

Relevant Subject Area of Comparison	THE CONSTITUTION OF ROME (3rd and 2nd century BC)	THE CONSTITUTION OF THE UK (1215 to date)	THE CONSTITUTION OF THE USA (1787/89 to date)	THE ITALIAN CONSTITUTION (1947/48 to date)	THE GERMAN BASIC LAW (1949 to date)	THE FRENCH CONSTITUTION (1958 to date)
Checks and Balances	Yes	Yes	Yes	Yes	Yes	Yes
Vetoing	Yes	Yes, e.g. the UK Government can intervene and veto a UK nation's bill	Yes, e.g. Presidential veto, which can only be overridden by a 2/3 majority of those voting in the Senate and the House of Representatives	Yes, e.g. Presidential veto, which can be overridden if the same law is passed again in Parliament	Yes, e.g. Presidential veto; the *Bundesrat* too can veto a bill, if such affects the interests of the German federal states	Yes, e.g. Presidential veto for reconsideration of a law by Parliament once on the basis that the Prime Minister has agreed to this
Fixed Terms	Yes, for magistrates but not for Senators	Yes	Yes	Yes	Yes	Yes
Power to Impeach	Yes, Censors could remove Senators	Yes, especially through a vote of no confidence	Yes, the Congress can remove the President	Yes, the Parliament can in a joint session through a majority request the removal of the President	Yes, the Federal Diet on the final approval of the Federal Constitutional Court can remove the President	Yes, the President can be removed through the procedure of destitution
Emergency Constitutional Offices/ Powers	Yes: Dictator Office (501–44 BC)/*Senatus Consulta Ultima* (121–40 BC)	Yes	Yes	Yes	Yes	Yes
Regular Voting	Yes	Yes	Yes	Yes	Yes	Yes

PART IV
CONCLUDING THOUGHTS

Chapter 15

A Constitution that Could Not Support Any More the Empire it Generated

15.1 INTRODUCTION

It is a historical fact that the Roman empire was created during and because of the Roman Republic, the Republic eventually having given way to the Roman Principate. The constitution of the Roman Republic was sacrificed in the process. This chapter, thus, explains that the constitution of the Republic could simply not accommodate Rome's transformation into an empire; nor could it withhold the powerful and often violent social and political forces that were ready to be unleashed in Rome when opportunity would arise in the 2nd and the 1st centuries BC. The chapter further explains that the Republic, by constitutional design, was about making it most challenging, if not impossible, for a single political figure in the form of a *Rex* (King) to become Rome's absolute ruler; at least, this was the Republic's constitutional intent. It also explains that the Republic was not originally designed with the idea of creating an imperial Republic either. As such, this chapter explores the legal, political, social and constitutional reasons as to the fact that, by late 2nd century BC, the Roman Republic's constitution was not fit for purpose for an empire that was constantly growing.

15.2 ROME'S RISE TO EMPIRE STATUS IN THE 2ND CENTURY BC

It was clear in the 2nd century BC already, that the Republic could simply not support the empire that it generated. Equally, at least according to Polybius, the peculiar[1] nature of the constitution of the Roman Republic and its mixed character were responsible for the restoration of Roman power over Carthage, Rome's conquests in parts of the Mediterranean world and its eventual rise to world domination.[2] Montesquieu, however, noted that the same constitution could not support the geopolitical giant it had created. He was quite illuminating in this respect: the sheer size of the imperial Republic led to its retreat to the Principate,

[1] Plb. 3.118.9.

[2] R Seager, 'Polybius' Distortions of the Roman "Constitution": A Simpl(istic) Explanation' in R Gibson and T Harrison (eds), *Polybius and his World. Essays in Memory of F. W. Walbank* (Oxford University Press 2013) 247–8 citing Polybius 3. 2. 6; 3. 118. 9; 6. 2. 9; 6. 3. 7; 39. 8. 7).

as the Roman Republic still had constitutional structures that would be geared mostly towards a city, Rome, rather than an empire.[3]

Yet, the particular constitution, at least until the beginning of the 2nd century's final quarter or so, was the constitution that generated the Roman empire in the first place, despite the fact that the Republic, as a constitutional order and political reality, started to crumble after 133 BC. As Eder states, 'something was rotten in [the Roman] state and society'.[4] It should also be noted that, even after the fall of the Republic, the Romans believed that it was the Republic that made Rome a superpower and that republicanism was part and parcel of the Roman psyche.[5] The Romans were right with regard to the former but not with regard to the latter: Rome indeed rose because of its sophisticated Republic and her constitution; this was a key factor for her rise. However, the Romans were probably wrong to identify themselves with republicanism per se, in that imperial Rome actually lasted more years through the Principate and the Dominate than the Roman Republic did, whilst the Second Rome, Constantinople, was always imperial in what later came to be the Eastern Roman Empire.

15.3 CONSIDERABLE PRESSURES ON THE REPUBLIC'S CONSTITUTION

Rome's excellence according to Polybius has been effectively the result of her mixed constitution.[6] Equally, Polybius himself, a person who at least in his writings, openly admired Rome's constitutional structures, put Rome's deterioration down to 'uncontestable interstate power and the rise of the popular element in political life'.[7] Peculiarly, however, while he was painting the Rome that he admired – at least from what one could observe through his writings – with grim colours, the Treaty of Apamea in 188 BC, between the Roman Republic and the Seleucid Empire, effectively made Rome operate as a major empire in the making in the Mediterranean world[8] rather than a geopolitical power that would confine its ambition to the Italian peninsula, the south part of seaside Illyria and certain coastal parts of the east and south Iberian peninsula. Of course, the Republic was already imperial in its overall outlook by 202 BC (post Roman victory over

[3] HI Flower, 'The Imperial Republic' in A Barchiesi and W Scheidel (eds), *The Oxford Handbook of Roman Studies* (Oxford University Press 2010) 528.

[4] W Eder, 'Republicans and Sinners: The Decline of the Roman Republic and the End of a Provisional Arrangement' in RW Wallace and EM Harris (eds), *Transitions to Empire: Essays in Greco-Roman History, 360–146 B.C., in Honor of* E. *Badian* (University of Oklahoma Press 1996) 440.

[5] E.g. Flower (n 3) 528.

[6] E.g. J Tan, 'Climate Change and Rome's Changing Republic' in M Balbo and F Santangelo (eds), *A Community in Transition: Rome between Hannibal and the Gracchi* (Oxford University Press 2023) 37 referring to Book 6 of Polybius' *Histories*.

[7] C Champion, 'Historiographic Patterns and Historical Obstacles in Polybius' *Histories*: Marcellus, Flaminius, and the Mamertine Crisis' in B Gibson and T Harrison (n 2) 143.

[8] IE Τζαμτζής, *Ο Μεσογειακός Κόσμος* (Εκδόσεις Σάκκουλα 2014, ανατύπωση 2018) 79.

Carthage at the battle of Zama)[9] and clearly an imperial power by the end of the Second Punic War in 201 BC but after 188 BC it was also a major geopolitical power in the Mediterranean world. Rome in the 2nd century BC, after Zama, became the aggressor in the Eastern Mediterranean.[10] However, the constitutional shell of the Roman Republic was in the process of cracking: Rome's policies would result in tensions with its Italian *socii* and *foederati* to the point that a social war, the Social War, would eventually ensue in the early 1st century BC between Rome and many of its disgruntled Italian allies.[11]

Even so, it is interesting that Polybius was concerned with Rome's deterioration, when the empire had been growing and becoming stronger for decades already. An explanation for this may be the fact that Polybius was, or at least would like to be seen as, a responsible critical friend of Rome to the point that he would inform it of a future downfall or deterioration, despite the fact that its empire was in the process of rising. In other words, Polybius may have ultimately foreseen the fall of the Republic (as opposed to the fall of the empire).

But the more ominous interpretation of Polybius' writings may concern the fact that democracy, as a system of government, was not necessarily favoured by him. In all this, he may have been impliedly right that the Rome of his time had been wrongly accelerating towards somewhat more democratic forms of government in an existing constitution that had, according to him, certain significant democratic features, amongst its monarchic and aristocratic features. However, Rome was traditionally mostly oligarchic and Polybius' implicit warning may have related to the fact that democracy and oligarchy are not best friends in a constitutional order. Thus, not only would the constitution of the Republic not be 'fit for purpose' for Rome's ever-growing empire and ambition, but it would also impliedly lack the practical political 'capability', at least for Polybius in 2nd century BC, and at least in the final 150 years of the Republic, to 'tolerate', let alone sustain, any constitutional reform towards a slightly more democratic reality for Rome.

It would also be important for one to appreciate that the Roman Republic's constitution of 509 BC was created for fear of returning to the one-man absolute state(s) in the final stages of the Roman Monarchy. The transition was from monarchy to a mixed constitution. Rome's mixed constitution was never created with an imperial republic in mind. If the ruling elites of Rome had wholly masterminded a republican constitution at the end of the 6th century, which, of course, seems highly likely, the proto-Republican atmosphere of Rome at the time would be a far cry from a constitution of imperial ambitions. Rome was, at the time, a small and rather insignificant republic in central Italy, merely fighting for survival and to sustain itself against its neighbours. Rome's imperial ambition started to grow only as late as the 3rd century BC; such ambition flourished further in the

[9] Cf. WV Harris, 'Power' in Barchiesi and Scheidel (n 3) 568.

[10] HI Flower, 'Epilogue – Periodization in Perspective: Further Thoughts about the Second Century BCE' in Balbo and Santangelo (n 6) 341.

[11] Ibid.

2nd century BC, while during the 1st century BC it was absolutely clear that Rome was a full-blown empire with little interest in maintaining its traditional republican roots and values. Yet, as its empire was growing, its republican constitution was retreating.

15.4 A CONSTITUTION CREATED FOR A CITY EVENTUALLY COULD NOT SUSTAIN AN EMPIRE

Constitutional disharmony had already been the case from the 2nd century BC: the Republic's constitution was created for a city, at most for Latium, but Rome was no longer merely an Italian geopolitical power. It was a Mediterranean geopolitical power. So too, the ambition of its elites spanned beyond Italy. Conventionally, it should be stated at this point that from the assassination of Tiberius Gracchus, the Republic of Rome's final days began. As stated, however, Rome's republican constitution was designed for the more limited purposes of a city and the region around it. Dramatically, the Roman Republic's fall started from within it,[12] from the very constitution that made it an empire. By design, therefore, it was not conceived as a constitution for an empire and it could just not support the empire that it actually generated.[13] In the 1st century BC, the Roman empire continued to grow at a pace that not only crushed the Republic's constitution but also created the very conditions for the rise of an emperor, the exact opposite of the Republic's raison d'être. Rome's republican constitutional engine was simply not potent enough to keep the empire; it was not designed for that. Rome needed a new constitutional engine. The point is also attested by taking a more political economy perspective: Rome's checks and balances had worked for about four centuries due to its limited and homogeneous population during this time.[14] However, a constitutional lawyer could maintain that the constitutional design behind the city of Rome would simply not be sufficient for the more heterogeneous and expanded Roman empire, which was the case in the 1st century BC. The more Rome expanded, the greater the pressure on its constitution, which of course collapsed altogether in 27 BC.

Moreover, it was not Tiberius Gracchus' assassination per se that led the Republic into chaos. It was the fact that his assassination would unleash some of the darkest forces in Roman history and society. The Republic was thereafter steadily becoming a mere shadow of its old self and, whilst the empire and Rome's ambition continued to grow, Rome was not a republic any more but a reality in which powerful personalities would effectively run city and empire with internal conflicts defining the day.

[12] Cf. Eder (n 4) 440.

[13] Cf. Eder (n 4) 439, citing Montesquieu, *Oeuvres complètes de Montesquieu* I (Paris, 1892) and W Dahlheim, *Die griechisch-römische Antike*, vol. 2: *Rom* (Paderborn, 1992) 156.

[14] EA Posner, 'The Constitution of the Roman Republic' in G Dari-Mattiacci and DP Kehoe (eds), *Roman Law and Economics: Institutions and Organizations Volume I* (Oxford University Press 2020) 36.

15.5 THE EMPIRE WEAKENED THE REPUBLIC'S CONSTITUTION TO ITS FINAL DEMISE

On the one hand, the Republic and, by extension its constitutional order, was responsible for the empire. On the other hand, the empire that was created weakened, to the point of dismantling,[15] the Republic and the constitution which were responsible for its creation. At the beginning of the 2nd century BC, the senatorial order of Rome had already become alarmed by the fact that certain nobles of Rome wished to influence the *populus* in order to promote their own personal interests.[16] The personal ambitions of powerful men in Rome would become ever greater and would stand in the way of Rome's constitution. This trend continued and became even stronger in the 1st century BC. Thus, Rome, for most of the final century of its Republic, was not ruled so much by its constitution any more but by powerful military personalities such as Sulla and Julius Caesar.[17] Apparently, rather paradoxically, close to the Republic's constitutional fall, the Roman masses were heard somewhat more than previously,[18] but there was to be no return for the Republic: the republic which for centuries fought tooth and nail against the rule of one man over Rome would wholly retreat and Rome would return to one man rule.

15.6 THE CURTAIN OF THE REPUBLIC FALLS: FROM A REPUBLIC OF INSTITUTIONS TO A REPUBLIC OF PERSONALITIES

The argument that Rome's constitution had not 'exceeded the bounds of its possibilities, but [its fall was due to the fact that its] institutional framework had never been thought out carefully'[19] is misleading. Let us elaborate on this: first and foremost, that is an easy argument to make but certainly a difficult one to sustain. For all its systemic weaknesses, the Republic was, before the beginning of its end, a rather well-organised and well-arranged constitutional order which actually matured over a good three centuries and a half (509–133 BC). It is the case, however, that after 133 BC in the Late Republic, the spirit of the Middle Republic effectively gave way to something that was a republic in name or, more precisely from the historical-political point of view, a sequence of governments in Rome that comprised a rather turbulent set of mini republics, atypical dictatorships and triumvirates. Legally, Rome's constitutional order was predominantly republican but not continuously any more. It was patchy. Second, many of the structures of the Republic were quite stable. For instance, the institutions of

15 Harris (n 9) 570.

16 M Bellomo, 'The Administration of the *Imperium Romanum* in the Second Century BCE' in Balbo and Santangelo (n 6) 175.

17 Harris (n 9) 570.

18 E.g. Harris (n 9) 570.

19 Eder (n 4) 440–1.

Consuls, the Dictator, the Senate itself, went back a number of centuries. Of course, these offices, these institutions, could have been designed even better but it could certainly be opined that the Republic of Rome was clearly quite mature, confident and well-functioning in the years of the Middle Republic. Finally, the strength of the Plebeian Tribunes can clearly be seen and ought to be seen as a democratic strength of the Republic; not as a thing that held the Republic back.[20] In fact, the opposite is true: Sulla made the constitution more anti-democratic to the point that the Plebeians would have a lesser voice than they did. That overall lessening of the Plebeian voice must have been a crucial factor in the fall of the Republic. A more authoritarian regime, the Principate, would replace the Republic.

This brings us to the next two points, which were also associated with the way the Republic was designed. Here one notes another well-known argument as to the fall of the Republic: 'the exigencies of administering an empire over-stressed the capacity of a city-state'.[21] The constitution of the Roman Republic was, of course, designed for a city and it would just not be able to deal with the needs of running an empire. In modern constitutional terms, this would be the equivalent of running the whole of the United States of America under the Laws of the City of New York. Another argument, our second point here, is the fact that the Roman Republic, an inherently conservative republic, 'missed opportunities to adapt the constitution of city-state to the administrative demands of an empire'.[22]

Finally, let us recall this: Rome's institutions despite reform could not thwart the Republic's demise. For example, Sulla's reforms could not avert powerful personalities from taking control of the Republic in the future, him having been another powerful personality who created a dictatorial republic in his years in power. In short, what was fundamentally a republic of institutions and magistrates deteriorated into a republic of personalities in the 1st century BC.[23] The wider connotations here concern the fact that the role of individuals in the face of constitutional legal history should not be underestimated. If so, the cynical but pragmatic argument would be that the Romans did not underestimate the effect of such powerful personalities as Tiberius Gracchus, Julius Caesar and Cicero but, by all accounts, the means chosen to remove these great men from Roman politics were wholly unacceptable.

[20] But cf. Eder (n 4) 441.

[21] Eder (n 4) 444.

[22] Eder (n 4) 445.

[23] Cf. Flower (n 3) 529; CF Noreña, 'The Early Imperial Monarchy' in Barchiesi and Scheidel (n 4) 533.

15.7 WHY THE ROMAN REPUBLIC'S CONSTITUTIONAL ENGINE FALTERED: BEYOND OVERSTRETCHING AND INITIAL DESIGN FLAWS THAT WERE NOT SUBSEQUENTLY RECTIFIED

Yet, it was not just the flaws in the initial design of Rome's constitutional engine that led to the Republic's demise; it was not just the fact that Rome's constitutional engine operated at a much higher level than it was configured for, overstretching to breaking point; it was not just the fact that the constitutional design flaws of a Republic, which would now control an empire, were not rectified. It was all these things in conjunction with other factors too: economic factors such as a rich centre (Rome) and a poorer periphery (countryside); Rome's constant engagement with warfare; the expansion of patronage in Roman society especially vis-à-vis the Roman army; the non-engagement with recurring military and economic matters; the ambition and competition of Rome's military leaders; the fact that political compromise would often become impossible, when Rome of the centuries before 133 BC would have flourished, in one way or another, on reasonable compromises between its different political classes; civil wars and civil strife; a Senate that would be but a shadow of its old self; the willingness to impose a state of emergency in Rome through *senatus ultima consulta* or by way of dictatorial figures as Sulla (as opposed to maintaining the republican order of things per se without use of such extraordinary measures); and the fact that those who would abuse Rome's constitution could do so without repercussion.[24] To this list, one should also add: corruption; the greed of the ruling classes of Rome for more power and more wealth, even to the detriment of the Roman people; a decadent political atmosphere closer to the final fall of the Republic; proscriptions that created a state of terror in Rome; a state of extensive violence in Rome (but also in other parts of the empire); and mistrust and deterioration of the constitutional characteristics that first made the Republic the great republic that it once was.

[24] Flower (n 3) 529.

Chapter 16

The Fall of the Republic (133–27 BC)

The [S]tate is dead[1]

'Non mos, non ius.' ... and out of the blood of Caesar the monarchy [was once] again born.[2]

16.1 INTRODUCTION

This chapter explores and explains the reasons, constitutional and otherwise, why the Republic, a republic that was praised by many for its strengths, was a republic but in name only in the period of decline of the Roman Republic. Whereas the Republic's purpose was to make it impossible for a *Rex* (King) to take control of it, dictators in the 1st century BC, moving away from the classical essence of the office of the Dictator, would effectively move Rome back to a more absolute constitutional type of order, the Republic eventually giving way to the Principate. This chapter also juxtaposes the apex of the constitution of the Roman Republic with this period, the period that was effectively the end of the Republic. The effect powerful personalities such as Sulla and Julius Caesar had on the Republic's constitution is explored in certain detail here, in addition to assessing the deterioration of the Senate in its operations, when the Senate was traditionally a body that would uphold the Republic.

16.2 THE ASSASSINATION OF TIBERIUS AS THE SYMBOLIC BEGINNING OF THE END OF THE REPUBLIC

It was the blood of Tiberius Gracchus in 133 BC, not the final victory of the Romans against the Carthaginians in 146 BC, that signified the symbolic beginning of the end[3] for the Roman Republic.[4] It was, of course, the blood of the assassinated Julius Caesar in 44 BC that would signal the final unravelling of the Republic until its full demise in 27 BC. Of course, conventionally, the Late Republic could stand

[1] C Steel, *The End of the Roman Republic, 146 to 44 BC: Conquest and Crisis* (Edinburgh University Press 2013) 167, citing *Att.* 2.21.1, *tota periit*; 2.25.2, *re publica nihil desperatius*.

[2] R Syme, *The Roman Revolution* (Oxford University Press 1939) 201, citing Tacitus, *Ann.* 3, 28.

[3] PA Zoch, *Ancient Rome* (University of Oklahoma Press 1998) 141; HI Flower, *Roman Republics* (Princeton University Press 2010) 61.

[4] But cf. Steel (n 1), arguing that the end of the Republic commenced in 146 BC (as opposed to it commencing with Tiberius Gracchus' death in 133 BC).

for the period between 146 and 27 BC but, in constitutional law terms, the assassination of Tiberius was the first major blow to what was a relatively stable and confident constitution and republic prior to his death. The brutal assassination of this promising young man, a man who wanted to reform land ownership, effectively unleashed the first social and political forces behind the slow and painful dissolution of the Republic, which lasted about 100 years until the Republic's final demise in 27 BC with the rise of the Roman Principate.

16.3 THE REPUBLIC'S FALL POST-133 BC

Major blows to the Republic followed one after another: the assassination of Tiberius' brother too, Gaius Gracchus, in 121 BC, again by Senators, on the 'rationale' that he 'championed the popular cause';[5] the corruption of Roman officials in the Jugurthine War (112–106 BC);[6] the *senatus consultum ultimum* of 100 BC, which led to significant violence in Rome; the Social War between 91 and 87 BC; the corruption of Roman soldiers by moral degradation and the pursuit of luxury;[7] the dictatorial Republic of Sulla of 82–80 BC, starting with the proscription of 82 BC; the perception that the Senate was widely abusing its powers in 67 BC;[8] the so-called Catilinarian conspiracy of 63–62 BC; the civil war between the forces of Julius Caesar and Pompey between 49 and 45 BC; the assassination of Julius Caesar in 44 BC; the proscription of 43 BC, which resulted in the same year in the execution of Cicero; and the civil war of Actium between Octavian and Mark Antony and Cleopatra's forces from 32 to 30 BC. These were all signs of a declining Republic and signs of a constitution that did not have an effect the way it did in the years of the Middle Republic. In the Late Republic, strong personalities could effectively manipulate Republic and constitution. This is, by far, the darkest period of the Roman Republic and one of the darkest periods in a given state in the face of human history.

The Roman Republic after 133 BC effectively ceased to be a republic any more, in the sense of Rome's classical republic. So too, the assassination of Tiberius Gracchus was more than a significant 'challenge to the legitimacy and unity of the ruling class'.[9] After Gracchus' assassination, the Republic, its constitution, started to show the first signs of significant decline. In this period of time, one could still nominally call the Republic a republic but powerful personalities such as Sulla, Cicero, Pompey and Julius Caesar were more important than the classic Republic's constitution, or what was now left of it. The phenomenon of powerful personalities attempting to save or abolish the Republic in the period between 133 and 27 BC is observed. But it was also the historical circumstances that enabled the

[5] Steel (n 1) 26.
[6] 'Everything is for sale at Rome' (*Romae omnia venalia esse*) Sallust, Iug. 8.1, 15–16 as cited in Steel (n 1) 70.
[7] Sal. Cat. 11.
[8] Steel (n 1) 145.
[9] Steel (n 1) 19.

flourishing of such personalities and their rise to power.[10] In any case, those who wished to destroy the remnants of the Republic were eventually successful.

> Thus, the highest officials of the *res publica* tore down the Republic piece by piece; one sin was followed by another until civil war broke out, because one of the sinners should not be allowed to be reelected consul.[11]

The constitution of the Republic was now crumbling. Rome's moral decline led to the deterioration of the Republic politically.[12] The Republic was but a shadow of its past glory days. The old office of the Dictator was abused, so was the *consultum ultimum* mechanism, and the constitution was steadily burning out. This was the constitution that created the Roman empire but was clearly one that could not support the empire any more: at this point, it should be recalled that the Republic's constitution was a constitution that was designed to serve first and foremost Rome itself and, by extension, its surrounding territories (e.g. Latium); not an empire.

The Republic itself was already entering a new phase from 146 BC, in that the end of the Third Punic War was a landmark in Roman history. Whereas the Republic was already imperial since 202 BC (victory of the Romans against the Carthaginians at the Battle of Zama), Rome was now a wholly imperial power. It was not fighting for its survival. It was fighting for expansion and its empire. Its interest was not just to conquer but to conquer, plunder and destroy. Roman imperialism had flourished between 220 and 167 BC, Polybius reporting that 'almost the whole inhabited world was conquered and brought under the dominion of the single city of Rome'.[13] In 146 BC, Rome ordered both Corinth and Carthage to be wholly destroyed and plundered, a major turning point in Rome's history. It was only unfortunate that the Roman generals, for lack of education, knew little of the intrinsic value of the things they would plunder.[14] Rome, while rising, was declining, in that the influence of Greek letters and arts was not felt throughout its ruling classes (let alone in the orders of the Plebeians). In fairness, Mummius and Scipio Aemilianus both proceeded with the destruction of Corinth and Carthage on what seemed to be instructions from Rome, Scipio Aemilianus shedding tears when he saw Carthage burning. In that respect, it was not Rome's executive military arms that had lost so much their soul; it was Rome's central constitutional organ that did – the Senate.

10 Cf. Steel (n 1) 248.

11 W Eder, 'Republicans and Sinners: The Decline of the Roman Republic and the End of a Provisional Arrangement' in RW Wallace and EM Harris (eds), *Transitions to Empire: Essays in Greco-Roman History, 360–146 B.C., in Honor of E. Badian* (University of Oklahoma Press 1996) 453.

12 E.g. AW Lintott, 'Imperial Expansion and Moral Decline in the Roman Republic' (1972) 21(4) *Historia: Zeitschrift für Alte Geschichte* 626, 626–38.

13 Plb. 1.1.

14 E.g. Steel (n 1) 62.

16.4 THE ROMAN EMPIRE CONTINUED TO GROW DESPITE THE FALL OF THE REPUBLIC

The reader would be reminded here that, while the Republic was disintegrating, failing and falling, the Roman empire which the Republic had generated was growing and growing. Thus, most interestingly, while the constitutional engine of the Republic was about to fall apart, the empire was becoming stronger. The invisible hand of the Roman Republic's constitution, responsible for the rise of Rome, was effectively no more.

Concurrently, the last Hellenistic kingdom, the Ptolemaic Kingdom in Egypt, fell into Roman hands in 30 BC with the Roman Republic transforming itself into the Principate in 27 BC. The constitutional decline of republican Rome seems to have left Rome's appetite for new dominions unaffected and could, probably, be explained from the fact that either the Republic's constitution was practically dead since the times of Sulla already or from the fact that, despite the Republic's powerful military element in its constitution, the Senate and, by extension, Rome's ruling classes, would wholly superimpose their ambitions over army and constitution. Powerful personalities raised private armies, this leading to considerable civil conflicts and wars.[15] A peculiar stratocratic, dictatorial, senatorial-plutocratic, mixed constitution was observed in the final five decades of the Roman Republic, a constitution that was clearly very different from the more balanced republic between 287 and 133 BC. Rome became a plutocracy with powerful and overambitious personalities ruling the day, ironically like the plutocracy of the city that Rome hated the most: Carthage.

Moreover, the nexus of power in the Roman Republic was effectively one that would traditionally address the tensions of the following two: first, the tensions between different members of the ruling elite of Rome; and, second, the tensions between the ruling elite and the citizens of Rome.[16] However, in the Late Republic this nexus of power became much more fragile and the tensions between the Senate and the people of Rome became ever-increasing. If the clinical death of the Republic was nominally declared in 27 BC, the Roman patient that the Late Republic was, became almost terminally ill from 80 BC, having sustained the first major hit already in 133 BC.

[15] Cf. R Jankowski, 'The Demise of the Roman Republic: A Faulty Constitution?' (2021) 32 *Constitutional Political Economy* 218, 226–7; CJ Dart, D Rafferty, FJ Vervaet, 'New Perspectives on Old Problems/Old Perspectives on New Problems' in FJ Vervaet, D Rafferty and CJ Dart (eds), *How Republics Die: Creeping Authoritarianism in Ancient Rome and Beyond* (De Gruyter 2025) 18.

[16] Cf. Steel (n 1) 252; A Schiavone, 'Introduzione: Una Storiografia di Confine' in J-L Ferrary, *Dall'ordine Repubblicano ai Poteri di Augusto. Aspetti della Legislazione Romana* (L'Erma di Bretschneider 2016) xiv.

16.5 THE ROMAN OLIGARCHIC AND PLUTOCRATIC ELITES WERE LEFT LARGELY UNAFFECTED BY THE FALL OF THE REPUBLIC

The Republic was, thus, close to terminal death for many decades before its final demise in 27 BC with the rise of the Principate, Augustus becoming Rome's first Emperor. The constitution of the Republic was practically dead for much of the Late Republican era and Rome was, during this time, but a republic in name only. In fact, at the time Rome was more of an imperial Republic maintaining practically a number of its classic constitutional characteristics fully intact and functional,[17] as these would have been observed at its apex in constitutional terms and otherwise. Eventually, however, in the years of the Principate and the Dominate, the roles of the magistrates of the Republic were eroded and diminished,[18] the role of the Plebeian Council was practically abolished to ceremonial status a little after the reign of Augustus,[19] while central legislative procedures of the Republic were deserted, even though many of the Republic's laws continued to live.[20] Later the Senate too lost its somewhat significant powers originally in the Principate and became more of an expression of the Emperor's will. Roman laws were codified in the 3rd, 4th and 5th centuries AD, the apex of codification and systematisation of Roman law being, of course, the codification ordered by Emperor Justinian in the 6th century AD.[21] Thenceforth, Roman law affected and was received by medieval and modern European legal systems[22] and, through them, all of the world's modern legal systems in one way or another, whether directly or indirectly.

As such, it would be a mistake to maintain that the Republic's institutions were abolished with the rise of the Principate: with the Republic dead, the Republic's institutions lived on, only that the offices behind them were consolidated in the hands of the Emperor,[23] these old offices having to work in new ways.[24] It would also be a mistake to maintain that Rome's profound constitutional re-ordering in 27 BC resulted in the abolition of Rome's class system or that Rome's oligarchic and plutocratic elites ceased to expand and flourish with the rise of the Principate. On the contrary, these elites continue to grow and grow, especially now that they were the elites of a vast empire. In short, the oligarchies of Rome

[17] E.g. W Kunkel, *An Introduction to Roman Legal and Constitutional History* (JM Kelly (tr), 2nd edn, Clarendon Press 1973) 48, 51.

[18] Kunkel (n 17) 51–2.

[19] Kunkel (n 17) 52–3.

[20] N Davies, *Europe: A History* (Pimlico 1996, reprinted with corrections 1997) 182–3.

[21] Davies (n 20) 183.

[22] R Zimmermann, 'Roman Law in the Modern World' in D Johnston (ed), *The Cambridge Companion to Roman Law* (Cambridge University Press 2015) 452–8, 463–6. Cf. L Winkel, 'Roman Law and Its Intellectual Context' in D Johnston (ed), *The Cambridge Companion to Roman Law* (Cambridge University Press 2015) 9.

[23] Davies (n 20) 182.

[24] Ibid.

continued to play a vital role[25] in the Principate's running,[26] even though there was now a single ruler, Rome's Emperor, albeit not a wholly absolute one in the first decades of the Principate.[27] For instance, the Senate acquired for a while, after Augustus, a new sense of constitutional importance, especially with the sidelining of Rome's popular assemblies, but its decisions probably required imperial approval.[28] Control of Rome's laws was practically now in the hands of the *Princeps* (i.e. the Emperor) and, of course, his counsellors.[29] In any case, the move of Rome from more republican forms of government to more imperial monarchic forms of government from 27 BC onwards would not have affected Rome's elites to any significant extent. They continued to thrive despite the Republic's retreat to the Principate.

16.6 POLYBIUS ON ROME'S COLLECTIVE DEGENERACY

For Polybius, the historian who praised the Republic, mostly justifiably, at other times unjustifiably, in his famous work *Histories*, 'Roman collective degeneracy was all too evident in [his] estimation'.[30] As we are aware, Polybius wrote his works as an historical attempt to explain, amongst other things, how Rome became an empire. The world would be a darker place without Polybius' *magnum opus*, *The Histories*. Polybius was not a jurist though. Polybius, in his efforts to praise Rome, otherwise excels in the use of rhetorical figures of speech that only some of the world's finest orators could match. The following are submitted on an indicative basis as examples where he uses rhetorical devices to praise Rome's establishment and constitution (in brackets the rhetorical device/fallacy used by him): Plb. 6.3 [11], omitting to state that Rome's 'aristocracy', the Senate, was actually an oligarchy (aposiopesis); 6.4 [3], omitting anew to state the same (aposiopesis); 6.11 [12], stating that the Senate was an aristocracy without any explanation (jumping to conclusion / lack of justification); 6.13 [8–9], stating that the constitution of Rome, because of the Senate, was imagined as an aristocracy (jumping to conclusion / suppressed evidence fallacy / generalisation) and 6.16, claiming that the Senate was controlled by the people and cannot neglect their feelings (jumping to conclusion / generalisation). However, he also seems to criticise the deterioration of the Roman character, such deterioration being 'the result of political and societal

[25] L Capogrossi Colognesi, *Law and Power in the Making of the Roman Commonwealth* (Cambridge University Press 2014) xxviii.

[26] Cf. WV Harris, 'Power' in A Barchiesi and W Scheidel (eds), *The Oxford Handbook of Roman Studies* (Oxford University Press 2010) 572 citing R Syme, *The Roman Revolution* (Oxford University Press 1939) 7.

[27] Harris (n 26) 573 citing Z Yavetz, 'Caligula, Imperial Madness and Modern Historiography' (1996) 78 *Klio* 105–29.

[28] E.g. J Harries, 'Law' in Barchiesi and Scheidel (n 26) 644.

[29] Harries (n 28) 644.

[30] C Champion, 'Historiographic Patterns and Historical Obstacles in Polybius' *Histories*: Marcellus, Flaminius, and the Mamertine Crisis' in B Gibson and T Harrison (eds), *Polybius and his World. Essays in Memory of F. W. Walbank* (Oxford University Press 2013) 145.

debasement'[31] the closer we come to 146 BC onwards.[32] Concurrently he criticises his fellow Greeks, the Macedonians for wishing to rise against the Romans,[33] and the Achaeans,[34] as if to put the blame on them for the Roman conqueror's act to destroy Corinth. Obviously, these conflicting accounts (both the Romans and the Achaeans and the Macedonians being in the wrong, when Rome was the perpetrator with the Achaeans and the Macedonians fighting for their freedom) were deliberate. As such, as much as one ought to praise Polybius for being one of the central historical sources of the Roman Republic's rise and fall, his historical narratives and analyses are not always wholly objective.[35] His work covers the period between 264 and 146 BC but, as stated, his main concern was the historical narration and exploration of Rome's rise to the status of an empire between 220 and 167 BC. We can otherwise only hypothesise that Polybius wrote his work between 146 and 118 BC, 118 BC being the year of his death. There is also the view that he wrote at least the first six books of his *Histories* before 150 BC as a political prisoner in Rome.[36] Furthermore, we are aware that he returned to Greece in the same year Corinth was destroyed. It is, therefore, well possible that he wrote a considerable amount of his famous work in Greece rather than in Rome. Nonetheless, his pro-Roman stance in his work, for reasons explained previously in this monograph, is beyond question. After all, he was a sort of a Roman *Gauleiter* in the occupied-by-the-Romans Greece. As one of Rome's collaborators in Greece and a less-than-always-democratic type of personality,[37] to put things mildly, the news of the assassination of the democratic Tiberius Gracchus might have been perceived by him in 133 BC, a turning point for the Republic, with apathy, if not with mild satisfaction. Even Polybius, however, could sense, after 146 BC to his death in 118 BC, that the Republic was failing. Remarkably, when reading Polybius it is as if a man who was missing Rome's republican glory occasionally criticises it between the lines. Polybius' histories were a milder version of Cato the Elder's narratives. Of course, the way he writes about Rome and her constitution has been deliberate: on the one hand, he must have been under certain considerable pressure to be viewed as an obedient Roman collaborator, while, on the other hand, his criticism was subtle, albeit real, so that he would appeal as a critical friend to Rome's conservative circles. In this respect, Polybius' deliberate narratives seem to have been the narratives of a less-than-wholly-free man, even if the Romans treated him better than his fellow Greeks.

[31] Champion (n 30) 144.
[32] Ibid.
[33] E.g. Plb. 36.17.12–13.
[34] Champion (n 30) 144.
[35] E.g. MB Hatzopoulos, *Ancient Macedonia* (De Gruyter 2020) 170–2. Cf. Steel (n 1) 66–7, Steel arguing that Polybius leans towards glorifying military Rome, especially considering his friendship with Scipio Aemilianus.
[36] Champion (n 30) 154, citing FW Walbank, *Polybius*, Sather Classical Lectures, 42 (Berkeley and Los Angeles), 19–25.
[37] E.g. Plb. 6.43.6–6.44.9.

16.7 SENATORIAL CLASS: FROM STABILISING FACTOR TO DESTABILISING FACTOR OF THE REPUBLIC

The Senate in the Late Republic was not the institution it used to be in the Middle Republic. Whereas internal conflicts within the Senatorial class could certainly be identified before 133 BC, the Senate ultimately became a highly destabilising factor for the Republic during the Late Republic, while it had previously been the constitutional glue that actually kept the Republic together. Moreover, the Senate was now often at odds with the Roman people,[38] unpopular[39] and largely perceived to be (or even was) incompetent.[40] Whereas the Republic continued its existence until 27 BC, when it was abolished through the rise of the Principate, already from 80 BC the Republic could not manage the tensions between its highly competitive members and the Roman people.[41] It seemed that the Senate that once kept the Republic together would not be able to stabilise it any more. As a matter of fact, its continuous moral decline contributed to the fall of the Republic.

16.8 THE FINAL DAYS OF THE REPUBLIC AND THE DIVIDED ROMAN REPUBLICANS

Rome's republican traditions were falling apart closer to the end of the second century BC and, of course, in the 1st century BC. The constitution of the Republic was not fit for purpose any more. Polybius had warned his Roman readership that the form of a state's constitution is 'the most powerful agent for success or failure'.[42] However, persons such as Pompey and Cicero just could not salvage it later in the 1st century BC. History crushed them, as it had crushed the Republic.

Rome's constitution was now caught between two opposing worlds: the stoic conservative republicans[43], such as Scipio Africanus the Younger; and the more democratic republicans, such as Tiberius Gracchus, who wanted reform of the republic by taking the interests of the Plebeians into greater account. The hand of the staunch republicans that assassinated Tiberius Gracchus could have been indirectly armed by Polybius, the majority of Rome's upper classes and their fears. The hand of the reformists, with Gracchus taking the lead and his supporters opposing the former, was armed by Blossius,[44] the philosopher,[45] and Diophanes[46],

[38] Steel (n 1) 42.
[39] Steel (n 1) 249.
[40] Ibid.
[41] Steel (n 1) 252.
[42] Plb. 6.1.
[43] E.g. DR Dudley, 'Blossius of Cumae' (1941) 31 *The Journal of Roman Studies* 94, 96–7.
[44] Dudley (n 43) 94, 94.
[45] Dudley (n 43) 94, 96.
[46] D.13.diophanes-bio-1 in W Smith, *A Dictionary of Greek and Roman Biography and Mythology* (Spottiswoode and Co.) as cited in the Perseus Digital Library.

the rhetorician,[47] and their hopes, these two being the key persons who seem to have recommended, if not instigated,[48] Tiberius Gracchus to proceed with his reforms. Metaphorically, the Roman hand that instigated the first major blow to the Republic, through the assassination of Tiberius Gracchus in 133 BC, was the same hand that instigated one of its final major blows to the Republic through the assassination of Julius Caesar in 44 BC. Their rationale? That Tiberius Gracchus and Julius Caesar would abolish the Republic by becoming kings (tyrants). In any case, these opposing forces within the constitution of the Republic, later received the epithet *optimates* (the stoic conservative republican Senators of Rome) and the *populares* (the pro-Plebeian democratic republican Senators of Rome). They were all predominantly members of the Roman nobility, whether of Patrician or Plebeian descent.

Historians will have different views as to the final year of the Republic. Nonetheless, there would be no doubt whatsoever that, in constitutional law terms, the rise of the Principate in 27 BC effectively coincided with the fall of the Republic in the same year. Thus, in constitutional law terms, the Republic ceased to exist with the installation of the Principate. Of course, the Republic was dying a long and painful death in constitutional law terms at least since 133 BC. However, the Republic did not exactly fully die with the assassination of Julius Caesar. In fact, the opposite is true: the assassins of Julius Caesar wanted to salvage the Republic through their abominable act, broken as the Republic had been for many decades already. The assassination of Julius Caesar can, therefore, more plausibly, if not definitively, be seen as an attempt to restore the Republic from the Caesarian 'deviation', the fact that Caesar had declared himself dictator in perpetuity.

Finally, even after the vote of the Roman people in 43 BC to constitute the Second Triumvirate (Lepidus, Mark Antony and Octavian), it could be contemplated that the Second Triumvirate was a constitutionally legitimised deviation, legally about ten years long, within the confines of the Republic: it was in the context of the republic and under the republic that the Second Triumvirate came to life. Thus, the 'constitutional deviation' of the Second Triumvirate could be perceived as one that was effected as the Republic's defence mechanism to reconstitute order and republic in Rome. Of course, one could argue that the considerable duration of the Second Triumvirate broke the continuity of the Republic to the point that the Republic ceased to exist in 43 BC but this seems relatively unlikely, in that, as stated, the Second Triumvirate was constituted under the Republic's mechanisms. What could also be plausibly argued would be the fact that the Second Triumvirate's despotic ambition laid the seed for the rise of the Principate in 27 BC, only six years after the Second Triumvirate ceased to legally exist.

[47] Dudley (n 43) 94, 96.

[48] At least in the case of Blossius, he himself stated that he was Tiberius' subordinate: Dudley (n 43) 94, 96.

Chapter 17

Implications for the Future

17.1 INTRODUCTION

This chapter concludes with the monograph's key findings. It further posits that not only modern scholars but also our world's modern republics can still benefit from appreciating the way these people, the Romans, built and developed the constitution of their Republic, many of whom must have been so very proud of it, mostly with good reason.

17.2 MAIN FINDINGS OF THIS MONOGRAPH

This monograph posited four things: first, the Roman Republic was a mixed polity, an Aristotelian polity+, a polity that combined monarchic/dyarchic, oligarchic, aristocratic and democratic elements into one. Second, Polybius and Cicero rounded and idealised the Republic. The core of the Roman Republic (for instance, the Senate), while an aristocracy to them, was actually an established and powerful oligarchy of plutocrats in perfect and full agreement with Aristotelian doctrine.[1] Third, the Romans never had a golden age Athenian style. Nevertheless, their proud and confident Republic was a relatively stable constitutional vessel between 287 and 133 BC in the face of magnificent adversity. Thus, the period between 287 and 133 BC seems to have been republican Rome's constitutional and political apogee in the wider republican era between 509 and 27 BC. Fourth, the constitution of the Republic, while fuzzy and mostly indistinct, aside from its clear-cut institutional layout, is responsible for transforming what was once a rustic, insignificant and pale republic somewhere in central Italy into a world empire. Rome's constitution was, thus, the condition precedent for her internal stability to eventually project herself into the world. This is Rome's greatest achievement in history: not her legions, not her conquests or victories but her stealthy and agile constitution based on an extensive set of checks and balances, institutions and magistrates.

17.3 THE RELEVANCE OF THE ROMAN REPUBLIC IN MODERNITY

Rome of the Republic stands after more than two millennia as modernity's constitutional factory. Indeed, what one observes in the modern world of mixed

[1] Aristot. Pol. 3.1279b–80a.

constitutions is mostly about adaptations of Platonic and Aristotelian doctrine and the Roman Republic's components on the ever-marching idea of democracy. Modern constitutional lawyers would only benefit if they rediscovered the Roman Republic's constitution, as would modern comparative lawyers but also political scientists, classicists, philosophers and sociologists.

Crucially, the central components of the Roman Republic (democratic, aristocratic, oligarchic and monarchic ones) are ones that can be found in one way or another in many modern constitutions. The mix of the Republic's constitutional components can create an infinite number of constitutional configurations. These components were, of course, first explored by Plato and Aristotle but it is in Rome that so many diverse components were manifestly put together and created a mixed polity, a republic, or an Aristotelian polity+, as maintained elsewhere in the analysis.

The Republic is also a sort of eternal reminder of the powerful effect of plutocratic elites, which, on many occasions, govern modern constitutions *lato sensu* too. For legal historians and classicists, there is not much to be said when it comes to the exploration of Rome and her constitution, as for them their engagement with the Roman Republic is a *res ipsa loquitur* matter. Close to this, it would also be important for the reader to appreciate that the constitutional miracle that occurred in Rome for a number of centuries was one which occurred in the face of considerable adversity for the Republic.

17.4 COMPARATIVE ELEMENTS IN THE CONSTITUTION OF THE REPUBLIC – FUTURE RESEARCH

Moreover, one must steer clear of the point that was made elsewhere that, when it comes to modern constitutional law, everything or almost everything leads back to Rome. Whereas one could not deny the fact that the constitution of the Roman Republic was mostly a Roman creation and the well-known fact that it has affected so many of our modern world's constitutions in one way or another (e.g. the Constitution of the USA is a classic example in this respect), the Romans must have been in communication, whether directly with the Greeks of south Italy or more indirectly with the Greeks of mainland Greece, and would have acquired comparative constitutional information[2] from places such as Sparta and Athens and, more provokingly, even from their greatest enemy, Carthage.

It would be odd if they did not, as it would be odd if the Romans had not acquired any cultural elements or constitutional ideas from the Etruscans by whom they were controlled and affected for a number of centuries. Mommsen's view that the foreign elements in Roman constitutional law were minute and unimportant simply because Rome expressed all the ideas of such law in Latin[3] is rejected *ab initio*, as the onomatology of the subject matter does not necessarily

[2] Cf. A Momigliano, *Alien Wisdom: The Limits of Hellenization* (Cambridge University Press 1975) 14.

[3] T Mommsen, *The History of Rome*, vol 1 (W Purdie Dickson (tr), Macmillan & Co. 1901) 105.

reveal its origin. Indeed, the Romans took great pains not to reveal the persons behind the Roman Republic's constitution. All foreign constitutional ideas that found their way into their Republic must have been latinised and romanised for the same reason. Moreover, certain of the oligarchic and monarchic elements of Rome's constitution must have come from north of Rome, from Etruria, where democracy never took off: the Roman genius, however, moved away from the monarchic core of Etruscan political thought by intelligently and decisively castigating the possibility of monarchic offices going out of control in Rome until the times of Sulla. That is the single most crucial element of the Roman Republic's constitution and that seems to be a Roman invention.

It is for future research to establish the precise comparative elements that found their way into the constitution of the Roman Republic but it would be naïve not to even consider the possibility that monarchic, dyarchic and oligarchic elements of constitutions beyond Rome did at least inspire the Romans, especially through their contacts with the Greeks, the Etruscans and the Carthaginians, to fine-tune, calibrate and configure their republic. For instance, the Greek and Phoenician traders may well have offered the Romans the opportunity to familiarise themselves with certain laws of the peoples of the Eastern Mediterranean.[4] Of course, here one could argue that the split of the old monarchic *Rex* into two republican Consuls may have been a Roman invention but it was one of these inventions that were strongly reminiscent of older dyarchies such as the two Kings of Sparta. Moreover, the possibility that certain constitutional characteristics of the Republic were taken from the Etruscans cannot be excluded either.

17.5 WIDER CONNOTATIONS FROM THE REPUBLICAN YEARS OF ROME

There are, however, wider connotations here for researchers and academic citizens as a whole. What one calls the stealthy but powerful constitution of the Republic is one of the best reflections of human nature, one of its finest manifestations, and exploring the constitutional elements of the Roman Republic is about opening one's intellectual horizons into the world of human nature itself: learning about the constitution of Rome ought to make us better human beings. It is about rediscovery, reinvigoration and the cultivation of the human spirit. For instance, the failures and the mistakes of the Romans, their double hybris in 146 BC and their deterioration as a republic in the 1st century BC must be constant reminders for our leaders, our countries and our citizens. Rome's constitutional successes and failures ought to be major guides in the way we will strengthen modernity's republics and build the societies of the future. Rome's militaristic spirit is not to be admired.[5] Nonetheless, in a lethargic Europe, in the complacent developed world

[4] J Clarkson, 'Roman Law in its Italic Context' in SW Bell and PJ du Plessis (eds), *Roman Law before the Twelve Tables* (Cambridge University Press 2020) 9.

[5] F Millar, *The Roman Republic in Political Thought* (University Press of New England 2002) 1.

more generally, Rome's fighting spirit and absolute resolve and determination to defend itself at all times against 'all enemies from within and from without'[6] must be kept in mind as the ideological *ultima ratio* of her constitution, as a leading principle and guide for self-preservation and prosperity against the tyrants or the potential tyrants of contemporaneity. Here, then, is the greatest lesson of Rome's original republican constitution per se: its absolute resolve to guard and fight against potential tyrants from within and from without Rome. *Libertas* as *civitas* at all times, at all costs, at any rate.

The Republic, despite its magnificent constitution, however, Rome's greatest and finest monument, was one that used certain of the most cynical, devious and ruthless ways in the face of human history to achieve its imperial goals.[7] Davies is illuminating on this: '[Rome's] psychological controls were built on fear and punishment–on the absolute certainty that anyone or anything that threatened the authority of Rome would be utterly destroyed'.[8] Our world's leaders must, therefore, recall and keep in mind that the Romans occasionally used magnificent power for magnificently wrong causes and that is something that we must guard against in modernity, now and in the future. The republican Romans were no angels and must be treated as such by the theoretical scientist. The proficient ways of the Romans in military matters and their frequent use of brutal force resulted in tragic outcomes for humanity.[9]

Equally, the constitutional lawyer ought to state here that the imperial hybris of Rome should not sacrifice Rome's finest achievement, her constitution, in the altar of blind attacks against all things Roman because of Rome's imperial credentials. The theoretical scholar, in the same way an experienced surgeon of impeccable chirurgical precision would operate, must distinguish the constitution of the Roman Republic from imperial Rome, even if that same constitution was a condition precedent for Rome's rise to empire status. It would, thus, be *neoteristic*, for the wrong reasons, to surrender the Roman Republic as easy theoretical prey to the continuous and relentless attacks of scholars, mostly from former colonial powers and the neo-imperial powers of our times, in their desperate and hopeless pursuit to wash away the historical sins of the past and the neocolonial sins of the present. The more balanced thesis would be not to praise the Romans of the Republic in the way European scholars did between c. 1800 and 1945 but also not to cast the stone of all blame for all the sins of colonial and neocolonial imperial powers of modernity to them as easy theoretical prey in the way many scholars did after 1945 to date.

[6] Cf. George Washington's correspondence to the American Senate on 22 November 1794 as to meeting 'enemies from within and from without': C Holloway and BP Wilson (eds), *The Political Writings of George Washington*, vol 2: 1788–1799 (Cambridge University Press 2023) 379.

[7] ES Gruen, *The Hellenistic World and the Coming of Rome* (University of California Press 1984, reprinted 1986) 346–7 citing Polybius.

[8] N Davies, *Europe: A History* (Pimlico 1996, reprinted 1997) 149.

[9] C Ando, 'Public Law and Republican Empire in Rome, 200–27 BCE' in E Cavanagh (ed), *Empire and Legal Thought: Ideas and Institutions from Antiquity to Modernity* (Brill Nijhoff 2020) 107.

One must tread carefully between these two worlds of scholars. After all, the point of the academic exercise is to be academically correct, not necessarily to be politically correct in the interests of sounding pleasant to the reactionary audiences and the angry masses of contemporaneity. By all means, in the interests of academic accuracy, the Romans created a fine constitution which mostly served them well. Of course, succumbing to natural *nomoteleia* but also the very weight of an empire, which the same constitution created, the Republic gave way to the Principate.

In relation to Rome, her constitution, her republic and her empire, the theoretician will always have to answer two sets of questions: (i) did Rome do well for itself herself and was the constitution of her Republic of appropriate standard for the Romans? and (b) did Rome use the magnificent geopolitical thrust, which her constitution offered her, to cause magnificent pain through her empire? Both questions, according to the author of this monograph, are answered in the affirmative. Rome did manage to create a constitution which stabilised Rome considerably to eventually project herself to the world. In this respect, Rome's constitution achieved its goals and served the Romans well. However, whereas Rome's constitution started as a defensive constitution, a constitution for a city attempting to stabilise and survive against its neighbours, it actually eventually caused her to more than significantly expand to the point of causing magnificent pain to humanity.

The vices of the Romans were many and ought not to be forgotten.[10] From duplicating the divide and conquer (*διαίρει και βασίλευε*) strategy of Philip II of Macedon to mastering the art of propaganda and proceeding as far as using a Hellenistic type of humanistic narrative[11] for expanding and justifying its *imperium* all over the Mediterranean world, the Black Sea and Gaul, the Rome of the Republic stands for a *locus classicus* of an imperial and constitutional power that expanded through objectionable means that caused more-than-considerable pain to herself, the Romans, the enemies of Rome and, by extension, humanity. It would also be fair to maintain that the harm Rome caused to herself pales into insignificance to the harm she caused to others. One's admiration for the constitution of the Republic ought not to result in one neglecting the political vices and the geopolitical mistakes of the Romans of the Republic, which were many and considerable. The Romans of the Republic, who would be initially called 'barbarians' by lay Greeks in the Italian peninsula, the latter mostly connoting the fact that the language that the Romans spoke was incomprehensible to them,[12] came to use the term 'barbarians' too for connoting the normally inferior character of the ones they would conquer or would have conquered.[13]

[10] E.g. Davies (n 8) 150.

[11] Cf. T Whitmarsh, 'Hellenism' in A Barchiesi and W Scheidel (eds), *The Oxford Handbook of Roman Studies* (Oxford University Press 2010) 735.

[12] On what seems like the original use of the term 'barbarian' without connotations beyond language incomprehensibility, see e.g. HDF Kitto, *The Greeks* (Penguin Books 1951, reprinted 1960) 7.

[13] E.g. Cic. Scaur. 38–45a.

More interestingly, the Romans of the Republic, especially in the Late Republic, would package their conquests with what seemed like Hellenistic ideals of peace and human values (*humanitas*)[14] when these would be nothing short of the execution and display of cynical imperial power. Thus, not only would the Romans expand their empire by advocating that they conquer 'inferior' peoples, but they would also do so in the name of humanism (*contradictio in absurdum*). Ironically, very similar devices to those the Romans of the Republic used against their enemies were used by Victorian imperialists:[15] divide and rule seems to have been used by them to impose and solidify their rule in India,[16] while they also justified their conquest as an opportunity for the locals and the Orientals to introduce themselves to modern European standards[17] – the Romans would do so in the Mediterranean world through the introduction of their 'humanistic' Hellenistic ideals to the conquered.

17.6 ROME'S CONSTITUTION AS A GUIDE FOR THE FUTURE

And yet this does not change the fact that Rome offers us lessons for the future. The exploration of Rome and her constitution allows us to understand our world, the world of modernity, our modern republics and our constitutions. Rome offers us the great opportunity to reflect on ourselves[18] and our societies.

The first and greatest victory one can achieve in life is the victory against oneself.[19] It would seem that the Romans attained that victory in the 3rd century BC by changing themselves and by fighting the demons they held well-kept in their soul. They, then, changed the world for centuries but the Republic retreated to the Principate. Rome became a world empire but the Romans eventually became decadent and lost their soul. Those who changed the world could not change and rediscover themselves any more, Rome giving way to Second Rome, Constantinople.

The constitution of the Roman Republic is an absolute triumph of the human spirit and intellect. Imperfect as it was, it strived for perfection. A republic, any genuine republic, stands as a matter of principle over and above any single man who aspires to abolish or violate it. A republic will always stand at a higher level than the individuals running it, for the republic caters for the general good, not for the individuals running it.[20] In all this, the guardians of a republic must make

14 E.g. Whitmarsh (n 11) 735.

15 Whitmarsh (n 11) 735 citing G Woolf, *Becoming Roman: The Origins of Provincial Civilization in Gaul* (Cambridge University Press 1998) 1–23.

16 E.g. S Tharoor, *Inglorious Empire: What the British Did to India* (Hurst 2017) 101 citing Lord Elphinstone.

17 Whitmarsh (n 11) 735–6 citing E Saïd, *Orientalism: Western Conceptions of the Orient* (2nd edn, Penguin 1995) 31–7.

18 M Beard, *SPQR: A History of Ancient Rome* (Liveright Publishing 2015) 15.

19 Plat. Laws 1.626e.

20 Aristot. Pol. 1.1252b-1.1253a; 8.1337a.

sure that they do not become monsters like the monsters they fight,[21] as the 'protectors of the Republic' in the form of the assassins of Julius Caesar once became.

Concurrently, one's admiration of the Colosseum as an architectural monument must come with a reminder of the perverse uses for which such a monument was used.[22] One's admiration of the constitution of the Roman Republic, especially the constitution of the Republic between 287 and 133 BC, Rome's constitutional apogee, must come with a reminder that, even though this was the constitution that made Rome rise to unimaginable heights of glory, prestige and accomplishment, all this was on the magnificent pain of so many in Rome's path;[23] all this was built on tears, greed and blood.

What is the point of man, a city or a state that would have built something so refined and so unique but, while doing so or after they would have done so, their most appealing characteristics, that is to say their human traits, the very traits that would have made them so great in the first place, would have all been sacrificed and lost in the process? What is the point of a man who would have conquered all he could conquer only for him to ultimately betray all his principles and all that he stood for?[24] By all means, what is the point of a republic that is so refined and balanced, imperfect as it could occasionally be, but one that would ultimately betray its constitution and its character, as the Roman Republic did after 133 BC? In all this, Rome and her instigators would do all they could to idealise her, even when they would criticise her. Polybius, for instance, did not only round the Republic's constitution to please his Roman patrons but he also implied that the fall of the Republic's constitution started in 168 BC,[25] when it was a generation after, in 133 BC, that Rome started its genuine decline until its full demise in 27 BC. It would seem, however, that the pro-Roman establishment voices, such as the voice of Polybius, threw even more fuel into Rome's socio-constitutional fire, which burnt Rome's old republican soul into pieces with the rise of the Principate.

The Republic, its constitution, the ways this people, the Romans, built their city, their state and their empire are some of the finest lessons one could take for life. The Romans of the Republic are an example to follow but also an example to avoid. Their constitution was used to stabilise the Republic but Rome concurrently engaged in its continuous bloodstained historical journey beyond *pomoerium* and Latium. However, unlike the colonial powers of modernity, there was no central design; no central planning;[26] no original configuration for an empire.[27] Nevertheless, the constitution of the Republic was ultimately the

21 F Nietzsche, *Beyond Good and Evil* (Helen Zimmern (tr), Modern Library 1917) 87, para. 146.

22 Davies (n 8) 150.

23 E.g. M Rostovtzeff, *The Social and Economic History of the Roman Empire* (Oxford University Press 1926) 7.

24 Cf. Matthew 16:26.

25 Plb. 6.57; J von Ungern-Sternberg, 'The End of the Conflict of the Orders' in KA Raaflaub (ed), *Social Struggles in Archaic Rome* (Blackwell 2005) 316.

26 Beard (n 18) 17, 163.

27 Gruen (n 7) 5 citing T Mommsen, *Römische Gesichte* I (Berlin, 1903, first published 1854).

single most crucial element that acted as a condition precedent for Rome's subsequent great empire. It was the same constitution, after it generated the Roman empire, that ultimately collapsed under the very weight of the empire it generated. Rome's Republic fell; so did its magnificent constitution. However, Rome lived on and grew ever stronger. Yet that old dream of the Roman republicans, before Rome became an empire, so reminiscent of certain characteristics of Plato's and Aristotle's ideal constitutions, of a city that would be built on honour, distinction, a frugal life of moderation and checks and balances was lost forever.

Addendum I

Chronology of Major Legal and Political Developments in Rome (287–133 BC)

- 287 BC: *Lex Hortensia*: democratisation of the Roman Republic's constitution with the Clash of the Orders coming to a conventional end: plebiscites would now be binding on the whole of the Republic
- 286 BC: *Lex Aquilia*: possible enactment of a law protecting citizens from theft and destruction of property by providing a framework of compensation
- 275 BC: assumed date when the office of *princeps senatus* is established[1]
- 242 BC: second Praetor office (*Praetor Peregrinus*) established
- 241 BC: reorganisation of the Army's Assembly (Centuriate Assembly)
- 228 BC: the number of Praetors increases to four
- 224 BC: Gaius Flaminius becomes the first Plebeian to hold the office of Consul
- 215 BC: *Lex Oppia*, the law restricting the display of wealth is passed
- 218 BC: the Claudian Law (*Plebiscitum Claudianum* or *Lex Claudia*) forbids Senators and their offspring to own large ships and proceed with enterprises that would result in business or bank profits
- 204 BC: *Lex Cincia*, probably a *plebiscitum*, limiting the value of gifts received and offered, it also prohibiting gifts in exchange for legal services
- 199 BC: First *Lex Porcia*: extended the *provacatio* (right to appeal against magistrates) of Roman citizens and soldiers 1,000 paces outside of Rome
- 197 BC: the number of Praetors increases to six
- 195 BC: Cato the Elder becomes Consul – probable year for the Second *Lex Porcia*: *provocatio ad populum* is extended; *Lex Oppia* is repealed
- 184 BC: Third *Lex Porcia*: provides for severe sanction against magistrates who do not recognise the right to *provocatio*
- 181 BC: *Lex Orchia*, the law against luxury, is passed
- 180 BC: *Lex Villia Annalis*: establishment of strict order of offices (*cursus honorum*)[2]
- 172 BC: for the first time, both Consuls of Rome were Plebeians[3]
- 171 BC: Senate's members reportedly examine for the first time allegations against Roman officials as to abuses of power, bribery and violent conduct in Iberia[4]

[1] FX Ryan, *Rank and Participation in the Republican Senate* (Franz Steiner Verlag 1998) 170.

[2] RE Mitchell, 'The Aristocracy of the Roman Republic' in R Howarth (ed), *Hearsay, History, and Heresy: collected Essays on the Roman Republic by Richard E. Mitchell* (Gorgias Press 2010) 138.

[3] Mitchell (n 2) 111.

[4] IE Τζαμτζής, *Ο Μεσογειακός Κόσμος* (Εκδόσεις Σάκκουλα 2014, ανατύπωση 2018) 123.

- 167 BC: Roman citizens in Italy are exempted from direct taxation (*tributum*)[5]
- 161 BC: the Senate bans philosophers and rhetoricians from Rome
- 155 BC: a Greek embassy comprising three philosophers is allowed to teach philosophy to the Romans
- 149 BC: establishment of a permanent jury court in Rome (*quaestio perpetua*)[6] – *Lex Calpurnia de pecuniis repetundis* allowed under civil and penal procedural rules the examination of Senators by Senators who would have previously acted as Rome's leading officials in provinces;[7] *Lex Atinia* allowed the plebeian Tribunes to automatically be members of the Senate
- 139 BC: introduction of secret voting in Rome's popular assemblies (*leges tabellariae*)[8]
- 137 BC: introduction of secret voting in Rome's popular trials except in *perduellio*[9]
- 133 BC: passage of the *Lex Agraria* and assassination of Tiberius Sempronius Gracchus

5 PA Zoch, *Ancient Rome* (Oklahoma University Press 1998) 91.

6 E.g. HI Flower, *Roman Republics* (Princeton University Press 2010) 69.

7 Τζαμτζής (n 4) 123.

8 E.g. Τζαμτζής (n 4) 103, 172.

9 E.g. Τζαμτζής (n 4) 172.

Addendum II

Chronology of Major Legal, Political and Military Developments beyond Rome as These Affected the Republic's Development (287–133 BC)

- 286/285 BC: Rome is requested for the first time its protection by a Greek colony, that of Thurii, against another Greek colony, that of Tarentum
- 284/283 BC: the Romans are defeated by Celts in Arretium; the Romans subsequently defeat Senone Celts
- 282 BC: Roman vessels on their way to Thurii were caught in a storm off Tarentum but the Tarentines taking offence from the incident attack the Romans and help the democrats of Thurii to take control of the city; as a result, the Romans withdrew their garrison from Thurii
- 281 BC: the Romans plunder Tarentum
- 280 BC: King Pyrrhus of Epirus arrives in Italy to defend the Tarantines and the rest of the Greeks there; Rome is defeated at the Battle of Heraclea by Pyrrhus; his Greek armies sustain considerable losses, as have the opposing armies of the Roman Republic at the same battle[1]
- 279 BC: Rome is defeated at the Battle of Asculum by King Pyrrhus of Epirus; however, his Greek armies suffer certain considerable losses again, as have the opposing armies of the Roman Republic at the same battle[2] – 4th[3] (or 3rd) Carthaginian-Roman treaty
- 278 BC: Carthaginians launch an offensive in Sicily
- 275 BC: Rome establishes full control over almost all of the Greek city states in south mainland Italy after it came out victorious against King Pyrrhus of Epirus at the Battle of Beneventum; King Pyrrhus leaves Italy; after a treaty with the Romans his remaining general there with the remaining Greek forces leave too.[4]
- 273 BC: Ptolemy II, ruler of Ptolemaic Egypt, exchanges embassies with Rome, Egypt thereby becoming the first Hellenistic Kingdom to recognise Rome[5]
- 272 BC: Rome conquers Tarentum, the last free Greek colony in south mainland Italy

[1] PA Zoch, *Ancient Rome* (Oklahoma University Press 1998) 87.

[2] Zoch (n 1) 88.

[3] If one takes the alleged 306 BC Roman-Carthaginian treaty as one that has historically occurred.

[4] Zoch (n 1) 89.

[5] D Hoyos, *Rome Victorious: The Irresistible Rise of the Roman Empire* (Bloomsbury Academic 2019, reprinted 2023) 9, 18.

- 270 BC: Rome's control extends from its borders with Cisalpine Gaul in the North all the way to south Italy[6]
- 268 BC: Rome founds the colony of Beneventum in Samnium;[7] Sabines in the proximity of Rome acquire Roman citizenship[8]
- 267 BC: Rome conquers Brundisium; Rome now controls the whole of south Italy[9]
- 264 BC: Rome is reported[10] to have broken the 3rd Carthaginian-Roman Treaty, the Philinus Treaty of 306 BC,[11] by setting claims over Sicily, otherwise an area reserved for the Carthaginian Empire; the Roman people overrule the Senate which would not decide on the invasion of Sicily; Rome controls most of peninsular Italy[12] – **beginning of 1st Punic War**
- 263 BC: Rome founds the colony of Aesernia in Samnium[13]
- 262 BC: Rome captures Agrigentum after it defeats Hanno's Carthaginian forces there; the Romans pursued fleeing Hannibal Gisco but eventually returned to Agrigentum to establish their control there; Rome decides to build a fleet[14]
- 252 BC: Carthage requests a loan of 2,000 talents from Ptolemy II Philadelphus, a request which is rejected
- 249 BC: Carthage defeats Rome at the naval Battle of Drepana
- 241 BC: highland Sabines acquire full Roman citizenship;[15] Rome defeats Carthage at the naval Battle of the Aegates – Rome establishes full control over the whole of Sicily except Syracuse; Carthage initially agrees to pay 2,000 Euboean talents to Rome over two decades and additionally remove its forces from Sardinia and pays another 200 talents to Rome; through the Treaty of Lutatius, Rome demands a total of 3,200 talents over ten years instead, 1,000 talents payable immediately, something which Carthage accepts – **end of 1st Punic War**
- 237 BC: Carthaginian forces commence the Iberian conquest; Carthage concedes Sardinia and Corsica to Rome and pays 1,200 talents to Rome[16]
- 229 BC: Rome orders 200 ships to Corcyra to raise the siege of the island which was now occupied by the Illyrians – Corcyra becomes a Roman protectorate after the previous Illyrian ally and garrison there surrenders with the aid of

[6] Hoyos (n 5) 18.

[7] E.g. M Crawford, *The Roman Republic* (2nd edn, Fontana Press 1992) 35.

[8] E Dench, *From Barbarians to New Men: Greek, Roman, and Modern Perceptions of Peoples of the Central Apennines* (Oxford University Press 1995) 15.

[9] L Capogrossi Colognesi, *Law and Power in the Making of the Roman Commonwealth* (Cambridge University Press 2014) 115.

[10] E.g. RE Mitchell, 'Roman-Carthaginian Treaties: 306 and 279/8 B.C.' in R Howarth (ed), *Hearsay, History, and Heresy: Collected Essays on the Roman Republic by Richard E. Mitchell* (Gorgias Press 2010) 48, 52.

[11] Livy attests that this treaty existed, the Philinus Treaty, has actually occurred. See Livy, *The History of Rome* 9 43.

[12] Zoch (n 1) 89.

[13] E.g. Crawford (n 7) 35.

[14] Hoyos (n 5) 19.

[15] Dench (n 8) 15.

[16] Plb. 1.88.

Demetrius of Pharos, who was initially an Illyrian ally; Roman forces make advances on the Illyrian coastline and a Consul remains in Illyria to oversee the newly protected lands of Rome – **beginning of 1st Illyrian War**

- 228 BC: Rome turns Illyria into a client state – a peace treaty agreed between Rome and Illyria is very favourable to Rome and is also well-received by the Greek Leagues – Rome now controls the strategic ports of Epidamnus, Apollonia and Corcyra – **end of 1st Illyrian War**
- 227 BC: both Sardinia and Corsica become a single Roman province – Hasdrubal the Fair founds[17] New Carthage (Carthago Nova) in Iberia
- 226 BC: the Carthaginians agree with the Romans not to cross Ebro[18] river in the Iberian peninsula
- 225 BC: Rome suffers a defeat from the Gauls at the Battle of Faesulae but subsequently defeats the Gauls at the Battle of Telamon
- 223 BC: invasion of Cisalpine Gaul in north Italy by the Romans
- 222 BC: the Insubrian Gauls surrender to Rome
- 221 BC: Rome orders a fleet attack against Histri – **beginning of 2nd Illyrian War**
- 219 BC: Rome attacks and conquers Illyrian Dimallum, a crucial city for the rebellious Demetrius of Pharos – elsewhere, in the Iberian peninsula, Saguntines and other Greeks seek the support of Rome[19] to defend Saguntum against the Carthaginians but none was sent (probably because the Carthaginian forces could legitimately be south of river Ebro, as agreed between Carthage and Rome in 226 BC)
- 219/218 BC: Rome quashes an attempt of the Illyrians to assert full control over their land with the island of Pharos falling in Roman hands[20] and its fortifications destroyed, whilst Demetrius flees to the Macedonian King's (Philip V) Court – in Iberia, Rome overturns its previous decision not to interfere south of the river Ebro in breach of its agreement of 226 BC with the Carthaginians and declares war against Carthage for its conquest of Saguntum – the Carthaginians defeat the Romans at the Battle of the Rhône Crossing, the Battle of Ticinus and the Battle of the Trebia River – **end of 2nd Illyrian War and beginning of 2nd Punic War**
- 218 BC: Rome formally declares war against Carthage in the Spring[21]
- 217 BC: the Carthaginians defeat the Romans at the Battle of Lake Trasimene – panic ensues in Rome[22] – the news reaches Macedonia and Demetrius of

[17] Hoyos puts the founding of New Carthage in 228 BC: Hoyos (n 5) 23.

[18] Polybius mistakenly stated Iber river in *Histories* 2.13 and the same mistake seems to have been repeated by Appian as Iberus river in *Wars in Spain* (Hisp. 2.7). It is also possible that Ebro's name was then called Iber or Iberus. E.g. IE Τζαμτζής, *Ο Μεσογειακός Κόσμος* (Εκδόσεις Σάκκουλα 2014, ανατύπωση 2018) 144.

[19] App. Hisp. 2.7.

[20] Hoyos (n 5) 21 reports a 219 BC date for the removal of Demetrius.

[21] Hoyos (n 5) 22.

[22] Liv. 22.7.

Pharos advises the Macedonian King, Philip V, to invade Italy[23] but his advice is discarded – thereafter the Carthaginians defeat the Romans at the Battle of Ager Falernus and the Battle of Geronium

- 216 BC: Rome now suffers continuous defeats by the Carthaginians, its latest defeat taking place at the Battle of Cannae (in August); most of Rome's forces are decimated with thousands of Roman soldiers fleeing – the news of the Carthaginian victory against the Romans at the Battle of Cannae reaches Macedonia – as a result, the Macedonian King, Philp V, sends ambassadors to Hannibal in Italy to negotiate an alliance with the Carthaginians to which they agree[24] – Rome achieves a minor victory against the Carthaginian forces in the First Battle of Nola
- 215 BC: Macedonia and Carthage form an alliance against Rome and its allies – Rome deploys military forces in Illyria – Rome manages to hold Nola against the Carthaginian forces in the Second Battle of Nola
- 214 BC: Rome loses most of its Samnite, Greek and Etruscan territories in south Italy and not only, them defecting *en masse* to Carthage; Rome crosses with its forces to Illyria and clashes with Macedonian forces – Rome manages to still hold Nola against the Carthaginian forces in the Third Battle of Nola – **beginning of 1st Macedonian War**
- 213 BC: Rome loses several Sicilian cities, them defecting to Carthage
- 212 BC: Rome suffers further continuous defeats at the Battle of Capua, the Battle of the Silarus and the First Battle of Herdonia – Rome and the Tarantine pro-Roman faction also suffer further defeat from Carthage and the Tarantine pro-Punic faction at the Battle of Tarentum; as a result of all these defeats for Rome, Carthage effectively controls most of Italy's Greek South except Rhegium – later this year, in the Autumn, Rome manages to conquer Syracuse, the largest and most prosperous city of Greater Greece,[25] after an Iberian captain and one of the prefects of Achradina, Moeriscus, lets the Romans enter the area near the Fountain of Arethusa[26] – as a result, Rome establishes its full control over the whole of the island of Sicily and explores the possibility of Greek allies in mainland Greece with the Aetolian League; Archimedes is killed by a Roman soldier
- 211 BC: Rome loses control over parts of Sicily; an alliance pact between Rome and the Aetolian league and its allies[27] of Elis, Messenia, Sparta, Pergamon and Illyria is signed; Roman forces are defeated by Carthaginian forces at the Battle of the Upper Baetis in Iberia; Rome captures Capua[28]

[23] Plb. 5.101.

[24] Zoch (n 1) 120.

[25] N Davies, *Europe: A History* (Pimlico, London 1996, reprinted with corrections 1997) 140.

[26] Davies (n 25) 144.

[27] ES Gruen, *The Hellenistic World and the Coming of Rome* (University of California Press 1984, reprinted 1986) 17.

[28] Hoyos (n 5) 22.

- 210 BC: Rome re-establishes control all over Sicily – Carthage defeats the Roman forces in the Second Battle of Herdonia and the Battle of Numistro
- 209 BC: Rome defeats the Carthaginians at the Battle of New Carthage (Carthago Nova); as a result, Rome controls the greater part of the Mediterranean coast of Iberia – elsewhere, in the Italian peninsula, the Carthaginians defeat the Romans at the Battle of Canusium but the Romans defeat the Carthaginian forces at the Battle of Tarentum, thereby capturing Tarentum
- 208 BC: Rome manages to regain control over many Italian cities that were lost to Carthage – in Iberia, Roman forces defeat Carthaginian forces at the Battle of Baecula
- 207 BC: Rome defeats the Carthaginian forces at the Battle of Grumentum and at the Battle of the Metaurus[29], thereby re-asserting control over most of the Italian peninsula
- 206 BC: Rome defeats the Carthaginian forces at the Battle of Ilipa in Iberia, parts of the Carthaginian army surrendering, one Carthaginian General fleeing to Africa and another eventually fleeing to the Balearics; Philip V conquers the betrayed-by-the -Romans Aetolians[30]
- 205 BC: Mago attempts to invade Liguria and captures Genua; the Roman Republic and the Kingdom of Macedon sign the Peace Treaty of Phoenice, the Macedonians moving away from their alliance with the Carthaginians and holding control of much of Greece and Illyria – **end of 1st Macedonian War**
- 204 BC: the Carthaginian forces repulse the Roman ones at one of the Battles of Croton
- 203 BC: Rome comes out victorious against the Carthaginian and the Numidian forces at the Battles of Utica and the Great Plains in Northern Africa and the Battle of Insubria in Northern Italy – Hannibal after almost fifteen years of fighting against the Romans in Italy is recalled to Carthage
- 202 BC: Rome defeats the Carthaginian forces at the Battle of Zama, imposing punitive conditions on Carthage
- 201 BC: Rome establishes its full control over Carthaginian Iberia; Rhodes and Pergamon seek the support of Rome to avoid destruction by the Macedonians – **end of 2nd Punic War**
- 200 BC: Rome's Centuriate Assembly rejects a call for war against the Kingdom of Macedon; Consul Publius Sulpicius Galba convinces the Centuriate Assembly at a second session to enter war with the Kingdom of Macedon – **beginning of 2nd Macedonian War**
- 198 BC: the Romans and the Macedonians clash at the Battle of Aous river – the Roman forces come out victorious
- 197 BC: Smyrna cutting off its ties with the Kingdom of Pergamum appeals to Rome to act as the defender of its freedom; the Romans and the Macedonians clash at the Battle of Cynoscephalae with the Roman forces coming out

[29] Zoch (n 1) 113–14.
[30] Zoch (n 1) 120.

victorious[31] – Rome neutralises the control of Macedonia over southern Greece, Thrace and parts of Anatolia – it is now the ruler of Greece in places where Macedonia would previously rule[32] – creation of two Roman provinces in Iberia

- 196 BC: Rome signs with favourable terms to it the Peace Treaty of Flamininus; Roman General and politician Titus Quinctius Flamininus proclaims in the Isthmian Games the 'freedom of the Greeks'; Rome withdraws from Greece but much of Greece is now in the orbit of the Roman Republic – **end of 2nd Macedonian War**
- 195 BC: Rome is deified throughout the empire in the form of Goddess Roma, which was invented by the people of Smyrna – Hannibal escapes arrest in Carthage and flees to Tyre; from there he finds protection in the court of Antiochus III
- 194 BC: Roman forces leave Greece[33]
- 193 BC: Rome offers to Antiochus III control over the Greeks of Asia Minor on the basis that his Empire would not make any claims to Eastern Europe[34]
- 192 BC: Roman forces start to return[35] to Greece in preparation for an attack against the Seleucid Empire
- 191 BC: Roman forces defeat the Seleucids and their allies at the Battle of Thermopylae[36]
- 190 BC: Rome defeats the army and the fleet of the Seleucid Empire in Magnesia ad Sipylum[37] and at the sea off Side respectively – Rome requests the surrender of Hannibal from Emperor Antiochus III
- 189 BC: Hannibal finds himself in Gortyna, Crete; Aetolia partially[38] submits to Rome through treaty[39]
- 188 BC: the Roman Republic and the Seleucid Empire sign the Peace Treaty of Apamea with very favourable terms for Rome, the Seleucid Empire abandoning both Europe and the area west of the Taurus Mountains in Anatolia; the Seleucid Empire was forced to offer 15,000 talents to the Romans over a period of twelve years[40] – post this treaty, Rome conclusively becomes a fully fledged international geopolitical power in its own right; after the Treaty of Apamea, a Spartan embassy resorts to Rome for help against the Achaean League[41]

31 Zoch (n 1) 122.
32 Plb. 18.45.
33 Zoch (n 1) 123.
34 Hoyos (n 5) 25.
35 Zoch (n 1) 123.
36 Zoch (n 1) 123.
37 E.g. Zoch (n 1) 124.
38 Gruen (n 27) 31–2.
39 Plb. 21.32.
40 Liv. 37 45.
41 Gruen (n 27) 330.

- 186 BC: *Senatus Consultum de Bacchanalibus* – the Senate bans the cult of Bacchanalia all over Italy with only limited exceptions authorised by the Senate itself, considering the cult a threat to the Republic
- 183 BC: Hannibal commits suicide in Libyssa, Bithynia[42]
- 181–179 BC: Rome submits a number of Celtiberian tribes after the siege of Aebura and a number of Roman campaigns in the area – **beginning and end of 1st Celtiberian War**
- 171 BC: Carteia in Iberia is declared a Roman colony; Roman forces enter Epirus; a Roman contingent attacks and defeats Boeotians in southern Greece – Illyrian King Gentius allies with the Romans – **beginning of 3rd Macedonian War**
- 170 BC: Rome seizes 54 Illyrian lembi in the port of Epidamnus – **beginning of 3rd Illyrian War**
- 169 BC: Illyrian King Gentius allies with the Macedonians under King Perseus against the Romans
- 168 BC: Illyrian King Gentius attacks the Roman Illyrian city of Bassania at the beginning of the year – Rome destroys the Illyrian Kingdom and divides it into lightly taxed allied areas and heavily taxed conquered areas – later, in the Summer, the Macedonians are defeated in the First Battle of Pydna;[43] Rome divides Macedonia into four client states[44] – Rome intervenes in favour of Ptolemy VI by presenting Antiochus IV a humiliating[45] ultimatum – **end of 3rd Illyrian War and end of 3rd Macedonian War**
- 167 BC: Rome plunders 70 Epirote towns and enslaves 150,000 Epirotes[46]
- 155 BC onwards: Carthaginian politics divided into three: Hanno III the Great supporting the pro-Roman Carthaginian nobility; Carthalo and Hamilcar the Samnite supporting the popular democratic Barcid Carthaginian fraction and Hannibal the Starling supporting the pro-Numidian fraction
- 153 BC: Roman ambassadors with Cato the Elder leading are sent to Carthage – the Romans realise during their visit that Carthaginian strength has increased
- 151 BC: Carthage expels forty members of the Carthaginian pro-Numidian fraction, them fleeing to Cirta, Numidia – Rome uses this event as pretext to intervene in Carthage – Carthage's debt to Rome is fully paid – Numidians cross Carthaginian borders
- 150 BC: Andriscus of Adramyttium claims the Macedonian throne – Utica breaks ranks with Carthage and willingly surrenders to Rome – **beginning of 4th Macedonian War**
- 149 BC: Roman forces are deployed in Utica but Rome loses the Battle of Lake Tunis against the Carthaginians; the Carthaginians are given the opportunity

[42] 183–181 BC has been offered as the range of years in which Hannibal committed suicide.
[43] E.g. Hoyos (n 5) 27.
[44] E.g. Hoyos (n 5) 27.
[45] E.g. Hoyos (n 5) 27.
[46] Hoyos (n 5) 27.

to capitulate but they refuse to abandon Carthage[47] – Cato the Elder, the Roman politician and soldier that opposed Carthage more than any other politician in the city of Rome, dies from natural causes; Andriscus leads a Macedonian army and defeats a Roman army[48] – **beginning of 3rd Punic War**

- 148 BC: Roman forces defeat Andriscus and the Macedonian forces in the Second Battle of Pydna; Rome annexes Macedonia and turns it into a Roman province – Carthaginian General Hasdrubal takes full control of Carthage – **end of 4th Macedonian War**
- 147 BC: Rome defeats the Carthaginian forces at the Battle of Nepheris, an area south of Carthage; call of the Achaean Greeks to turn against Rome and Sparta
- 146 BC: Rome defeats the Achaean League's forces at the Battle of Scarpheia; the Achaean League is disintegrated;[49] Roman forces, on the instruction of the Senate, destroy both Carthage and Corinth in the same year;[50] 50,000 Carthaginians are sold as slaves;[51] all of mainland Greece is now under full Roman control as is what remained of the Carthaginian Empire – **end of 3rd Punic War and beginning and end of Achaean War**
- 137 BC: Roman forces and Consul Mancinus surrender to Numantian Celtiberians[52]
- 134 BC: Rome destroys Numantia
- 133 BC: Rome asserts control over almost the whole of the Iberian peninsula and is bequeathed[53] the Kingdom of Pergamum by Attalus III
- 242 BC: second Praetor office (*Praetor Peregrinus*) established
- 167 BC: Roman citizens in Italy are exempted from direct taxation (*tributum*)[54]
- 155–139 BC: the continuous revolts of the Lusitanians are put down by Rome – **beginning and end of the Lusitanian War**
- 154–133 BC: Rome submits the Numantines after a long period of resistance of the Celtiberians, peace thereby being established in Iberia for more than half a century – **beginning and end of 2nd Celtiberian War**

47 Hoyos (n 5) 30–1.
48 Hoyos (n 5) 29.
49 Zoch (n 1) 128.
50 Hoyos (n 5) 29.
51 Hoyos (n 5) 31.
52 Hoyos (n 5) 29.
53 E.g. Hoyos (n 5) 32.
54 Zoch (n 1) 91.

Addendum III

Foundation of Key Cities, Settlements and Alliances in the Wider Mediterranean World

- Corinth: 7th millenium BC
- Pylos: 7th millenium BC
- Orchomenus: 6th millenium BC
- Mycenae: 5th millenium BC
- Tiryns: 5th millenium BC
- Troy: 4th millenium BC
- Athens: 3rd millenium BC
- Jerusalem: 3rd millenium BC
- Tyre: 3rd millenium BC
- Gortyn: 3rd millenium BC
- Argos: 3rd millenium BC
- Iolcus: 2nd millenium BC
- First Greek Settlers from the Peloponnese (Arcadians) in Southern Italy: 2nd millenium BC
- Lavinium: 1181 BC
- Alba Longa: 1151 BC
- Utica: 11th century BC
- Aegae/Aigai: 11th century BC
- Sparta: 10th century BC
- Veii: 10th century BC
- Villanovan Culture: 9th century BC
- Caere: 9th century BC
- Populonia: 9th century BC
- Vulci: 9th century BC
- Kingdom of Macedon: 9th century BC
- Carthage: 814 BC
- Latin League: 793 BC
- Pithecusae/Aenaria: 775 BC
- **Rome: 753 BC (first settlements from 17th century BC)**[1]
- Illyrian Kingdom: 8th century BC
- Parthenope/Neapolis: 8th century BC/507 BC
- Cumae: 8th century BC[2]

[1] M Beard, *SPQR: A History of Ancient Rome* (Liveright Publishing 2015) 84.

[2] Beard (n 1) 85.

- Rhegium: 8th century BC
- Zancle/Messina: 8th century BC
- Catania: 8th century BC
- Tharros: 8th century BC
- Tarquinia: 8th century BC
- Volaterrae: 8th century BC
- Veii: 8th century BC
- Sybaris: 720 BC
- Karaly: 8th century BC/7th century BC
- Sis/Panormos: 734 BC/5th century BC
- Naxos, Sicily: 734 BC
- Syracuse: 734 BC
- Taormina: 734 BC
- Sybaris: 720 BC
- Croton: 710 BC
- Taras/Tarentum: 706 BC
- Metapontium: 700 BC
- Gela: 688 BC
- Selinous: 654 BC/650 BC/628 BC
- Massalia: 600 BC
- Poseidonia: 6th century BC
- Capua: 6th century BC
- Irnthi: 6th century BC
- Monoikos: 6th century BC
- Acragas: 582 BC
- Alalia: 566 BC/560 BC
- Peloponnesian League: 550 BC
- Hyele/Elea: 538 BC
- Dion: 5th century BC
- Achaean League (classical years): 5th century BC
- Pyxus: 471 BC
- Thurii: 443 BC
- Heraclea: 433 BC
- Pella: 4th century BC
- Ancona: 387 BC
- Arcadian League: 370 BC
- Hellenic League: 338 BC
- Peak of the Macedonian Empire: 323 BC
- Thessalonica: 315 BC
- Seleucid Empire: 312 BC
- Kingdom of Lysimachus: 306 BC
- Ptolemaic Kingdom: 305 BC
- Kingdom of Cassander: 305 BC
- Achaean League (Hellenistic years): 280 BC

Bibliography

Abbott FF, *A History and Description of Roman Political Institutions* (Ginn & Company 1901, rev. edn 1907)

Adams J, *A Defence of the Constitutions of Government of the United States of America*, vol. I (John Stockdale 1794)

Ando C, 'Public Law and Republican Empire in Rome, 200–27 BCE' in E Cavanagh (ed), *Empire and Legal Thought: Ideas and Institutions from Antiquity to Modernity* (Brill 2020)

Ando C, *Roman Social Imaginaries: Language and Thought in the Context of Empire* (University of Toronto Press 2015)

Ando C, 'Self, Society, Individual, and Person in Roman Law' in MR Niehoff and J Levinson (eds), *Self, Self-Fashioning and Individuality in Late Antiquity: New Perspectives* (Mohr Siebeck 2019)

Arena V, 'Varro, the Name-Givers, and the Lawgivers: The Case of the Consuls' (2021) 38 *Polis* 588

Astin AE, 'Regimen Morum' (1988) 87 *The Journal of Roman Studies* 14

Aubert J-J, 'The Republican Economy and Roman Law: Regulation, Promotion, or Reflection?' in HI Flower (ed), *The Cambridge Companion to the Roman Republic* (2nd edn, Cambridge University Press 2014)

Barchiesi A, and Scheidel W (eds), *The Oxford Handbook of Roman Studies* (Oxford University Press 2010)

Beard M, *SPQR: A History of Ancient Rome* (Liveright Publishing 2015)

Bell SW, and du Plessis PJ (eds), *Roman Law before the Twelve Tables* (Cambridge University Press 2020)

Bellomo M, 'The Administration of the *Imperium Romanum* in the Second Century BCE' in M Balbo and F Santangelo (eds), *A Community in Transition: Rome between Hannibal and the Gracchi* (Oxford University Press 2023)

Bernard S, Mignone L, and Peralta DP (eds), *Making the Middle Republic: New Approaches to Rome and Italy, c.400–200 BCE* (Cambridge University Press 2023)

Betts RF, 'The Allusion to Rome in British Imperialist Thought of the Late Nineteenth and Early Twentieth Centuries' (1971) 15 *Victorian Studies* 149

Bickerman EJ, 'Origines Gentium' (1952) *Classical Philology* 65

Biondi C-A, 'Aristotle on the Mixed Constitution and its Relevance for American Political Thought' (2007) 24 *Social Philosophy and Policy* 176

Boardman J, *The Archaeology of Nostalgia: How the Greeks Re-created their Mythical Past* (Thames & Hudson 2002)

Boatwright MT, *Peoples of the Roman World* (Cambridge University Press 2012)

Bowes K, 'Roman Agriculture from Above and Below: Words and Things' in C Courrier and JC Maglahães de Oliveira (eds), *Ancient History from Below: Subaltern Experiences and Actions in Context* (Routledge 2023)
Bradley G, *Early Rome to 290 BC: The Beginnings of the City and the Rise of the Republic* (Edinburgh University Press 2020)
Bradley K, 'Freedom and Slavery' in A Barchiesi and W Scheidel (eds), *The Oxford Handbook of Roman Studies* (Oxford University Press 2010)
Brant PA, 'Reflections on British and Roman Imperialism' (1965) 7 *Comparative Studies in Society and History* 267
Brennan TC, 'Power and Process under the Republican "Constitution"' in HI Flower (ed), *The Cambridge Companion to the Roman Republic* (2nd edn, Cambridge University Press 2014)
Brennan TC, *The Fasces: A History of Ancient Rome's Most Dangerous Political Symbol* (Oxford University Press 2023)
Brennan TC, *The Praetorship in the Roman Republic*, vol. 1 (Oxford University Press 2000)
Butler SJ, *Britain and Its Empire in the Shadow of Rome: The Reception of Rome in Socio-Political Debate from the 1850s to the 1920s* (Bloomsbury Academic 2012)
Capogrossi Colognesi L, *Law and Power in the Making of the Roman Commonwealth* (Cambridge University Press 2014)
Champion C, 'Historiographic Patterns and Historical Obstacles in Polybius' *Histories*: Marcellus, Flaminius, and the Mamertine Crisis' in B Gibson and T Harrison (eds), *Polybius and his World. Essays in Memory of F. W. Walbank* (Oxford University Press 2013)
Chen AHY, and Lo PY, 'The Constitutional Orders of "One Country, Two Systems": A Comparative Study of the Visible and Invisible Bases of Constitutional Review and Proportionality Analysis in the Chinese Special Administrative Regions of Hong Kong and Macau' in R Dixon and A Stone (eds), *The Invisible Constitution in Comparative Perspective* (Cambridge University Press 2018)
Cifani G, *The Origins of the Roman Economy: From the Iron Age to the Early Republic in a Mediterranean Perspective* (Cambridge University Press 2020)
Clark JH, 'Were Tribuni Militum First Elected in 362 or 311 BCE?' (2016) 63 *Historia: Zeitschrift für Alte Geschichte* 275
Clarkson J, 'Roman Law in its Italic Context' in SW Bell and PJ du Plessis (eds), *Roman Law before the Twelve Tables* (Cambridge University Press 2020)
Comay del Junco E, 'Aristotle on Comparison' (2022) 61 *Oxford Studies on Ancient Philosophy* 103
Connolly J, 'Political Theory' in A Barchiesi and W Scheidel (eds), *The Oxford Handbook of Roman Studies* (Oxford University Press 2010)
Cornell TJ, *The Beginnings of Rome: Italy and Rome from the Bronze Age to the Punic Wars (c. 1000–264 BC)* (Routledge 1995)
Courrier C, and de Oliveira JCM (eds), *Ancient History from Below: Subaltern Experiences and Actions in Context* (Routledge 2023)
Crawford M, *The Roman Republic* (2nd edn, Fontana Press 1992)

Culham P, 'Women in the Roman Republic' in HI Flower (ed), *The Cambridge Companion to the Roman Republic* (2nd edn, Cambridge University Press 2014)

Cunningham LS, and Reich JJ, *Culture and Values: A Survey of the Humanities* (7th edn, Thompson/Wadsworth 2006)

Dart CJ, Rafferty D, and Vervaet FJ, 'New Perspectives on Old Problems/Old Perspectives on New Problems' in FJ Vervaet, D Rafferty and CJ Dart (eds), *How Republics Die: Creeping Authoritarianism in Ancient Rome and Beyond* (De Gruyter 2025)

Davies N, *Europe: A History* (Pimlico 1996, reprinted with corrections 1997)

De Laix RA, 'Aristotle's Conception of the Spartan Constitution' (1974) 12 *Journal of the History of Philosophy* 21

Dench E, *From Barbarians to New Men: Greek, Roman, and Modern Perceptions of Peoples of the Central Apennines* (Oxford University Press 1995)

Dench E, 'Roman Identity' in A Barchiesi and W Scheidel (eds), *The Oxford Handbook of Roman Studies* (Oxford University Press 2010)

Derow P, *Rome, Polybius, and the East* (A Erskine and J Crawley Quinn (eds)) (Oxford University Press 2014)

Drogula FK, 'Plebeian Tribunes and the Government of Early Rome' (2017) 51 *Antichthon* 101

Drogula FK, *Commanders and Command in the Roman Republic and Early Empire* (University of North Carolina Press 2015)

Dudley DR, 'Blossius of Cumae' (1941) 31 *The Journal of Roman Studies* 94

Earl DC, *The Moral and Political Tradition of Rome* (Cornell University Press 1967)

Eco U, 'Eternal Fascism' in *The New York Review of Books* (New York, 22 June 1995)

Eder W, 'Republicans and Sinners: The Decline of the Roman Republic and the End of a Provisional Arrangement' in RW Wallace and EM Harris (eds), *Transitions to Empire: Essays in Greco-Roman History, 360–146* B.C., *in Honor of E. Badian* (University of Oklahoma Press 1996)

Eder W, 'The Political Significance of the Codification of Law in Archaic Societies: An Unconventional Hypothesis' in KA Raaflaub (ed), *Social Struggles in Archaic Rome: New Perspectives on the Conflict of the Orders* (2nd edn, Blackwell Publishing 2005)

Epstein DF, 'Caesar's Personal Enemies on the Ides of March' (1987) 46 *Latomus* 566

Erskine A, 'Polybios and Barbarian Rome' (2000) 3 *Mediterraneo Antico* 165

Fantham E, 'Literature in the Roman Republic' in HI Flower (ed), *The Cambridge Companion to the Roman Republic* (2nd edn, Cambridge University Press 2014)

Ferrary J-L, 'Cicéron et les Institutions Rhodiennes (De re publica 3, 35, 48)' Romaine' in J-L Ferrary (ed), *Rome et le Monde Grec* (Les Belles Lettres 2017)

Ferrary J-L, 'L'Empire de Rome et Les Hégémonies de Cités Grecques chez Polybe' in J-L Ferrary (ed), *Rome et le Monde Grec* (Les Belles Lettres 2017)

Ferrary J-L, 'La Géographie de l'Hellénisme sous la Domination Romaine' in J-L Ferrary (ed), *Rome et le Monde Grec* (Les Belles Lettres 2017)

Ferrary J-L, 'Le Jugement de Polybe sur la Domination Romaine: État de la Question' in J-L Ferrary (ed), *Rome et le Monde Grec* (Les Belles Lettres 2017)

Ferrary J-L, 'Le Monde Hellénistique, Rome et La Notion d'Équilibre International' in J-L Ferrary (ed), *Rome et le Monde Grec* (Les Belles Lettres 2017)

Ferrary J-L, 'Les Romains de la République et les Démocraties Grecques' in J-L Ferrary (ed), *Rome et le Monde Grec* (Les Belles Lettres 2017)

Ferrary J-L, *Philhellénisme et Impérialisme* (BEFAR 1988)

Ferrary J-L, 'Rome, Athènes et le Philhellénisme dans l'Empire Romain, d'Auguste aux Antonins' in J-L Ferrary (ed), *Rome et le Monde Grec* (Les Belles Lettres 2017)

Flower HI, 'Epilogue – Periodization in Perspective: Further Thoughts about the Second Century BCE' in M Balbo and F Santangelo (eds), *A Community in Transition: Rome between Hannibal and the Gracchi* (Oxford University Press 2023)

Flower HI, *Roman Republics* (Princeton University Press 2010)

Flower HI (ed), *The Cambridge Companion on the Roman Republic* (2nd edn, Cambridge University Press 2014)

Flower HI, 'The Imperial Republic' in A Barchiesi and W Scheidel (eds), *The Oxford Handbook of Roman Studies* (Oxford University Press 2010)

Forsén B, and Lampinen A, 'Barbarians and Empire: Greek and Roman Conceptions of the East' in B Forsén and A Lampinen (eds), *Oriental Images: Stereotypes and Identity Creation in the Ancient World* (Franz Steiner 2024)

Forsythe G, *A Critical History of Early Rome* (University of California Press 2006)

Fraschetti A, *The Foundation of Rome* (Marian Hill and Kevin Windle (trs), Edinburgh University Press 2005)

Freeman P, 'British Imperialism and the Roman Empire' in J Webster and N Cooper (eds), *Roman Imperialism: Post-colonial Perspectives* (School of Archaeological Studies, University of Leicester 1996)

Freeman P, *Julius Caesar* (Simon & Schuster 2008)

Frier BW, Book Review (1977) *The Classical Journal* 379

Fulminante F, *The Rise of Early Rome: Transportation Networks and Domination in Central Italy, 1050–500 BC* (Cambridge University Press 2023)

Graziadei M, 'The Functionalist Heritage' in P Legrand and R Munday (eds), *Comparative Legal Studies: Traditions and Transitions* (Cambridge University Press 2003)

Gregory J, 'Cicero and Plato on Democracy: a Translation and its Source' (1991) 50 *Latomus* 639

Gruen ES, 'Augustus and the Making of the Principate' in K Galinsky (ed), *The Cambridge Companion to the Age of Augustus* (Cambridge University Press 2005)

Gruen ES, *Culture and National Identity in Republican Rome* (Cornell University Press 1992)

Gruen ES, *The Hellenistic World and the Coming of Rome* (University of California Press 1984, reprinted 1986)

Gruen ES, 'The Origins of the Achaean War' (1976) 96 *The Journal of Hellenic Studies* 46

Hamza G, 'The Classification (divisio) into "Branches" of Modern Legal Systems (Orders) and Roman Law Traditions' [2006] *European Journal of Law Reform* 361

Hansen MH, 'The Mixed Constitution Versus the Separation of Powers: Monarchical and Aristocratic Aspects of Modern Democracy' (2010) 31 *History of Political Thought* 509

Harries J, 'Law' in A Barchiesi and W Scheidel (eds), *The Oxford Handbook of Roman Studies* (Oxford University Press 2010)

Harries J, 'Roman Law Codes and the Roman Legal Tradition' in JW Cairns and PJ du Plessis (eds), *Beyond Dogmatics: Law and Society in the Roman World* (Edinburgh University Press 2007)

Harris WV, 'Power' in A Barchiesi and W Scheidel (eds), *The Oxford Handbook of Roman Studies* (Oxford University Press 2010)

Harris WV, 'The Roman Father's Power of Life and Death' in RS Bagnall and WV Harris (eds), *Studies in Roman Law in Memory of AA Schiller* (EJ Brill 1986)

Hatzopoulos MB, *Ancient Macedonia* (De Gruyter 2020)

Henderson MM, 'Tiberius Gracchus and the Failure of the Roman Republic' (1968) 31 *Theoria: A Journal of Social and Political Theory* 51

Herman A, *The Cave and the Light: Plato Versus Aristotle and the Struggle for the Soul of Western Civilization* (Random House 2014)

Herman Hansen M, 'Was Sparta a Normal or Exceptional Polis?' in S Hodkinson (ed), *Sparta: Comparative Approaches* (The Classical Press of Wales 2009)

Hin S, 'Population' in HI Flower (ed), *The Cambridge Companion to the Roman Republic* (2nd edn, Cambridge University Press 2014)

Hingley R, 'Attitudes to Roman Imperialism' (1993) TRAC 1991 *Theoretical Roman Archaeology Journal* 23

Hodkinson S, 'Introduction' in S Hodkinson (ed), *Sparta: Comparative Approaches* (The Classical Press of Wales 2009)

Hodkinson S, 'Was Sparta an Exceptional Polis?' in S Hodkinson (ed), *Sparta: Comparative Approaches* (The Classical Press of Wales 2009)

Hölkeskamp K-J, *Rekonstruktionen einer Republik: die politische Kultur des antiken Rom und die Forschung der letzten Jahrzehnte* (Oldenbourg Wissenschaftsverlag 2004, reprinted 2014)

Holloway C, and Wilson BP (eds), *The Political Writings of George Washington*, vol. 2: 1788–1799 (Cambridge University Press 2023)

Hoyos D, *Rome Victorious: The Irresistible Rise of the Roman Empire* (Bloomsbury Academic 2019, reprinted 2023)

Humbert M, 'Libertas id est Civitas: Autour d'un Conflit Négatif de Citoyennetés au IIe s. avant J.-C.' in M Humbert (ed), *Antiquitatis Effigies: Recherches sur le Droit Public et Privé de Rome* (IUSS Press 2013)

Husa J, 'The Comparatist and Plato's Cave' in L Siliquini-Cinelli, D Gianti and M Balestrieri (eds), *The Grand Strategy of Comparative Law: Themes, Methods, Developments* (Routledge 2024)

Jankowski R, 'The Demise of the Roman Republic: A Faulty Constitution?' (2021) 32 *Constitutional Political Economy* 218

Kahlos M, 'Charismatic Leadership in Ancient Rome' in JP Zúquete (ed), *Routledge International Handbook of Charisma* (Routledge 2021)

Kalyvas A, 'The Tyranny of Dictatorship: When the Greek Tyrant Met the Roman Dictator' (2007) 35 *Political Theory* 412

Kamm A, *The Romans* (Routledge 2006)

Katz JT, 'Linguistics' in A Barchiesi and W Scheidel (eds), *The Oxford Handbook of Roman Studies* (Oxford University Press 2010)

Keyser PT, 'Science' in A Barchiesi and W Scheidel (eds), *The Oxford Handbook of Roman Studies* (Oxford University Press 2010)

Kiernan B, 'The First Genocide: Carthage, 146 BC' (2004) 51 *Diogenes* 27

Kitto HDF, *The Greeks* (Penguin Books 1951, reprinted 1960)

Koptev A, 'The Five-Day Interregnum in the Roman Republic' (2016) 66 *The Classical Quarterly* 205

Krikona E, 'Aristotle's Theory on the Mixed Spartan Regime and the Athenian Father-State' (2017) 2 *Conatus – Journal of Philosophy* 73

Kunkel W, *An Introduction to Roman Legal and Constitutional History* (JM Kelly (tr), 2nd edn, Clarendon Press 1973)

Kunkel W, and Wittmann R, *Staasordnung und Staatspraxis der römischen Republik: Die Magistratur* (C.H. Beck 1995)

Lampinen A, 'Explaining the East: Forming and Applying Eastern Stereotypes in the Graeco-Roman Tradition' in B Forsén and A Lampinen (eds), *Oriental Images: Stereotypes and Identity Creation in the Ancient World* (Franz Steiner 2024)

Lanfranchi T, 'Legislation, Politics and Social Change in the Early Second Century BCE' in M Balbo and F Santangelo (eds), *A Community in Transition: Rome between Hannibal and the Gracchi* (Oxford University Press 2023)

Lanni A, and Vermeule A, 'The Design of Ancient Constitutions' (2012) 64 *Stanford Law Review* 907

Latte K, 'The Origin of the Roman Quaestorship' (1936) 67 *Transactions and Proceedings of the American Philological Association* 24

Lee D, *Popular Sovereignty in Early Modern Constitutional Thought* (Oxford University Press 2016)

Legrand P, 'The Same and the Different' in P Legrand and R Munday (eds), *Comparative Legal Studies: Traditions and Transitions* (Cambridge University Press 2003)

Linderski J, 'Religious Aspects of the Conflict of the Orders: The Case of *Confarreatio*' in KA Raaflaub (ed), *Social Struggles in Archaic Rome: New Perspectives on the Conflict of the Orders* (2nd edn, Blackwell Publishing 2005)

Lintott A, *The Constitution of the Roman Republic* (Clarendon Press 1999)

Lintott AW, 'Imperial Expansion and Moral Decline in the Roman Republic' (1972) 21(4) *Historia: Zeitschrift für Alte Geschichte* 626

Loomis WT, 'The Introduction of the Denarius' in RW Wallace and EM Harris (eds), *Transitions to Empire: Essays in Greco-Roman History, 360–146* B.C., *in Honor of E. Badian* (University of Oklahoma Press 1996)

Maglahães de Oliveira JC, and Courrier C, 'Ancient History from Below: An Introduction' in C Courrier and JC Maglahães de Oliveira (eds), *Ancient History from Below: Subaltern Experiences and Actions in Context* (Routledge 2023)

Mathisen RW, *Ancient Roman Civilization: History and Sources* (Oxford University Press 2019)

Matyszak P, *Greece Against Rome: The Fall of the Hellenistic Kingdoms 250–31* BC (Pen & Sword 2001)

Metcalf WE, 'Numismatics' in A Barchiesi and W Scheidel (eds), *The Oxford Handbook of Roman Studies* (Oxford University Press 2010)

Millar F, *The Crowd in Rome in the Late Republic* (University Michigan Press 1998)

Millar F, *The Roman Republic in Political Thought* (University Press of New England 2002)

Millender E, 'The Spartan Dyarchy: A Comparative Perspective' in S Hodkinson (ed), *Sparta: Comparative Approaches* (The Classical Press of Wales 2009)

Mitchell RE, *Patricians and Plebeians: The Origin of the Roman State* (Cornell University Press 1990)

Mitchell RE, 'The Aristocracy of the Roman Republic' in R Howarth (ed), *Hearsay, History, and Heresy: Collected Essays on the Roman Republic by Richard E. Mitchell* (Gorgias Press 2010)

Mitchell RE, 'The Definition of *Patres* and *Plebs*: An End to the Struggle of the Orders' in KA Raaflaub (ed), *Social Struggles in Archaic Rome: New Perspectives on the Conflict of the Orders* (2nd edn, Blackwell Publishing 2005)

Mitchell RE, 'The Fourth Century Origin Roman Didrachms' in R Howarth (ed), *Hearsay, History, and Heresy: Collected Essays on the Roman Republic by Richard E. Mitchell* (Gorgias Press 2010) 13

Momigliano A, *Alien Wisdom: The Limits of Hellenization* (Cambridge University Press 1975)

Momigliano A, 'The Rise of the *Plebs* in the Archaic Age of Rome' in KA Raaflaub (ed), *Social Struggles in Archaic Rome: New Perspectives on the Conflict of the Orders* (2nd edn, Blackwell Publishing 2005)

Mommsen T, *Römisches Staatsrecht*, vols 1–3 (S Hirzel 1876–88)

Mommsen T, *The History of Rome*, vol. 1 (W Purdie Dickson (tr), Macmillan & Co. 1901)

Moore K, 'Rome's Decemviral Commission to Greece: Fact, Fiction or Otherwise?' (2019) 5 *Athens Journal of History* 123

Morrell K, 'Enabling Laws, Rule of Law, and the Transformation of the Roman Republic' in FJ Vervaet, D Rafferty and CJ Dart (eds), *How Republics Die: Creeping Authoritarianism in Ancient Rome and Beyond* (De Gruyter 2025)

Mouritzen H, *Politics in the Roman Republic* (Cambridge University Press 2017)

Nelson E, *The Greek Tradition in Republican Thought* (Cambridge University Press 2004)

Nicolet C, *The World of the Citizen in Republican Rome* (PS Falla (tr), University of California 1980)

Nietzsche F, *Beyond Good and Evil* (Helen Zimmern (tr), Modern Library 1917) 87, para. 146.

Noreña CF, 'The Early Imperial Monarchy' in A Barchiesi and W Scheidel (eds), *The Oxford Handbook of Roman Studies* (Oxford University Press 2010)

Oakley SP, 'The Early Republic' in HI Flower (ed), *The Cambridge Companion on the Roman Republic* (2nd edn, Cambridge University Press 2014)

Örücü E, *The Enigma of Comparative Law: Variations on a Theme for the Twenty-First Century* (Brill Academic Publishers 2004)

Panila Peralta D, *Making the Middle Republic: New Approaches to Rome and Italy, c. 400–200* BCE (Cambridge University Press 2023)

Pasquino P, 'Classifying Constitutions: Preliminary Conceptual Analysis' (2013) 34(3) *Cardozo Law Review* 999

Pasquino P, 'Machiavelli and Aristotle: The Anatomies of the City' (2009) 35 *History of European Ideas* 397

Perlikowski Ł, 'How Does One Understand the Stability of Political Regimes from a Theoretical Point of View?' (2019) 6 (63) *Politeja* 111

Petrochilos N, *Roman Attitudes to the Greeks* (National and Capodistrian University of Athens 1974)

Pina Polo F, *The Consul at Rome: The Civil Functions of the Consuls in the Roman Republic* (Cambridge University Press 2011)

Pina Polo F, and Díaz Fernández A, *The Quaestorship in the Roman Republic* (De Gruyter 2019)

Posner EA, 'The Constitution of the Roman Republic' in G Dari-Mattiacci and DP Kehoe (eds), *Roman Law and Economics: Institutions and Organizations Volume I* (Oxford University Press 2020)

Powell JGF, 'The Embassy of the Three Philosophers to Rome in 155 BC' in C Kremmydas and K Tempest (eds), *Hellenistic Oratory: Continuity and Change* (Oxford University Press 2013)

Purcell N, 'Urbanism' in A Barchiesi and W Scheidel (eds), *The Oxford Handbook of Roman Studies* (Oxford University Press 2010)

Raaflaub KA, 'Born to Be Wolves? Origins of Roman Imperialism' in RW Wallace and EM Harris (eds), *Transitions to Empire: Essays in Greco-Roman History, 360–146* B.C., *in Honor of E. Badian* (University of Oklahoma Press 1996)

Raaflaub KA, 'From Protection and Defense to Offense and Participation: Stages in the Conflict of the Orders' in KA Raaflaub (ed), *Social Struggles in Archaic Rome: New Perspectives on the Conflict of the Orders* (2nd edn, Blackwell Publishing 2005)

Raaflaub KA (ed), *Social Struggles in Archaic Rome: New Perspectives on the Conflict of the Orders* (2nd edn, Wiley-Blackwell 2005)

Raaflaub KA, 'The Conflict of the Orders in Archaic Rome: A Comprehensive and Comparative Approach' in KA Raaflaub (ed), *Social Struggles in Archaic Rome: New Perspectives on the Conflict of the Orders* (2nd edn, Blackwell Publishing 2005)

Rawson B, 'Family and Society' in A Barchiesi and W Scheidel (eds), *The Oxford Handbook of Roman Studies* (Oxford University Press 2010)

Richard J-C, 'Patricians and Plebeians: The Origin of a Social Dichotomy' in KA Raaflaub (ed), *Social Struggles in Archaic Rome: New Perspectives on the Conflict of the Orders* (2nd edn, Blackwell Publishing 2005)

Richardson JS, 'Old Statutes Never Die: A Brief History of Abrogation' in M Austin, J Harries and C Smith (eds), *Modus Operandi: Essays in Honour of Geoffrey Rickman* (Institute of Classical Studies – School of Advanced Study, University of London 1998)

Riesbeck DJ, 'The Unity of Aristotle's Theory of Constitutions' (2016) 49 *Apeiron* 93

Robb MA, *Beyond Populares and Optimates: Political Language in the Late Republic* (Franz Steiner Verlag Stuttgart 2010)

Roselaar ST, 'The Concept of *Commercium* in the Roman Republic' (2013) 66 *Phoenix* 381

Roselaar ST, 'The Concept of *Conubium* in the Roman Republic' in PJ du Plessis (ed), *New Frontiers: Law and Society in the Roman World* (Edinburgh University Press 2013) 102–122.

Roselaar ST, 'The Grand Strategy? Spoils and Colonization in the Fourth and Third Centuries BCE' in M Helm and ST Roselaar (eds), *Spoils in the Roman Republic: Boon and Bane* (Franz Steiner Verlag 2023)

Rosenstein N, *Rome and the Mediterranean 290 to 146 BC: The Imperial Republic* (Edinburgh University Press 2012)

Rossi A, 'The Tears of Marcellus: History of a Literary Motif in Livy' (2000) 47(1) *Greece and Rome* 56

Rostovtzeff M, *The Social and Economic History of the Roman Empire* (Oxford University Press 1926)

Ryan FX, *Rank and Participation in the Republican Senate* (Franz Steiner Verlag 1998)

Scarciglia R, *Methods and Legal Comparison: Challenges for Methodological Pluralism* (Edward Elgar 2023)

Schiavone A, 'Introduzione: Una Storiografia di Confine' in J-L Ferrary, Dall'ordine Repubblicano ai Poteri di Augusto. Aspetti della Legislazione Romana (L'Erma di Bretschneider 2016) xiv.

Scott SP, *The Civil Law* (The Central Trust Company 1932)

Seager R, 'Polybius' Distortions of the Roman "Constitution": A Simpl(istic) Explanation' in R Gibson and T Harrison (eds), *Polybius and his World. Essays in Memory of F. W. Walbank* (Oxford University Press 2013)

Sedley D, 'Philosophy' in A Barchiesi and W Scheidel (eds), *The Oxford Handbook of Roman Studies* (Oxford University Press 2010)

Segev M, *The Value of the World and of Oneself: Philosophical Optimism and Pessimism from Aristotle to Modernity* (Oxford University Press 2022)

Sellers MNS, 'The Roman Republic and the French and the American Revolutions' in HI Flower (ed), *The Cambridge Companion to the Roman Republic* (2nd edn, Cambridge University Press 2014)

Shatzman I, *Senatorial Wealth and Politics* (Latomus 1975)

Shatzman I, 'The Roman Republic: From Monarchy to Julius Caesar' in JA Olsen and CS Gray (eds), *The Practice of Strategy: From Alexander the Great to the Present* (Oxford University Press 2011)

Smiley CN, 'Stoicism and Its Influence on Roman Life and Thought' (1934) 29 *The Classical Journal* 645

Smith C, 'Becoming Political: Middle Republican Quandaries' in S Bernard, LM Mignone and D Padilla Peralta (eds), *Making the Middle Republic: New Approaches to Rome and Italy, c. 400–200* BCE (Cambridge University Press 2023)

Steel C, *The End of the Roman Republic, 146 to 44* BC*: Conquest and Crisis* (Edinburgh University Press 2013)

Stevens B, 'Aeolism: Latin as a Dialect of Greek' (2006/7) 102 *The Classical Journal* 115

Straumann B, *Crisis and Constitutionalism: Roman Political Thought from the Fall of the Republic to the Age of Revolution* (Oxford University Press 2016)

Straumann B, *The Just State: Greek and Roman Theories of Justice and Their Legacy in Western Thought* (Wiley-Blackwell 2024)

Syme R, *The Roman Revolution* (Clarendon Press 1939)

Tan J, 'Climate Change and Rome's Changing Republic' in M Balbo and F Santangelo (eds), *A Community in Transition: Rome between Hannibal and the Gracchi* (Oxford University Press 2023)

Tarwacka A, *The Censors as Guardians of Public and Family Life in the Roman Republic* (Routledge 2025)

Terrenato N, 'Early Rome' in A Barchiesi and W Scheidel (eds), *The Oxford Handbook of Roman Studies* (Oxford University Press 2010)

Tharoor S, *Inglorious Empire: What the British Did to India* (Hurst 2017)

Trikkaliotis D, Mouratidou AA, and Anastasiou A, 'The Fate of Sickly and Disabled New-born Babies in Ancient Greece (Sparta and Athens)' [2018] *The Journal of Physical Activity, Nutrition and Rehabilitation* 519

Van den Bergh R, 'Roman Women: Sometimes Equal and Sometimes Not' (2006) 12 *Fundamina* 113

Várhelyi Z, 'The Specters of Roman Imperialism: The Live Burials of Gauls and Greeks at Rome' (2007) 26 *Classical Antiquity* 277

Verhasselt G, 'Heraclides' Epitome of Aristotle's *Constitutions* and *Barbarian Customs*: Two Neglected Fragments' (2020) 69 *The Classical Quarterly* 672

Vervaet FJ, Dart CJ, and Rafferty D, 'Reform Unwillingness and the Death of the Roman Republic' in FJ Vervaet, D Rafferty and CJ Dart (eds), *How Republics Die: Creeping Authoritarianism in Ancient Rome and Beyond* (De Gruyter 2025)

Vlassopoulos K, 'Subaltern Community Formation in Antiquity: Some Methodological Reflections' in C Courrier and JC Magalhães de Oliveira (eds), *Ancient History from Below: Subaltern Experiences and Actions in Context* (Routledge 2023)

Von Fritz K, *The Theory of the Mixed Constitution in Antiquity: A Critical Analysis of Polybius' Political Ideas* (Columbia University Press 1954)

Von Ungern-Sternberg J, 'The Crisis of the Republic' in HI Flower (ed), *The Cambridge Companion to the Roman Republic* (2nd edn, Cambridge University Press 2014)

Von Ungern-Sternberg J, 'The End of the Conflict of the Orders' in KA Raaflaub (ed), *Social Struggles in Archaic Rome: New Perspectives on the Conflict of the Orders* (2nd edn, Blackwell Publishing 2005)

Walbank F, 'A Greek Looks at Rome: Polybius VI Revisited' (1998) 17 *Scripta Classica Israelica* 45

Wallace R, 'The Latin Alphabet and Orthography' in J Clarkson (ed), *A Companion to the Latin Language* (Wiley-Blackwell 2011)

Wallace-Hadrill A, 'To be Roman, Go Greek: Thoughts on Hellenization at Rome' in M Austin, J Harries and C Smith (eds), *Modus Operandi: Essays in Honour of Geoffrey Rickman* (Institute of Classical Studies – School of Advanced Study, University of London 1998)

Westbrook R, 'Vitae Necisque Potestas' (1999) 48 *Historia: Zeitschrift für Alte Geschichte* 203

Whitmarsh T, 'Hellenism' in A Barchiesi and W Scheidel (eds), *The Oxford Handbook of Roman Studies* (Oxford University Press 2010)

Wilson MB, *Dictator: The Evolution of the Roman Dictatorship* (University of Michigan Press 2021)

Winkel L, 'Roman Law and Its Intellectual Context' in D Johnston (ed), *The Cambridge Companion to Roman Law* (Cambridge University Press 2015)

Winters JA, *Oligarchy* (Cambridge University Press 2011)

Wittgenstein L, *Tractatus Logico-Philosophicus* (Kegan Paul, Trench, Trubner & Co. 1922)

Xella P, Quinn J, Melchiorri V, and van Dommelen P, 'Cemetery or Sacrifice? Infant Burials at the Carthage Tophet: Phoenician Bones of Contention' (2013) 87 (338) *Antiquities* 1

Xu R, 'Roman Conception of Self and Others' (2018) (10) *Review of European Studies* 139

Zimmermann R, 'Roman Law in the Modern World' in D Johnston (ed), *The Cambridge Companion to Roman Law* (Cambridge University Press 2015)

Zoch PA, *Ancient Rome: An Introductory History* (University of Oklahoma Press 1998)

Zweigert K, and Kötz H, *An Introduction to Comparative Law* (Tony Weir (tr), 3rd edn, Oxford University Press 1998)

Τζαμτζής ΙΕ, *Carthago Καρχηδών* (Εκδόσεις Σάκκουλα 2023)

Τζαμτζής ΙΕ, *Ο Μεσογειακός Κόσμος* (Εκδόσεις Σάκκουλα 2014, ανατύπωση 2018)

Classical Sources Cited

Appian, *Civil Wars* (App. BC)
Appian, *Punic Wars* (App. Pun.)
Appian, *Samnite History* (App. Sam.)
Appian, *Wars in Spain* (App. Hisp.)
Aristotle, *Politics* (Aristot. Pol.)
Athenaeus, *Deipnosophistae* (Ath.)
C. Suetonius Tranquillus, *Divus Augustus* (Suet. Aug.)
C. Suetonius Tranquillus, *Tiberius* (Suet. Tib.)
Cassius Dio, *Roman History* (Dion. Cass.)
Cato the Elder, *De Agri Cultura*
Cicero, *De Legibus* (Cic. Leg.)
Cicero, *de Natura Deorum* (Cic. N.D.)
Cicero, *De Officiis* (Cic. Off.)
Cicero, *De Oratore* (Cic. de Orat.)
Cicero, *De Republica* (Cic. Rep.)
Cicero, *For Aemilius Scaurus* (Cic. Scaur.)
Cicero, *For Archias* (Cic. Arch.)
Cicero, *For Sestius* (Cic. Sest.)
Dionysius of Halicarnassus, *Antiquitates Romanae* (D.H.)
Gaius, *The Institutes*
Herodotus, *The Histories* (Hdt.)
Hesiod, *Works and Days* (Hes. WD)
Juvenal, *Satires* (Juv.)
Livy, *The History of Rome* (Liv.)
Maurus Servius Honoratus, *Commentary on the Aeneid of Vergil* (Serv. A.)
P. Vergilius Maro, *Aeneid* (Verg. A.)
Plato, *Crito* (Plat. Crito)
Plato, *Laws* (Plat. Laws)
Plato, *Phaedo* (Plat. Phaedo)
Plato, *Republic* (Plat. Rep.)
Plato, *Timaeus* (Plat. Tim.)
Pliny the Elder, *The Natural History* (Plin. Nat.)
Plutarch, *Camillus* (Plut. Cam.)
Plutarch, *Fabius Maximus* (Plut. Fab.)
Plutarch, *Lycurgus* (Plut. Lyc.)
Plutarch, *Marcus Cato* (Plut. Cat. Ma.)
Plutarch, *Pyrrhus* (Plut. Pyrrh.)
Plutarch, *Quaestiones Romanae* (Plut. Quaes. Rom.)
Polybius, *Histories* (Plb.)
Q. Horatius Flaccus (Horace), *Epistles* (Hor. Ep.)
Q. Horatius Flaccus (Horace), *The Art of Poetry: To the Pisos* (Hor. Ars)
Sallust, *Conspiracy of Catiline* (Sal. Cat.)

Seneca, *De Tranquillitate Animi* (Sen. Tranq.)
Thucydides, *History of the Peloponnesian War* (Thuc.)

Classical works are normally cited according to the Perseus Digital Library's abbreviations for such.

Index

EU Authorised Representative:
Easy Access System Europe Mustamäe tee 50, 10621 Tallinn, Estonia
gpsr.requests@easproject.com

Printed and bound by CPI Group (UK) Ltd, Croydon, CR0 4YY
17/02/2026
02055182-0009